Activiti in Action

Activiti in Action

EXECUTABLE BUSINESS PROCESSES IN BPMN 2.0

TIJS RADEMAKERS

MANNING

Shelter Island

Manning Publications Co.
20 Baldwin Road
PO Box 261
Shelter Island, NY 11964

Development editor: Sebastian Stirling
Technical proofreader: Andy Verberne
Copyeditor: June Eding
Proofreader: Nermina Miller
Typesetter: Gordan Salinovic
Cover designer: Marija Tudor

ISBN 9781617290121
Printed in the United States of America
1 2 3 4 5 6 7 8 9 10 – MAL – 17 16 15 14 13 12

brief contents

v

contents

foreword by tom baeyens

Business processes represent the core functions of an organization. If these core functions are implemented inefficiently, a company gives its competitors an easy advantage. Business Process Management (BPM) is nothing more than ensuring that an organization is run well and remains in good shape. For small companies, a single person might be able to oversee everything that is going on and deal with situations as they occur. But when companies grow larger and processes expand, it's harder to maintain control. Work is delegated, people start optimizing their own responsibilities, and an overview can quickly get lost. Over the long run, constant monitoring and improving of business processes are what separates good organizations from excellent ones.

One aspect of managing business processes is automation. Despite big advancements in software technology in the last decade, building custom software to support business processes remains expensive for enterprises.

Traditional BPM Systems (BPMSs) have attempted to simplify the creation of software for monitoring business processes. The biggest advantage of BPMSs is that they're based on flowchart diagrams. Business managers and technical team members can understand these diagrams, which helps bring communication of requirements to a new level.

The bottleneck of traditional BPMSs has been flexibility. BPMSs that focus on technical integration with backend systems over web services (for example, BPEL) are not suited for business people. And BPMSs that focus on business diagrams are typically limited in backend integration and scripting.

This lack of flexibility is why I started building a home-brewed process engine back in 2002. Initially, the goal was to build an interpreter for state machines. It was much later that I heard from many developers that they had gone through the same initial phase. Originally, my process engine was intended as an internal project for which I was doing Java consulting.

Without expectations and without really knowing what I was getting myself into, I published the project on SourceForge as jBPM. My reaction to the first forum post was, "Cool! Someone found my engine!"—and this motivated me to improve. Many more forum posts kept me going until JBoss came along and asked me to develop it further.

After the Business Process Model and Notation (BPMN) standard was introduced, we realized that it would be crucial to have an Apache-licensed implementation of BPMN. jBPM's LGPL could pose a problem for mass adoption. At the same time, Alfresco needed an Apache-based BPMN engine, so the company hired me, and that is how Activiti was born. Because of the different licenses, we couldn't use any of the jBPM code, so we had to write it from scratch at Alfresco: but this became an opportunity to revisit all the key architectural decisions that had been made before.

During the evolution of jBPM, leading up to Activiti, I took a new approach to the old problem. Initially, the focus was on state machines, but eventually we constructed an engine to match the way business people and developers collaborate. We designed the engine in such a way that it would allow business people to define the graphical flow of the process and, at the same time, give developers the opportunity to bind program logic inside the process flows. In addition, the engine was light-weight and integrated easily into any Java environment. The result was what we call embeddable BPM.

BPMN is a recent standard that has emerged from a long list of predecessors in the BPM space. It describes the shapes and connections for drawing business-process diagrams as well as their meanings and file formats. BPMN is different because of its clear focus on the business side and process modeling, whereas earlier standards focused more on the technical aspects.

In this book, Tijs has included concrete instructions for developers, technical managers, and business analysts to start building BPMN process solutions with Activiti. The book includes a comprehensive overview of the Activiti framework, the Activiti Engine, and BPMN. But Tijs goes beyond the basics and describes how to integrate these with a rule engine and web-based services.

The reader will get a thorough understanding of BPM technology as it is applied in today's enterprise environments. This is definitely the most practical guide to BPMN using Activiti as the engine.

TOM BAEYENS
ACTIVITI AND JBPM FOUNDER
CHIEF BPM ARCHITECT, ALFRESCO

foreword by joram barrez

A picture is worth a thousand words

I believe this is a saying that exists in every culture around the world. And, truly, our minds are impressive image-processing machines, spotting structure and anomalies in a fraction of a second. Yet we tend to base much of our daily communication, both personal and professional, on the written word.

As software developers, we live in the most interesting of times, with the World Wide Web, the mobile (r)evolution, and the movement to the cloud with a clear focus on consumers. Yet the building process of that software remains complex—we produce pages and pages of lengthy documents to describe what we would like to see emerge from that ocean of zeroes and ones.

What if there were a way to improve this situation? As it happens, improving this situation is the main goal of those who are involved with BPM.

I started my career as a typical Java developer, a generalist doing tids and tads of everything involving Java. One day, out of the blue, I was assigned to a jBPM project. At that point, I had never heard of BPM or anything close to it. Long story short: I fell in love. I devoted my days, nights, and weekends to understanding the inner workings of the engine. Open source is a powerful potion, and I drank it. The community was hard to please (I got an "rtfm" on my first post) but responsive to those who were willing to learn and to share their knowledge.

It was, as the French would say, a *coup de foudre* (love at first sight). I worked on BPM projects coding during the day, and I lurked on the forums at night. And then it happened. About a year after my first encounter with BPM, I met Tom Baeyens, the project lead of jBPM at the time, at a seminar where we both were speakers. We connected immediately as fellow geeks. A year later, I joined his team at JBoss and followed him subsequently to help build Activiti at Alfresco.

Why the switch? The answer is simple. There was no room for an Apache-licensed engine at JBoss at that time, but we knew that an Apache license was crucial due to the advent of the BPMN 2.0 standard. If we weren't going to do it, someone else would.

Putting all our experiences together—what worked, what didn't work, and what rocked—we started to build a BPMN 2.0 engine at the beginning of 2010, an engine that would do exactly what I started my story with: improve communication between those who need software solutions and those who build software by using flowchart-like diagrams. Expressing how your business works with diagrams is hard, but it is worth the effort. Visualization is a powerful tool and, in the past, I often saw clients change their way of working after seeing how the different steps connected. The BPMN 2.0 standard is of great value here. It may seem simplistic, but by defining how certain shapes have specific meanings, not only can you visualize your workflows, you can find others in the industry who speak the same language. The fact that version 2.0 also includes execution semantics adds the next level of power: not only do the diagrams become standardized, but now you can switch the engine that's executing the diagrams with any BPMN 2.0–compliant engine—not that there is any reason to switch from Activiti, of course!

As a Java developer, I used to loathe BPM suites—big black boxes that cost tons of money to produce pictures. Every sane developer understands that pictures will never make it into stable, performant software. That is why you will love Activiti: it is built with benefits for business users in mind, without forgetting the developers. All the code is open source—if something bothers you or isn't clear, you can join our discussions on the forum. Activiti in its simplest form is a library, a JAR, one among many, embeddable in every Java project, be it EE, Spring, or OSGi. With Activiti, you write unit tests just as you are used to doing. But instead of testing code, you are testing processes—based on diagrams that you and the business people discussed and understood—enriched with Java code to make them do exactly what you want them to do. Then you integrate them with other components exactly as you envisioned.

I touch only briefly here on the benefits of BPM and the power of Activiti. Tijs does an outstanding job of covering every facet of Activiti in great detail, and I'm excited and thankful that he put so much time into this book project. Software and open source frameworks in general rise or fall with the available documentation, and it's my belief that this is a superb book that provides much-needed, detailed information. There currently is no better source of knowledge on Activiti and BPMN 2.0. Period.

Think about it: processes are all around us. Without processes, a company wouldn't exist or, at least, it wouldn't make money for long. Every company needs processes to fulfill its goals. And in this quickly changing world, opportunities exist everywhere, from mobile integration in the workflow to massive cloud services orchestrations. It's up to you to grab them.

JORAM BARREZ
COFOUNDER OF ACTIVITI
CORE ACTIVITI DEVELOPER, ALFRESCO

preface

Writing this book was a life-changer for me. After I wrote *Open Source ESBs in Action* for Manning a few years ago, I focused on my daily job for some time, working with open source enterprise integration frameworks like Mule, Camel, ServiceMix, and Spring Integration. My work, over time, drove me to designing and developing processes and BPM, and I started using jBPM and WebSphere Process Server. Then I learned that the founder of the jBPM project, Tom Baeyens, was leaving JBoss to work on a new open source project, which was in stealth mode at that time (early 2010). When the first alpha version of Activiti was released, I told myself I had to contribute to that project, one way or another.

A piece that was missing in the first stages of the Activiti project was an Eclipse plug-in. I had some email conversations with Tom about contributing the plug-in to Activiti. We met and he told me that his goal was to disrupt the process engine space with the Activiti project. My enthusiasm grew even more and I offered my time to start working on a first version of the Activiti Designer. Together with my former colleagues, Tiese Barrell, Yvo Swillens, and Ron van Liempd, we were able to deliver a first version within a couple of months.

As we became part of the Activiti developer community, my hands were itching to start writing a book about Activiti. I felt that a great open source process engine would need a detailed book to describe all the possibilities and potential it offers. Manning was eager to publish a book about Activiti, and, together with Ron, we started writing in the autumn of 2010. We had a hard time keeping up with the frequent releases and the new functionality that kept on coming. But, it also was a lot of fun to be able to write about a new functionality that was just (or about to be) released.

After a few meet-ups with the Activiti developer community and a couple of nice dinners with the Activiti team, we began discussing the possibility of my joining Alfresco to work on Activiti. In May 2011, I accepted the offer and was able to begin working on Activiti full-time.

In the meantime, the writing of this book fell a little behind schedule. There was so much interesting work to be done developing the Activiti Designer, working on the Activiti Engine, and starting in a new job, that time caught up with me. After I had settled in a bit, I took up the writing task again and began working on the remaining chapters.

So here I am, at the end of the process. I've switched from being a consultant to an open source software engineer, and I'm close to completing my second book. And, just like with my previous book, I have a new family addition coinciding with the book's release. I hope you will enjoy reading this book as much as I loved writing it!

acknowledgments

Many people deserve thanks for helping me with this book project. First of all, I want to thank Ron for starting this adventure with me and for his contributions to the book.

A big thank you to the guys on the Activiti team—Tom, Joram, and Frederik—for starting this great open source project and for all the help they gave me during the writing of the book. Special thanks to Tom and Joram for kindly contributing the forewords.

I'd also like to thank the guys at camunda (Bernd and Daniel, in particular) for their contribution to the Activiti project and for their help when I was writing about the camunda fox cycle and the Activiti CDI module.

Thanks to Balsamiq Studios and Giacomo "Peldi" Guilizzoni for providing licenses for their great Balsamiq tool. I really enjoyed creating the graphics for this book.

Thanks to Tiese Barrell and Yvo Swillens for their enthusiasm and development work on the Activiti Designer. Together we became part of the great Activiti developer community.

A special thank-you to Andy Verberne for his work on the technical proofread of the final manuscript (again).

Without the patience of my lovely Ankie, the writing of this book would not have been possible. She managed to love me, even after long working days and in spite of my sometimes grumpy communication when examples were not working as expected. Liv and Noah, thank you for all the joy you bring to my life. Thanks to my parents and parents-in-law for their love and interest in my writing.

Thanks also to the following reviewers of the manuscript who read it and provided feedback during the various stages of its development: Gil Goldman, Michał Minicki,

Sven Vintges, Joram Barrez, Jeff Davis, Gordon Dickens, Roy Prins, Claus Ibsen, Federico Tomassetti, Greg Helton, Mykel Alvis, and Nicolas Leroux.

Finally, my appreciation to everyone at Manning, starting with publisher Marjan Bace, my editor Sebastian Stirling, and the production team of June Eding, Nermina Miller, Mary Piergies, Gordan Salinovic, and Janet Vail.

about this book

Activiti is an open source Business Processing Model and Notation (BPMN) 2.0 process engine framework that provides an environment for running your business and technical processes. It's a project funded by Alfresco and established by jBPM founder Tom Baeyens. Activiti provides much more functionality than simply running BPMN 2.0 processes in a rock-solid way. It provides a web-based modeling tool for business analysts, an Eclipse plug-in for developers, and a web application to work with and manage the processes. In addition, Activiti community members, including SpringSource, FuseSource, MuleSoft, and camunda, have implemented further functionality like full Spring integration, an OSGi bundle, Mule and Camel integration, and a CDI module.

This book is written by one of the Activiti core developers and the lead developer of the Activiti Designer component. It contains loads of examples to help you understand the BPMN 2.0 language and how to work with all the extensions Activiti provides. In the final chapters, the book goes beyond Activiti's core functionality and shows how to do CMIS communication from a process definition and how to implement a business activity monitoring environment using the open source Esper framework.

You should not expect to find examples of all the nitty-gritty details of the BPMN 2.0 specification. Instead, the focus is on Activiti-supported elements and the most common use cases for developing process definitions.

You also won't find in-depth discussions of the business side of BPM. Many other books focus on the business perspectives of BPM; this book focuses on the technical aspects of BPM, mostly on BPMN 2.0 and Activiti.

Who should read this book?

This book is written for everyone who's interested in learning about Activiti. In addition, it's a great way to learn about BPMN 2.0 from a practical perspective. Every developer, process designer and analyst, or architect will benefit from the information and examples provided to learn about the basics and details of the Activiti framework. With the technical perspective offered in this book, you shouldn't be afraid of the Java and XML code listings.

Roadmap

The book has 14 chapters divided into 4 parts:

- Part 1 Introducing BPMN 2.0 and Activiti
- Part 2 Implementing BPMN 2.0 processes with Activiti
- Part 3 Enhancing BPMN 2.0 processes
- Part 4 Managing BPMN 2.0 processes

There are also two appendixes. Appendix A explains how to work with the source code examples, and appendix B covers elements supported by Activiti BPMN 2.0.

Part 1 shows you how to get started with the Activiti framework and explains the background of the BPMN 2.0 standard. You are introduced to the different components of the Activiti framework and developing with the Activiti API.

Chapter 1 introduces the Activiti framework and shows you how to set up the Activiti default environment. At the end of the chapter, you implement your first simple BPMN 2.0 process definition and test it with a simple JUnit test.

Chapter 2 provides a short introduction to Business Process Management. Here, you'll learn about the background of the BPMN 2.0 standard, compared with other standards like WS-BPEL. Finally, you are introduced to core BPMN 2.0 elements.

Chapter 3 provides an overview of all the components of the Activiti framework, including the Activiti Modeler, Activiti Designer, Activiti Explorer, and the camunda fox cycle. Using a simple process example, we walk through the components and you'll learn how to model, design, and deploy a BPMN 2.0 process definition.

Chapter 4 gives an overview of the Activiti API, starting with short code examples illustrating the main Activiti interfaces. Then, you'll learn how to implement Java logic in a BPMN 2.0 process definition and how to work with Spring beans.

In part 2, we shift the focus from understanding the Activiti framework and BPMN 2.0 to using them to develop process definitions. We discuss and use most of the supported BPMN 2.0 elements and talk about important topics like error handling and deploying process definitions to an Activiti Engine. In the final chapter, we explore additional modules provided by the Activiti framework, such as CDI and OSGi.

Chapter 5 shows how to implement a full-blown process definition using Activiti. We explore the workflow and form capabilities of the Activiti Engine and you'll learn how to use an email task to send emails during process execution.

Chapter 6 introduces a number of advanced BPMN 2.0 constructs and Activiti extensions. You'll learn about multiple execution paths using the parallel gateway and how to structure larger process definitions using standalone or embedded subprocesses. You also are introduced to the JPA and listener Activiti extensions.

Chapter 7 describes ways to deal with error handling in BPMN 2.0 processes. You can use the standard error end event and boundary error event or implement an approach using Java exceptions and multiple outgoing sequence flows.

Chapter 8 talks about ways to deploy the Activiti Engine in your environment. You can choose an embedded approach, using only Activiti JARs, or go for a standalone approach using the Activiti REST API. At the end of chapter, you'll also learn how to implement an additional REST service when necessary.

Chapter 9 shows how to make use of the Activiti OSGi bundle and the CDI module. With the OSGi bundle, you can deploy Activiti on an OSGi container like Apache Karaf and take advantage of the flexibility offered by that platform. The Activiti CDI module provides integration with the Contexts and Dependency Injection JEE framework. You can use handy annotations to quickly build a JSF process and workflow application.

In part 3, we focus on more advanced features and extensions to the Activiti framework. In the previous two parts, we looked at the basic functionality of Activiti and BPMN 2.0, so now it's time to step up and talk about advanced ways of using Activiti. We integrate Activiti with the Drools rule engine, the Alfresco document management system, Mule and Camel for external communication, and Esper for business activity monitoring.

Chapter 10 discusses advanced workflow features with subtasks, task delegation, and the four-eye principle workflow pattern. We also show how to use an LDAP server for identity management and how to use the BPMN 2.0 multi-instance construct. And, finally, we look at how to implement additional form types and go for an external form-rendering approach.

Chapter 11 shows how you can communicate with external services and applications to execute business logic that is necessary during process execution. With the Activiti Mule and Camel modules, it's simple to use the powerful features these frameworks provide to implement all kinds of communication logic.

Chapter 12 provides a detailed overview of how to use the Drools rule engine with Activiti business rule tasks. We start with an introduction to the Drools framework and implement a couple of rule examples. After you implement a process definition containing two business rule tasks, you'll learn how to implement a Vaadin web application where you can change deployed rules in real time.

Chapter 13 shows how Activiti is used in the open source Alfresco product and how you can use the CMIS standard (with Apache Chemistry) to communicate with Alfresco from a process definition.

Chapter 14 introduces business activity monitoring with Activiti using the open source Esper framework. You'll learn how to fire events to Esper using Activiti listeners and how to implement eventing logic in Esper to combine events into useful management information. Finally, you'll see how you can implement a simple Vaadin dashboard to monitor business processes running on the Activiti Engine.

In part 4, we leave behind the development of process definitions and focus on running process definitions on the Activiti Engine in a production environment. This part consists of one chapter.

Chapter 15 discusses important topics that are needed to run processes on the Activiti Engine successfully. First, we look at the database model of the Activiti Engine in detail, and then we move on to dealing with process versioning. Then, you'll see how jobs are handled in the Activiti Engine using the asynchronous job executor implementation. And, finally, you'll learn how you can extend the Activiti Explorer with additional management functionality, like a report of all running and completed process instances.

Appendix A provides an overview of all the projects you'll find in the book's source code. Pointers are given on where each project is used in which chapter of the book. Appendix B provides a detailed overview of the BPMN 2.0 elements supported by the Activiti Engine.

Code conventions and downloads

Source code in listings or in text appears in a `fixed-width font like this` to separate it from ordinary text. Code annotations accompany many of the listings, highlighting important concepts. In some cases, numbered cueballs link to additional explanations that follow the listing.

There are many code examples in this book. The process definitions are described using XML code that shows the BPMN 2.0 XML elements. The process logic, like Java service tasks and listeners, is implemented in Java.

The source code for the book is divided into a number of projects. The `bpmn-examples` project contains the most example code and the other projects are used to implement special artifacts like web applications. For a full description of the source code projects, please refer to appendix A.

Source code for the examples in this book can be downloaded from the publisher's website at www.manning.com/ActivitiinAction. There's also a special website devoted to this book at www.bpmnwithactiviti.org.

Author Online

Purchase of *Activiti in Action* includes free access to a private web forum run by Manning Publications where you can make comments about the book, ask technical questions, and receive help from the author and from other users. To access the forum and subscribe to it, point your web browser to www.manning.com/ActivitiinAction. This page provides information on how to get on the forum once you're registered, what kind of help is available, and the rules of conduct on the forum.

Manning's commitment to our readers is to provide a venue where a meaningful dialog between individual readers and between readers and the author can take place. It's not a commitment to any specific amount of participation on the part of the author, whose contribution to the forum remains voluntary (and unpaid). We suggest you try asking the author some challenging questions lest his interest stray!

The Author Online forum and the archives of previous discussions will be accessible from the publisher's website as long as the book is in print.

About the author

Tijs Rademakers is a senior software engineer at Alfresco, where he is a member of the Activiti core development team. He is an Activiti committer to the Activiti Engine and lead developer for the Activiti Eclipse Designer. Tijs is coauthor of *Open Source ESBs in Action* (Manning, 2008) and has over 10 years of software engineering experience, with a focus on open source BPM and enterprise integration frameworks. He lives in Valkenswaard in the Netherlands with his girlfriend and two children.

about the cover illustration

The figure on the cover of *Activiti in Action* is captioned "Member of the Eastern Goths," also known as the Ostrogoths, an ancient Germanic tribe that in the late fifth century AD established a large kingdom in Italy. Their descendants still live in northern Italy today. This illustration is taken from a recent reprint of Balthasar Hacquet's *Images and Descriptions of Southwestern and Eastern Wenda, Illyrians, and Slavs* published by the Ethnographic Museum in Split, Croatia, in 2008. Hacquet (1739–1815) was an Austrian physician and scientist who spent many years studying the botany, geology, and ethnography of many parts of the Austrian Empire, as well as the Veneto, the Julian Alps, and the western Balkans, inhabited in the past by peoples of many different tribes and nationalities. Hand drawn illustrations accompany the many scientific papers and books that Hacquet published.

The rich diversity of the drawings in Hacquet's publications speaks vividly of the uniqueness and individuality of Alpine and Balkan regions just 200 years ago. This was a time when the dress codes of two villages separated by a few miles identified people uniquely as belonging to one or the other, and when members of an ethnic tribe, social class, or trade could be easily distinguished by what they were wearing. Dress codes have changed since then and the diversity by region, so rich at the time, has faded away. It is now often hard to tell the inhabitant of one continent from another and today's inhabitants of the picturesque towns and villages in the Italian Alps are not readily distinguishable from residents of other parts of Europe.

We at Manning celebrate the inventiveness, the initiative, and the fun of the computer business with book covers based on costumes from two centuries ago brought back to life by illustrations such as this one.

Part 1

Introducing
BPMN 2.0 and Activiti

This first part of the book provides an introduction to the Activiti framework and the background about the BPMN 2.0 standard. In chapter 1, we'll cover how to set up an Activiti environment, starting with the download of the Activiti framework. In chapter 2, you'll be introduced to the main elements of the BPMN 2.0 standard in order to create process definitions. Chapter 3 offers an overview of the Activiti framework's main components, including the Activiti Designer and Explorer. Finally, in chapter 4, we'll discuss the Activiti API with several short code examples.

Introducing
the Activiti framework

1

This chapter covers

- Introduction to Activiti
- Installing the Activiti framework
- Implementing a BPMN 2.0 process

Every day, your actions are part of different processes. For example, when you order a book in an online bookstore, a process is executed to get the book paid for, packaged, and shipped to you. When you need to renew your driver's license, the renewal process often requires a new photograph as input. Activiti provides an open source framework to design, implement, and run processes. Organizations can use Activiti to implement their business processes without the need for expensive software licenses.

This chapter will get you up and running with Activiti in 30 minutes. First, we'll take a look at the different components of the Activiti tool stack, including a Modeler, Designer, and a REST web application. Then, we'll discuss the history of the Activiti framework and compare its functionality with its main competitors, jBPM and BonitaSoft.

Before we dive into code examples in section 1.4, we'll first make sure the Activiti framework is installed correctly. At the end of this chapter, you'll have a running Activiti environment and a deployable example.

First, let's look at Activiti's tool stack and its different components, including the modeling environment, the engine, and the runtime explorer application.

1.1 *The Activiti tool stack*

The core component of the Activiti framework is the process engine. The process engine provides the core capabilities to execute Business Process Model and Notation (BPMN) 2.0 processes and create new workflow tasks, among other things. You can find the BPMN specification and lots of examples at www.bpmn.org, and we'll go into more detail about BPMN in chapter 2. The Activiti project contains a couple of tools in addition to the Activiti Engine. Figure 1.1 shows an overview of the full Activiti tool stack.

Let's quickly walk through the different components listed in figure 1.1. With the Activiti Modeler, business and information analysts are capable of modeling a BPMN 2.0-compliant business process in a web browser. This means that business processes can easily be shared—no client software is needed before you can start modeling. The Activiti designer is an Eclipse-based plugin, which enables a developer to enhance the modeled business process into a BPMN 2.0 process that can be executed on the Activiti process engine. You can also run unit tests, add Java logic, and create deployment artifacts with the Activiti Designer.

In addition to the design tools, Activiti provides a number of supporting tools. With Activiti Explorer, you can get an overview of deployed processes and even dive into the database tables underneath the Activiti process engine. You can also use Activiti Explorer to interact with the deployed business processes. For example, you can get a list of tasks that are already assigned to you. You can also start a new process instance and look at the status of that newly created process instance in a graphical diagram.

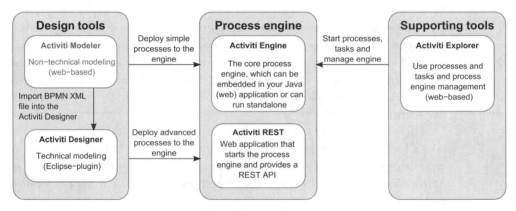

Figure 1.1 An overview of the Activiti tool stack: in the center, the Activiti process engine, and on the right and left sides, the accompanying modeling, design, and management tools. The grayed-out components are add-ons to the core Activiti framework.

Finally, there's the Activiti REST component, which provides a web application that starts the Activiti process engine when the web application is started. In addition, it offers a REST API that enables you to communicate remotely with the Activiti Engine.

The different components are summarized in table 1.1.

Table 1.1 An overview of the different components of the Activiti tool stack

Component name	Short description
Activiti Engine	The core component of the Activiti tool stack that performs the process engine functions, such as executing BPMN 2.0 business processes and creating workflow tasks.
Activiti Modeler	A web-based modeling environment for creating BPMN 2.0-compliant business process diagrams. This component is donated by Signavio, which also provides a commercial modeling tool, named the Signavio Process Editor.
Activiti Designer	An Eclipse plugin that can be used to design BPMN 2.0-compliant business processes with the addition of Activiti extensions, such as a Java service task and execution listeners. You can also unit test processes, import BPMN 2.0 processes, and create deployment artifacts.
Activiti Explorer	A web application that can be used for a wide range of functions in conjunction with the Activiti Engine. You can, for example, start new process instances and get a list of tasks assigned to you. In addition, you can perform simple process management tasks, like deploying new processes and retrieving the process instance status.
Activiti REST	A web application that provides a REST interface on top of the Activiti Engine. In the default installation (see section 1.1.3), the Activiti REST application is the entry point to the Activiti Engine.

You can't start developing without a clear understanding of the Activiti framework and the architecture that's built around a state machine. Let's take a closer look at the history of the Activiti framework and discuss the Activiti Engine in more detail.

1.2 Getting to know Activiti

When you start working with a new framework, it's always good to know some project background and have an understanding of the main components. In this section, we'll be looking at exactly that.

1.2.1 A little bit of history

The Activiti project was started in 2010 by Tom Baeyens and Joram Barrez, the former founder and the core developer of jBPM (JBoss BPM), respectively. The goal of the Activiti project is to build a rock-solid open source BPMN 2.0 process engine. In the next chapter, we'll talk in detail about the BPMN 2.0 specification, but in this chapter we'll focus on the Activiti framework itself and getting it installed and up and running with simple examples.

Activiti is funded by Alfresco (known for its open source document management system of the same name; see www.alfresco.com and chapter 13 for more details), but Activiti acts as an independent, open source project. Alfresco uses a process engine to support features such as a review and approval process for documents, which means that the document has to be approved by one user or a group of users. For this kind of functionality, Activiti is integrated into the Alfresco system to provide the necessary process and workflow engine capabilities.

> **NOTE**   jBPM was used in the past instead of Activiti to provide this process and workflow functionality. jBPM is still included in Alfresco, but it may be deprecated at some point in time.

Besides running the Activiti process engine in Alfresco, Activiti is built to run standalone or embedded in any other system. In this book, we'll focus on running Activiti outside the Alfresco environment, but we'll discuss the integration opportunities between Activiti and Alfresco in detail in chapter 13.

In 2010, the Activiti project started off quickly and succeeded in producing monthly (!) releases of the framework. In December 2010, the first stable and production-ready release (5.0) was made available. The Activiti developer community, including companies like SpringSource, FuseSource, and Mulesoft, has since been able to develop new functionality on a frequent basis. In this book, we'll explore this contributed functionality, such as the Spring integration (chapter 4) and the Mule and Apache Camel integration (chapter 11).

But first things first. What can you do with a process engine? Why should you use the Activiti framework? Let's discuss the core component, the Activiti Engine.

1.2.2   *The basics of the Activiti Engine*

Activiti is a BPMN 2.0 process-engine framework that implements the BPMN 2.0 specification. It's able to deploy process definitions, start new process instances, execute user tasks, and perform other BPMN 2.0 functions, which we'll discuss throughout this book.

But at its core, the Activiti Engine is a state machine. A BPMN 2.0 process definition consists of elements like events, tasks, and gateways that are wired together via sequence flows (think of arrows). When such a process definition is deployed on the process engine and a new process instance is started, the BPMN 2.0 elements are executed one by one. This process execution is similar to a state machine, where there's an active state and, based on conditions, the state execution progresses to another state via transitions (think again of arrows). Let's look at an abstract figure of a state machine and see how it's implemented in the Activiti Engine (figure 1.2).

In the Activiti Engine, most BPMN 2.0 elements are implemented as a state. They're connected with leaving and arriving transitions, which are called sequence flows in BPMN 2.0. Every state or corresponding BPMN 2.0 element can have attached a piece of logic that will be executed when the process instance enters the state. In figure 1.2, you can also look up the interface and implementing class that are used in the Activiti Engine. As you can see, the logic interface `ActivityBehavior` is implemented by a lot of classes. That's because the logic of a BPMN 2.0 element is implemented there.

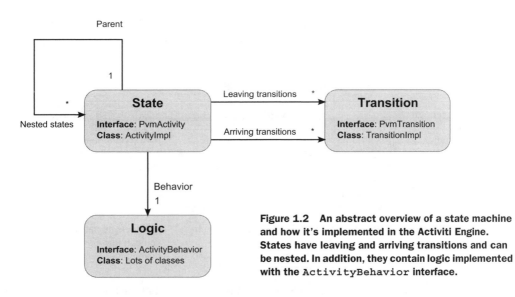

Figure 1.2 An abstract overview of a state machine and how it's implemented in the Activiti Engine. States have leaving and arriving transitions and can be nested. In addition, they contain logic implemented with the `ActivityBehavior` interface.

When you see a complex BPMN 2.0 example later on in the book, remember that, in essence, it's a rather simple state machine. Now let's look at a couple other open source process engines that offer functionality similar to Activiti, and also consider the differences.

1.2.3 *Knowing the competitors*

When you're interested in an open source process engine like Activiti, it's always good to know a little bit more about the competing open source frameworks. Because the main developers of Activiti were previously involved with the JBoss BPM or jBPM framework, there's also some controversy surrounding this discussion. It's obvious that jBPM and Activiti share a lot of the same architectural principles, but there are also many differences. We'll only discuss the two main open source competitors of Activiti:

- *JBoss BPM or jBPM*—An open source process engine that first supported the custom jPDL process language, but, because version 5.0 supports BPMN 2.0, the jBPM project has merged with the JBoss Drools project (an open source business-rule management framework) and replaced Drools Flow as the rule flow language for the Drools framework.
- *BonitaSoft*—An open source process engine that provides support for the BPMN 2.0 process language. The main differentiators of BonitaSoft are the large set of supported elements and the integrated development environment.

Let's discuss the similarities and differences between Activiti and its two competitors in a bit more detail.

ACTIVITI AND JBPM
Activiti and jBPM have a lot in common: they're both developer-oriented process engine frameworks built around the concept of a state machine (see section 1.2.2).

Because jBPM 5 also implements the BPMN 2.0 specification, a lot of similar functionality can be found. But there are a number of differences that are important to mention; see table 1.2.

Table 1.2   Main differences between Activiti and jBPM

Description	Activiti	jBPM
Community members	Activiti has a base team consisting of Alfresco employees. In addition, companies like SpringSource, FuseSource, and Mule-Soft provide resources on specific components. There are also individual open source developers committing to the Activiti project.	jBPM has a base team of JBoss employees. In addition, there are individual committers.
Spring support	Activiti has native Spring support, which makes it easy to use Spring beans in your processes and to use Spring for JPA and transaction management.	jBPM has no native Spring support, but you can use Spring with additional development effort.
Business rules support	Activiti provides a basic integration with the Drools rule engine to support the BPMN 2.0 business rule task.	jBPM and Drools are integrated on a project level, so there's native integration with Drools on various levels.
Additional tools	Activiti provides modeler (Oryx) and designer (Eclipse) tools to model new process definitions. The main differentiator is the Activiti Explorer, which provides an easy-to-use web interface to start new processes, work with tasks and forms, and manage running processes. In addition, it provides ad hoc task support and collaboration functionality.	jBPM also provides a modeler based on the Oryx project and a Eclipse designer. With a web application, you can start new process instances and work with tasks. The form support is limited.
Project	Activiti has a strong developer and user community with a solid release schedule of two months. Its main components are the Engine, Designer, Explorer, and REST application.	jBPM has a strong developer and user community. The release schedule isn't crystal clear, and some releases have been postponed a couple of times. The Designer application is (at the moment of writing) still based on Drools Flow, and the promised new Eclipse plugin keeps getting postponed.

It's always difficult to compare two open source frameworks objectively, and this book is about Activiti. This book by no means presents the only perspective on the differences between the frameworks, but it identifies a number of differences that you can consider when making a choice between them.

Next up is the comparison between Activiti and BonitaSoft.

ACTIVITI AND BONITASOFT

BonitaSoft is the company behind Bonita Open Solution, an open source BPM product. There are a number of differences between Activiti and BonitaSoft:

- Activiti is developer-focused and provides an easy-to-use Java API to communicate with the Activiti Engine. BonitaSoft provides a tool-based solution where you can click and drag your process definition and forms.
- With Activiti, you're in control of every bit of the code you write. With Bonita-Soft, the code is often generated from the developer tool.
- BonitaSoft provides a large set of connectivity options to a wide range of third-party products. This means it's easy to configure a task in the developer tool to connect to SAP or query a particular database table. With Activiti, the connectivity options are also very broad (due to the integration with Mule and Camel), but they're more developer focused.

Although both frameworks focus on supporting the BPMN 2.0 specification and offering a process engine, they take different implementation angles. BonitaSoft provides a development tool where you can draw your processes and configure and deploy them without needing to write one line of code. This means that you aren't in control of the process solution you're developing. Activiti provides an easy-to-use Java API that will need some coding, but, in the end, you can easily embed it into an application or run it on every platform you'd like.

As you can see, Activiti is not the only open source process engine capable of running BPMN 2.0 process models, but it's definitely a flexible and powerful option, and one that we'll discuss in detail in this book. Now that you know the different components of Activiti, let's get the framework installed on your development machine.

1.3 Installing the Activiti framework

The first thing you have to do is point your web browser to the Activiti website at www.activiti.org. You'll be guided to the latest release of Activiti via the download button. Download the latest version and unpack the distribution to a logical folder, such as

```
C:\activiti (Windows)
/usr/local/activiti (Linux or Mac OS)
```

This isn't the beginning of a long and complex installation procedure—with Activiti, there's a setup directory that contains an Ant build file that installs the Activiti framework. The directory structure of the distribution is shown in figure 1.3.

Before you go further with the installation procedure, make sure that you've installed a Java 5 SDK or higher, pointed the JAVA_HOME environment variable to the Java installation directory, and installed a current version (1.8.x or higher) of Ant (http://ant.apache.org). Shortcuts to the Java SDK and the Ant framework are also provided on the Activiti download page.

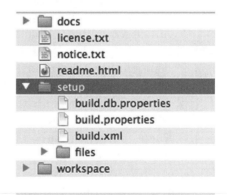

Figure 1.3 The directory structure of the Activiti distribution with the setup directory and the Ant build.xml file as the main parts for the installation procedure.

The last thing to confirm is that you have an internet connection available without a proxy, because the Ant build file will download additional packages. If you're behind a proxy, make sure you've configured the Ant build to use that proxy (more info can be found at http://ant.apache.org/manual/proxy.html).

When you open a terminal or command prompt and go to the setup directory shown in figure 1.3, you only have to run the ant command (or ant demo.start). This will kick off the Activiti installation process, which will look for a build.xml file in the setup directory. The installation performs the following steps:

1   An H2 database is installed to /apps/h2, and the H2 database is started on port 9092.
2   The Activiti database is created in the running H2 database.
3   Apache Tomcat 6.0.x is downloaded and installed to /apps/apache-tomcat-6.0.x, where x stands for the latest version.
4   Demo data, including users, groups, and business processes, are installed to the H2 database.
5   The Activiti REST and Activiti Explorer WARs are copied to the webapps directory of Tomcat.
6   Tomcat is started, which means that the Activiti Explorer and REST applications are running.
7   Depending on on your OS, a web browser is started by the installation script with the Activiti Explorer URL. On Windows 7, no web browser is started; in other versions of Windows, the web browser is only started if you have Firefox installed.

When the Ant script has finished, you have the Activiti tool stack installed and running. That's not bad for about a minute of installation time. The Ant build file isn't only handy for installing Activiti but also for doing common tasks, like stopping and starting the H2 database (ant h2.stop, ant h2.start) and the Tomcat server (ant tomcat.stop, ant tomcat.start) and for re-creating a vanilla database schema (ant internal.db.drop, ant internal.db.create). It's worth the time to look at the Ant targets in the Ant build file.

The installation of Activiti consists foremost of two web applications being deployed to a Tomcat server and a ready-to-use H2 database being created with example processes, groups, and users already loaded. Figure 1.4 shows the installation result in a schematic overview.

Notice that we haven't yet installed the Activiti Modeler and Designer applications. These components aren't part of the installation script and have to be installed separately. We'll discuss how to do this in chapter 3.

To verify whether the installation has succeeded, the Activiti Explorer, listed in table 1.3, should be available via your favorite web browser. You can use the user kermit with password kermit to log in. To work with the Activiti REST application, you can use a REST client, such as the REST client Firefox plugin. You can read more about the Activiti REST API in chapter 8.

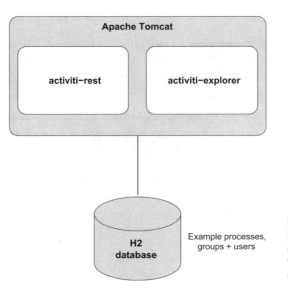

Figure 1.4   An overview of the installation result of the Activiti tool stack, including a running Tomcat server and H2 database with the two Activiti web applications already deployed.

Table 1.3   The URI of the Activiti Explorer and REST web applications available for you after the installation of Activiti

Application name	URI	Short description
Activiti Explorer	http://localhost:8080/activiti-explorer	The Explorer application can be used to work with the deployed processes. This is a good starting point from which to try the example processes.
Activiti REST	http://localhost:8080/activiti-rest/service	The REST application can be used to gain remote access to the Activiti Engine via a REST interface. For all available REST services, you can look in the Activiti user guide that can be found on the Activiti website.

By trying the Activiti Explorer application, you can verify whether the installation was successful. After logging in and clicking on the Process tab, you should get a list of the examples processes that are deployed on the Activiti Engine.

Working with demo processes is fun, but it's even better to try out your own developed business process.

1.4   *Implementing your first process in Activiti*

Let's try to implement a simplified version of a book order process. We could use the Activiti Modeler to first model the process, and the Activiti Designer to implement and deploy the process, but it's better to start off with a BPMN 2.0 XML document for learning purposes. There won't be any drag-and-drop development, but get ready for some XML hacking.

1.4.1 *Say hello to Activiti*

We'll keep things simple for now; if you don't understand every construct already, don't be worried—we'll discuss the BPMN 2.0 elements in more detail in chapter 2.

In the following listing, a starter for the BPMN 2.0 XML definition of the book order process is shown with only a start event, an end event, and a sequence flow to connect the two.

Listing 1.1 bookorder.simple.bpmn20.xml document with only a start and end event

```xml
<?xml version="1.0" encoding="UTF-8"?>
<definitions xmlns="http://www.omg.org/spec/BPMN/20100524/MODEL"
            targetNamespace="http://www.bpmnwithactiviti.org">

  <process id="simplebookorder" name="Order book">
    <startEvent id="startevent1" name="Start"/>
    <sequenceFlow id="sequenceflow1"
        sourceRef="startevent1" targetRef="endevent1"/>
    <endEvent id="endevent1" name="End"/>
  </process>
</definitions>
```

A BPMN 2.0 XML definition always starts with a `definitions` element that is identified with a namespace from the OMG BPMN specification. Each process definition must also define a namespace; here, you define a `targetNamespace` with the book's website as its attribute value. Activiti also provides a namespace, which enables you to use Activiti extensions to the BPMN 2.0 specification, as you'll see in chapter 4. You can now run this simple process to test if you've correctly defined the process definition and the environment setup in the right manner.

To test this process, you have to create a Java project in your favorite editor. In this book, we'll use Eclipse for the example description, because the Eclipse Designer is only available as an Eclipse plugin. But it's easier to download the source code from the book's website at Manning (or you can go directly to the Google code repository at http://code.google.com/p/activitiinaction) and import the examples from there.

When you import the `bpmn-examples` project (used in this chapter), the Activiti libraries have to be added to the Java build path. The book's source code uses Maven to retrieve all the necessary dependencies. The sample project's code structure is explained in detail in chapter 4 and appendix A. But, starting from Eclipse Indigo (version 3.7.x), there's good built-in Maven support, so it's easy to get it working. Activate the Maven project capabilities by choosing the Configure–Convert to Maven Project option in the project menu when you right-click on the `bpmn-examples` project in Eclipse. Eclipse will download all the necessary dependencies and configure the classpath for you.

With the dependencies in place, you can look for the `SimpleProcessTest` unit test in the `org.bpmnwithactiviti.chapter1` package of the `bpmn-examples` project. The `SimpleProcessTest` class contains one test method, shown in the following listing.

Listing 1.2 First example of a JUnit test for a Activiti process deployment

```
public class SimpleProcessTest {

  @Test
  public void startBookOrder() {
    ProcessEngine processEngine = ProcessEngineConfiguration
        .createStandaloneInMemProcessEngineConfiguration()
        .buildProcessEngine();

    RuntimeService runtimeService =
        processEngine.getRuntimeService();
    RepositoryService repositoryService =
        processEngine.getRepositoryService();
    repositoryService.createDeployment()
        .addClasspathResource(
            "bookorder.simple.bpmn20.xml")
        .deploy();

    ProcessInstance processInstance =
        runtimeService.startProcessInstanceByKey(
            "simplebookorder");
    assertNotNull(processInstance.getId());
    System.out.println("id " + processInstance.getId() + " " +
        processInstance.getProcessDefinitionId());
  }
}
```

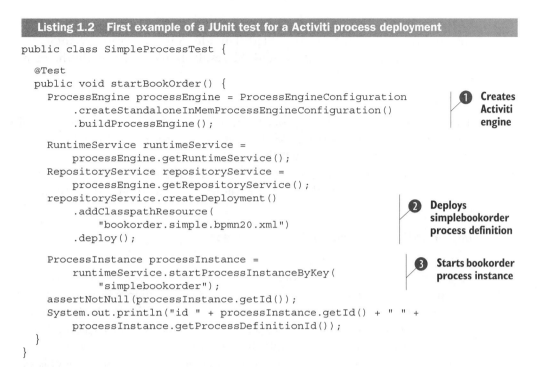

❶ Creates Activiti engine

❷ Deploys simplebookorder process definition

❸ Starts bookorder process instance

In just a few lines of code, you're able to start up the Activiti process engine, deploy the book order process XML file from listing 1.1 to it, and start a process instance for the deployed process definition.

The process engine can be created with the ProcessEngineConfiguration ❶, which can be used to start the Activiti engine and the H2 database. In this case, the process engine is started with an in-memory H2 database. There are different ways to start up an Activiti engine, and we'll look at the options in detail in chapter 4.

> **NOTE** Activiti can also run on database platforms other than H2, such as Oracle or PostgreSQL.

The next important step in listing 1.2 is the deployment of the bookorder.simple.bpmn20.xml file from listing 1.1. To deploy a process from Java code, you need to access the RepositoryService from the ProcessEngine instance. Via the RepositoryService instance, you can add the book order XML file to the list of classpath resources to deploy it to the process engine ❷. The process engine will validate the book order process file and create a new process definition in the H2 database.

It's easy to start a process instance based on the newly deployed process definition by invoking the startProcessInstanceByKey method ❸ on the RuntimeService instance, which is also retrieved from the ProcessEngine instance. The key bookorder, which is passed as the process key parameter, should be equal to the process id attribute from the book order process of listing 1.1. A process instance is stored to the H2 database, and a process instance ID that can be used as a reference to this specific process instance is created. This identifier is very important.

You can now run the unit test and the result should be green. In the console, you should see a message like this:

```
id 4 simplebookorder:1:3
```

This message means that the process instance ID is 4 and the process definition that was used to create the instance was the `simplebookorder` definition with version 1 and the process definition database ID is 3.

Now that we've covered the basics, let's implement a bit more of the book order process; then you can use the Activiti Explorer to claim and finish a user task for your process.

1.4.2   *Implementing a simple book order process*

It would be a shame to finish chapter 1 with an example that only contains a start and an end event. Let's enhance your simple book order process with a script task and a user task so you can see a bit of action on the Activiti engine. First, the script task will print an ISBN number that will be provided as input to the book order process when it's started in a unit test (like this example) or in the Activiti Explorer. Then, a user task will be used to manually handle the book ordering.

Activiti allows you to use the scripting language you want, but Groovy is supported by default. We'll use a line of Groovy to print the ISBN process variable. The following listing shows a revised version of the book order process.

Listing 1.3   A book order process with a script and user task

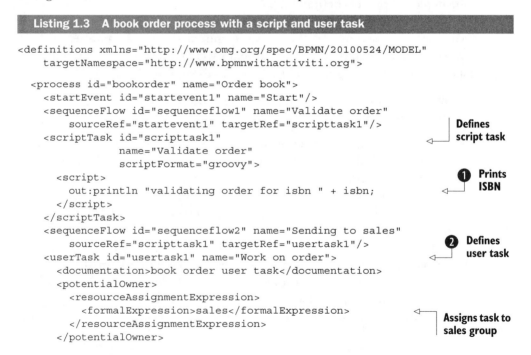

```
<definitions xmlns="http://www.omg.org/spec/BPMN/20100524/MODEL"
    targetNamespace="http://www.bpmnwithactiviti.org">

  <process id="bookorder" name="Order book">
    <startEvent id="startevent1" name="Start"/>
    <sequenceFlow id="sequenceflow1" name="Validate order"
        sourceRef="startevent1" targetRef="scripttask1"/>        ⎤ Defines
    <scriptTask id="scripttask1"                                 ⎦ script task
                name="Validate order"
                scriptFormat="groovy">
      <script>                                                   ❶ Prints
        out:println "validating order for isbn " + isbn;           ISBN
      </script>
    </scriptTask>
    <sequenceFlow id="sequenceflow2" name="Sending to sales"
        sourceRef="scripttask1" targetRef="usertask1"/>          ❷ Defines
    <userTask id="usertask1" name="Work on order">                 user task
      <documentation>book order user task</documentation>
      <potentialOwner>
        <resourceAssignmentExpression>
          <formalExpression>sales</formalExpression>             ⎤ Assigns task to
        </resourceAssignmentExpression>                          ⎦ sales group
      </potentialOwner>
```

```
    </userTask>
    <sequenceFlow id="sequenceflow3" name="Ending process"
        sourceRef="usertask1" targetRef="endevent1"/>
    <endEvent id="endevent1" name="End"/>
  </process>
</definitions>
```

With the two additional tasks added to the process definition, the number of lines in the XML file grows quite a bit. In chapter 3, we'll look at the Activiti Designer, which does the BPMN 2.0 XML generation for you and provides a drag-and-drop type of process development.

The script task contains a out:println variable ❶, which is a Groovy reserved word within the Activiti script task for printing text to the system console. Also notice that the isbn variable can be used directly in the script code without any additional programming.

The user task ❷ contains a potential owner definition, which means that the task can be claimed and completed by users that are part of the group sales. When you run this process in a minute, you'll see in the Activiti Explorer that this user task is available in the task list for the user kermit, who is part of the sales group.

Now that you've added more logic to the process, you also need to change your unit test. One thing you need to add is an isbn process variable when starting the process. To test whether the user task is created, you also need to query the Activiti engine database for user tasks that can be claimed by the user kermit.

Take a look at the changed unit test in the next code listing. You can again find this unit test class in the bpmn-examples project in the org.bpmnwithactiviti.chapter1 package.

Listing 1.4   A unit test with a process variable and user task query

```
public class BookOrderTest {

  @Test
  public void startBookOrder() {
    ProcessEngine processEngine = ProcessEngineConfiguration
        .createStandaloneProcessEngineConfiguration()
        .buildProcessEngine();

    RepositoryService repositoryService =
        processEngine.getRepositoryService();
    RuntimeService runtimeService =
        processEngine.getRuntimeService();
    IdentityService identityService =
        processEngine.getIdentityService();
    TaskService taskService =                            ❶ Gets TaskService
        processEngine.getTaskService();                     instance
    repositoryService.createDeployment()
        .addClasspathResource("bookorder.bpmn20.xml")
        .deploy();

    Map<String, Object> variableMap =
        new HashMap<String, Object>();
```

```
variableMap.put("isbn", "123456");
identityService.setAuthenticatedUserId("kermit");
ProcessInstance processInstance =
    runtimeService.startProcessInstanceByKey(
        "bookorder", variableMap);
assertNotNull(processInstance.getId());
List<Task> taskList = taskService.createTaskQuery()
    .taskCandidateUser("kermit")
    .list()
assertEquals(1, taskList.size());
System.out.println("found task " +
    taskList.get(0).getName());

    taskService.complete(taskList.get(0).getId());
  }
}
```

The `BookOrderTest` unit test starts a process instance with a `Map` of variables ❷ that contains one variable with a name of `isbn` and a value of `123456`. In addition, when the process instance has been started, a `TaskService` instance ❶ is used to retrieve the tasks available to be claimed by the user `kermit`. Because there's only one process instance running with one user task, you test that the number of tasks retrieved is 1.

Also note that you're not using the in-memory database anymore but have switched (`createStandaloneProcessEngineConfiguration`) to the default stand-alone H2 database that's installed as part of the Activiti installation procedure. This means that, before running the unit test, the H2 database should be running (`ant h2.start` or `ant demo.start`). Now you can run the unit test to see if your changes work. In the console, you should see a similar output to

```
validating order for isbn 123456
found task Work on order
```

The first line is printed by the Groovy script task in the running process instance. The last line confirms that one user task is available for claim for the user `kermit`. Because a user task is created, you should be able to see this task in the Activiti Explorer. Confirm that Tomcat has been started (`ant tomcat.start` or `ant demo.start`).

Now, point your browser to http://localhost:8080/activiti-explorer and log in with the user `kermit` and the same password. When you click on the link Queued, you should see one task in the group `Sales`. When you click on this `Sales` group, you should see a screen with one user task with the name of Work on Order like the screenshot shown in figure 1.5.

For the sake of completeness, you can claim the user task and see that it becomes available in the Inbox page. There you can complete the task, which triggers the process instance to complete to the end state. But, before you do that, you can click on the process link, Part of process: 'Order Book', to see details about the running process instance, as shown in figure 1.6.

In the process instance overview, you can get the details about the user tasks that aren't yet completed and the process variables of the running instance. The Activiti

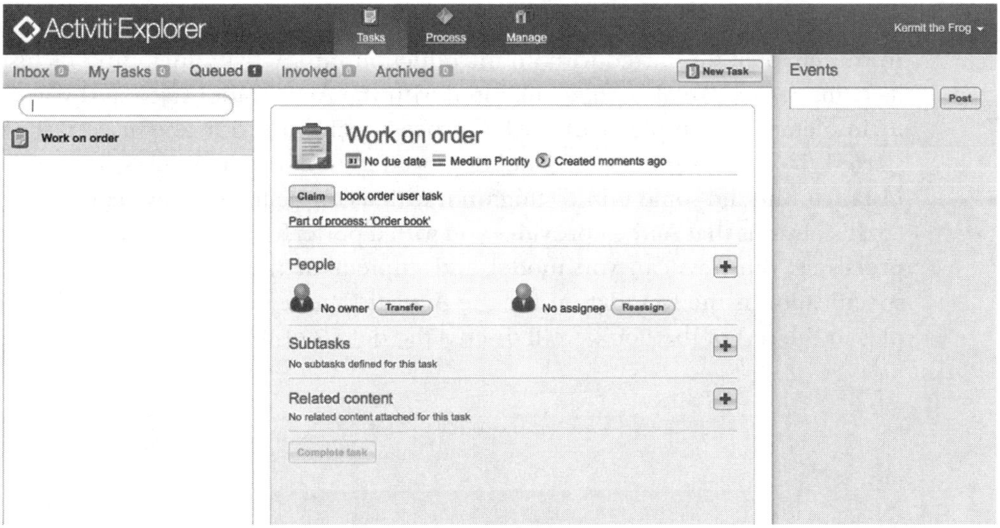

Figure 1.5 A screenshot of the Activiti Explorer showing the user task of the book order process.

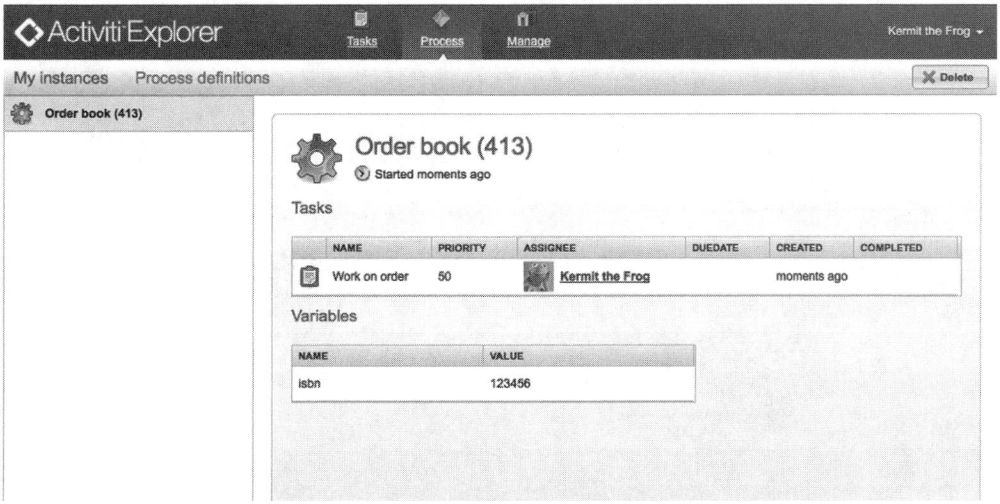

Figure 1.6 A screenshot of the Activiti Explorer application showing the details of a running process instance with open user tasks and the process instance variables.

Explorer contains a lot more functionality, which we'll discuss throughout the book, starting in chapter 3.

This completes our first journey in the Activiti framework. In the coming chapters, we'll take a more detailed look at the Activiti tool stack and explore how to use Activiti's Java API to, for example, create processes or retrieve management information. But, first, we'll look more closely at BPMN 2.0.

1.5   *Summary*

In this chapter, we started with an introduction into Activiti, including its history and its competitors. We also got acquainted with the Activiti tool stack and you were able to implement a simple book order process using a script and user task. You also started the Activiti process engine, deployed a book order process, started a process instance, and did some unit testing on it with a couple lines of Java code.

It's obvious that Activiti provides you with a powerful API and tool stack to run your processes. But how can you model and implement these processes? The BPMN 2.0 specification is the foundation for the Activiti Engine, and, to prepare for the examples in the rest of the book, we'll discuss the details of BPMN 2.0 in the next chapter.

BPMN 2.0:
what's in it for developers?

This chapter covers

- Introducing the BPM discipline
- Categorizing the BPMN 2.0 palette into three levels
- Designing processes with BPMN 2.0

This chapter stands out from the others in this book because it doesn't contain a single code example. To get your head around developing BPMN 2.0 processes, it's necessary to have a thorough understanding of BPM and the main elements of the BPMN 2.0 palette. If you're already familiar with BPM and BPMN 2.0, feel free to skip this chapter and move on to exploring the Activiti framework in chapter 3.

The definition of business process management (BPM) is broad, and BPM vendors are broadening the term even further every day. Because I can't (and don't want) to cover the full spectrum of what's covered by BPM, this chapter defines the boundaries that we'll cover in this book. You'll find that this book isn't about, for example, the theory behind business processes, business rules, business activity monitoring, and straight-through processing. Rather, this book will show you how to develop and deploy business processes with BPMN 2.0 and the Activiti process engine.

But, before we start implementing code examples (in chapter 4), we'll first take a look at the topic of BPM. Once you have a good sense of this broad world, we'll look at the BPMN 2.0 specification and see why it's such an important industry standard. Then, the theoretical foundation for this book is presented, and we'll look at BPMN 2.0 purely from a developer's perspective.

2.1   *Taking a closer look at BPM*

I've already mentioned that BPM covers a wide spectrum. That's because BPM has an ambitious goal: improving processes continuously and promoting efficiency and effectiveness. You can imagine that achieving that goal involves a lot of different roles and players, including management, end users, business analysts, information analysts, architects, developers, and system controllers.

Goals like promoting efficiency and effectiveness are typical targets that the management of an organization tries to achieve. BPM can be regarded as a management discipline and, therefore, it's obvious that these kinds of goals are part of the targets set by implementing BPM. In this book, although we won't focus on the management side of BPM, I fully comprehend the importance of it. We'll concentrate on the technical aspects of BPM with process engines and business process management suites.

Our starting point and the central component within BPM is a business process. Simple examples of business processes are a vacation request process or a book order process. Such a process consists of several activities that eventually result in your receiving a vacation request confirmation or the book you bought. Let's look at a sample book order process in figure 2.1.

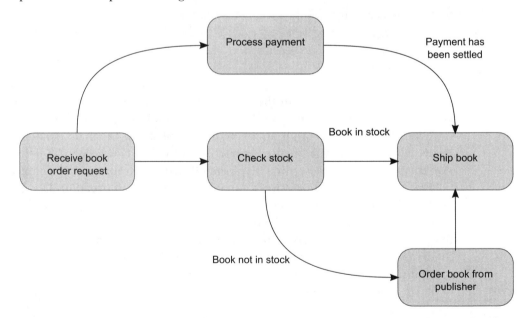

Figure 2.1   A sample book order business process that processes book payment and eventually ships the book to the customer

The book order business process consists of six activities that may need to be executed. Once the book order request is received, the payment is processed to make sure the money is received, and the stock of the book is checked. When the book is in stock, it's shipped to the customer and a confirmation email is sent. But, when the book isn't in stock, it needs to be ordered from the publisher before it can be shipped. So the "Order book from publisher" activity is *optional; it's only* executed *when the condition* "Book not in stock" is *met.*

As you can see, this business process is fairly simple—and incomplete. For example, what happens when the process payment fails? Error handling is one of the challenging aspects of developing a business process. Dealing with error handling is covered in chapter 7.

Another element that the example doesn't cover is how the shipping process will be triggered when a book is ordered from a publisher and arrives at the bookstore. Because there are a lot of additional activities involved, like sending the order to the publisher and following up with the publisher when the book doesn't arrive on time, the "Order book from publisher" activity could be modeled as a subprocess. Subprocesses are a good solution to abstract a main process flow from all the details and to structure process logic for the purpose of reuse. In chapter 6, we'll look into subprocesses in more detail.

To be able to implement even a simple business process like the example in figure 2.1, a number of steps have to be performed. We'll now look at these important steps in the BPM life cycle.

2.1.1　*Walking around the BPM life cycle*

Creating a fully functional business process involves five steps, often referred to collectively as the BPM life cycle, shown in figure 2.2.

Each of these five steps represents an important development phase in implementing a successful process solution:

- *Design*—The first step consists of activities that define the business process: identifying high-level activities, discussing possible organizational changes, defining service level agreements, and specifying process details such as actors, notifications, and escalations.

Figure 2.2　The five steps of the business process management discipline: design, modeling, execution, monitoring, and optimization

- *Modeling*—In this step, the business process is fully specified and validated. The process flow is formalized, for example, by using BPMN; additionally, process variables are defined and candidate services that can be used to execute an activity are identified. To validate the business process, "what-if" scenarios are performed with process simulation.

- *Execution*—The modeled business process is implemented in a business process application, often using a business process management system (BPMS) such as Activiti. You still need to add technical details to the business process before you can execute it. The process is implemented with a process language like WS-BPEL or BPMN 2.0.

- *Monitoring*—The processes are monitored for business goals that are defined by key performance indicators (KPIs). Examples of KPIs are "the average number of orders received in a day should be at least 30" and "the time to send a proposal to a customer based on a web inquiry shouldn't exceed eight hours."

- *Optimization*—Based on new insights, changing business requirements, and monitoring results, the implemented business processes will need to be optimized. When the optimization phase is done, the business process goes into the design phase again and the cycle is completed.

The BPM life cycle shows that implementing business processes is an ongoing process due to the everchanging business environment and need for optimization. How long it takes to walk through all five steps of the BPM life cycle depends greatly on the business environment and the ability of a business to execute. In some businesses, it may take years to complete the cycle; in others, it can be done in weeks or even days. In this book, we'll focus on the execution step of the BPM life cycle because this book is aimed at running business processes on the Activiti process engine.

To get processes implemented and deployed on the Activiti Engine, you need a thorough understanding of the BPMN 2.0 language. Let's see how the BPM industry evolved to support the BPMN 2.0 specification as the dominant process language.

2.2   Evolution to BPMN 2.0

Now that you have a good grasp of BPM terminology, it's time to look at a language that implements a business process: Business Process Model and Notation (BPMN) 2.0. Before we start looking at the BPMN 2.0 language constructs, though, it's good to know a bit about the history of the Object Management Group (OMG). OMG is a well-known standardization organization that develops and maintains the Unified Modeling Language (UML) standard, for example.

2.2.1   Wasn't there a standard called WS-BPEL?

Right! From a developer's perspective, the first industry standard for implementing business processes was the Web Services Business Process Execution Language (WS-BPEL) specification. Although BPMN 1.0 had been standardized and was widely used by information and business analysts from 2004 on, WS-BPEL was the first BPM language that was used by developers to run processes on a process engine. In figure 2.3, the timeline of the WS-BPEL standard is shown.

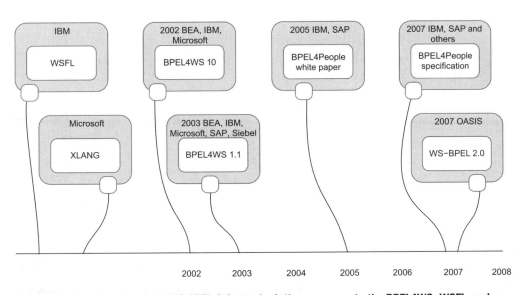

Figure 2.3   The timeline of the WS-BPEL 2.0 standard, the successor to the BPEL4WS, WSFL, and XLANG process languages

The timeline shows that we already had executable process languages before 2002 with IBM's web services flow language (WSFL) and Microsoft's XLANG specification. But, because other software vendors didn't use these languages, there was a traditional vendor lock-in scenario. It was 2002 before BEA, IBM, and Microsoft made the business process execution language for web services (BPEL4WS) publicly available. The purpose of this team of software vendors was to standardize version 1.1 of BPEL4WS at OASIS. In 2007, OASIS finally standardized the specification and renamed it WS-BPEL 2.0.

Although the WS-BPEL 2.0 standard was quite successful at defining an execution model for business processes, important constructs were lacking. One important missing element is human task or workflow support, which is used to allocate work to a group of people or an individual. In figure 2.3, the BPEL4People specification is included, because this add-on specification to WS-BPEL 2.0 does provide this functionality. But BPEL4People isn't standardized and it isn't fully embraced by BPM software vendors.

Another construct that's lacking in WS-BPEL is cyclic control flow. That sounds a bit complex, but it's nothing more than looping back to a previous activity in a process. In WS-BPEL, this can't be done (other than by using a while loop with all kinds of difficult conditional logic). But, let's not stay too long in the past; let's look at the new standard for implementing business processes, BPMN 2.0.

2.2.2   And then there was BPMN 2.0

Although WS-BPEL was standardized in 2007, BPMN 1.0 was already standardized by the Business Process Management Initiative (BPMI) in 2004. BPMN 1.x is widely used as a modeling notation for business processes. As a process developer, you may have received a BPMN 1.x model for requirements or documentation purposes from information or

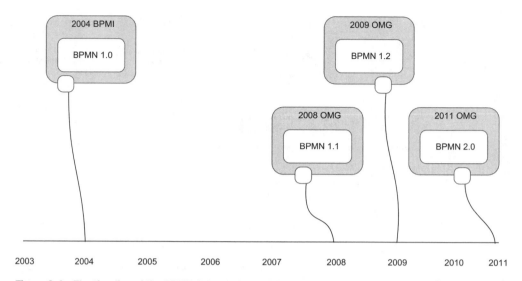

Figure 2.4   The timeline of the BPMN 2.0 standard, which was the successor to the BPMN 1.x modeling notations

business analysts. But, then you had to convert those models into an execution language, such as WS-BPEL.

Now, as figure 2.4 shows, we have BPMN 2.0 "to the rescue."

Now we have a standard for modeling business processes *and* implementing a process execution model. There's a real opportunity for business-oriented individuals and developers to speak with the same vocabulary and share business models without the need for conversion.

And, because the BPMN 2.0 standard provides an opportunity to bring business and IT closer together, there's a real need for collaboration tools. A business process will be defined and implemented by a lot of people with different backgrounds, and it's a real challenge to provide a toolset that can enable everyone to do their jobs.

Now that you know a bit about the history of BPMN 2.0, we can look at the elements of the language itself and start modeling.

2.2.3   *Getting your head around all the BPMN 2.0 constructs*

You only need to take a quick look at the BPMN 2.0 specification at the Object Management Group (OMG) website (www.omg.org/spec/BPMN) and it becomes obvious that it's a rather substantial specification, filling around 550 pages and including over 100 BPMN 2.0 constructs. It can be overwhelming to get started with BPMN 2.0 and try to comprehend the basics of the specification. Therefore, it's important to start by structuring the BPMN 2.0 into different groups of modeling detail.

An important advocate of grouping the constructs is Bruce Silver, author of *BPMN Method & Style*. The book is a good read and a great guide to getting started with modeling BPMN 1.x and 2.0 processes. In addition, Silver groups the BPMN constructs into three different levels:

- Level 1 is described as descriptive BPMN, which can be used for high-level modeling with a restricted palette of BPMN constructs.
- Level 2 can be used for detailed modeling, including event and exception handling, and is described as analytical BPMN. It uses a wide range of BPMN constructs.
- Level 3 is the execution model of BPMN (which is new in BPMN 2.0), which can be deployed on a process engine.

With these different levels in mind, it's easier to start with BPMN by using the level 1 group of BPMN constructs.

Another important advocate of categorizing BPMN constructs is the Workflow Management Coalition (WfMC). The WfMC, and Robert Shapiro in particular, grouped the BPMN 2.0 constructs into four different categories (see the PowerPoint presentation at http://bit.ly/qYRHiQ for more details), shown in figure 2.5.

The categorization of the WfMC, as shown in figure 2.5, is similar to the levels created by Silver. The descriptive category can be compared to level 1, DODAF (an architecture framework of the United States Department of Defense) to level 2, and the complete palette to level 3. The main difference is the simple category, which can be used for high-level modeling of business processes. Even then, you can question whether a vital construct of business process modeling, such as pool and lane, shouldn't belong to the simple category as well. But, it's obvious that Silver's level 1

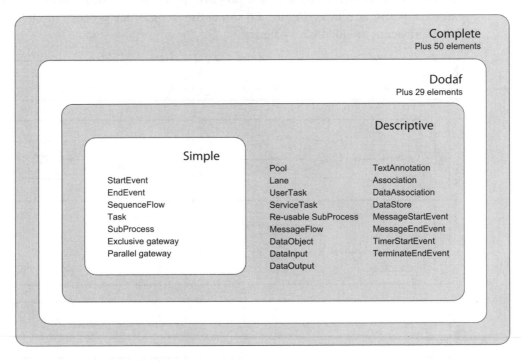

Figure 2.5　A categorization of BPMN 2.0 constructs by the WfMC. The simple category can be used for high-level business modeling without a lot of restrictions. The descriptive category can be used for more detailed modeling by business and information analysts.

palette of and the descriptive category of WfMC are better starting points than the complete palette of the BPMN 2.0 standard.

Now that you understand the history of BPMN 2.0, it's time to start looking at the BPMN constructs and do some modeling!

2.3   *Introducing BPMN 2.0 from a developer's viewpoint*

To become familiar with the important constructs of BPMN, we'll first start with a high-level business process model before we design a more detailed process model with constructs like error events, similar to the different levels and categories of WfMC (shown in figure 2.5) and Silver's book. Level 3 of Silver's categorization is the implementation of the process in BPMN 2.0 XML; we'll skip that step for now and stick with the modeling levels.

2.3.1   *High-level modeling with BPMN 2.0*

In section 2.1, we looked at a sample book order business process. In figure 2.1, the book order process was modeled without a real model notation. With the simple or level 1 palette in mind, we'll take another look at the book order process and convert it into a real BPMN 2.0 business process model.

This means that we have to add a more formal notation to describe the book order process. In the BPMN 2.0 book order process, we'll use start and end events, parallel gateways, pools, and tasks. Figure 2.6 shows the book order process, modeled with a simple subset of the BPMN 2.0 palette.

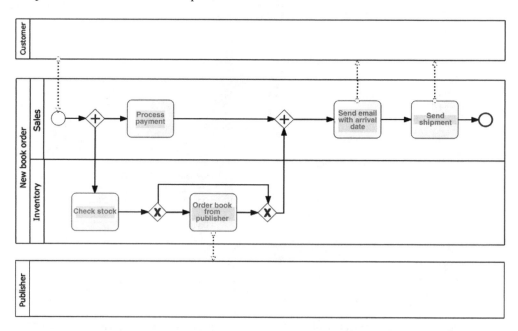

Figure 2.6   A high-level BPMN 2.0 model describing the book order process with a simple subset of the BPMN 2.0 construct palette

Before discussing the process in more detail, let's first look at the individual BPMN 2.0 constructs in table 2.1.

Table 2.1　Overview of the BPMN 2.0 constructs used in figure 2.6

BPMN 2.0 icon	BPMN 2.0 name	Description
○	Start event	A start event is the trigger to start a new process instance.
◯	End event	An end event is the last step before the process instance is completed. Note that the end event has a thicker circular border than the start event.
New book order (pool)	Pool	A pool represents the container for the activities of a process. Best practice is to use the process name for the pool name.
Sales (lane)	Lane	A lane represents a role within a process model. In most cases, this is an organizational unit or a role definition.
Process payment	Task	A task is a piece of work that has to be executed as part of the process definition. A task can be an automated activity or a manual activity.
◇+	Parallel gateway	A parallel gateway is used to indicate that activities can be executed simultaneously or that all incoming activities must be completed before the process progresses to the next activity.
◇X	Exclusive gateway	An exclusive gateway is used for conditional logic. Based on a condition, only one of the outgoing sequence flows will be followed.
⌑- - - - - - - -▷	Message flow	A message flow is used to send a signal or message from one pool to another. It may not be used to connect activities within one pool.
⟶	Sequence flow	A sequence flow connects activities, gateways, and events to each other within one pool. Therefore, It represents the orchestration of the process definition.

Now that you know the meaning of the individual BPMN 2.0 constructs, let's walk through the full process model. One of the eye-catching differences between the models in figures 2.1 and 2.6 is the use of pools and lanes. In figure 2.6, there are three pools: Customer, New book order, and Publisher. The pools describe either the business process itself or different external participants that interact with the business process. In the New book order pool, there are two lanes that characterize the different organizational units within the bookstore company. Because the bookstore in this example is a small company, there are only sales and inventory organizational units.

In this business process model, we focus on the bookstore, but we could also include the process activities that are necessary for the publisher to complete the order process. The process begins with a customer order request, pictured here as a message flow (the dashed line) initiating a start event (a circle).

When the process is started, two tasks should be completed: the process payment and the check stock tasks. Because these tasks can be executed in parallel, a parallel gateway is modeled after the start event. After the stock is checked, an exclusive gateway is used for the conditional logic of the book being in stock or not. When the book isn't in stock, it's ordered from the publisher by an additional task.

When the book is in stock, either because it was already or because there was an extra order sent to the publisher, the book is ready for shipment. But, before the book can be shipped, we must be sure that the payment has been successfully completed. A parallel gateway is used to join the tasks, meaning that the process won't go further until both these tasks have been completed.

After the parallel gateway, two additional tasks are executed to inform the customer about the arrival date and ship the book to the customer before the process is completed by an end event. As you can see, the high-level model doesn't contain stuff like error handling or the definition of the type of a task; that's what we'll add in the next section.

2.3.2   *Detailed process modeling*

Although a book ordering process may seem simple at first, when looking at it in more detail, it's clear that a lot of process logic is needed. In this section, we'll focus on detailing the process payment task by adding validation and error-handling logic. This also means we'll need BPMN 2.0 constructs that are part of the descriptive or level 2 palette. Figure 2.7 shows the subprocess payment, which is a more detailed model of the process payment task from figure 2.6.

As you can see, we're using a number of additional BPMN 2.0 constructs in the process model in figure 2.7. Let's first look at these extra elements' definitions in table 2.2.

In figure 2.7, the tasks have been made more specific by adding type identifiers. For example, the invoice credit card task is modeled as a service task, because the validity of the credit card can be checked by invoking a web service. There's also a user task to indicate that the task has to be performed by a human. The contact customer

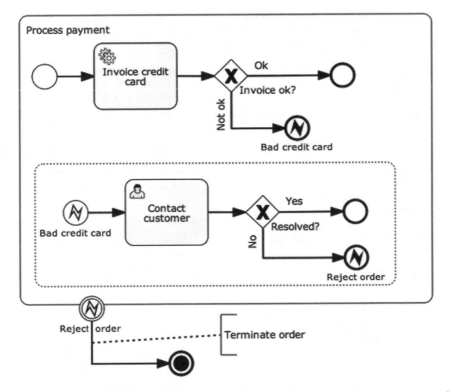

**Figure 2.7   The extracted process payment subprocess from the book order process model.
The subprocess shows the use of end error and start error events and a terminate end event.**

Table 2.2   Overview of the additional BPMN 2.0 constructs used in figure 2.7

BPMN 2.0 icon	BPMN 2.0 name	Description
Bad credit card	End error event	An error end event is a specific kind of end event, which can be used to throw an error inside the process model definition.
Bad credit card	Start error event	A start error event can be used to catch a specific error thrown by an error end event, such as one within a subprocess.
Reject order	Intermediate error event	An intermediate error event can be used to catch a fault on a task or a subprocess boundary.

Table 2.2   Overview of the additional BPMN 2.0 constructs used in figure 2.7 *(continued)*

BPMN 2.0 icon	BPMN 2.0 name	Description
◉	Terminate end event	A terminate end event is a special kind of end event that causes the process to be terminated. If a terminate end event is used in a subprocess, it only causes the subprocess to be terminated, not the parent process.
Invoice credit card	Service task	A service task is a specific type of task that represents an automated activity. For example, a service task could be a web service call or a Java class invocation.
Contact customer	User task	A user task is a specific type of human task that is performed via a computer interface. A user task can be claimed and completed by a configured individual or group of users.
Process payment	Subprocess	A subprocess is a compound activity that can contain multiple other activities, including tasks, gateways, and events. A subprocess can be embedded in the parent process or be a standalone process model that can be invoked by the parent process via a call activity.
Terminate order	Text annotation	A text annotation can be used to add documentation to specific elements of the process model.

activity is a user task because an employee of the bookstore has to get in contact with the customer to solve the bad credit card problem.

In the process payment subprocess shown in figure 2.7, you can see a couple of other new BPMN 2.0 constructs. First, note that a subprocess always starts with a start event. To begin, the credit card information is validated by invoking an automated task. Then you check the outcome of this credit card validation with an exclusive gateway. If the credit card validation is successful, the payment is finished and the subprocess is ended.

If the credit card validation doesn't succeed, an error end event throws an exception. This exception is caught within the subprocess by the error start event that's handling the bad credit card exception. In this case, the customer is contacted personally by a bookstore employee to determine whether the credit card information was entered incorrectly or if the customer can pay in another way. If the payment can be settled with the customer, a normal end event in the exception handler is reached and the subprocess is completed.

But, if the payment can't be settled, another error end event throws a reject order exception. This exception isn't handled within the subprocess, but with an error boundary event. This error boundary event handles the exception by forwarding it to a terminate end event, which causes the whole book order process to be terminated immediately.

We covered many of the most important parts of the BPMN 2.0 palette in this section, but we haven't discussed the full palette, and by no means have we talked about every BPMN 2.0 construct in detail. Nevertheless, this should provide you with a good start in BPMN 2.0 modeling, and we'll be discussing more details of BPMN 2.0 throughout the rest of the book. Now it's time to get more familiar with the different components of the Activiti framework.

2.4   *Summary*

We started this chapter with a gentle introduction to business process management and BPM vocabulary. You also saw a bit of history when we talked about WS-BPEL, BPMN 1.x, and, eventually, BPMN 2.0. At that point, we took a closer look at the way you can do modeling with BPMN 2.0, and we looked at the different categorization strategies WfMC and Bruce Silver use to make BPMN 2.0 understandable and user friendly for different users.

Finally, we got acquainted with a large set of BPMN 2.0 elements with a high-level process model and a detailed subprocess. You now have a good enough foundation in BPMN 2.0 to work with the examples in the remainder of this book. But, before we dive deeper into developing BPMN 2.0 processes, we'll first look at the different components of the Activiti tool stack in the next chapter.

Introducing
the Activiti tool stack

3

This chapter covers
- Installing and using the Activiti Modeler
- Working with the Activiti Eclipse Designer
- Guided tour of the Activiti Explorer

Now that you know more about what BPMN 2.0 can do for you in terms of developing, it's time to take a closer look at the Activiti tool stack. We'll start by looking in more detail at the Activiti tools that you saw in the first chapter, and you'll learn a bit about the background of where the tools come from. Then, one by one, we'll look at all the tools and see them in action!

We'll start with the Activiti Modeler. You'll model a simple process definition as a means to get started in modeling business processes with the Activiti Modeler. Then, we'll take a look at Activiti's Eclipse-based development environment, the Activiti Designer. You'll implement a simple process and unit test it on a local Activiti Engine distribution. You'll also import the process model created in the Activiti Modeler into the Activiti Designer.

With the Activiti Explorer, we'll take a look at how to deploy process definitions, start new process instances, and work with user tasks. The Activiti Explorer provides an easy-to-use web interface that can work with the Activiti Engine—without the need to write code.

We've got lots of ground to cover—time to get started with the Activiti Modeler!

3.1 Working with the Activiti Modeler

To run processes on a runtime environment like the Activiti Engine, you first need to define a business process. You could do this by using the Activiti Designer Eclipse tool or by writing the BPMN 2.0 XML yourself. But, as you saw in the first chapter, BPMN 2.0 creates a real opportunity for business-oriented people and developers to use the same vocabulary.

Therefore, a typical workflow of defining a business process is started with business-oriented people modeling their processes graphically, for example, with Activiti Modeler. Let's see how Modeler provides the means to do this.

3.1.1 Installing the Activiti Modeler

The Activiti Modeler is an add-on component to the core Activiti framework and has to be deployed via a separate installation script. We'll look at how to perform the installation by building from the sources, but you can also download the WAR deployable directly from the book's website (www.bpmnwithactiviti.org).

The Activiti Modeler sources are available from the Signavio Core Components Google repository (http://code.google.com/p/signavio-core-components). First, you have to check out the sources. In the root directory, you can find a build.properties file that needs to be edited to get the Activiti Modeler application. The following code snippet shows the values that need to be changed:

```
version=1.0.05.9
war = signaviocoreactiviti-modeler
configuration = defaultActiviti
fileSystemRootDirectory = c:/repo../../../workspace/
        ➥ activiti-modeler-examples
```

Once you've changed the Properties file, you can start the Ant build script with the following command:

```
ant build-all-in-one-war
```

This will create a target/activiti-modeler.war file that can be deployed in the webapps directory of the Tomcat application that's part of the Activiti installation directory. When you copy that WAR file and start up the Tomcat container, you'll be able to start the Activiti Modeler application by pointing your web browser (Firefox and Chrome are supported; Internet Explorer isn't supported) to http://localhost:8080/activiti-modeler. You should see the startup screen as shown in figure 3.1.

With the Activiti Modeler installed, we can now take a look at how you can start modeling new processes.

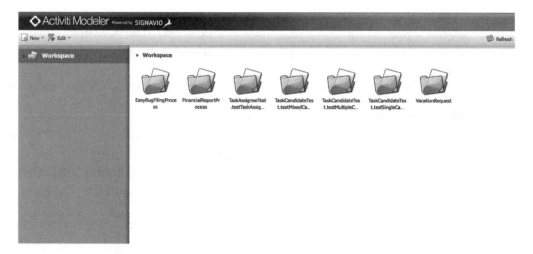

Figure 3.1   The Activiti Modeler's startup screen showing the example processes that are part of the Activiti distribution

3.1.2   *Modeling processes with the Activiti Modeler*

Let's take the simple bookstore process from chapter 2 and model it in the Activiti Modeler to see how the tool works. Point your browser at http://localhost:8080/activiti-modeler again. Browse a bit through the examples that you see in your workspace and investigate how to create a folder structure in the Modeler to organize your models. You can find the folders you create with the Modeler on the filesystem in the Activiti installation directory under workspace/activiti-modeler-examples. When you take a look in this directory, you'll see that the directories already contain sample BPMN 2.0 models created with the Activiti Modeler.

Now let's design a basic process with the Activiti Modeler, save it, and check out how this process is stored in the model repository. Again, you'll use the basic book ordering process example from chapter 2 and implement the process model as shown in figure 3.2.

Start by choosing New > Business Process Diagram (BPMN 2.0) from the top left corner of the Activiti Modeler startup screen. When your browser finishes loading the

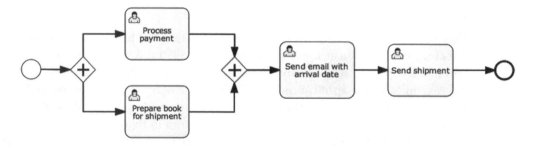

Figure 3.2   The sample book order process that you'll model with the Activiti Modeler

modeling page, you'll see all of the BPMN constructs that the Activiti Modeler supports in the shape repository in the left pane. You can now start dragging and dropping the BPMN constructs onto the modeling pane.

NOTE The Activiti Engine doesn't support all of these BPMN elements. To find out which of the BPMN elements the Activiti Engine supports, you can look at appendix B or the Activiti user guide (see www.activiti.org/ userguide).

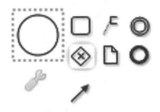

Let's begin with a start event, which you can find in the Start Events folder of the palette. Drag and drop it onto the modeling pane. When you hover over the start event, a context menu appears, as shown in figure 3.3. This menu can help you to quickly add a new BPMN element to your process model. Let's pick the exclusive gateway construct.

In the book order process, you have the "Process payment" and the "Prepare book for shipment" tasks, which should be executed in parallel (see figure 3.2). You need to change the exclusive gateway into a parallel gateway. You can do that by clicking on the transform shape icon when hovering over the Exclusive Gateway and then choosing the Parallel Gateway from the pop-up menu, as shown in figure 3.4.

Figure 3.3 A context menu from the modeling pane in the Activiti Modeler, which enables you to quickly draw tasks, gateways, events, and sequence flows

Now you can add a new task, "Process payment," and change its type by opening the attributes view on the right side of the screen, selecting the task in the modeler pane, and browsing in the Properties view to add a TaskType of type User (figure 3.5).

You can now complete the book order process model (refer to figure 3.2). When you've finished modeling the book order process, you can save the diagram to the default file repository, located in the Activiti installation directory under workspace/ activiti-modeler-examples. Take a look at the BPMN 2.0 file that's saved in your filesystem in the Activiti Modeler repository and you'll see that, next to the process definition itself, the file contains elements with the `bpmndi` prefix. The BPMN DI schema contains elements that declare information concerning the graphical representation of the process constructs. You can use this diagram information to import the process model into the Activiti Designer and add technical details to it.

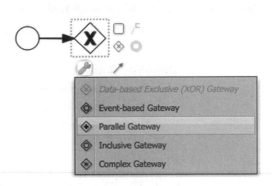

Figure 3.4 A pop-up menu that allows you to transform an exclusive gateway to another gateway type

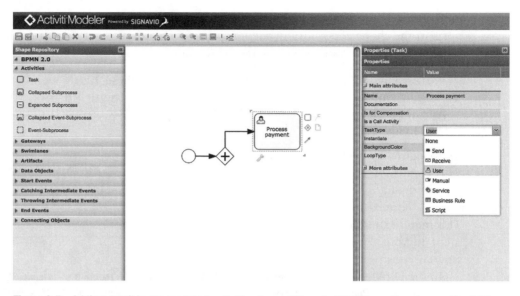

Figure 3.5   Adding detail to the modeled activities is possible using the Properties view on the right side of the modeling canvas. In the Properties view, you can, for example, specify the type of task.

3.2   *Adding technical details with the Activiti Designer*

At some point, the business/process analyst will finish modeling the business process in the Activiti Modeler. Then, you need to add technical details to the process before it's ready to run on a process engine. For example, you may need to include Java classes to implement the service task logic.

The Activiti Designer can be used to add technical details to an imported process model. But, it can also be used to model new processes from scratch. In addition, the Designer provides functionality to test processes and create deployment artifacts.

First, let's install the Activiti Designer and get it up and running.

3.2.1   *Getting up and running with Activiti Designer*

Installing the Eclipse-based Designer tool is a simple process that takes only a few minutes:

1 Download and install an Eclipse Indigo distribution (the previous version, Helios, is not supported).
2 Install the Activiti Designer plugin from the Activiti update site http://activiti.org/designer/update. Note that you should keep the option "Contact All Update Sites During Install to Find Required Software" checked.
3 Restart Eclipse.

You should now be able to create your first Activiti Designer Eclipse project by using the Activiti Project option in the New Project Eclipse wizard, as shown in figure 3.6.

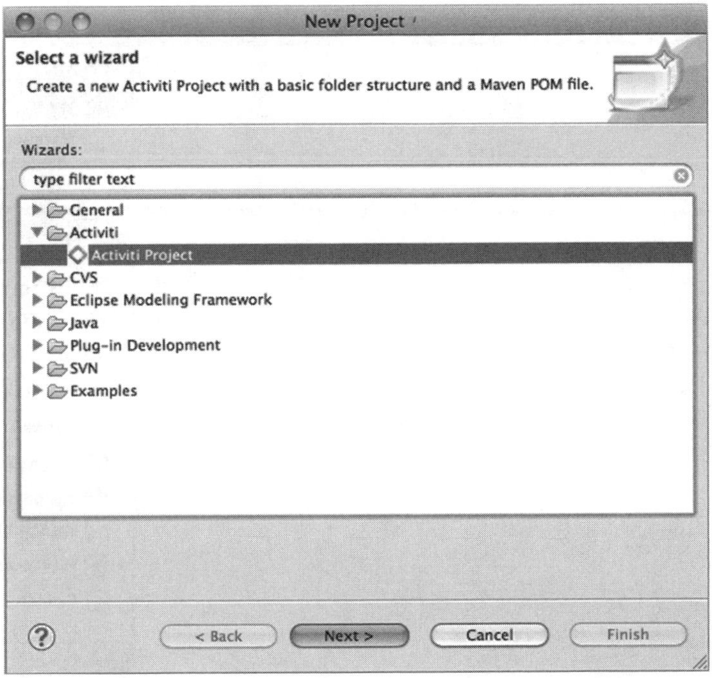

Figure 3.6 Creating a new Activiti project with the Activiti Designer via Eclipse's New Project wizard

When you look at the Java project the Activiti Designer has just created, you can see the source folders adhering to the Apache Maven standards. The resources directories in these folders will contain the models you create with the Designer tool later on.

Now that the Activiti Designer is installed and up and running, you can start developing a simple process to get familiar with its functionality.

3.2.2 Designing a process from scratch

In this section, you'll create a basic process with only a simple Groovy script task to show the Activiti Designer functionality. Once you're familiar with the Designer, we'll take a look at how to do more complicated stuff in later chapters.

Right-click with the mouse on the newly created project to open the context menu in Designer and then go to New > Other and choose Activiti Diagram. After you've provided a filename for the new process, the editor pane will open and on the right side you'll see the palette with the supported BPMN 2.0 constructs. See figure 3.7.

You can start dragging and dropping BPMN 2.0 constructs onto the pane. In addition, when you hover over a node in the diagram, you can see that a context menu appears. You can use this context menu to quickly develop a new process model, which is similar to using the Activiti Modeler. Let's start with designing a simple process model and creating a diagram that has a start event, a script task, and an end event.

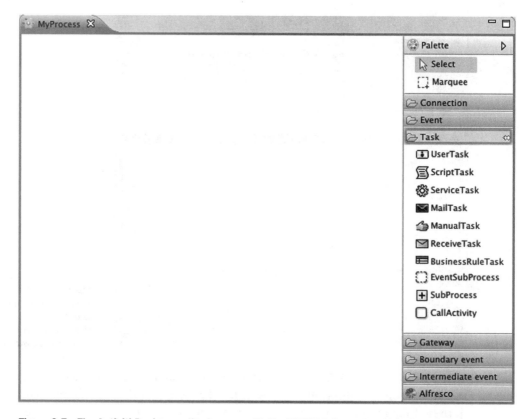

Figure 3.7   The Activiti Designer editor's pane with the BPMN 2.0 constructs in the palette

First, drag a start event to the diagram and then hover over the start node and select the new element icon, as shown in figure 3.8.

Choose the Create Script Task item from the pop-up menu. This action will create a new script task next to the start event and automatically add a sequence flow. Now, add an end event to complete this simple process (figure 3.9).

Now you need to test this process, and it's currently not doing anything, so you have to add scripting logic to the script task. Open the Properties

Figure 3.8   The hover capabilities of the Activiti Designer allow you to quickly add a new task, gateway, or end event to the diagram.

Figure 3.9   A simple process with a script task designed with the Activiti Designer

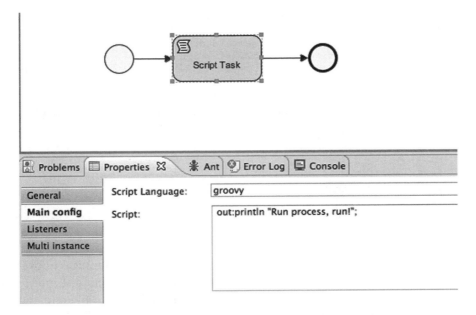

Figure 3.10   Adding a piece of Groovy scripting code in the script task Properties view

view of the script task by selecting it (make sure the Properties view is open in your Eclipse canvas). Then select Groovy from the drop-down menu next to Script Language, and add the following line of Groovy code: out:println "Run process, run!"; (figure 3.10).

Now that you've designed the process model and implemented a line of scripting code, you're ready to test it. Let's take a look at how to test processes with a generated JUnit test.

3.2.3   *Testing processes with the Activiti Designer*

In order to test the newly created process, you need a BPMN 2.0 XML file. When you save the diagram, the BPMN XML content is generated in the model file that is created when you complete the create diagram wizard. You can view the XML content by opening the model file in the Eclipse XML editor. The generated XML should look similar to the XML content shown in the next code listing.

Listing 3.1   BPMN 2.0 XML generated by the Activiti Designer

```
<?xml version="1.0" encoding="UTF-8"?>
<definitions xmlns="http://www.omg.org/spec/BPMN/
        ➥ 20100524/MODEL"
    targetNamespace="http://www.activiti.org/test"
    xmlns:activiti="http://activiti.org/bpmn">

  <process id="MyProcess" name="MyProcess">
    <documentation>
```
BPMN 2.0 root element with namespace declarations

```
        Place documentation for the 'MyProcess' process here.
      </documentation>
      <startEvent id="startevent1" name="Start"></startEvent>
      <scriptTask id="scripttask1" name="Script Task"
          scriptFormat="Groovy">
        <script>
          <![CDATA[out:println "Run process, run!";]]>
        </script>
      </scriptTask>
      <sequenceFlow id="flow1" name="" sourceRef="startevent1"
          targetRef="scripttask1">
      </sequenceFlow>
      <sequenceFlow id="flow2" name="" sourceRef="scripttask1"
          targetRef="endevent1">
      </sequenceFlow>
      <endEvent id="endevent1" name="End"></endEvent>
    </process>
  </definitions>
```

> **Groovy scripting code definition**

> **End event definition**

Note that I didn't include the BPMN DI XML containing the graphical information in this listing because that isn't relevant for now. To generate a unit test, you can select the model file in the package explorer view. Right-click on the file and you'll see a context menu appear (figure 3.11).

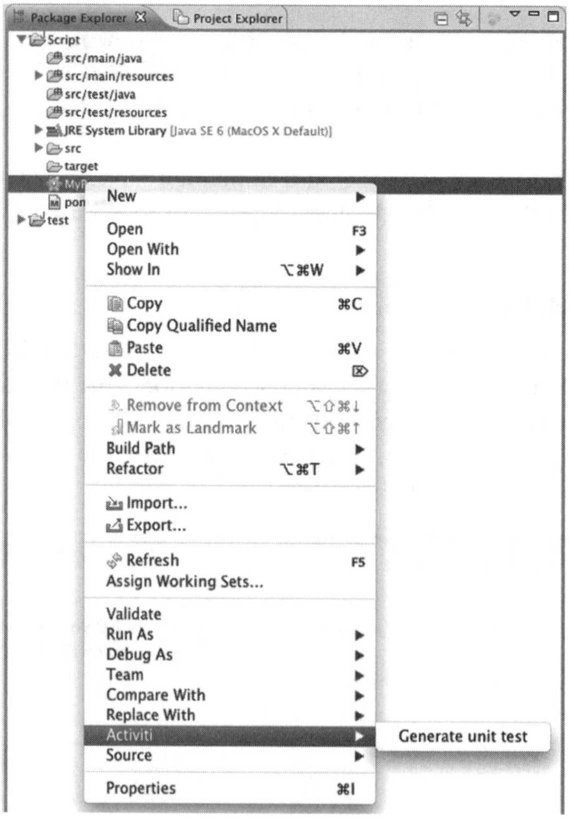

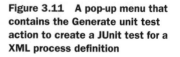

Figure 3.11 A pop-up menu that contains the Generate unit test action to create a JUnit test for a XML process definition

Click on the "Generate unit test" action and a JUnit test will be generated in the
`org.activiti.designer.test` package. To get the necessary project dependencies in
place, you can run the Maven `mvn eclipse:eclipse` command or use the M2Eclipse
plugin. Make sure you have configured in your Eclipse workspace a `M2_REPO` classpath
variable that points to the Maven repository (which, by default, is located in the .m2/
repository in your user home directory).

Before running the test, take a look at the generated code in the following listing.

Listing 3.2   The JUnit test class generated by the Activiti Designer

```
public class ProcessTestMyProcess {

  private String filename =
      "/Users/trademakers/workspace/Script/MyProcess.bpmn";

  @Rule
  public ActivitiRule activitiRule = new ActivitiRule();

  @Test
  public void startProcess() {
    RepositoryService repositoryService =
        activitiRule.getRepositoryService();
    repositoryService.createDeployment()
        .addInputStream("process.bpmn20.xml",            ❶ Deploys process
            new FileInputStream(filename)).deploy();        definition
    RuntimeService runtimeService =
        activitiRule.getRuntimeService();
    Map<String, Object> variableMap =
        new HashMap<String, Object>();
    variableMap.put("name", "Activiti");
    ProcessInstance processInstance = runtimeService        ❷ Starts a new
        .startProcessInstanceByKey("MyProcess",              process instance
            variableMap);
    assertNotNull(processInstance.getId());
    System.out.println("id " + processInstance.getId() + " "
        + processInstance.getProcessDefinitionId());
  }
}
```

As you can see, the code differs a bit from the unit test implemented in chapter 1.
Here, you make use of the `ActivitiRule` class, which is a utility class that sets up the
Activiti Engine in a unit test. (I'll talk in more detail about this handy class in the next
chapter.) The BPMN 2.0 XML file is deployed via the `RepositoryService` that reads
the BPMN file from an `InputStream` ❶.

NOTE   process.bpmn20.xml is used as the filename for the process definition input stream. Activiti 5.9 only accepts process definition files with an
extension of .bpmn20.xml. Starting from Activiti 5.10, .bpmn extensions are
also supported.

The `RuntimeService` is used to start a new process instance of the process ❷. When
you run this unit test, you can see `Run process, run!` appear in the Eclipse console,
and the process instance and process definition identifiers are printed out.

This simple example only shows the typical workflow in the Activiti Designer. Let's return to the process definition created with the Activiti Modeler in section 3.1 and import it into the Activiti Designer.

3.2.4 Importing a Modeler process into the Designer

It's easy to import a process definition created with the Activiti Modeler into the Designer. What you need is the BPMN 2.0 XML file created by the Activiti Modeler. When you implement the process model in section 3.1, a BPMN 2.0 XML file is generated in the workspace/ activiti-modeler-examples folder of your Activiti installation directory. Look for a file starting with the name you chose when saving the model and ending with bpmn20.xml. The sample Modeler file can also be found in the `bpmn-examples` project under modeler/chapter3 (see this book's source code).

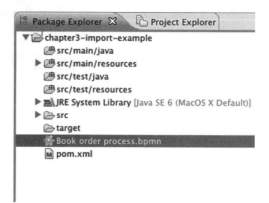

Figure 3.12 A BPMN 2.0 file can be imported by just copying the file to an Activiti Designer project.

Create a new Activiti project in the Activiti Designer and then copy the Activiti Modeler bpmn20.xml file to the Activiti Designer project and rename the file extension to .bpmn (see figure 3.12).

When you open the .bpmn file, the Activiti Designer will read the BPMN 2.0 elements and create and open a new diagram, as shown in figure 3.13.

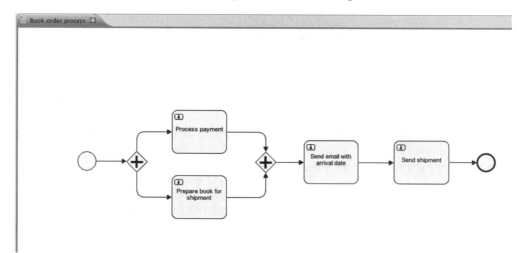

Figure 3.13 A BPMN 2.0 XML file can be imported into the Activiti Designer and a new diagram will be created and opened, as shown here.

The newly created diagram looks similar to the Activiti Modeler diagram shown in figure 3.2.

> **NOTE** The process identifier of the imported process can contain spaces. Make sure that the spaces are removed, because the id attribute isn't allowed to contain spaces according to the BPMN 2.0 specification. You can do this by clicking on a white space in the diagram and filling in the id field in the Properties view.

You can now add new BPMN 2.0 elements and detailed information, such as the person or group to which the four user tasks have to be assigned. You can also quickly change a task type. Let's take a look at how to do that with the "Process payment" user task and change it into a simple script task. Hover over the "Process payment" element and choose the icon with the small pencil. There, you can change the element into a script task (figure 3.14).

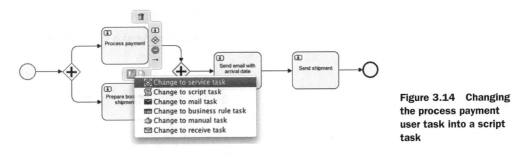

Figure 3.14 Changing the process payment user task into a script task

When the "Process payment" user task is transformed to a script task, you can add scripting logic to it. When you want to add Java logic, the service task would be the task type of choice. But, for this example, you add a log line by filling in the script text box in the Properties view of the script task, as shown in figure 3.15.

What's left is the assignee configuration for the three remaining user tasks. Fill in a value of "kermit" in the assignee Property field of every user task (figure 3.16). This will assign every user task directly to the *kermit* user.

Problems	Properties ⊠	Ant	Error Log	Console

General	Script Language:	groovy
Main config	Script:	out:println "Processing payment";
Listeners		
Multi instance		

Figure 3.15 A piece of scripting logic can be configured for a script task.

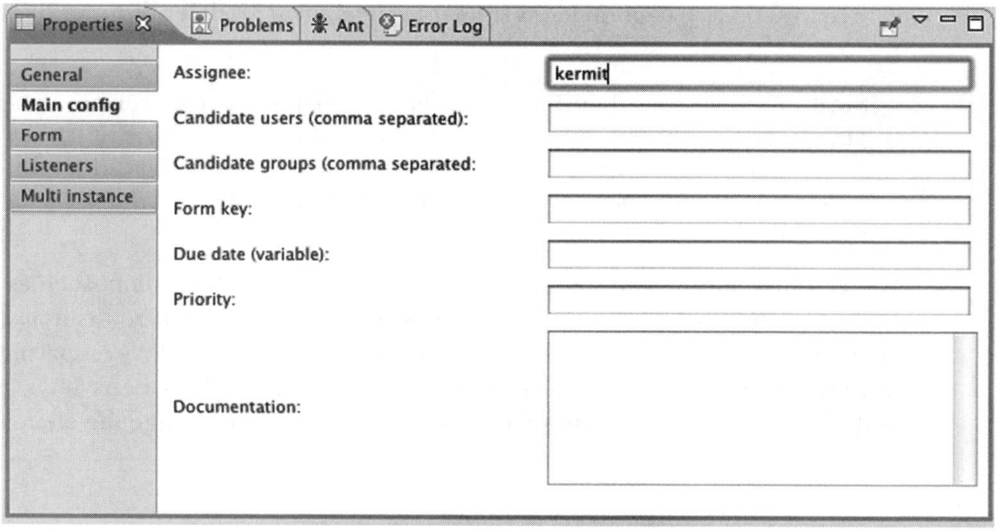

Properties ⊠	Problems	Ant	Error Log	

General	Assignee:	kermit
Main config	Candidate users (comma separated):	
Form	Candidate groups (comma separated:	
Listeners	Form key:	
Multi instance	Due date (variable):	
	Priority:	
	Documentation:	

Figure 3.16   The user task Properties view contains a lot of configuration items, including the assignment definition.

When you save the diagram, you've completed the book order process implementation and you're ready to deploy it to the Activiti Engine. The Activiti Designer can ease the deployment task with the generation of a BAR file, which is nothing more than a zipped file that contains the BPMN 2.0 XML process definition and Java class files that are available in the project. The BAR file will be generated when you right-click on an Activiti project and choose the "Create deployment artifacts" option from the pop-up menu. See figure 3.17.

When you click to generate the deployment artifacts, a deployment folder is created in the root of the corresponding Activiti project. There, you can find the BAR file that can be deployed on the Activiti Engine. It's time to see your book order process in action using the Activiti Explorer.

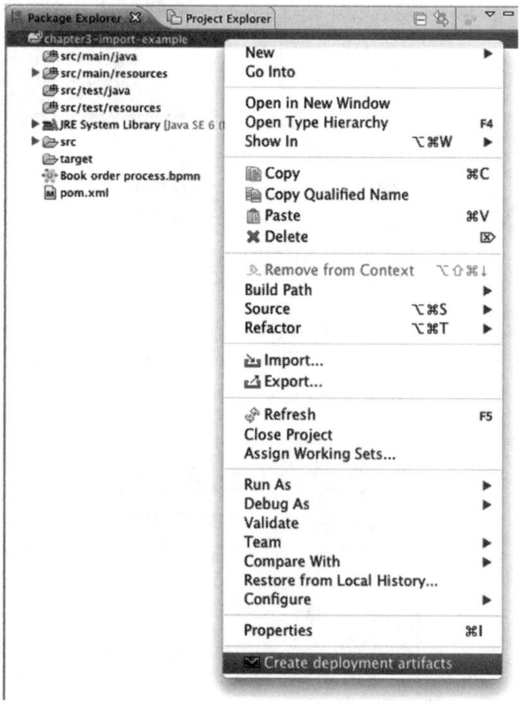

Package Explorer ⊠	Project Explorer	
chapter3-import-example		
src/main/java	**New**	▶
src/main/resources	Go Into	
src/test/java	Open in New Window	
src/test/resources	Open Type Hierarchy	F4
JRE System Library (Java SE 6 (	Show In	⌥⌘W ▶
src		
target	Copy	⌘C
Book order process.bpmn	Copy Qualified Name	
pom.xml	Paste	⌘V
	Delete	⌦
	Remove from Context	⌥⇧⌘↓
	Build Path	▶
	Source	⌥⌘S ▶
	Refactor	⌥⌘T ▶
	Import...	
	Export...	
	Refresh	F5
	Close Project	
	Assign Working Sets...	
	Run As	▶
	Debug As	▶
	Validate	
	Team	▶
	Compare With	▶
	Restore from Local History...	
	Configure	▶
	Properties	⌘I
	Create deployment artifacts	

Figure 3.17   The BAR deployment artifact containing the BPMN 2.0 XML process definition can be generated by right-clicking on an Activiti project and choosing the "Create deployment artifacts" option.

3.3 *Managing the Engine using the Activiti Explorer*

The Activiti Explorer can be used to execute a wide variety of tasks. In this section, we'll explore the Activiti Engine management capabilities and, in the next section (3.4), we'll focus on the process and task functionality. Now that you've created a BAR file in the Activiti Designer, you can use the Activiti Explorer to deploy the BAR file to the Activiti Engine.

Make sure the Tomcat server running the Activiti Explorer application is started. Then, open a browser and go to http://localhost:8080/activiti-explorer. Log in as *kermit*, with the password *kermit*. As you can see in the Users tab, Kermit is registered as system administrator and, therefore, allowed to perform management tasks in the Activiti Explorer. The other example users, Fozzie and Gonzo, aren't allowed to do this because they don't have the system administrator security role. See figure 3.18 for Kermit's user details—this is the view in the Activiti Explorer where you'll do user and group administration.

When you click on the Deployments tab, you can upload a new deployment artifact. In the pop-up menu, you can choose to open a File dialog box to select the BAR file or to drag and drop the BAR file onto the web page. Choose your preferred way of uploading the BAR deployment artifact to the Activiti Explorer and you'll see a new view showing the details of the new deployment. When you click on the book order

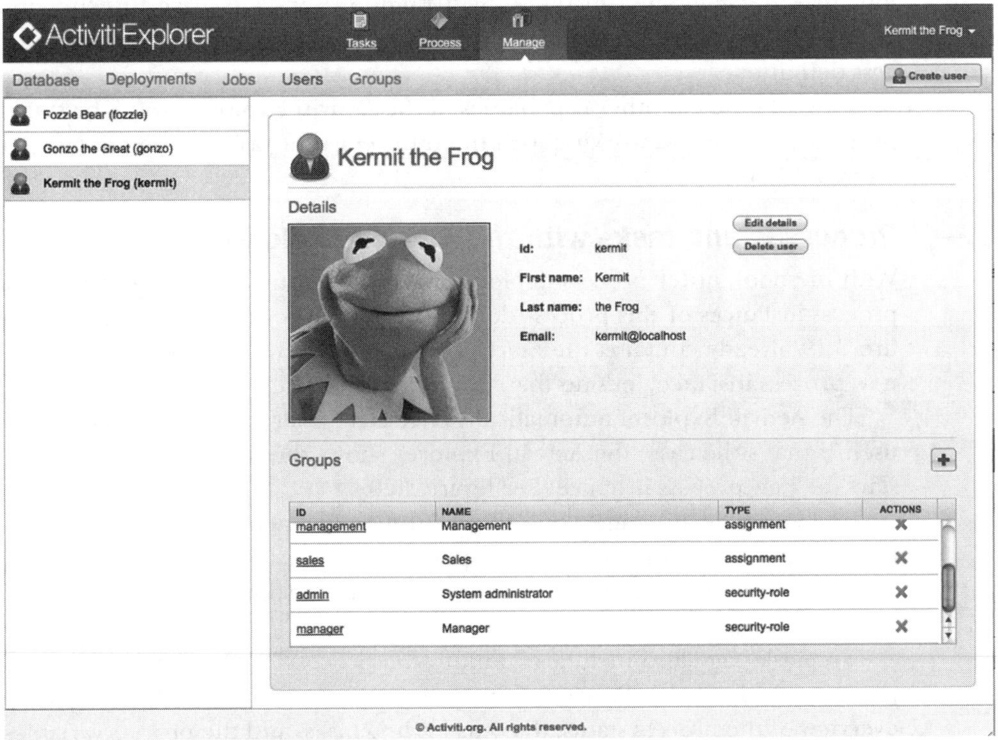

Figure 3.18   The user administration page in the Activiti Explorer, showing the user details of Kermit

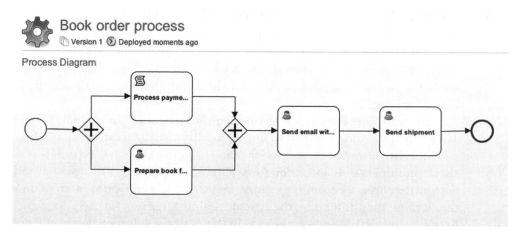

Figure 3.19   Graphical overview of the deployed book order process definition

process definition, you can see the graphical overview of the process model, as shown in figure 3.19.

In addition to the deployment and user and group management capabilities of the Activiti Explorer, you can also get a view of every database table and look at the jobs that are scheduled in the Activiti Engine. But we'll leave this functionality for later chapters, starting with chapter 5, where you'll implement a more complex process definition.

Now let's look at other capabilities of the Activiti Explorer. You'll be starting a new process instance and working with the different user tasks of the book order process model.

3.4   *Processes and tasks with the Activiti Explorer*

With the book order process deployed on the Activiti Engine, you can now start new process instances of this process definition. The process definition view shown in figure 3.19 already contains the Start process button in the top-right corner to start a new process instance; let's do that.

The Activiti Explorer automatically checks if a user task is created for the logged-in user. If that's the case, the Activiti Explorer shows the task detail page right after you start the new process instance. See figure 3.20.

In the task details page, you can perform several actions on the user task. You can, for example, add a document that's part of the user task or reassign the user task to somebody else. You can also create new subtasks to split up a large task into multiple smaller tasks.

The task page also includes a link to the process instance status overview: Part of process: 'Book Order Process'. The process instance overview provides a graphical overview of the process status, the outstanding tasks, and the process variables. See figure 3.21.

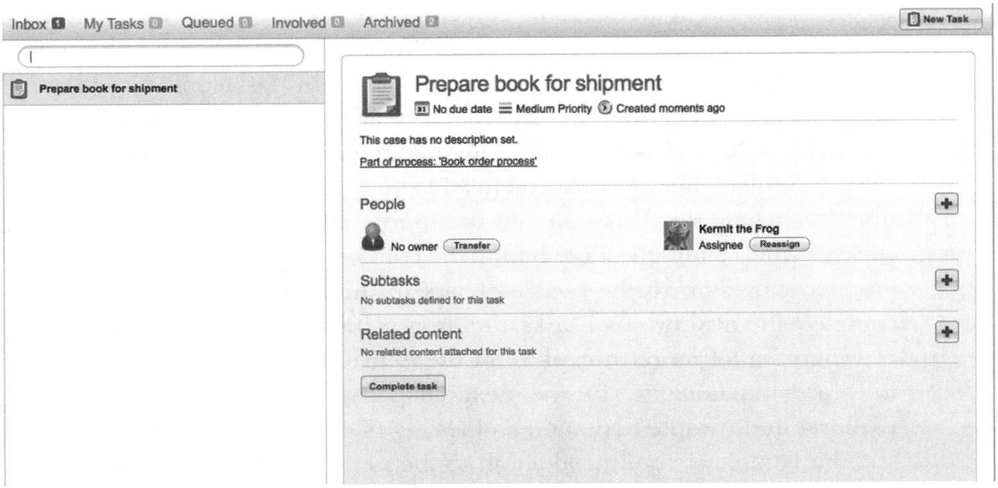

Figure 3.20 The task details page of the first user task created in the book order process. The task is assigned to Kermit.

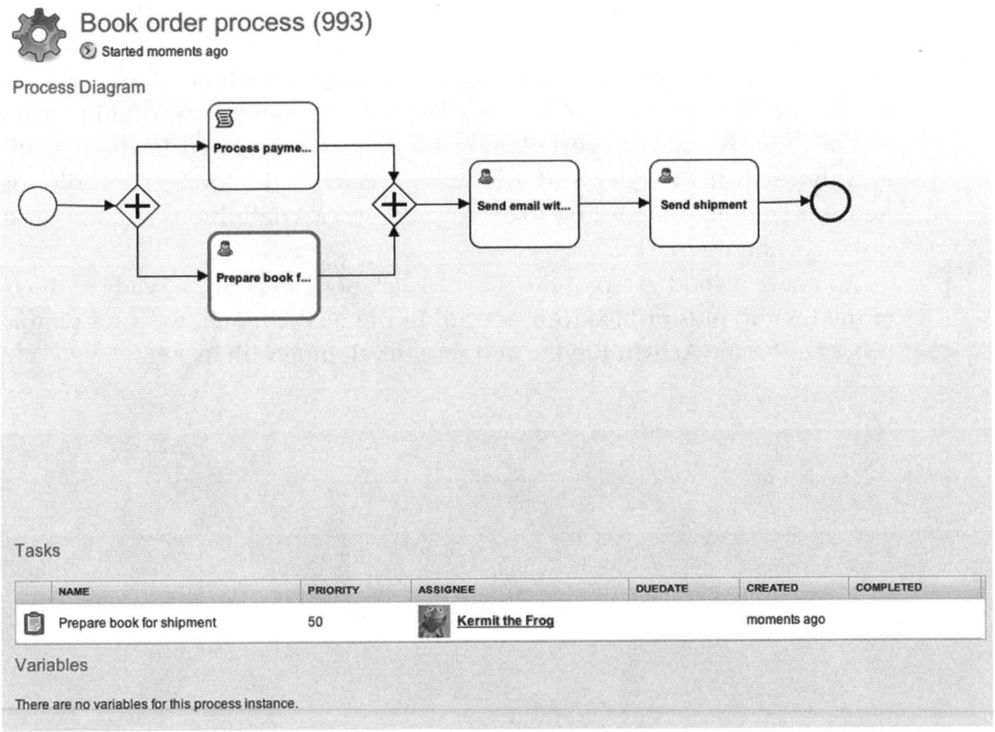

Figure 3.21 The process instance overview page, showing the process instance status, the open user tasks, and the process variables

As you can see in figure 3.21, the current open task in the process instance is the "Prepare book for shipment" user task. The "Process payment" script task has already been executed and completed. But the "Process payment" task could also have been a user task that hadn't been completed yet. In that case, the process instance's graphical overview would have two user tasks highlighted with red rectangles.

To complete the user task, you need to go back to the task details page. This is possible by clicking the Tasks tab and the Inbox link. On the task details page, you can click on the Complete Task button to complete the user task. Then, the process instance moves on to the next user task in the book order process. When you also complete the next two user tasks, the process instance will be completed.

There's a lot more to explore in the Activiti Explorer, but we've already covered the core functionality. In the next chapters, you'll frequently be using Activiti Explorer in the implementation and testing of example processes.

This completes the introduction to the Activiti tool stack and the add-on components that you can download and install separately.

3.5   Summary

We've covered a lot of ground in this chapter. If you worked your way through the examples, you'll now have a good idea of what Activiti is all about.

You saw how the Activiti Modeler works and played a bit with it to get a feel for modeling business processes. You discovered the Eclipse-based Designer environment and learned how to test processes in a fast and convenient way without having to write lots of code. You also imported an example process created in the Activiti Modeler into the Activiti Designer and eventually created a deployable BAR file for it. With Activiti Explorer, you saw how to deploy new process definitions and work with process instances and user tasks.

You have a good grasp of the Activiti stack now, and you're ready to discover more of the ins and outs of BPM with Activiti. In the next chapter, we'll start implementing processes on the Activiti Engine and start developing with its API.

Working with
the Activiti process engine

4

This chapter covers

- Setting up a development environment
- Understanding the Activiti API
- Implementing processes with plain Java
- Using Spring with Activiti

It's time to take a look at the core asset of the Activiti platform, the Activiti process engine. We already looked at a simple example in chapter 1 and at the Activiti tool stack in chapter 3, but, in this chapter, we'll discuss how you can use the Activiti Java API to interact with and use the process engine in a lot more detail.

To develop business process applications, you first have to set up a decent development environment, including a Maven configuration. We'll cover this first. Then, we'll take a look at the Activiti API, which will provide the necessary interfaces to start new processes, claim user tasks, and query the process engine for specific process instances, for example. After that, we'll explore the Java service tasks of Activiti, which provide a way to implement BPMN 2.0 processes with plain Java logic. When there's no need for web service interfaces or other external interfaces, the Java service tasks provide an easy-to-use framework to build processes. We'll also discuss how to execute these Java service tasks asynchronously. Finally, we'll look at how to apply Spring beans inside the BPMN 2.0 processes and even run the whole Activiti engine within a Spring container.

Let's get started by setting up a development environment so you can work with Activiti and explore some examples.

4.1 Creating an Activiti development environment

In this chapter, you'll be developing a lot of code snippets and unit tests. Instead of using a simple text editor, you might like to use your favorite development tool to develop processes, process logic, and unit tests. In this section, you'll be introduced to the different Activiti libraries you can use and how to set up a Maven project structure.

Logging is an important tool for understanding what's going on in a complex framework, like a process engine. First you'll learn how you can tune the log levels for your needs. Then you'll see a couple of options for running the Activiti engine.

Let's begin by taking a closer look at the Activiti library structure.

4.1.1 Getting familiar with the Activiti libraries

In chapter 3, you saw that the Activiti distribution consists of several modules, including the Activiti Explorer and the add-on components Activiti Modeler and camunda fox cycle. Each of these modules have their dependencies and project structure. In this section, we'll only focus on the Activiti Engine module, which provides the core component of the project.

But the Activiti engine also consists of several layers, as shown in figure 4.1. The first layer is the engine itself, which provides the engine interfaces we'll discuss in section 4.2 and which implements the BPMN 2.0 specification. The engine component also includes a process virtual machine abstraction, which translates the BPMN 2.0 engine logic into a state machine model, as discussed in chapter 1. This process virtual machine, therefore, is capable of supporting other process languages and provides the foundational layer of the Activiti Engine. The engine component is implemented in the activiti-engine-*version* JAR file.

An optional layer is the Spring container integration for the Activiti engine, which we'll discuss in detail in section 4.4. This layer makes the Activiti engine available for use inside a Spring container and provides functionality to invoke Spring beans directly from service tasks. This layer is provided with the activiti-spring-version JAR file that's available in the workspace/activiti-spring-examples/libs-runtime directory of the Activiti distribution.

As you can see in figure 4.1, each layer of the Activiti Engine adds a specific set of functionality. Before you can use the Activiti Engine in the development environment, the dependent libraries must also be available. In the next section, you'll see a Maven-based project structure that will provide you with the necessary dependencies. But you can also reference the library dependencies from the Activiti workspace directory. Notice that you then have to start by running the setup as described in chapter 1.

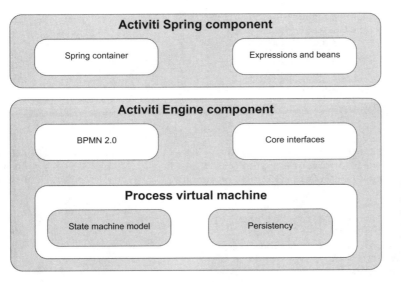

Figure 4.1 Overview of the different layers of the Activiti Engine, including the process virtual machine, the engine, and the Spring integration layers

After the Activiti installation script (see chapter 1) has been executed, you can find the Activiti Engine libraries in the workspace/activiti-engine-examples directory. The runtime libraries can be found in the libs-runtime directory, and the libraries necessary to test the examples are provided in the libs-test directory of every example project. If you don't want to use Maven for your project, you can retrieve the necessary libraries from the workspace/activiti-spring-examples directory, but, you'll see in the next section that a Maven project structure makes life a bit easier.

4.1.2 *Mavenizing your Activiti project*

Apache Maven can be considered the default choice for dependency management and project build management in general, and Activiti makes it easy to set up your project with Maven. In this section, you'll learn about the Maven configuration that's used in the source code of this book's examples. The examples in the Activiti distribution also have a Maven structure and a pom.xml file. To create a new Activiti project with a Maven configuration from scratch, you can create a new Maven project in the Eclipse IDE. In the presented wizard, you can fill in the necessary group and artifact identifier and choose a project name.

The pom.xml in the root of the new project needs some work; you have to add the Activiti dependencies. The following listing shows a Maven pom.xml that contains the minimal set of dependencies you need when starting an Activiti project. For a full list of all the dependencies you'll use throughout this book, you can look at the pom.xml file in the root of the `bpmn-examples` project in the book's source code.

Listing 4.1   A standard Maven configuration for an Activiti project

```
<project>
  <modelVersion>4.0.0</modelVersion>
  <groupId>org.bpmnwithactiviti</groupId>
```

```
<artifactId>your-project</artifactId>
<packaging>jar</packaging>
<version>1.0-SNAPSHOT</version>
<name>your-project</name>

<properties>
  <activiti-version>5.9</activiti-version>
</properties>

<dependencies>
  <dependency>
    <groupId>org.activiti</groupId>
    <artifactId>activiti-engine</artifactId>
    <version>${activiti-version}</version>
  </dependency>
  <dependency>
    <groupId>com.h2database</groupId>
    <artifactId>h2</artifactId>
    <version>1.2.132</version>
    <scope>test</scope>
  </dependency>
  <dependency>
    <groupId>junit</groupId>
    <artifactId>junit</artifactId>
    <version>4.8.1</version>
    <scope>test</scope>
  </dependency>
</dependencies>
  <repositories>
  <repository>
    <id>Activiti</id>
    <url>http://maven.alfresco.com/nexus/content/
        ➥ repositories/activiti</url>
  </repository>
</repositories>
</project>
```

1 Activiti Engine dependencies

2 H2 database driver

3 Alfresco Maven repository for Activiti

In the listing, the Maven namespace declarations are left out to make the configuration more readable. To include the Activiti Engine dependencies, you only have to include the activiti-engine dependency **1**. This dependency will also get all the third-party libraries, which are necessary to run the Activiti Engine. Notice that, in this Maven configuration, the Activiti Spring module isn't included because you don't need it for your first examples, but the module is included in the book's example source code.

To be able to test with an in-memory H2 database, you must also add the H2 database dependency **2**. The H2 database dependency also provides the database driver to connect to both the standalone H2 database provided with the Activiti distribution as well as the in-memory H2 database.

Because the Activiti Engine dependency isn't yet available from a central Maven repository, you also need to add the Alfresco Maven repository for the Activiti project **3**. If you're using the Eclipse development tool, you can now use the Maven Update Project Configuration menu item to create the necessary Eclipse project and classpath files.

NOTE Similar Maven archetypes are available for IntelliJ IDEA and other IDEs, and you can still use the good old command line to execute Maven commands.

Now all the Java libraries needed to run the Activiti Engine are available inside the IDE. This means that you can start implementing Activiti logic in your project. In the `bpmn-examples` project available in the book's source code, you can see that we also used a Maven configuration and defined the Activiti Engine dependencies. Now let's discuss how to tune logging in the Activiti Engine.

4.1.3 *Logging in the Activiti Engine*

Logging statements can help a lot when you're debugging, but they're also essential for getting good error descriptions from a production system. When you're using multiple open source frameworks in one project—like you do in this chapter with Activiti and Spring—you may run into different logging systems.

Activiti uses the standard Java java.util.logging API, also known as JDK 1.4 logging, and Spring uses Apache commons logging. This means that, by default, it's not possible to have one logging configuration file. Luckily, there's the Simple Logging Façade for Java (SLF4J—http://www.slf4j.org) framework that can translate log messages from different frameworks into the log message of your choice.

In this book, we'll use Log4J (http://logging.apache.org/log4j/1.2) as the logging system of choice, but you can easily change this to Apache Commons Logging, for example. SLF4J provides support for Log4J as well as Apache Commons Logging. For JDK 1.4 logging statements to be translated by SLF4J to Log4J, you have to do some coding.

You'll be using a lot of unit tests to work with the Activiti BPM platform, so the next code snippet shows the `AbstractTest` class you'll be extending from in every unit test to initialize your logging framework:

```java
import java.util.logging.Handler;
import java.util.logging.LogManager;
import java.util.logging.Logger;

import org.activiti.engine.impl.util.LogUtil;
import org.slf4j.bridge.SLF4JBridgeHandler;

public abstract class AbstractTest {

  @BeforeClass
  public static void routeLoggingToSlf4j() {
    LogUtil.readJavaUtilLoggingConfigFromClasspath();
    Logger rootLogger =
        LogManager.getLogManager().getLogger("");
    Handler[] handlers = rootLogger.getHandlers();
    for (int i = 0; i < handlers.length; i++) {
      rootLogger.removeHandler(handlers[i]);
    }
    SLF4JBridgeHandler.install();
  }
}
```

This abstract unit test class first makes sure that the `logging.properties` for the JDK 1.4 logging of the Activiti Engine are read from the classpath. By default, the JDK 1.4 logging reads the log configuration of your JAVA_HOME/lib/logging.properties—and that's not what you want. In the logging.properties file of the `bpmn-examples` project, the log level is set to FINEST so you can get all the logging information out of the Activiti Engine when you want to.

Next in the code snippet, the log handlers are removed from the `java.util.logging.Logger` class; otherwise, the JDK 1.4 logging framework still performs the logging. At the end of the code snippet, the `install` method of the SLF4J bridge is invoked, which will direct all JDK 1.4 logging output to SLF4J. Because you have the SLF4J Log4J library on the classpath, you can now define the log level of the Activiti Engine, the Spring framework, and other external frameworks in a default log4j.xml file. With this configuration, all logging is redirected to Log4j and you can define the desired logging level in the `log4j.xml` that's available on the classpath.

This means you can define a log level of DEBUG when you want to do some debugging, and you can set the level to ERROR when you don't want extra information logged in your unit tests. In the source code examples implemented in the `bpmn-examples` project, you extend the `AbstractTest` class in all unit test classes.

Now that the logging configuration is in place, let's discuss the options available for running the Activiti Engine.

4.1.4   *Developing and testing with the Activiti Engine*

The primary component you have to deal with when designing and developing BPMN 2.0 processes with Activiti is the Activiti Engine. The engine is your entry point to deploying new process definitions, starting new process instances, querying for user tasks, and so on. But what are the options for running the Activiti Engine during development? In the following subsections, we'll discuss the following three options:

- Running the Activiti Engine in the JVM with an in-memory database (H2)
- Running the Activiti Engine in the JVM with a standalone database (H2)
- Running the Activiti Engine on an application server (Apache Tomcat) with a standalone database (H2)

Let's look at the first of these options now.

RUNNING THE ACTIVITI ENGINE WITH AN IN-MEMORY DATABASE

A good way to test a BPMN 2.0 process is to run the Activiti Engine inside the Java Virtual Machine (JVM) with an in-memory database. In this deployment scenario, the unit tests can also be run within a continuous build environment without the need for external server components. The whole process engine environment runs from within the JVM and the unit test. Figure 4.2 illustrates this method of deployment.

In the source code examples we'll discuss in the rest of this chapter, this deployment alternative is used because it's the easiest to use from within an IDE. In the next subsection, we'll take a look at another option: using a standalone database.

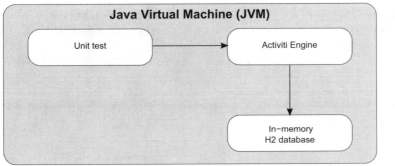

Figure 4.2 The deployment scenario where the Activiti Engine runs within the JVM with an in-memory database

RUNNING THE ACTIVITI ENGINE WITH A STANDALONE DATABASE

If you want to work with process definitions or instances that are deployed and running on a standalone environment, you need another deployment alternative. You must be able to run the Activiti Engine connected to a standalone database. This enables possibilities, such as querying the standalone database for specific running process instances. This type of deployment is shown in figure 4.3.

In the first example of this book, shown in chapter 1, you used this deployment option; an Activiti Engine is created from within a unit test and connected to a standalone H2 database. The H2 database is already installed and started as part of the Activiti installation setup. This type of setup isn't suitable for unit testing because the outcome of the unit test may vary with each run depending on what's already present in the database unless you clean the database before each run. But, it can be handy for integration testing, where you also want to use the Activiti Explorer together with a process you create from your local development environment.

RUNNING THE ACTIVITI ENGINE ON APACHE TOMCAT WITH A STANDALONE DATABASE

The previous deployment options are useful for unit and integration testing. But, eventually, you'll want to deploy your business processes on a production-like environment and do some basic testing there, too. This means that you can't start an Activiti Engine from within a unit test, because it runs on a separate application server environment.

What you can do is use the REST API provided with the Activiti Engine to interact with the process engine. The deployment of a new process definition must then be

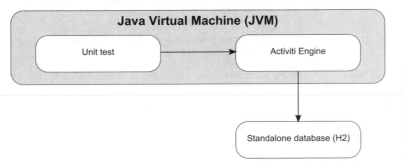

Figure 4.3 The deployment alternative where the Activiti Engine runs within the same JVM as the unit test and connects to a standalone database

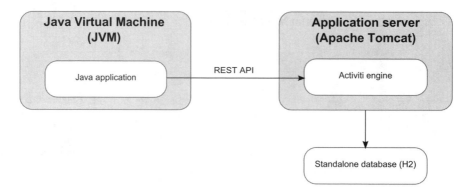

Figure 4.4 A typical Activiti Engine environment where the process engine runs on an application server, such as Apache Tomcat, with a standalone database. The REST API provides the necessary interface to interact with the process engine.

done via Activiti Explorer (like you did in chapter 3) or an Ant script by deploying a Business Archive file. This alternative is shown in figure 4.4.

In an environment like the one shown in figure 4.4, the need for unit tests is typically low because the deployment alternatives discussed earlier are more likely to be used for unit and integration testing. But, you will still need to communicate with the process engine when tools like the Activiti Explorer don't provide all the information you need or in cases where you want to communicate with the process engine from other applications. An example would be when you want to build a custom user interface for users to interact with the user tasks in a particular process. The REST API provides a great way to implement the necessary communication.

In chapter 8, we'll take close look at the possibilities of the REST API. But first, it's time to learn about the Java interfaces you can use to talk with the Activiti Engine.

4.2   *Using the Activiti Engine API*

The Activiti Engine API is divided into seven core interfaces, each targeted at interacting with different functionality of the process engine. Table 4.1 summarizes the core interfaces.

Table 4.1   Overview of the seven core interfaces of the Activiti API

Interface	Description
FormService	To work with the user task forms generated by the Activiti form engine, the form service provides several methods.
HistoryService	To retrieve information about completed process instances, you can use the history service interface.
IdentityService	The identity service provides an interface on the authentication component of the Activiti process engine.

Table 4.1   Overview of the seven core interfaces of the Activiti API *(continued)*

Interface	Description
`ManagementService`	The management service can be used to query the Activiti tables and execute jobs.
`RepositoryService`	The repository service provides functionality to deploy, query, delete, and retrieve process definitions.
`RuntimeService`	The runtime service provides an interface to start and query process instances. In addition, process variables can be retrieved and set, and processes can be signaled to leave a wait state.
`TaskService`	With the task service you can do a lot of things with user tasks. For example, you can create a new task and query Activiti for a list of tasks that a specific user can claim.

In this section, we'll discuss most of these interfaces with small and easy-to-use code examples, starting with the `RuntimeService`. We won't be covering the `FormService` and the `ManagementService` here because they provide specific functionality. The `FormService` can be used to interact with a user task or start event forms (we'll discuss this in chapter 5), and the `ManagementService` can be used to access jobs and query the Activiti tables (the job architecture is discussed in chapter 15).

4.2.1   *Starting process instances with the RuntimeService*

The primary usage of the `RuntimeService` is to start new process instances based on a specific process definition. But this isn't the sole purpose of this interface; it also provides simple query functionality and methods to set and retrieve process variables, among other operations.

Let's first look at how to use the `RuntimeService` to start a new process instance.

Listing 4.2   Start a new process instance with the `RuntimeService`

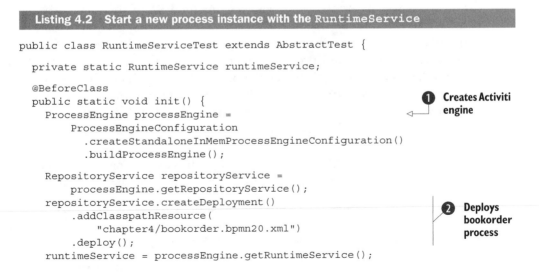

```
public class RuntimeServiceTest extends AbstractTest {

  private static RuntimeService runtimeService;

  @BeforeClass
  public static void init() {                            ❶ Creates Activiti
    ProcessEngine processEngine =                            engine
        ProcessEngineConfiguration
          .createStandaloneInMemProcessEngineConfiguration()
          .buildProcessEngine();

    RepositoryService repositoryService =
        processEngine.getRepositoryService();
    repositoryService.createDeployment()                 ❷ Deploys
        .addClasspathResource(                              bookorder
            "chapter4/bookorder.bpmn20.xml")                process
        .deploy();
    runtimeService = processEngine.getRuntimeService();
```

```
    }
    @Test
    public void startProcessInstance() {
      Map<String, Object> variableMap =
          new HashMap<String, Object>();
      variableMap.put("isbn", "123456");
      ProcessInstance processInstance =
          runtimeService.startProcessInstanceByKey(
              "bookorder", variableMap);
      assertNotNull(processInstance.getId());
      System.out.println("id " + processInstance.getId() + " "
          + processInstance.getProcessDefinitionId());
  }

    @Test
    public void queryProcessInstance() {
      List<ProcessInstance> instanceList = runtimeService
          .createProcessInstanceQuery()
          .processDefinitionKey("bookorder")
          .list();

      for (ProcessInstance queryProcessInstance : instanceList) {
        assertEquals(false, queryProcessInstance.isEnded());
        System.out.println("id " + queryProcessInstance.getId() +
            ", ended=" + queryProcessInstance.isEnded());
      }
    }
  }
}
```

❸ Starts new process instance

❹ Queries for running bookorder instances

To implement a unit test class with multiple test methods, it's a good practice to create the Activiti engine ❶ in an init method annotated with @BeforeClass. This makes the Activiti engine available in every test method. Then the book order process used in chapter 1 is deployed on the engine ❷. Figure 4.5 shows the simple book order process.

To start a new process instance for the book order process shown in figure 4.5, you can use the startProcessInstanceByKey method ❸ of the RuntimeService interface. With this method, the latest version of the specified process definition name is started. You can optionally provide a map of process variables as in this example. The other way to start a new process instance is to use the startProcessInstanceById method, which starts a specific version of a process definition. The process definition identifier is stored within the Activiti Engine database and is provided when you deploy a process definition with the RepositoryService. But, most of the time, you'll want to use the startProcessInstanceByKey method because you want to use the latest version of the process.

In the last step of the unit test, you query the Activiti engine for running process instances of the book order process ❹. Note that you use the processDefinitionKey

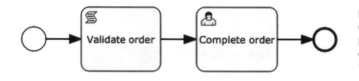

Figure 4.5 The process diagram of a simple book order process, containing a "Validate order script" task and a "Complete order user" task.

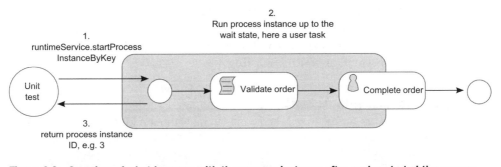

Figure 4.6   Overview of what happens with the process instance after you've started the process instance in the unit test

method here, which means all running process instances for all versions of the book order process are returned. To retrieve only the running process instances of a specific version of the book order process definition, you have to use the processDefinitionId method and provide the process definition identifier value.

When you run this unit test, you'll see one running process instance with the process instance query because you only started one new process instance. Let's see what happened inside the Activiti engine with the book order process instance after you started the process instance (figure 4.6).

The Activiti Engine executes the process instance immediately after the book order process is started with the startProcessInstanceByKey method. Because this is a synchronous execution in a single transaction and thread, the unit test will wait until the process instance identifier is returned. Activiti executes the process until a wait state is encountered. A user task is an example of such a wait state because somebody has to claim and complete the task before the process instance will proceed to the next activity. "Validate order" is a script task, which isn't a wait state and, therefore, it executes synchronously in the current thread. In section 4.3, you'll see how to define an automatic task, like a script or a Java service task, to run asynchronously.

For the unit test example, the Activiti engine executes the "Validate order" script task and initiates the "Complete order" user task. Then the wait state is activated and the process instance identifier is returned to the unit test. When you query the Activiti engine for running processes, you find exactly one instance, which has a current activity of the type user task. Now let's look at how to deal with this user task using the TaskService.

4.2.2   *Working with user tasks via the TaskService*

The TaskService provides a lot of functionality surrounding user tasks for the Activiti engine. You can, for example, use the TaskService to query the engine for specific tasks or to create a new standalone task for a specific user. In this section, we'll walk through most of the functionality the TaskService interface provides, starting with querying for running user tasks.

QUERYING FOR USER TASKS WITH THE TASKSERVICE

In the previous section, we looked at the usage of the `RuntimeService` with a rather large unit test. From now on, you'll use the unit testing functionality that the Activiti framework provides, as you'll see listing 4.3.

Unit testing with Activiti

When you want to test your process definition without a lot of plumbing code, you can use the unit testing functionality of the Activiti framework. The unit testing functionality of Activiti using JUnit 4 is centered on the use of the `ActivitiRule` class. The `ActivitiRule` class is a subclass of the JUnit `TestWatchman` class, which intercepts test method calls so it can provide the setup and teardown functionality. If you want to use JUnit 3 to create your tests, you can use the `AbstractActivitiTestCase` abstract base class.

But, first things first. At the creation of an `ActivitiRule` instance, an Activiti Engine is created using the activiti.cfg.xml configuration file found on the classpath by default. This can be overwritten if you want to. The activiti.cfg.xml configuration file contains, for example, the definition of the Activiti Engine and configures the database (embedded or standalone) that's used by the Activiti Engine. We'll discuss all the configuration options of the activiti.cfg.xml file in chapter 8.

The main usage of the `ActivitiRule` instance is that you can deploy a process definition before a test method is executed. This can be done by including the `@Deployment` annotation. By default, a process definition with the name testclassname.testmethodname.bpmn20.xml in the same package as the test class is deployed, but this can be overridden by specifying one or more bpmn20.xml files with the `resources` element of the `@Deployment` annotation. The `@Deployment` annotation also makes sure that after the test method has executed, running process instances, user tasks, and jobs are deleted. This is handy for keeping the database clean while running your unit tests.

In addition, the `ActivitiRule` instance can be used to retrieve the seven core interfaces we discuss in this section (section 4.2). You can also specify a specific `java.util.Date` with the `setCurrentTime` method, which can be used to test timers and due dates.

Listing 4.3   Querying for user tasks with the `TaskService` interface

```
public class TaskServiceTest extends AbstractTest {

  @Rule
  public ActivitiRule activitiRule = new ActivitiRule(          ❶ Initiates
      "activiti.cfg-mem.xml");                                    Activiti unit
                                                                  testing
  private void startProcessInstance() {
    RuntimeService runtimeService =
        activitiRule.getRuntimeService();
    Map<String, Object> variableMap =
        new HashMap<String, Object>();
    variableMap.put("isbn", "123456");
    runtimeService.startProcessInstanceByKey(                   ❷ Starts new
        "bookorder", variableMap);                                process instance
```

```
  }

  @Test
  @Deployment(resources={                                    ◄─┐   Deploys book
      ➥ "chapter4/bookorder.bpmn20.xml"})                    ❸   order process
  public void queryTask() {
    startProcessInstance();
    TaskService taskService = activitiRule.getTaskService();
    Task task = taskService.createTaskQuery()                ◄    ❹  Queries
        .taskCandidateGroup("sales")                                 for user
        .singleResult();                                             tasks
    assertEquals("Complete order", task.getName());
    System.out.println("task id " + task.getId() +
        ", name " + task.getName() +
        ", def key " + task.getTaskDefinitionKey());
  }
}
```

This unit test makes use of the powerful unit testing functionality Activiti provides with the `ActivitiRule` class ❶. This reduces the plumbing code necessary to test a process definition to a minimum. With the `@Deployment` annotation ❸, the book order process definition is deployed to the Activiti engine. But, you still have to start a new process instance ❷ before you can proceed with the actual testing logic.

Querying for user tasks is done via the `TaskQuery` interface where you can, for example, specify candidate user or group criteria and define ordering instructions. In this example, you query for user tasks that can be completed by users belonging to the sales group ❹. The user task defined in the book order process definition has a group definition that's equal to the name `sales`:

```
<userTask id="usertask1"
    name="Complete order"
    activiti:candidateGroups="sales">
  <documentation>book order user task</documentation>
</userTask>
```

Because you know that only one user task is running inside the unit test, you can use the `singleResult` method to return one `Task` instance.

Now let's move on to creating a new task and completing it.

CREATING AND COMPLETING USER TASKS VIA THE TASKSERVICE

The most common functionalities of the `TaskService` that you'll be using are the `claim` and `complete` methods. When a user task is created for a process instance, a person has to claim and complete the user task before the process instance proceeds to the next activity. Claiming a task means that the person who claims the task becomes the owner (assignee) of the task. It also means that the claimed task isn't available anymore for the other potential task owners to claim or complete it.

> **NOTE** The `TaskService` doesn't prohibit you from completing a task before it has been claimed. But, it's a best practice to claim a task with a particular user first and then complete it. This ensures that a full audit trail, including the name of the user who completed the task, is available.

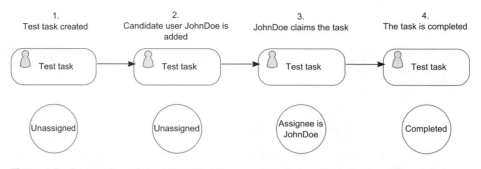

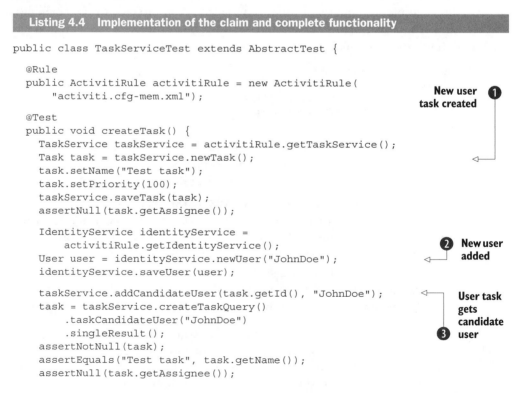

Figure 4.7 An overview of the different states a user task goes through when it's created, claimed, and completed

In the next example, you're going to create a standalone user task and claim and complete it. A standalone user task isn't bound to a specific process instance and can be created at any point in time in the Activiti Engine. The claim and complete functionality is no different for a process-bound user task. Figure 4.7 shows the different states the user task will have in this example.

The next listing implements the different states shown in figure 4.7 in a unit test method. The `createTask` test method is implemented in the same unit test class as the previous listing.

Listing 4.4 Implementation of the claim and complete functionality

```
public class TaskServiceTest extends AbstractTest {

  @Rule
  public ActivitiRule activitiRule = new ActivitiRule(
      "activiti.cfg-mem.xml");

  @Test
  public void createTask() {
    TaskService taskService = activitiRule.getTaskService();
    Task task = taskService.newTask();
    task.setName("Test task");
    task.setPriority(100);
    taskService.saveTask(task);
    assertNull(task.getAssignee());

    IdentityService identityService =
        activitiRule.getIdentityService();
    User user = identityService.newUser("JohnDoe");
    identityService.saveUser(user);

    taskService.addCandidateUser(task.getId(), "JohnDoe");
    task = taskService.createTaskQuery()
        .taskCandidateUser("JohnDoe")
        .singleResult();
    assertNotNull(task);
    assertEquals("Test task", task.getName());
    assertNull(task.getAssignee());
```

❶ New user task created

❷ New user added

❸ User task gets candidate user

```
        taskService.claim(task.getId(), "JohnDoe");               ◁─┐  User task
        task = taskService.createTaskQuery()                        ④  claimed
            .taskAssignee("JohnDoe")
            .singleResult();
        assertEquals("JohnDoe", task.getAssignee());

        taskService.complete(task.getId());                       ◁─┐  User task
        task = taskService.createTaskQuery()                        ⑤  completed
            .taskAssignee("JohnDoe")
            .singleResult();
        assertNull(task);
    }
}
```

To create a standalone user task, you can use the newTask method ❶ of the TaskService interface. In this example, the user task name and priority are set and the task is saved with these new values.

> **TIP** The priority attribute of a user task can be used to define the urgency of the work to be done. By default, this value is 50, but you define any value from 0 to 100 (where 100 is the highest priority level and 0 the lowest). The Activiti Engine itself doesn't use the priority attribute, but it can be used by your workflow application.

When the new user task is created, the assignee attribute is empty, meaning that there is no specific user allocated yet to do the work associated with the user task. To be able to claim the user task with a specific user, you first add a new user to the Activiti Engine. This is done via the IdentityService and the newUser method ❷. Note that the user isn't created before the saveUser method is invoked. Once the John Doe user is created, you can add a candidate user to the user task ❸. This means that John Doe is the candidate who'll execute the work associated with the user task.

> **NOTE** In Activiti, there's no validation if the user who claims the user task is also part of the candidate user or group. The Engine doesn't even validate whether the user is known. This makes it easy to plug in your own identity management solution, which can, for example, be an LDAP repository. We'll take a look at various options to implement identity management in chapter 10. It's a best practice to define a list of candidate users or groups and only claim the user task with a user that's on this list. The validation logic that checks if a user exists in your identity management system and whether the user is part of a specific group must be implemented by you.

In the next step of the unit test, the user task is claimed with the John Doe user ❹. Now the assignee attribute of the user task is filled with the user identifier of the claimer, which in this example, is John Doe. To complete the user task, the complete method is used ❺. When the user task is completed, it can't be found with a task query anymore. The only way to retrieve the user task at this point is via the HistoricActivityInstanceQuery, which we'll discuss in section 4.2.5. First, let's look at how to delete a process definition via the RepositoryService.

4.2.3 *Deleting process definitions with the RepositoryService*

You already used the `RepositoryService` interface in section 4.2.1 to deploy a process definition; it can also be used to query the Activiti engine for deployment artifacts and process definitions. In this section, you'll also use the delete functionality, which the `RepositoryService` interface provides. Let's work through an example where you deploy a new process definition and delete it at the end (see the next listing).

Listing 4.5   Deleting a deployment with the `RepositoryService`

```java
public class RepositoryServiceTest extends AbstractTest {

    @Rule
    public ActivitiRule activitiRule = new ActivitiRule(
        "activiti.cfg-mem.xml");

    @Test
    public void deleteDeployment() {
        RepositoryService repositoryService =
            activitiRule.getRepositoryService();
        String deploymentID = repositoryService.createDeployment()
            .addClasspathResource("chapter4/bookorder.bpmn20.xml")
            .deploy()
            .getId();

        Deployment deployment = repositoryService
            .createDeploymentQuery()
            .singleResult();
        assertNotNull(deployment);
        assertEquals(deploymentID, deployment.getId());
        System.out.println("Found deployment " + deployment.getId()
            + ", deployed at " + deployment.getDeploymentTime());

        ProcessDefinition processDefinition = repositoryService
            .createProcessDefinitionQuery()
            .latestVersion()
            .singleResult();
        assertNotNull(processDefinition);
        assertEquals("bookorder", processDefinition.getKey());
        System.out.println("Found process definition " +
            processDefinition.getId());

        RuntimeService runtimeService =
            activitiRule.getRuntimeService();
        Map<String, Object> variableMap =
            new HashMap<String, Object>();
        variableMap.put("isbn", "123456");
        runtimeService.startProcessInstanceByKey(
            "bookorder", variableMap);

        ProcessInstance processInstance = runtimeService
            .createProcessInstanceQuery()
            .singleResult();
        assertNotNull(processInstance);
        assertEquals(processDefinition.getId(),
            processInstance.getProcessDefinitionId());
```

Annotations:
1. Deploys new process definition
2. Queries engine for deployments
3. Retrieves the deployed process definition
4. Starts new process instance

```
    repositoryService.deleteDeployment(deploymentID, true);          Deletes
                                                                      process
    deployment = repositoryService                                   definition
        .createDeploymentQuery()                                     and
        .singleResult();                                          5  instances
    assertNull(deployment);
    processDefinition = repositoryService
        .createProcessDefinitionQuery()
        .singleResult();
    assertNull(processDefinition);
    processInstance = runtimeService
        .createProcessInstanceQuery()
        .singleResult();
    assertNull(processInstance);
  }
}
```

This is quite a bit of coding, but, as you can see, you do a lot of querying to validate the results of the deployment activities. First, you start with deploying the book order process definition ❶ like you did in section 4.2.1. The difference here is that you keep track of the deployment identifier that's generated by the Activiti Engine. This deployment identifier will be needed later on.

When the deployment has been executed, you can query the process engine for deployment artifacts with the DeploymentQuery ❷. Because you're using an in-memory database, you'll expect to find only the deployment done in this unit test. In addition to the deployment artifact query, you can also query the engine for the latest version of the deployed process definitions via the ProcessDefinitionQuery ❸.

NOTE A deployment can contain multiple resources, including a process definition. But, it can also contain other resources, such as a business rule and a process definition image.

Because you want to show the ability to delete the process definition, including possible running process instances and process history information, a new process instance is started ❹ in the unit test. The RepositoryService interface provides two types of delete methods:

- The deleteDeployment method with a deployment identifier and a false input parameter, which only deletes the deployment and not the corresponding process instance data. When there are still running process instances, you'll get an exception when running this method.
- The deleteDeployment method with a deployment identifier and a true input parameter, which deletes all information regarding the process definition, running instances, and history. If you want all process data, including running process instances, to be deleted, you should use a Boolean value of true for the second input parameter.

Because you've been running process instances in this unit test, you must use the Boolean value of true ❺, or you'll receive an exception. In the last part of the unit test, you validate that the deployment, process definition, and instance are deleted. You can execute this unit test to ensure it runs successfully. Let's move on to the `Iden-tityService` interface and see how to create new group memberships.

4.2.4 Creating users, groups, and memberships with the IdentityService

In section 4.2.2, we talked about assigning, claiming, and completing user tasks with the `TaskService` interface. You've already seen how to create a new user within the Activiti identity module by using the `IdentityService`. The `IdentityService` interface does provide a lot more functionality, including query functions and group membership functions. This can be handy if you want to query the Activiti Engine for users belonging to a specific group or assign users a new group membership.

In the next listing, a new user, group, and group membership are created and the newly created group membership is tested using the book order process example you've seen before.

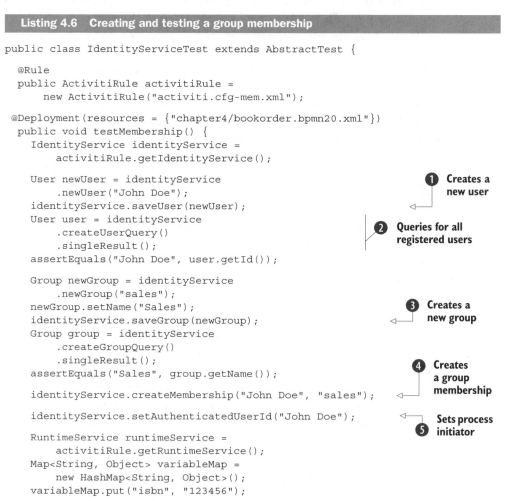

Listing 4.6   Creating and testing a group membership

```
public class IdentityServiceTest extends AbstractTest {

  @Rule
  public ActivitiRule activitiRule =
      new ActivitiRule("activiti.cfg-mem.xml");

  @Deployment(resources = {"chapter4/bookorder.bpmn20.xml"})
  public void testMembership() {
    IdentityService identityService =
        activitiRule.getIdentityService();

    User newUser = identityService                    ❶ Creates a
        .newUser("John Doe");                            new user
    identityService.saveUser(newUser);
    User user = identityService                       ❷ Queries for all
        .createUserQuery()                              registered users
        .singleResult();
    assertEquals("John Doe", user.getId());

    Group newGroup = identityService
        .newGroup("sales");
    newGroup.setName("Sales");                        ❸ Creates a
    identityService.saveGroup(newGroup);                new group
    Group group = identityService
        .createGroupQuery()
        .singleResult();
    assertEquals("Sales", group.getName());

    identityService.createMembership("John Doe", "sales");   ❹ Creates
                                                               a group
                                                               membership

    identityService.setAuthenticatedUserId("John Doe");   ❺ Sets process
                                                            initiator
    RuntimeService runtimeService =
        activitiRule.getRuntimeService();
    Map<String, Object> variableMap =
        new HashMap<String, Object>();
    variableMap.put("isbn", "123456");
```

```
    runtimeService.startProcessInstanceByKey(
        "bookorder", variableMap);
    TaskService taskService = activitiRule.getTaskService();
    Task task = taskService.createTaskQuery()
        .taskCandidateUser("John Doe")
        .singleResult();
    assertNotNull(task);
    assertEquals("Complete order", task.getName());
  }
}
```

6 Queries to validate group membership

You again create a new user **1**, but now you also query the Engine to see if the user was created correctly **2**. Because you eventually want to test whether the newly created `John Doe` user will be a candidate user for the user task in the book order process, you also create a new group **3**, `sales`, which is used in the group assignment in that process.

Having created the user and group, you can now create a group membership of `John Doe` for the `sales` group **4**. As you can see, this is all easy to do when using the `IdentityService` interface. The `IdentityService` also enables you to set the authenticated user **5**; in this example, it's used to set the user who starts or initiates the process instance. In the process definition, a process variable can be configured whereby this user identifier will be available during process execution:

```
<startEvent id="startEvent" activiti:initiator="starter" />
```

When you start a book order process instance, you can now test whether your new user is a candidate user for the `Complete order` user task. To test this, you use a task query with a candidate user criterion, which is equal to `John Doe` **6**. When the group membership has been created successfully, the retrieved user task name should be equal to `Complete order`.

It's nice to be able to start new process instances and work with user tasks using the Activiti API. But, what happens if a process instance is finished or terminated? Will you still be able to retrieve information about these process instances, such as for reporting? Yes; and that's what the next section about the `HistoryService` interface is about.

4.2.5 A sneak peek into the past with the HistoryService

When information about ended process instances is needed, or previous activities from a running execution must be retrieved, the `HistoryService` provides an interface to query this kind of data. But before we dive into a code example of how to use the `HistoryService` interface, let's first look at how the historic data about process instances and activities is stored inside the Activiti engine database. You'll again use the book order process for this and start a new process instance, as shown in figure 4.8.

Note that a historic process instance is stored right away when a new process instance is started. A query on historic process instances will also give results when all created process instances are still running; they don't have an end time yet. The database table in which you can find the historic process instances is the ACT_HI_PROCINST table. When the process instance enters its first activity state, such as `Validate order`, a record in the

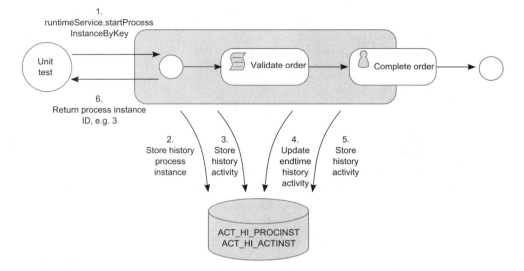

Figure 4.8   Overview of the historic data of process instances and activities, which is stored by the Activiti engine in the database when starting the example book order process

historic activity table (ACT_HI_ACTINST) is made. When the activity is finished, the record is updated with the end time of the activity. Figure 4.9 finishes the book order process example and shows what happens if the "Complete order" user task is completed.

When the user task is completed, the end time of the corresponding history activity instance is updated with the time at completion. Then the book order process instance reaches its final end state and the end time of the historic process instance is filled in. Because the process instance has finished its execution at this point, the Activiti Engine

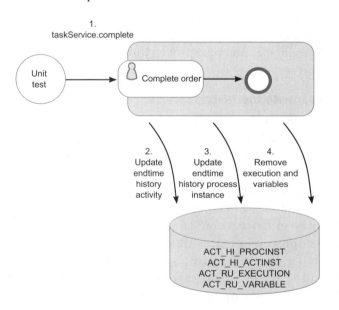

Figure 4.9   The complete story of what's stored in the Activiti engine database when the book order process user task is completed

will also delete the runtime execution information other than the history from the database. The deleted data is the execution instance stored in the ACT_RU_EXECUTION table and the process variables persisted in the ACT_RU_VARIABLE table.

The execution data is deleted to reduce the number of rows in the running process instance tables to improve performance. The historic tables don't have any foreign keys so they can be backed up easily. Note that the process variables aren't automatically stored in the history tables. The updates to process variables are only stored in a historic table, named ACT_HI_DETAIL, when you set the level of historic information to keep to full. We'll discuss how to configure the level of historic information that's logged shortly.

First, let's look at a unit test that uses the HistoryService interface to query the Activiti Engine for history process instances and history activities.

Listing 4.7 Querying for process instances and historic activities

```java
public class HistoryServiceTest extends AbstractTest {

  @Rule
  public ActivitiRule activitiRule = new ActivitiRule(
      "activiti.cfg-mem-fullhistory.xml");

  private String startAndComplete() {
    RuntimeService runtimeService =
        activitiRule.getRuntimeService();
    Map<String, Object> variableMap =
        new HashMap<String, Object>();
    variableMap.put("isbn", "123456");
    String processInstanceID = runtimeService
        .startProcessInstanceByKey(
            "bookorder", variableMap)
        .getId();

    TaskService taskService = activitiRule.getTaskService();
    Task task = taskService.createTaskQuery()
        .taskCandidateGroup("sales")
        .singleResult();
    variableMap = new HashMap<String, Object>();
    variableMap.put("extraInfo", "Extra information");
    variableMap.put("isbn", "654321");
    taskService.complete(task.getId(), variableMap);
    return processInstanceID;
  }

  @Test
  @Deployment(resources={"chapter4/bookorder.bpmn20.xml"})
  public void queryHistoricInstances() {
    String processInstanceID = startAndcomplete();
    HistoryService historyService =
        activitiRule.getHistoryService();
    HistoricProcessInstance historicProcessInstance =
        historyService
            .createHistoricProcessInstanceQuery()
            .processInstanceId(processInstanceID)
            .singleResult();
```

❶ Starts a new process instance

❷ Completes a user task with variables

❸ Queries for historic process instances

```
        assertNotNull(historicProcessInstance);
        assertEquals(processInstanceID, historicProcessInstance
            .getId());
        System.out.println("history process with definition id " +
            historicProcessInstance.getProcessDefinitionId() +
            ", started at " +
                historicProcessInstance.getStartTime() +
            ", ended at " + historicProcessInstance.getEndTime() +
            ", duration was " +
                historicProcessInstance.getDurationInMillis());
    }

    @Test
    @Deployment(resources={"chapter4/bookorder.bpmn20.xml"})
    public void queryHistoricActivities() {
      startAndcomplete();
      HistoryService historyService =
          activitiRule.getHistoryService();
      List<HistoricActivityInstance> activityList =
          historyService
              .createHistoricActivityInstanceQuery()
              .list();
      assertEquals(3, activityList.size());
      for (HistoricActivityInstance historicActivityInstance :
          activityList) {
        assertNotNull(historicActivityInstance.getActivityId());
        System.out.println("history activity " +
            historicActivityInstance.getActivityName() +
            ", type " +
                historicActivityInstance.getActivityType() +
            ", duration was " +
                historicActivityInstance.getDurationInMillis());
      }
    }
  }
}
```

❹ Queries
for historic
activities

The `startAndComplete` method starts a new process instance ❶ and completes the user task with an update to the `isbn` process variable and the addition of a new process variable `extraInfo` ❷. This corresponds to the execution logic in figures 4.8 and 4.9. The variables that are passed onto the process instance at the user task completion will be used later on, in listing 4.8.

In the first unit test implemented using the `HistoricProcessInstanceQuery`, the historic process instance started and completed in the `startAndComplete` method is retrieved ❸. Note that `HistoricProcessInstanceQuery` would also have returned the book order process instance if the user task wasn't completed and the process instance was still running, as illustrated in figure 4.4. The information that can be retrieved from a `HistoricProcessInstance` is basic; for example, the start and end times.

More interesting is the information that can be retrieved via the `HistoricActivity-InstanceQuery` ❹, which can provide a list of activities that have been executed by the Activiti Engine. In this example, the query will return three activities: the start event plus the "Validate order" and "Complete order" tasks from the book order process definition. This kind of information can be handy when you want to see the audit trail whose route has been executed in a specific process instance.

In this example, the default history settings of Activiti were used. But you can configure four levels of history archiving:

- *None*—No history information is archived.
- *Activity*—All process and activity instance information is archived.
- *Audit (default)*—All process, activity instance, and form properties information is archived.
- *Full*—The highest level of archiving; all audit information is archived and, additionally, the updates to process variables and user task form properties are stored.

When you don't want to use the default setting of audit for history archiving, you can specify an alternative value in the Activiti configuration file, which by default is activiti.cfg.xml. To do this, add the following property to the process engine configuration:

```
<property name="history" value="full" />
```

In this example, you've specified the highest level of history archiving, but this can be any of the four levels mentioned previously. In the highest level, the updates to process variables are logged in the history table ACT_HI_DETAIL. The next listing shows a unit test method—the same HistoryServiceTest class used in listing 4.7—which retrieves these process variable updates.

Listing 4.8 Retrieving process variable updates with the HistoryService interface

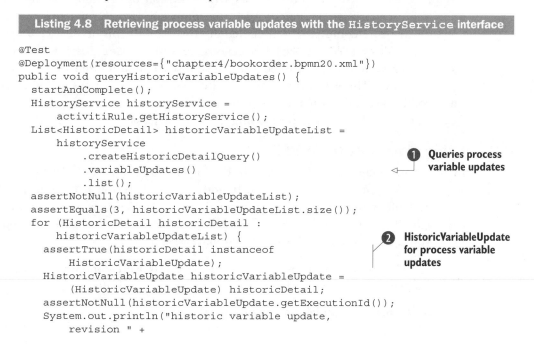

```
@Test
@Deployment(resources={"chapter4/bookorder.bpmn20.xml"})
public void queryHistoricVariableUpdates() {
  startAndComplete();
  HistoryService historyService =
      activitiRule.getHistoryService();
  List<HistoricDetail> historicVariableUpdateList =
      historyService
          .createHistoricDetailQuery()                     ❶ Queries process
          .variableUpdates()                                  variable updates
          .list();
  assertNotNull(historicVariableUpdateList);
  assertEquals(3, historicVariableUpdateList.size());
  for (HistoricDetail historicDetail :
      historicVariableUpdateList) {                        ❷ HistoricVariableUpdate
    assertTrue(historicDetail instanceof                      for process variable
        HistoricVariableUpdate);                              updates
    HistoricVariableUpdate historicVariableUpdate =
        (HistoricVariableUpdate) historicDetail;
    assertNotNull(historicVariableUpdate.getExecutionId());
    System.out.println("historic variable update,
        revision " +
```

```
        historicVariableUpdate.getRevision() +
    ", variable type name " +
        historicVariableUpdate.getVariableTypeName() +
    ", variable name " +
        historicVariableUpdate.getVariableName() +
    ", Variable value '" +
        historicVariableUpdate.getValue()+"'");
  }
}
```

❸ Gets new process variable value

When the history level is set to full, the historic detail query can be used to retrieve process variable updates ❶. This means that, when a new process variable is created, an update row is created. But an update row also is created when the value of a process variable is changed, as you saw with the isbn variable in listing 4.7.

The process variable updates can be retrieved using HistoricVariableUpdate instances ❷. In this unit test, you don't do a lot of testing, but you print all the variable update information for learning purposes, like the new process variable value ❸. When you run this unit test, you should see the following console output:

```
historic variable update, revision 0, variable type name string, variable
    name isbn, Variable value '123456'
historic variable update, revision 1, variable type name string, variable
    name isbn, Variable value '654321'
historic variable update, revision 0, variable type name string, variable
    name extraInfo, Variable value 'Extra information'
```

The first entry is created at the start of the process instance, when the isbn process variable is set. The second entry shows a new revision of the isbn variable, created when the user task is completed. And, the same goes for the last process variable update entry. This completes our detailed discussion of the history service interface.

We haven't covered the ManagementService and FormService interfaces yet. In the previous sections, you worked with the most frequently used interfaces of the Activiti Engine. These two, less common interfaces will be discussed in chapter 5, when you'll use a task form and a boundary timer event.

Now, though, let's look at developing Java service tasks.

4.3   *Using plain Java to do BPM*

By now, you're familiar with the Activiti Engine API, but we haven't discussed the use of Java inside a process definition yet. In addition to the script, web service, and user tasks available to define a process, you can also use Java classes to implement the process logic. When there's no web service that can be executed to deal with business logic, you can use a Java service task to do that work.

NOTE   The use of Java to implement a service task isn't standard BPMN 2.0 functionality but is provided as an add-on by the Activiti framework.

The Java service task can be used in four ways:

- Java service task class
- Java service task class with field extensions
- Java service task with method or value expressions
- A delegate expression that defines a variable that is resolved to a Java bean at runtime

In the following sections, we'll look at each of these four options with short code examples.

4.3.1 Java service task with class definition

The simplest way of using a Java service task is to create a simple Java class that extends the JavaDelegate convenience class and defines the fully qualified class name (package name and the class name) in the service task of the process definition.

Let's use the book order process example again and implement the validate order functionality in a Java class.

Listing 4.9 A validate order class that extends the JavaDelegate class

```java
public class ValidateService implements JavaDelegate {

  @Override
  public void execute(DelegateExecution execution) {
    System.out.println("execution id " + execution.getId());
    Long isbn = (Long) execution.getVariable("isbn");
    System.out.println("received isbn " + isbn);
    execution.setVariable("validatetime", new Date());
  }
}
```

A typical Java service task must implement the JavaDelegate class, which makes it easy to implement a bit of process logic. This convenience class takes care of leaving the Java service task when it has finished to all the outgoing transitions for which the sequence flow condition, if present, doesn't evaluate to false. When the Java service task is executed in the process instance, the execute method will be invoked by the Activiti Engine. The DelegateExecution instance provides an interface to retrieve and set the process variables. In this simple listing, the isbn process variable is retrieved and the validatetime variable is set with the current date and time.

The only thing you have to change in the process definition is the service task for the validate order step; but, in the following listing, the full process definition is included to make it more comprehensible.

Listing 4.10 The book order process definition with a Java service task class

```xml
<?xml version="1.0" encoding="UTF-8"?>
<definitions
    xmlns="http://www.omg.org/spec/BPMN/20100524/MODEL"
    targetNamespace="http://www.bpmnwithactiviti.org"
    xmlns:activiti="http://activiti.org/bpmn">
```

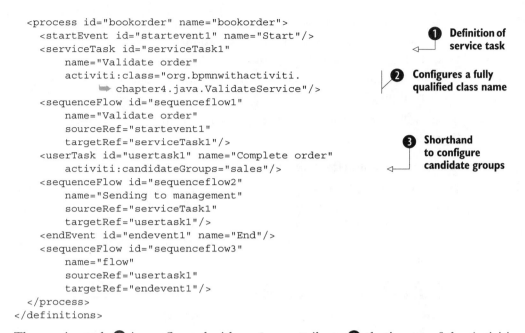

```
<process id="bookorder" name="bookorder">
  <startEvent id="startevent1" name="Start"/>
  <serviceTask id="serviceTask1"
      name="Validate order"
      activiti:class="org.bpmnwithactiviti.
          ➥ chapter4.java.ValidateService"/>
  <sequenceFlow id="sequenceflow1"
      name="Validate order"
      sourceRef="startevent1"
      targetRef="serviceTask1"/>
  <userTask id="usertask1" name="Complete order"
      activiti:candidateGroups="sales"/>
  <sequenceFlow id="sequenceflow2"
      name="Sending to management"
      sourceRef="serviceTask1"
      targetRef="usertask1"/>
  <endEvent id="endevent1" name="End"/>
  <sequenceFlow id="sequenceflow3"
      name="flow"
      sourceRef="usertask1"
      targetRef="endevent1"/>
</process>
</definitions>
```

1 Definition of service task

2 Configures a fully qualified class name

3 Shorthand to configure candidate groups

The service task **1** is configured with a `class` attribute **2** that's part of the Activiti BPMN extensions namespace. Note that you configured the `ValidateService` class shown in listing 4.8. The user task is changed a bit because you use the shorthand `candidateGroups` attribute here **3**. Activiti provides an easier way to define candidate users and groups with extension attributes because the BPMN 2.0 specification is a little bit verbose on this point. The same candidate group assignment would look like the following code snippet with BPMN 2.0–compliant XML:

```
<userTask id="usertask1" name="Complete order">
  <documentation>book order user task</documentation>
  <potentialOwner>
    <resourceAssignmentExpression>
      <formalExpression>sales</formalExpression>
    </resourceAssignmentExpression>
  </potentialOwner>
</userTask>
```

To test your book order process with a Java service task, you can develop a simple unit test like the one shown in the next listing.

Listing 4.11   Unit test that tests the book order process with Java service task

```
public class JavaBpmnTest extends AbstractTest {

  @Rule
  public ActivitiRule activitiRule = new ActivitiRule(
      "activiti.cfg-mem.xml");

  private ProcessInstance startProcessInstance() {
    RuntimeService runtimeService =
```

```
        activitiRule.getRuntimeService();
    Map<String, Object> variableMap =
        new HashMap<String, Object>();
    variableMap.put("isbn", 123456L);
    return runtimeService.startProcessInstanceByKey(
        "bookorder", variableMap);
}

@Test
@Deployment(resources={
    "chapter4/bookorder.java.bpmn20.xml"})
public void executeJavaService() {
    ProcessInstance processInstance = startProcessInstance();
    RuntimeService runtimeService =
        activitiRule.getRuntimeService();
    Date validatetime = (Date) runtimeService.getVariable(
        processInstance.getId(), "validatetime");
    assertNotNull(validatetime);
    System.out.println("validatetime is " + validatetime);
}
}
```

1 Starts new process instance

2 Deploys Java book order process

3 Gets validatetime process variable

To test the execution of the Java service task, you first have to start a new process instance **1** of the book order process in listing 4.10. To deploy the process definition with only one line of coding, you use the @Deployment annotation **2**. Because the ValidateService class invoked in the Java service task sets a process variable with the name validatetime, you test if that variable is set **3**. This shows you don't need a large unit test to verify a successful execution of a process definition.

Up to this point, you've been executing processes in a synchronous manner, until you encounter non-automatic tasks, such as a user task. In the next section, you'll see how to use async continuations to execute a service task asynchronously.

4.3.2 *Introducing asynchronous behavior*

In figure 4.6, you saw that Activiti executes automatic tasks like a service task in the same transaction and thread as the transaction and thread the process was started in. This means that the Java class that starts a process instance will have to wait until all automatic tasks have been executed in a process definition. When a service task contains long-running logic, like the invocation of an external web service or the construction of a large PDF document, this may not be the desired behavior.

Activiti provides a solution for these cases in the form of async continuations. From a BPMN 2.0 XML perspective, the definition of an asynchronous service task (or another type of task) is easy. You only have to add an async attribute to the service task configuration:

```
<serviceTask id="serviceTask1"
  name="Validate order"
  activiti:async="true"
  activiti:class="org.bpmnwithactiviti.chapter4.java.LongValidateService"/>
```

When we define a service task with the async attribute set to true, the execution of the service task logic will be executed in a separate transaction and thread. The process

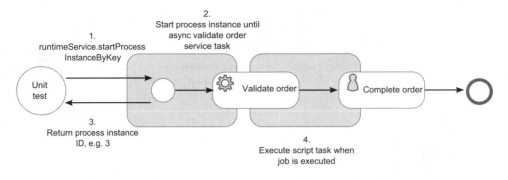

Figure 4.10   Asynchronous execution of the validate order service task using an Activiti async continuation

state is persisted to the Activiti database and a job is created to handle the service task execution. Figure 4.10 shows the book order process definition with the asynchronous validate order service task.

As you can see in figure 4.10, the unit test class (JavaBpmnTest) that starts the process instance will get a response right after the Activiti Engine stores the process state and creates a job to execute the "Validate order" service task. The Activiti job executor component that executes these jobs will be discussed in detail in chapter 15. For now, think of it as a standalone component that executes jobs in a separate transaction and thread. In the executeAsyncService method of the JavaBpmnTest class, you can find a unit test that executes the book order process as described in figure 4.10.

Besides a service task, you can also configure async continuations on other automatic tasks like a business rule task, call activity, or script task, and even on a subprocess. Furthermore, you can configure an async continuation on a non-automatic task like a user task or a receive task, which results in the execution listener being executed in a separate thread. (Execution listeners are introduced in chapter 6.)

You can also enhance the Java service task by injecting process variables or string values. In the next section, the book order example is changed a bit to include field extensions.

4.3.3   *Java service task with class definition and field extensions*

In section 4.4, you'll learn how to use the Activiti Engine inside a Spring container, which provides many ways to implement dependency injection. But the Activiti engine also provides some simple functionality regarding dependency injection. To be able to implement dependency injection, you'll have to change the ValidateService a bit, like the example in the following listing.

Listing 4.12   Java service task class with dependency injection

```
public class ValidateServiceWithFields
    implements JavaDelegate {

  private Expression validatetext;
```

```
    private Expression isbn;

    @Override
    public void execute(DelegateExecution execution) {
        System.out.println("execution id " + execution.getId());
        System.out.println("received isbn " +
            (Long) isbn.getValue(execution));
        execution.setVariable("validatetime", new Date());
        System.out.println(
            validatetext.getValue(execution).toString() +
                execution.getVariable("validatetime"));
    }
}
```

Get isbn expression value **1**

The `ValidateServiceWithFields` class defines two attributes that can be injected by the Activiti Engine: the `isbn` and `validatetext` attributes. Notice that the attributes are of type `org.activiti.engine.impl.el.Expression`. The `Expression` class is used by Activiti to support simple string attribute values as well as complex expressions.

> **NOTE** You might have expected a String type attribute for the `validatetext` parameter. But a service task has only one instance inside the Activiti Engine, which is reused for every process instance. Therefore, multiple threads can access a service task class at the same time, and class level attributes aren't thread safe. Activiti introduces an `Expression` class and the attribute value is retrieved by passing a `DelegateExecution` instance to the `Expression` instance, which can then evaluate the `Expression` value for that specific process instance.

In this example, the `isbn` expression consists of some logic to give the `isbn` at least a value that consists of more than six digits, as you'll see in the next code snippet. To get the value of the `isbn` number with the expression calculated, you can invoke the `getValue` method with the `DelegateExecution` instance as a parameter **1**.

Now you only have to change the service task definition of the book order process, shown in listing 4.10, according to the following code snippet:

```
<serviceTask id="serviceTask1" name="Validate order"
    activiti:class="org.bpmnwithactiviti.chapter4.
        ➥ java.ValidateServiceWithFields">
  <extensionElements>
    <activiti:field name="validatetext"
        stringValue="Validaton done at "/>
      <activiti:field name="isbn">
      <activiti:expression>
        ${isbn > 999999 ? isbn : 1000000 + isbn}
      </activiti:expression>
    </activiti:field>
  </extensionElements>
</serviceTask>
```

With this `extensionElements` XML element, fields to be injected into the `ValidateServiceWithFields` class can be specified. This can be a simple `String` value, like the `validatetext` field, or an expression using, for example, process variables like the isbn field. Note that you can directly use process variables in a process definition for the Activiti engine. You don't need additional coding. Because this new process definition can be tested with a unit test similar to the one shown in listing 4.11, we won't cover this in more detail.

In addition to using classes inside a Java service task, you can also use method or value expressions; this is what we'll explore in the next section.

4.3.4   *Java service task with method and value expressions*

When you don't want to be dependent on the `JavaDelegate` interface in your service class, you can define a method or value expression for a Java service task. Let's look at two simple examples to get you introduced to this type of Java service task.

When you have a `BookOrder` class with a `validate` method like the following code snippet, you can use a method expression:

```
public class BookOrder implements Serializable {

  private static final long serialVersionUID = 1L;

  public Date validate(Long isbn) {
    System.out.println("received isbn " + isbn);
    return new Date();
  }
}
```

The method expression will invoke the `validate` method and proceed to next transition. Note that you now have an `isbn` instance as a parameter in the `validate` method. How the `isbn` instance is passed on is defined in the method expression of the Java service task:

```
<serviceTask id="serviceTask1" name="Validate order"
    activiti:expression="#{bookOrder.validate(isbn)}"
    activiti:resultVariableName="validatetime"/>
```

If necessary, you can still pass a `DelegateExecution` instance as a parameter into the method by using the implicit `execution` variable, as illustrated in section 4.4.2. The attribute `resultVariableName` is used to make the return value of the method available as a process variable with the name `validatetime`. To be able to use the `BookOrder` instance inside the process definition, you must make sure the class is made available as a process variable with a name of `bookOrder`. This can be done when the process is started, like you did in the unit test of listing 4.11.

> **NOTE** When you use a Java bean as a process variable, make sure the bean implements the `Serializable` interface because the process variable will be persisted to the Activiti Engine database.

Another use of expressions inside a Java service task is a value expression. A value expression defines an attribute inside a Java bean for which the corresponding getter method will be invoked. This isn't a common use of Java service tasks, but it looks like the following XML snippet:

```
<serviceTask id="serviceTask1" name="Validate order"
    activiti:expression="#{bookOrder.isbn}"
    activiti:resultVariableName="isbn"/>
```

In this example, the `getIsbn` method will be invoked on the `BookOrder` process variable and the resulting value is assigned to the `isbn` process variable.

We haven't discussed the `delegateExpression` attribute yet, which is the fourth way to define a Java service task. With a delegate expression, you can configure a variable that is evaluated at runtime to a Java class that must implement the `JavaDelegate` interface. Here's a simple example:

```
<serviceTask id="serviceTask1" name="Validate order"
    activiti:delegateExpression="#{orderValidator}"/>
```

The `orderValidator` variable should evaluate to a bean name that is defined in the Spring configuration or to a fully qualified class name.

In the next section, we'll explore richer functionality and the use of the Spring container with the Activiti Engine.

4.4 Using Spring with Activiti

Activiti is able to run on various platforms, including the plain Java approach we've taken until now and on a servlet container or application server like Apache Tomcat. But, it's also easy to run the Activiti Engine within a Spring application context. By using the Spring container to execute the Activiti Engine, you can, for example, use the Spring dependency injection functionality and invoke a Spring bean from a service task in the BPMN process. In the second subsection, you'll see that it's easy to develop unit tests with Spring and Activiti; but, first, you must define the Spring configuration to integrate with the Activiti Engine.

4.4.1 Creating a generic Spring configuration for Activiti

To set up the Spring container to start up the Activiti engine, you need a generic application context configuration. You can use the Spring configuration shown in the following listing every time you want to use a Spring container to start up the Activiti Engine. For convenience reasons, the namespace declarations that are part of the root element beans are left out of the listing, but they can be found in the source code of the book.

Listing 4.13 Generic Spring configuration to start up the Activiti Engine

```
<beans>
  <bean id="dataSource" class="org.springframework.jdbc.          ❶ Defines H2
      datasource.TransactionAwareDataSourceProxy">                   datasource
    <property name="targetDataSource">
      <bean class="org.springframework.jdbc.
            datasource.SimpleDriverDataSource">
        <property name="driverClass" value="org.h2.Driver" />
        <property name="url"
            value="jdbc:h2:mem:activiti;DB_CLOSE_DELAY=1000" />
```

```
            <property name="username" value="sa" />
            <property name="password" value="" />
        </bean>
    </property>
</bean>

<bean id="transactionManager"
    class="org.springframework.jdbc.
        ➥ datasource.DataSourceTransactionManager">
    <property name="dataSource" ref="dataSource" />
</bean>

<bean id="processEngineConfiguration"
    class="org.activiti.spring.
        ➥ SpringProcessEngineConfiguration">
    <property name="databaseType" value="h2" />
    <property name="dataSource" ref="dataSource" />
    <property name="transactionManager"
            ref="transactionManager" />
    <property name="databaseSchemaUpdate" value="true" />
    <property name="deploymentResources"
        value="classpath*:chapter4/bookorder.spring.bpmn20.xml" />
        <property name="jobExecutorActivate" value="false" />
</bean>

<bean id="processEngine"
    class="org.activiti.spring.ProcessEngineFactoryBean">
    <property name="processEngineConfiguration"
            ref="processEngineConfiguration" />
</bean>

<bean id="repositoryService"
    factory-bean="processEngine"
    factory-method="getRepositoryService" />
<bean id="runtimeService"
    factory-bean="processEngine"
    factory-method="getRuntimeService" />
<bean id="taskService"
    factory-bean="processEngine"
    factory-method="getTaskService" />
<bean id="historyService"
    factory-bean="processEngine"
    factory-method="getHistoryService" />
<bean id="managementService"
    factory-bean="processEngine"
    factory-method="getManagementService" />
</beans>
```

❷ Wraps transaction manager

❸ Creates Activiti process engine configuration

❹ Deploys book order process

❺ Creates a RuntimeService instance

In this listing, you can see that many things you developed programmatically in Java in the previous examples are now defined in the Spring configuration file. For example, you have to define a process engine configuration ❸, which will be used to define the configuration options of the Activiti Engine.

In this Spring configuration, you defined an in-memory H2 data source ❶ in a so-called transaction-aware data source definition. Because the data source is wrapped in a transaction manager ❷, you can use the standard Spring JDBC transaction manager.

With the data source and the transaction manager defined, you can instantiate the SpringProcessEngineConfiguration with these components ❸. This means the Activiti Engine configuration is created with an in-memory data source when the Spring container is started. You can also specify a number of processes or task forms that have to be deployed to the Activiti Engine when it has started with the deploymentResources property ❹. You'll see how this makes unit testing even easier in a moment. Note that this property definition is specific to the example you'll implement in this section. The SpringProcessEngineConfiguration is used to instantiate the ProcessEngineFactoryBean that starts the Activiti Engine with the configured resources and settings.

In addition to the instantiation of the Activiti Engine, the Spring container can also create the core interface classes to the Activiti Engine for you. For example, the RuntimeService is created via the getRuntimeService method of the processEngine bean ❺. With this generic Spring configuration defined, you can now proceed to define a unit test that uses this Spring configuration to test a specific process.

4.4.2 *Implementing a Spring-enabled unit test for Activiti*

Because you've already defined all the necessary configuration of the Activiti engine, your unit test can be kept simple. The next listing shows a unit test that starts a new process instance of the book order process definition and completes the user task.

Listing 4.14   A unit test that takes advantage of the Spring configuration

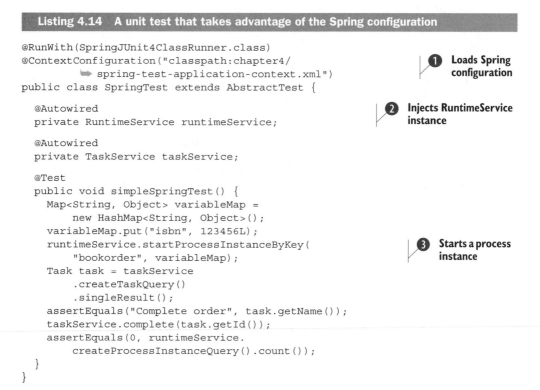

```
@RunWith(SpringJUnit4ClassRunner.class)
@ContextConfiguration("classpath:chapter4/
       ➥ spring-test-application-context.xml")
public class SpringTest extends AbstractTest {

  @Autowired
  private RuntimeService runtimeService;

  @Autowired
  private TaskService taskService;

  @Test
  public void simpleSpringTest() {
    Map<String, Object> variableMap =
        new HashMap<String, Object>();
    variableMap.put("isbn", 123456L);
    runtimeService.startProcessInstanceByKey(
        "bookorder", variableMap);
    Task task = taskService
        .createTaskQuery()
        .singleResult();
    assertEquals("Complete order", task.getName());
    taskService.complete(task.getId());
    assertEquals(0, runtimeService.
        createProcessInstanceQuery().count());
  }
}
```

❶ Loads Spring configuration

❷ Injects RuntimeService instance

❸ Starts a process instance

As you can see, the unit test is simple because you don't have to create the Activiti engine yourself. With the standard Spring annotations `@RunWith` and `@Context-Configuration` ❶, the Spring configuration you defined in listing 4.13 is used as part of this unit test.

With the `@Autowired` annotation, you can let the Spring container inject an instance of the `RuntimeService` in your unit test class ❷. This means you don't have to do any plumbing before you can start a new process instance of the book order process definition ❸. Because the book order process is already deployed as part of the Activiti Engine creation in the Spring configuration, you don't have to deploy the process first, either.

To complete the unit test, you query the Activiti engine for any running user tasks. Because you run this unit test with an in-memory database, you can be sure that no user task is running other than the `Complete Order` user task defined in the book order process. When this task is completed, you can make sure that there's no running process instance anymore by running a process instance query.

To make this unit test work, you have to implement the process definition of the `bookorder.spring.bpmn20.xml` file. This process definition has some small differences when compared to the bookorder.bpmn20.xml file you've used before. In this process definition, a Spring bean is used to implement the validation order activity that was first implemented with a script task. Let's take a quick look at the revised XML definition of the service task:

```
<serviceTask id="serviceTask1"
            name="Validate order"
            activiti:expression="#{order.validate(execution)}"/>
```

Because you run the Activiti Engine within the Spring container, you can directly reference Spring beans from a service task.

NOTE A Spring service task isn't standard BPMN 2.0 functionality, but is implemented as an add-on by the Activiti framework.

The `expression` attribute can be used to define a Spring bean name with the method that must be invoked, which, in this case, is the `order` Spring bean and the `validate` method. As you saw in section 4.3, you can pass on a `DelegateExecution` instance with the reserved keyword `execution`. Because you didn't configure the Spring bean `order` in section 4.3.1, the following code snippet must be added to the generic Spring configuration from listing 4.13:

```
<bean id="order"
    class="org.bpmnwithactiviti.chapter4.spring.OrderService" />
```

The last step is to implement the Spring bean class `OrderService` before you can finally run the unit test. This class is really simple and only prints a message to the system console:

```
public class OrderService {
  public void validate(DelegateExecution execution) {
    System.out.println("validating order for isbn " +
        execution.getVariable("isbn"));
  }
}
```

As you can see, this needs no explaining. Now you can run the unit test provided in listing 4.14 and see that it runs successfully.

A more flexible deployment strategy

In addition to the definition of deployment resources in the Spring configuration used in the previous example, you can also define a deployment per test method. To implement this strategy, an `ActivitiRule` Spring bean must be added to the Spring configuration:

```
<bean id="activitiRule" class="org.activiti.engine.test.ActivitiRule">
  <property name="processEngine" ref="processEngine" />
</bean>
```

The `ActivitiRule` Spring bean must also be injected into the Spring-enabled unit test via the `@Autowire` annotation:

```
@Autowired
@Rule
public ActivitiRule activitiSpringRule;
```

Now you can add a `@Deployment` annotation to every test method where you want to deploy a specific process definition to test the process logic. The advantage of this deployment strategy is that it's finer grained. You can define a specific process definition to be deployed before a test method is executed, and it will be undeployed afterwards. When you define the deployment resources as part of the Spring configuration, they will be available for every test method.

The unit test shown in the next listing can be rewritten to use the more flexible deployment strategy by using the `@Deployment` annotation.

Listing 4.15   Use of the `@Deployment` annotation in an unit test

```
@RunWith(SpringJUnit4ClassRunner.class)                          ❶ Spring configuration
@ContextConfiguration("classpath:chapter4/                          without deployment
        ➥ spring-nodeployment-application-context.xml")            resources
public class SpringWithDeploymentTest extends AbstractTest {

    @Autowired
    private RuntimeService runtimeService;

    @Autowired
    private TaskService taskService;

    @Autowired
    @Rule
    public ActivitiRule activitiSpringRule;                      ❷ ActivitiRule instance
                                                                    for test convenience
```

```
@Test
@Deployment(resources = {                                    ③  Process definition
    "chapter4/bookorder.spring.bpmn20.xml" })                    to be deployed
public void simpleProcessTest() {
  runtimeService.startProcessInstanceByKey("bookorder");
  Task task = taskService.createTaskQuery().singleResult();
  assertEquals("Complete order", task.getName());
  taskService.complete(task.getId());
  assertEquals(0, runtimeService
      .createProcessInstanceQuery()
      .count());
}
}
```

In this unit test, you use a Spring configuration that has no deployment resources defined ❶—unlike the Spring configuration you saw in section 4.4.1. To be able to use the @Deployment annotation, you have to inject the ActivitiRule instance ❷, which provides a hook into the Activiti Engine to deploy and undeploy process definitions. As shown with the simpleProcessTest method ❸, you can now configure a process definition file as part of the @Deployment annotation.

There are plenty of possibilities for using the strength of the Spring framework together with the Activiti process engine, such as using Spring's transaction handling. The information provided in this section should get you started. In chapter 6, you'll see how Spring can be used to retrieve and update entity objects from a database.

4.5   *Summary*

You now know a lot about the different ways you can develop and test with the Activiti Engine. You can query the process engine with all kinds of criteria to retrieve process definitions, instances, and user tasks. Because the Activiti Engine provides a service task that invokes a Java class, we also took a look at how to use this BPMN construct within a BPMN 2.0 process definition. This provides a powerful feature if you need process logic inside your business process. You also saw that you can make a service task asynchronous by adding an async continuation attribute to its definition.

We also covered the Spring integration module, which provides functionality to run the Activiti Engine within a Spring container. Running the Activiti Engine in a Spring container makes it possible to use Spring beans from a service task or expressions inside conditions or variable assignments. Because Spring provides functionality like transaction and security management and easy hooks to implement data access and messaging logic (among other things), the integration of Spring with Activiti provides lots of possibilities.

In the next chapter, we'll move away from the short code examples you've seen so far, and we'll look at a larger business process that you can implement using the Activiti Designer and the Eclipse IDE.

Part 2

Implementing BPMN 2.0 processes with Activiti

Now that we've covered the basic functionality of Activiti and the most common BPMN 2.0 elements, it's time to start implementing process definitions. We start off in chapter 5 with a detailed guide on how to implement a process definition from scratch with workflow and email functionality. In chapter 6, you'll be introduced to more advanced BPMN 2.0 constructs, like the embedded subprocess and the parallel gateway. Next, in chapter 7, we'll cover the importance of a good error handling approach using standard BPMN 2.0 constructs and some custom functionality. In chapter 8, we'll discuss best practices for using the Activiti Engine in your environment and how to use and extend the Activiti REST API. Finally, we'll explore the Activiti OSGi and CDI modules in chapter 9.

Implementing
a BPMN 2.0 process

This chapter covers

- Implementing a full-blown BPMN 2.0 process
- Adding logic to processes using a script and service task
- Using Activiti forms for starting a process and user tasks
- Conditional logic using the exclusive gateway
- Sending emails with the Activiti email service task

In the first chapter, I mentioned how big the BPMN 2.0 specification was. To be honest, if you took a look at all the constructs that are available and the number of pages the specification covers, you'll probably feel hesitant to ever take another look. But if you take a practical approach to BPMN, the specification suddenly becomes a whole lot easier to handle; you don't have to know all the nitty-gritty details of BPMN 2.0 to do business process modeling in your enterprise. In this chapter, we'll examine a practical approach to implementing a BPMN 2.0 business process.

We'll start by looking at a loan request business process that we'll use throughout the chapter. After considering it from a functional point of view, we'll get down to the BPMN 2.0 XML step by step. First, we'll add business logic to the process by implementing a script task and a service task. Then we'll add a start form to the process and cover the workflow functionality with user tasks. In the fourth section, we'll cover the exclusive gateway and the email task with a mail server.

Then, when the process is finished, we'll check out deployment options to get the process running on Activiti Engine. Finally, we'll test the process with Activiti Explorer.

We've got a lot of things to do. Let's start with modeling a loan request business process.

5.1   *Introducing a real business process*

This section will introduce the loan request process that you'll implement in the upcoming sections. Throughout the chapter, tasks are enhanced or implemented in alternative ways for illustration purposes, so you'll get a complete picture of the possibilities with BPMN 2.0 and Activiti. In the end, you'll have the loan request process up and running on the Activiti Engine.

Let's start by exploring the loan request process from a business perspective.

5.1.1   *Analyzing the loan request process*

The company that wants you to build a process with Activiti is the *Loan Sharks* organization, and the first process they'd like to see running is, of course, the loan request process. Loan Sharks wants to handle loan requests efficiently from their newly created website. The process contains automated steps for checking the credit amount in relation to the income of the potential customer. Not all steps in the process will need to be automated, though, because Loan Sharks management believes that each loan request should be evaluated by one of the employees.

The first step is to visualize the loan request business model so Loan Sharks management can approve the approach you want to take with the process implementation. The loan request process is modeled with Activiti Modeler, and the result is shown in figure 5.1.

A loan request process starts when Loan Sharks receive a request for a loan. This request is accompanied by some basic information, like the customer's name, email address, current income, and the amount of money the customer wants to borrow. Before the loan request is passed on to a Loan Sharks employee, a credit check is performed. The credit check ensures that the requested loan amount isn't higher than half of the income of the applicant. The result of the credit check has no direct influence on the process flow but is stored as additional process information.

When the credit check has been executed, an evaluation workflow of the loan request is started. Fozzie, an employee of Loan Sharks (and one of the standard users in the Activiti process engine), receives a task in his task list to perform a loan request evaluation, and he has to hurry! As you can see in the process model of figure 5.1, a

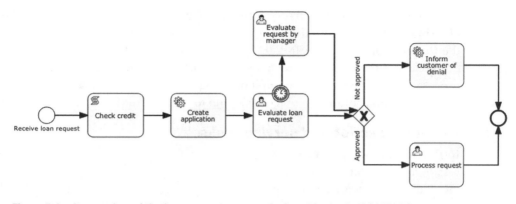

Figure 5.1   An overview of the loan request process designed in the Activiti Modeler

timer symbol is attached to the "Evaluate loan request" task. In BPMN 2.0 this is called a *timer boundary event*. If Fozzie isn't fast enough at completing the "Evaluate loan request" task, the task is escalated to a member of the management group. Considering the default users of the Activiti process engine, this means that Kermit will receive a task in the management group.

Either Fozzie or Kermit will need to evaluate the loan request, and, based on the outcome of that evaluation, the request is either processed or denied. In cases where the request isn't approved, an email is sent to the customer with information about why the loan request was denied. Otherwise, the request is approved, and another employee of Loan Sharks will create a formal loan agreement and finalize the request for the customer.

Now that it's clear what the process should do, let's take it a step further and implement the process activities to get it running on Activiti Engine!

5.1.2   Taking a process model to an XML process file

In the previous chapters, you've seen that there are different ways to develop business processes in Activiti.

Your first option is to create the model in Activiti Modeler and import it into the Activiti Designer Eclipse plugin to implement the technical parts, such as a Java service task. For some processes, it's even possible to skip the Activiti Designer because no additional technical implementation is needed.

A second option is to start in the Activiti Designer and implement the business process with the technical parts right away. From the Designer, you eventually create a Business Archive (BAR) file that can be deployed to the Activiti Engine using Activiti Explorer.

The last option is to use your favorite XML editor to develop the BPMN 2.0 XML. For smaller processes, this is workable; for larger processes, this becomes quite tedious, but it's a good way to become more familiar with the BPMN 2.0 XML. That's why we're going for the direct XML editing approach in this chapter.

When you're more familiar with the BPMN 2.0 constructs, you'll probably be better off using the Modeler and the Designer. Also, when you take an XML editing approach, the Designer provides a BPMN 2.0 XML editor that has XML code completion.

In each of the upcoming sections, we'll work out a part of the overall loan request process. The first part we'll be implementing is the credit check and the construction of the loan application Java object. It's time to start coding!

5.2   *Developing script and service tasks*

In this section, we'll focus on the process logic tasks that need to be implemented for the loan request process. Figure 5.2 shows the first activities of the loan request process.

Figure 5.2   Fragment of the loan request process from the Activiti Modeler containing a script and Java service task and a start event to kick off the process

First, we'll take a look at the script task. Then you'll implement the Java service task. (We'll cover the Java service tasks in less detail because the previous chapter already provided the necessary information about Java service tasks.) At the end of this section, we'll take a look at the BPMN 2.0 XML you've created so far and test the first part of the process with a unit test.

5.2.1   *Scripting in the Activiti Engine*

The first task you encounter when you look at the loan request process is the credit check activity. You'll use a script task to implement the credit check, but you could also have used a Java service task or a business rule task.

UNDERSTANDING SCRIPT TASKS IN BPMN 2.0

The script task is an official BPMN 2.0 construct. In figure 5.2, you can see the symbol that BPMN 2.0 prescribes for the script task—it has the same rectangular shape as a regular service task. The process engine will execute the script logic that's defined in the script task. An analyst will define the task in the model, and a developer has to implement the script with a language the engine can interpret. When the script is executed, the script task completes and the engine moves on toward the next activity.

The configurable options of the script task BPMN 2.0 construct are the `scriptFormat` attribute and the `script` child element. The `scriptFormat` attribute defines the format of the script (JavaScript, Groovy, and so on) and is mandatory. The optional `script` child element contains the actual script that needs to be executed. If no script is defined, the task will complete without doing anything.

WORKING WITH SCRIPT TASKS IN ACTIVITI

For the Activiti Engine to execute the script task, the `scriptFormat` attribute must have a value that's compatible with JSR-223 ("Scripting for the Java Platform"). The supported languages include Groovy, Clojure, JRuby, Jython, and JavaScript. For more information, you can check out the JSR-223 specification at http://jcp.org/en/jsr/detail?id=223.

Because the Groovy jar is shipped by default with the Activiti distribution, we'll use Groovy as the script language in the "Check credit" task. If you want to use another JSR-223 compatible scripting language, it's sufficient to add the corresponding jar file to the classpath and use the appropriate name in the script task configuration. If you use Java 6, you get the JavaScript scripting engine for free because it's part of the Java 6 implementation.

All the process variables are accessible in the script because the script has access to the execution that arrives in the task. You can, for example, use the process variable inputArray, an array of integers, as shown in the following code snippet:

```
<script>
    sum = 0;
    for ( i in inputArray ) {
      sum += i
    }
</script>
```

There's no boilerplate code necessary to get hold of process variables. Besides reading variables, it's also possible to set process variables in a script by using an assignment statement. In the previous example, the sum variable will be stored as a process variable after the script has been executed. If you want to avoid this default behavior, you can use script-local variables. In Groovy, you must use the keyword def: def sum = 0. In that case, the sum variable isn't stored as a process variable.

An alternative way to set process variables is by explicitly using the execution variable that's available in the script task the same way you saw it used in the previous chapter in the Java service task:

```
<script>
    def bookVar = "BPMN 2.0 with Activiti"
    execution.setVariable("bookName", bookVar);
</script>
```

Now let's return to the process and the "Check credit" script task.

IMPLEMENTING THE CREDIT CHECK SCRIPT TASK

Loan Sharks agrees to let a customer pass the credit check when their income divided by two is bigger than the requested loan amount. The following listing shows the BPMN 2.0 XML fragment that defines the script task.

Listing 5.1 The BPMN 2.0 XML fragment defining the credit check script task

```
<scriptTask id="checkCredit" scriptFormat="groovy">
  <script>
    out:println "Checking credit for " + name;
    creditCheckOk = false;
    if((income / 2) > loanAmount) {
      creditCheckOk = true;
    }
    out:println "Checked credit for " + name
        + " outcome is " + creditCheckOk;
  </script>
</scriptTask>
```

In the script, you use the `name` variable to print a logging statement on the console so you can follow the process flow. Then you create a new process variable, `creditCheckOk`, that will contain the credit check outcome. As long as your loan requestor has an income that's more than twice the requested loan amount, the credit check will pass.

You now have your first script task in the process under control; let's move on to the Java service tasks.

5.2.2 Implementing a Java service task

In this section, we'll implement the "Create application" task. The "Create application" task gathers all the information produced so far into a `LoanApplication` Java bean, and puts it in the process context as a process variable. This makes all the information regarding the loan request available in one Java object that can be used in the remaining activities of the process.

> **TIP** If you need more background about the ins and outs of the Java service task, go back to chapter 4, section 4.3. There you can find all the details of the Java service task.

IMPLEMENTING THE CREATE APPLICATION JAVA SERVICE TASK

The `CreateApplicationTask` service task gathers all the data that was produced in the previous steps into one container object and sets it as a process variable. In the later tasks, you'll see how you can access this object from the forms in the user tasks and in the email task to retrieve customer information.

The next listing displays the service task implementation.

Listing 5.2   The `CreateApplicationTask` service task implementation

```
public class CreateApplicationTask implements JavaDelegate {

  public void execute(DelegateExecution execution) {
    LoanApplication la = new LoanApplication();
    la.setCreditCheckOk((Boolean) execution
      .getVariable("creditCheckOk"));
    la.setCustomerName((String)
      execution.getVariable("name"));
    la.setIncome((Long) execution.getVariable("income"));
    la.setRequestedAmount((Long)
      execution.getVariable("loanAmount"));
    la.setEmailAddres((String)
      execution.getVariable("emailAddress"));
    execution.setVariable("loanApplication", la);
  }
}
```

Retrieves process variable ❶ to populate bean

In the `execute` method of the `ApplicationCreator` Java service task class, you create the `LoanApplication` instance. Remember that this object has to implement the `Serializable` interface; otherwise, the Activiti Engine won't be able to store it as a process variable in the process database. The values that are used to populate the object are retrieved from the start form you'll build in section 5.3.2 and from the credit check script task ❶. At the end, don't forget to store the variable in the execution.

Now that you have your business logic together, we'll take a look at the first part of the loan request BPMN 2.0 XML and then we'll build a unit test.

5.2.3 Creating the BPMN 2.0 XML file

To be able to test the first part of the loan request process, we'll implement a BPMN 2.0 XML file with the three activities we've covered so far. Listing 5.3 shows what the loan request process looks like so far.

Listing 5.3 BPMN 2.0 XML for the first part of the loan request process

```
<process id="loanrequest"
        name="Process to handle a loan request">
  <startEvent id="theStart" />
  <sequenceFlow sourceRef="theStart"
      targetRef="checkCredit" />
  <scriptTask id="checkCredit" scriptFormat="groovy">
    <script>
      out:println "Checking credit for " + name;
      creditCheckOk = false;
      if((income / 2) > loanAmount) {
        creditCheckOk = true;
      }
      out:println "Checked credit for " + name
          + " outcome is " + creditCheckOK;
    </script>
  </scriptTask>
  <sequenceFlow sourceRef="checkCredit"
      targetRef="createApplication" />
  <serviceTask id="createApplication"
      activiti:class="org.bpmnwithactiviti.
          ➥ chapter5.CreateApplicationTask"/>
  <sequenceFlow sourceRef="createApplication"
      targetRef="theEnd" />
  <endEvent id="theEnd" />
</process>
```

❶ Credit check script task

❷ Creates loan application service task

After the process is started, the process execution is forwarded to the `checkCredit` script task ❶. Then the process continues to the `createApplication` Java service task ❷. (We already looked at the implementation details of these tasks in the previous sections.)

> **NOTE** Listing 5.3 doesn't use the `definitions` element. It was left out to be brief, but remember that it's needed when you want to execute the BPMN 2.0 XML. You can find the full code example in the book's source code.

All the constructs used in the process can be easily tested in a JUnit test. It's good practice to test as early as possible; you want to get rid of possible bugs in the BPMN process before you deploy the process to a QA environment. Let's give the process a spin!

5.2.4   *Testing the process with JUnit*

In the previous chapter, we looked at unit testing with Activiti. We're now going to put what you learned there into practice. We'll use the ActivitiRule class to get the RuntimeService and use the @Deployment annotation to deploy the process. Take a look at the following listing to see how it's done.

Listing 5.4   Testing the first part of the loan request process

```
public class LoanRequestTest {

  @Rule
  public ActivitiRule activitiRule =
      new ActivitiRule("activiti.cfg-mem-fullhistory.xml");

  @Test
  @Deployment(resources={"chapter5/
      ➥ loanrequest_firstpart.bpmn20.xml"})
  public void creditCheckTrue() {
    Map<String, Object> processVariables =
        new HashMap<String, Object>();
    processVariables.put("name", "Miss Piggy");
    processVariables.put("income", 100l);
    processVariables.put("loanAmount", 10l);
    processVariables.put("emailAddress",
        "miss.piggy@localhost");
    activitiRule.getRuntimeService()
        .startProcessInstanceByKey(
            "loanrequest", processVariables);

    List<HistoricDetail> historyVariables =
        activitiRule.getHistoryService()
            .createHistoricDetailQuery()
            .variableUpdates()
            .orderByVariableName()
            .asc()
            .list();

    assertNotNull(historyVariables);
    assertEquals(7, historyVariables.size());
    HistoricVariableUpdate loanAppUpdate =
        ((HistoricVariableUpdate) historyVariables.get(5));
    assertEquals("loanApplication",
        loanAppUpdate.getVariableName());
    LoanApplication la = (LoanApplication)
        loanAppUpdate.getValue();
    assertEquals(true, la.isCreditCheckOk());
  }
}
```

1 Starts process with variables map

2 Retrieves process variable updates

3 Gets LoanApplication variable updates

Because you haven't implemented a start form for the process yet, you need to pass the necessary process variables when you start a new process instance **1**. When the startProcessInstanceByKey method has been executed, the process is already finished because there are no wait states in the loan request process. Because you want to test whether the "Credit check" and the "Create loan application" tasks have been executed as expected, you need a way to retrieve the process variables.

In chapter 4, you learned that you can use the `HistoryService` to get all process variable updates for a finished process instance. To store all process variable updates, you have to configure the Activiti Engine with a `history` parameter value of `full`. You do this in the `activiti.cfg-mem-fullhistory.xml` configuration file, as follows:

```
<bean id="processEngineConfiguration"
    class="org.activiti.engine.impl.cfg.
        ➥ StandaloneInMemProcessEngineConfiguration">
  <property name="databaseSchemaUpdate" value="true"/>
  <property name="history" value="full" />
  <property name="jobExecutorActivate" value="false" />
</bean>
```

In the unit test, you query the Activiti Engine database for all process variable updates sorted by variable name ❷. This means that the `loanApplication` variable set by the `CreateApplicationTask` service task should be at the sixth place of the result list ❸. If the `creditCheckOk` attribute of the `LoanApplication` object equals `true`, this means that the script and the service task are executed as expected.

Now you can give the unit test a spin to see if it's working as expected. You've seen how to implement business logic with scripts and Java service tasks and how to test it with a simple unit test. Let's add some workflow logic and a start form to the process to get it ready to run with the Activiti Explorer.

5.3 Interacting with user tasks and Activiti forms

To implement a human workflow in a process, you need a way to interact with it. The BPMN 2.0 specification doesn't define how to implement this user interaction besides the user task. But Activiti provides task forms to create a GUI application to work with user tasks.

In this section, you'll learn all about these Activiti task forms and how to apply them in the loan request process. First, we'll take a look at forms in Activiti in general, and then we'll create a start form so you can submit a loan request that starts the process. After the form is made, we'll explore how to test the capabilities of forms using the `FormService`. Finally, you'll see some workflows in action with escalation and the timer boundary event.

First things first, though: how do you create forms with Activiti?

5.3.1 Creating forms in Activiti

Activiti supports two ways of rendering forms. You can use the Activiti Explorer's form rendering by defining form properties on a start event or a user task. Or, if you want to render the forms yourself, you can use your own template technology and define the template with the `activiti:formKey` attribute, which can be specified on a start event or a user task. This is an example of using the `formKey` attribute on a start event:

```
<startEvent id="theStart" activiti:formKey="your.form" />
```

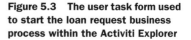

Process to handle a loan request

Version 1 · Deployed one day ago

Name	
Email address	
Income	
Loan amount	

Start process   Cancel

Figure 5.3   The user task form used to start the loan request business process within the Activiti Explorer

In this chapter, we'll be using the form rendering of the Activiti Explorer. The external form rendering will be discussed further in chapter 10.

Figure 5.3 gives you an idea how a form will be rendered with Activiti Explorer. It shows the start form for the loan request that we'll define in this section.

To use the built-in rendering, the form properties have to be defined with the start event or a user task. Let's start with the initial start event form for the loan request process.

5.3.2   Adding a task form on a start event

To start an instance of the loan request process, we'll use a form on the start event. Employees of Loan Sharks can use this form to fill out data about a customer who wants to borrow money. The following listing shows the form properties of the start event that will be rendered in the Activiti Explorer (as illustrated in figure 5.3).

Listing 5.5   The loan request start form using only simple HTML elements

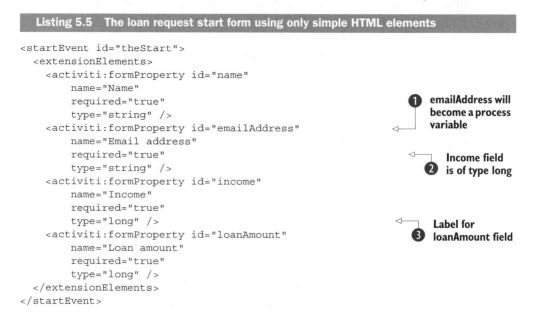

```
<startEvent id="theStart">
  <extensionElements>
    <activiti:formProperty id="name"
        name="Name"
        required="true"
        type="string" />
    <activiti:formProperty id="emailAddress"
        name="Email address"
        required="true"
        type="string" />
    <activiti:formProperty id="income"
        name="Income"
        required="true"
        type="long" />
    <activiti:formProperty id="loanAmount"
        name="Loan amount"
        required="true"
        type="long" />
  </extensionElements>
</startEvent>
```

❶ emailAddress will become a process variable

❷ Income field is of type long

❸ Label for loanAmount field

After the form is submitted, the fields in the form will be stored in the process context as process variables. The emailAddress field will be accessible in the process context with the process variable emailAddress **❶**. You can define in the form whether a certain value is required and what type it is **❷**. The default type is string; other supported types are long, Boolean, enum, and date. When you choose a date type field, the Activiti Explorer will render a date picker object. The name attribute value **❸** is used by the Activiti Explorer to create a label for the form property.

We can now test the form property definition functionality using the FormService.

5.3.3 Testing forms using the FormService

In chapter 4, we took a look at the main Activiti interfaces. One of them was the FormService. You'll use this interface now to test your newly created form from listing 5.5. The FormService gives access to the form properties of a user task or start event and can be used to submit the form fields to complete a specific user task.

Let's write a unit test that shows the FormService API for the form defined in listing 5.5.

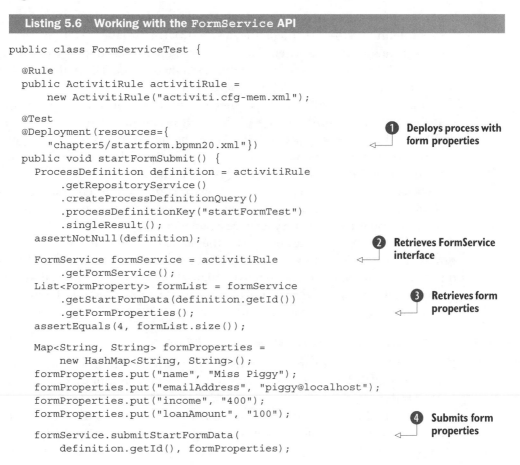

Listing 5.6 Working with the FormService API

```java
public class FormServiceTest {

  @Rule
  public ActivitiRule activitiRule =
      new ActivitiRule("activiti.cfg-mem.xml");

  @Test
  @Deployment(resources={
      "chapter5/startform.bpmn20.xml"})          ❶ Deploys process with
  public void startFormSubmit() {                    form properties
    ProcessDefinition definition = activitiRule
        .getRepositoryService()
        .createProcessDefinitionQuery()
        .processDefinitionKey("startFormTest")
        .singleResult();
    assertNotNull(definition);

    FormService formService = activitiRule          ❷ Retrieves FormService
        .getFormService();                             interface
    List<FormProperty> formList = formService
        .getStartFormData(definition.getId())       ❸ Retrieves form
        .getFormProperties();                          properties
    assertEquals(4, formList.size());

    Map<String, String> formProperties =
        new HashMap<String, String>();
    formProperties.put("name", "Miss Piggy");
    formProperties.put("emailAddress", "piggy@localhost");
    formProperties.put("income", "400");
    formProperties.put("loanAmount", "100");
                                                    ❹ Submits form
    formService.submitStartFormData(                   properties
        definition.getId(), formProperties);
```

```
List<HistoricDetail> historyVariables = activitiRule
    .getHistoryService()
    .createHistoricDetailQuery()
    .formProperties()
    .list();

assertNotNull(historyVariables);
assertEquals(4, historyVariables.size());

HistoricFormProperty formProperty = (HistoricFormProperty)
    historyVariables.get(0);
assertEquals("loanAmount", formProperty.getPropertyId());
assertEquals("100",
    formProperty.getPropertyValue());

formProperty = (HistoricFormProperty)
    historyVariables.get(1);
assertEquals("income", formProperty.getPropertyId());
assertEquals("400",
    formProperty.getPropertyValue());
  }
}
```

⑤ View history query for form properties

The form properties are configured on the start event of the startform.bpmn20.xml process definition ❶. Through the ActivitiRule instance, you can retrieve the FormService interface ❷. Then you can retrieve the form properties for the deployed process definition using the getStartFormData method ❸. The Activiti Explorer uses this method to render the task form component.

To fill in the form properties, you need to store the form values in a map. Notice that this map holds all the values of the form properties as strings, not as the type defined in the start event (see listing 5.5). At the start of the process, these properties are converted into process variables of the correct type. Then the FormService can be used to submit the form with the form properties map ❹.

When the submitStartFormData method execution is finished, your simple process is completed as well. This is because there are no wait states in the process definition. Therefore, you use the HistoryService again ❺ to validate whether the form properties income and loanAmount are equal to the values you submitted. Form properties are stored in the Activiti history database tables by default (the history level of audit). You don't need additional process engine configuration like you did in section 5.2.4.

Now that you have a form to start the process, let's move on to the user tasks that are needed to perform the loan request evaluation. They need forms too!

5.3.4   *Adding user tasks with an escalation workflow*

Now you have the first part of your loan request process in place; next, you need to add the workflow logic. Figure 5.4 shows the user task activities that we'll implement in this section.

In the "Evaluate loan request" task that's assigned to Fozzie, a form will be presented containing the information that's kept in the LoanApplication process variable you created in listing 5.2. This way, Fozzie will be able to see the result of the

"Check credit" script task and can look into the process variables that are passed on as form properties at the start of the process instance.

The timer symbol attached to the "Evaluate loan request" task is called a timer boundary event. A timer boundary event acts as a stopwatch or alarm clock. The timer starts when the execution arrives in the activity with the timer boundary event. When the timer fires after a specified interval, the activity is interrupted and the sequence flow going out of the timer boundary event is followed. When the user task is assigned to Fozzie, the clock starts ticking and, in this example, Fozzie will have no more than one minute to complete the task (you'll see this soon, in the BPMN 2.0 XML of listing 5.8).

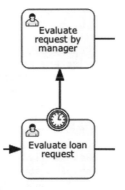

Figure 5.4 The part of the loan request process that implements the workflow and escalation logic with user tasks and a timer boundary event

If Fozzie doesn't complete his work on time, the task will be escalated. The "Evaluate loan request" task is cancelled and deleted, and the "Evaluate request by manager" user task is created and added to the candidate management group. When a manager claims the user task, the same task form will be shown as the "Evaluate loan request" task.

Now let's start implementing the new task form and create the escalation workflow logic, including the timer boundary event.

DEFINING AN APPROVAL TASK FORM

You already saw that it's easy to use process variables in the credit check script task implemented earlier on. When defining task forms, you can use a similar syntax to include process variable values. Activiti uses the JUEL expression language (http://juel.sourceforge.net) for this.

The next listing shows how you can use the `LoanAplication` process variable in your approval task form definition.

Listing 5.7 The user task form used to evaluate the loan request

```
<userTask id="evaluateLoanRequest"
    name="Evaluate loan request"
    activiti:assignee="fozzie">
  <extensionElements>
    <activiti:formProperty id="customerName"
        name="Customer name"
        expression="${loanApplication.customerName}"
        writable="false"/>
    <activiti:formProperty id="income"
        name="Income of customer"
        expression="${loanApplication.income}"
        writable="false"/>
    <activiti:formProperty id="requestedAmount"
        name="Requested loan amount"
```

❶ Displays customerName process variable

❷ Sets field as read-only

```
                expression="${loanApplication.requestedAmount}"
                writable="false"/>
            <activiti:formProperty id="creditCheckOk"
                name="Outcome of credit check"
                expression="${loanApplication.creditCheckOk}"
                writable="false"/>
            <activiti:formProperty id="requestApproved"
                name="Do you approve the request?"
                required="true"
                type="enum">
              <activiti:value id="true" name="Yes"/>
              <activiti:value id="false" name="No"/>
            </activiti:formProperty>
            <activiti:formProperty id="explanation"
                name="Explanation"/>
          </extensionElements>
        </userTask>
```

③ Defines new requestApproved process variable

In the ${loanApplication.customerName} expression ❶, the loanApplication process variable is used. At runtime, the variables in the expressions are resolved to their values in the process instance. A form property can be defined as read-only by configuring the writable attribute with value false ❷.

Based on the read-only information, Fozzie or a manager will have to make a decision concerning the loan request ❸ and, in case of denial, an explanation should be given. You'll use this explanation in the email task implemented later on.

DEFINING AN ESCALATION WORKFLOW WITH A TIMER BOUNDARY EVENT

The "Evaluate loan request" user task must have a timer boundary event to cancel the task after one minute. The next listing shows a fragment of the loan request process in which the user tasks and the timer boundary event are declared. Note that the form properties definition is left out because it was already defined in listing 5.7.

Listing 5.8 The loan request user tasks and timer boundary event definition

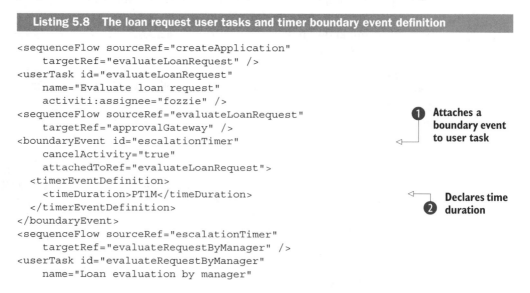

```
<sequenceFlow sourceRef="createApplication"
    targetRef="evaluateLoanRequest" />
<userTask id="evaluateLoanRequest"
    name="Evaluate loan request"
    activiti:assignee="fozzie" />
<sequenceFlow sourceRef="evaluateLoanRequest"
    targetRef="approvalGateway" />
<boundaryEvent id="escalationTimer"
    cancelActivity="true"
    attachedToRef="evaluateLoanRequest">
  <timerEventDefinition>
    <timeDuration>PT1M</timeDuration>
  </timerEventDefinition>
</boundaryEvent>
<sequenceFlow sourceRef="escalationTimer"
    targetRef="evaluateRequestByManager" />
<userTask id="evaluateRequestByManager"
    name="Loan evaluation by manager"
```

❶ Attaches a boundary event to user task

❷ Declares time duration

```
        activiti:candidateGroups="management" />
    <sequenceFlow sourceRef="evaluateRequestByManager"
        targetRef="approvalGateway" />
```

Adds task to management group ❸

The boundary event is a standard BPMN 2.0 construct ❶ that has a time duration definition attached to the event. The value is set to PT1M ❷, and this notation conforms to the ISO 8601 standard as required by the BPMN 2.0 specification. PT1M stands for Period Time 1 Minute. You can find more about the notation on the ISO 8601 page of Wikipedia: http://en.wikipedia.org/wiki/ISO_8601#Durations.

When the timer goes off, the evaluateLoanRequest user task is canceled and the job of evaluating the loan is escalated to the user task evaluateRequestByManager. This user task is made available to the users of the management group, to be claimed ❸.

After these two user tasks, the customer will either have approval for the loan request or not. Let's take a look at what we do with this decision and meet the exclusive gateway.

5.4 Handling decisions and sending email

In this section, we'll examine two new constructs in the loan request process. First, we'll take a look at the exclusive gateway BPMN 2.0 construct that helps to control execution flow in the loan request handling. We'll then explore how Activiti extends BPMN 2.0 functionality by implementing an Activiti-specific construct, the email task. Figure 5.5 shows the remaining part of the loan request process.

Either Fozzie or Kermit (as sole member of the management group) has evaluated the loan request in the last steps we covered. This evaluation will trigger some actions. If the loan request is approved, the request is processed

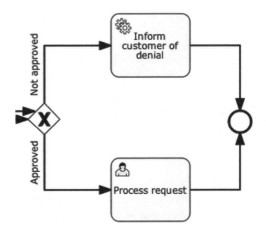

Figure 5.5 An exclusive gateway is used to implement conditional logic after the evaluation of the loan request. Based on the evaluation outcome, an execution path is chosen.

and the customer will receive the requested amount of money. If the employees of the Loan Sharks decide not to approve the loan request, an email will be sent to inform the customer that the request has been denied and explain why. First, we'll take a look at how to deal with the outcome of the evaluation, and then you'll start sending an email message.

5.4.1 Controlling flow with an exclusive gateway

Gateways are the BPMN 2.0 way of controlling the flow of execution. A gateway is graphically visualized as a diamond shape, with an icon inside. In the parallel gateway, this icon is a + symbol. When you need conditional logic, you can use an exclusive gateway, also called the *XOR gateway*. The BPMN 2.0 icon for this type of gateway is an X, as you can see in figure 5.5.

When the process execution arrives at an exclusive gateway, the condition expressions on the outgoing sequence flows are evaluated. The sequence flow corresponding to the first condition expression that evaluates to true will be executed. When more than one condition expression evaluates to true, only the first sequence flow will be executed, and the other condition expressions aren't even evaluated. If no condition expression evaluates to true, the Activiti Engine will throw an exception. To prevent this, you can define a default flow on the exclusive gateway in case no condition expression evaluates to true.

In the following code snippet, you can see how the exclusive gateway used in the loan request process is implemented in BPMN 2.0 XML:

```
<exclusiveGateway id="approvalGateway" />
<sequenceFlow sourceRef="approvalGateway"
    targetRef="informCustomer">
  <conditionExpression xsi:type="tFormalExpression">
    ${requestApproved == false}
  </conditionExpression>
</sequenceFlow>
<sequenceFlow sourceRef="approvalGateway"
    targetRef="processRequest">
  <conditionExpression xsi:type="tFormalExpression">
    ${requestApproved == true}
  </conditionExpression>
</sequenceFlow>
```

The `conditionExpression` element that's nested in a `sequenceFlow` uses the same type of expression you saw earlier in the forms. In these two condition expressions, you use the `requestApproved` process variable that's set by one of the two loan request evaluation user tasks executed in the previous step of the process.

Because the loan request evaluation leads either to approval or denial, there are only two sequence flows leaving the exclusive gateway. This isn't a restriction; you're allowed to define as many sequence flow paths as you want.

5.4.2   *Implementing an email service task*

When the employees of the Loan Sharks decide not to approve a loan request, the customer receives an email. The email service task is the last step in the loan request process in the case of denial.

> **NOTE** The email task isn't part of the BPMN 2.0 specification, so it doesn't have a dedicated icon and is shown as a regular service task. Activiti provides a default email service task that can be used to send emails to one or more recipients, including support for CC, BCC, and HTML content. It's a bonus!

Before you can execute the email task in the loan request process, you need to set up a mail server. We'll use the Apache James project for that and we'll look at how to get the mail server up and running. Then we'll implement a small process example to test the email task and send Miss Piggy a message. This way you can see how the email task works and make sure that the James environment is configured correctly.

GETTING UP AND RUNNING WITH APACHE JAMES MAIL SERVER

Download Apache James from http://james.apache.org and unzip the file in a directory of your choice. Because not all operating systems allow the use of ports like 25 for SMTP and 110 for POP, we'll configure James to use ports 1025 for SMTP and 1110 for POP for these examples.

You can configure this by editing the config.xml file in the apps/james/SAR-INF directory of your Apache James installation. Notice that the config.xml file is created only after James is started for the first time. You can start the server by executing the run.sh or run.bat file in the james_install_dir/bin directory. Search in the config.xml file for the following items and configure the ports as specified in the following configuration snippet:

```
<pop3server enabled="true">
    <port>1110</port>
</pop3server>

<smtpserver enabled="true">
  <port>1025</port>
</smtpserver>

<nntpserver enabled="true">
  <port>1119</port>
</nntpserver>
```

Now you can restart the server.

Once the server is up, you'll need to add a user account so you have somebody to send email to from the process. Start a telnet session with localhost on port 4555; you can log in with the preconfigured root user, password root. Then add a user with the following command:

```
adduser miss.piggy piggy
```

A user called miss.piggy is added with the email address miss.piggy@localhost and the password piggy. To check if Miss Piggy's account is added, you can execute the listusers command to verify it. The screenshot in figure 5.6 gives a view of the telnet session to summarize things.

That's all there is to it. The James mail server is configured correctly and is waiting to receive mail on port 1025. Back to Activiti!

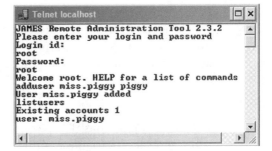

Figure 5.6 Screenshot of a telnet session that adds the Miss Piggy user to the Apache James mail server

IMPLEMENTING THE EMAIL TASK IN BPMN 2.0 XML

Now that your mail server is up, you're ready to define an email task in a BPMN 2.0 XML process definition. Take a look at the BPMN 2.0 XML in the next listing.

Listing 5.9   Simple email task process to test the James configuration

```
<process id="simpleEmailProcess" >
  <startEvent id="theStart" />
  <sequenceFlow sourceRef="theStart" targetRef="sendMail" />       ❶ Defines mail
  <serviceTask id="sendMail" activiti:type="mail">                    service task
    <extensionElements>
      <activiti:field name="to"
        stringValue="miss.piggy@localhost"/>
                                                                   ❷ Declares recipient
      <activiti:field name="subject"                                 and subject
        expression="Hello ${name}"/>

      <activiti:field name="html">
        <activiti:expression>
          <![CDATA[
            <html>
            <body>                                                 ❸ Uses name
              Hello ${name},<br/><br/>                               process variable
              Your loan request has been denied.<br/><br/>
              Kind regards,<br/>
              Loan Sharks
            </body>
            </html>
            ]]>
        </activiti:expression>
      </activiti:field>
    </extensionElements>
  </serviceTask>
  <sequenceFlow sourceRef="sendMail" targetRef="theEnd" />
  <endEvent id="theEnd" />
</process>
```

The mail service task is defined by adding an Activiti-specific attribute to a regular service task ❶. The email address is defined in the to field and the subject with the subject attribute ❷.

The email address that you send in listing 5.9 is hardcoded in the BPMN 2.0 XML, but in the loan request process you want this property to be flexible because it depends on who is filing for a loan. To solve that problem, you can use the expression attribute to define the address:

```
<activiti:field name="to" expression="${loanApplication.emailAddress}" />
```

The email you use has HTML content. You can see that in the email task you also have access to process variables; in this case, you use the name process variable ❸.

You can now run the process within Eclipse but you need a mail server to can test the email service task. The following listing shows an elegant way to write a unit test for this. Notice that you must first stop the James server.

Listing 5.10 Testing a process definition with an email service task

```java
public class MailTaskTest {
  @Rule
  public ActivitiRule activitiRule =
      new ActivitiRule("activiti.cfg-mem-mail.xml");

  @Test
  @Deployment(resources={"chapter5/testSimpleMail.bpmn20.xml"})
  public void sendMailLocalTest() throws Exception {
    Wiser wiser = new Wiser();
    wiser.setPort(1025);
    wiser.start();
    Map<String,Object> processVariables =
        new HashMap<String,Object>();
    processVariables.put("name", "Miss Piggy");
    activitiRule.getRuntimeService()
        .startProcessInstanceByKey("simpleEmailProcess",
            processVariables);
    List<WiserMessage> messages = wiser.getMessages();
    assertEquals(1, messages.size());
    WiserMessage message = messages.get(0);
    MimeMessage mimeMessage = message.getMimeMessage();
    assertEquals("Hello Miss Piggy",
        mimeMessage.getHeader("Subject", null));
    wiser.stop();
  }
}
```

1 Starts engine with mail client

2 Checks that one email was received

Make sure that the mail server port in the activiti.cfg-mem-mail.xml file ❶ is configured for port 1025. By default, Activiti expects the mail server to run on SMTP port 25; you have to override the port by defining the following mail server:

```xml
<mail server="localhost" port="1025" />
```

The Activiti project uses a mail server that's great for unit testing and is called Sub-Etha SMTP (http://code.google.com/p/subethasmtp/). This mail server project provides a class named `Wiser`, which can be used to start a mail server with a few lines of code. And when you want to check if an email has been sent to the mail server, you can use the `getMessages` method ❷. In this unit test, you validate whether the subject of the email is the one you defined in the process definition of listing 5.9.

In addition to writing a unit test using the SubEtha mail server project, you can also use Apache James as you will do in the loan request business process. You can use a unit test similar to the one in listing 5.10 but remove the `Wiser` mail test class and start a new process instance. Also, make sure you've started Apache James. To view the email, you can install an email client such as Mozilla Thunderbird. Remember that Apache James is using port 1110 for SMTP. In Thunderbird, the email should look similar to the one shown in figure 5.7.

In the previous sections, you implemented a number of activities of the loan request process definition. Because it would be a waste of paper to show the full BPMN 2.0 XML definition, now is a good time to look at the loanrequest.bpmn20.xml file in the source

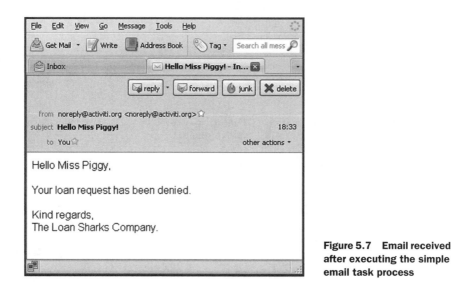

Figure 5.7   Email received after executing the simple email task process

code of this book (bpmn-examples/src/main/resources/chapter5). Notice that we skipped one activity in the process, which is the "Process request" user task that's executed when the loan request is approved. You already implemented two user tasks earlier on, and this activity contains no new configuration items.

> **NOTE**   When you want to use the email task in a process definition deployed on the Activiti Explorer, you need to set the mail server and SMTP port correctly in the applicationContext.xml file because, by default, the emails are sent to port 25 on localhost. You can find the Spring configuration file that the Activiti Explorer uses in the Tomcat webapps/activiti-explorer/WEB-INF directory. In the `processEngineConfiguration` bean, add the element `<property name="mailServerPort" value="1025"/>`.

In the next section, we're going to package the loan request process definition in a BAR file and deploy it to Activiti Explorer to see it running!

5.5   Deploying processes to the Activiti Engine

Before you can test the loan request process with the Activiti Explorer, you need to deploy it. We'll look into three options for deploying a process archive: using Java, Ant, or Activiti Explorer. At the end of this section, we'll take a quick look at using Activiti Explorer to check the outcome of a deployment.

5.5.1   Understanding the Activiti BAR file

The unit of deployment on Activiti Engine is a business archive (BAR) file. A business archive is equivalent to a standard Java JAR file and, therefore, a zip file. It can contain BPMN 2.0 processes, custom task templates, rules, and any other type of file. A business archive is a collection of resources.

When a business archive file is deployed, it's scanned for files with a bpmn20.xml extension. Each file that has this extension will be parsed and can contain multiple process definitions.

NOTE The Java classes that are added in the BAR file aren't added to the classpath. All the classes the process needs at runtime, such as the Java service tasks or implementations of event listeners, should be present on the Activiti Engine classpath for the processes in the business archive to run. In the loan request example, running on the Activiti Explorer on the default Tomcat instance, you need to put a JAR file containing the Java service task in the webapps/activiti-explorer/WEB-INF/lib directory.

We've created an Ant build.xml file in the src/main/resources/chapter5 directory of the book's source code to generate a BAR file containing the process definition. When you run this Ant target, a BAR file is created in the src/main/resources/chapter5/dist directory that contains the loan request process definition. In the same directory, a JAR file containing the Java service task class is created.

To run the example, you have to copy the newly created loanrequest.jar file to the webapps/activiti-explorer/WEB-INF/lib directory of the Tomcat distribution in Activiti (inside the apps folder).

Now that you have the Java classes on the Tomcat classpath and you've created a BAR file with the loan request process definition, you can deploy the loan request example to the Activiti Engine. Let's take a look at two options for doing so.

5.5.2 *Deploying processes to the Activiti Engine*

To deploy business archives on the Activiti Engine, you have three options. Deployments can be done via Java using the RepositoryService, using an Ant target, or—the easiest option—using Activiti Explorer. Let's take a look at the Java and Activiti Explorer options.

We'll skip the Ant target option, but you can find an example in the Ant build file we used earlier to create the BAR and JAR files. Make sure the H2 database and the Tomcat server are running. You can do this by running the ant demo.start command from the setup directory of the Activiti distribution, as explained in chapter 1.

DEPLOYING PROCESSES PROGRAMMATICALLY

The first option we'll explore is deploying the loan request process using the Activiti API. Take a look at the next listing; it shows how you can use a standalone J2SE application to deploy the archive.

Listing 5.11   Deploying a BAR file programmatically with the Activiti API

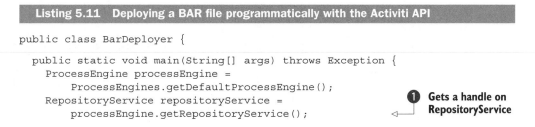

```
public class BarDeployer {

  public static void main(String[] args) throws Exception {
    ProcessEngine processEngine =
        ProcessEngines.getDefaultProcessEngine();
    RepositoryService repositoryService =              ① Gets a handle on
        processEngine.getRepositoryService();              RepositoryService
```

```
    String barFileName =
        "src/main/resources/chapter5/dist/loanrequest.bar";
    ZipInputStream inputStream = new ZipInputStream(new
        FileInputStream(barFileName));
    String deploymentID = repositoryService.createDeployment()
        .name(barFileName)
        .addZipInputStream(inputStream)
        .deploy()
        .getId();
    List<String> deployedResources = repositoryService
        .getDeploymentResourceNames(deploymentID);
    for(String deployedResource : deployedResources){
        System.out.println("Deployed : " + deployedResource);
    }
    inputStream.close();
  }
}
```

2 Reads in bar file

3 Deploys contents of file

First, you need to get a handle on a `ProcessEngine` instance. You use the `getDefault-ProcessEngine` method to get this. Then you use the `RepositoryService` **1**, read the BAR file **2** in a `ZipInputStream`, and deploy it **3**. With the deployment ID that you get back after the deployment, you can query the `RepositoryService` to display the deployed resources.

If you try this and see the deployed resources displayed in the console, everything is correctly deployed.

Let's take a look at the Activiti Explorer deployment option now.

DEPLOYING PROCESSES WITH THE ACTIVITI EXPLORER

To deploy the loanrequest.bar file with Activiti Explorer, you only have to start a web browser with http://localhost:8080/activiti-explorer, log in, and choose the Manage tab. There, you can deploy new BAR files using the "Choose a file" button, as shown in figure 5.8.

When the loan request process archive is uploaded to the Activiti engine, it's automatically deployed, versioned, and available in the Activiti Explorer for starting a new process instance. In the same deployment screen of Activiti Explorer, you can also delete a deployment archive.

When you deploy multiple versions of a process, you'll find multiple deploy-

Upload new deployment

Select a file (.bar, .zip or .bpmn20.xml) or drop a file in the rectangle below.

Choose a file

or

Drop a file here

Figure 5.8   A pop-up menu showing the Activiti Explorer deployment function

ments in the deployment view as well. Another place to look for deployment information is the database link in the Activiti Explorer. You can, for example, find the loan request process definition in the ACT_RE_PROCDEF table.

> **Process versioning**
>
> BPMN itself doesn't have a notion of versioning, but Activiti does. The version of a process is defined during deployment. Before the `ProcessDefinition` is stored in the Activiti database, a version will be assigned to it. The first time a process with a certain process identifier, which is defined in the BPMN 2.0 XML, is deployed, the version value is set to 1. For every subsequent deployment, the version number is increased by 1. You can have instances of multiple versions of a process running at the same time.

But, enough about deployments and database tables; let's see some action.

5.6 *Testing the process with Activiti Explorer*

Because you need to fill out a start form to get a loan request process instance running, go to the Activiti Explorer page at http://localhost:8080/activiti-explorer and log in as *fozzie* (password is also *fozzie*). In the Process tab, the list of deployed process definitions is shown, including the loan request process. The process definition name corresponds to the `name` attribute in the BPMN 2.0 XML file.

When you click the "Start process" button, the start form should automatically appear. Let's start a loan request for Miss Piggy and fill out the form, as shown in figure 5.9.

Fill in all the fields—they're all defined as mandatory in the form definition. Make sure you fill in `miss.piggy@localhost` in the email address field. Then click the "Start process" button.

You can now see that the "Evaluate loan request" task appears in Fozzie's task list. Be fast now because, if you don't click the "Complete task" button within one minute, the task will be escalated to Kermit the manager—the timer is running from the moment the task was assigned to Fozzie.

Unfortunately, Fozzie isn't the fastest worker on the planet, and the task disappeared from his task list. Let's log out and log in as Kermit. The "Evaluate loan request by manager" task was not assigned to Kermit explicitly in the process definition but to

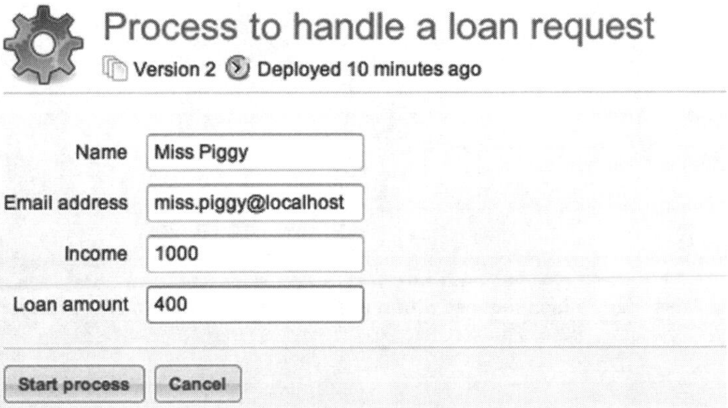

Process to handle a loan request
📄 Version 2 ⊙ Deployed 10 minutes ago

Name	Miss Piggy
Email address	miss.piggy@localhost
Income	1000
Loan amount	400

[Start process] [Cancel]

Figure 5.9 Start form for a loan request by Miss Piggy using the Activiti Explorer

the management group. Kermit has to open the Queued list and claim the task before he can work on it; and after he does that, nobody else can work on it. When you've claimed the task as Kermit, you can work on it and end it by clicking the "Complete task" button, as shown in figure 5.10.

Although Miss Piggy passed the credit check, Kermit denies her the loan. After you click "Complete task," an email will be sent to Miss Piggy's email account to inform her about the unfortunate event. You will see an email arrive in your email client.

That concludes our trip to implement your first complete business process with Activiti. Of course, you can play around a bit with the process to see, for example, how the checks behave with different input or to grant Miss Piggy the loan and see how the process finishes.

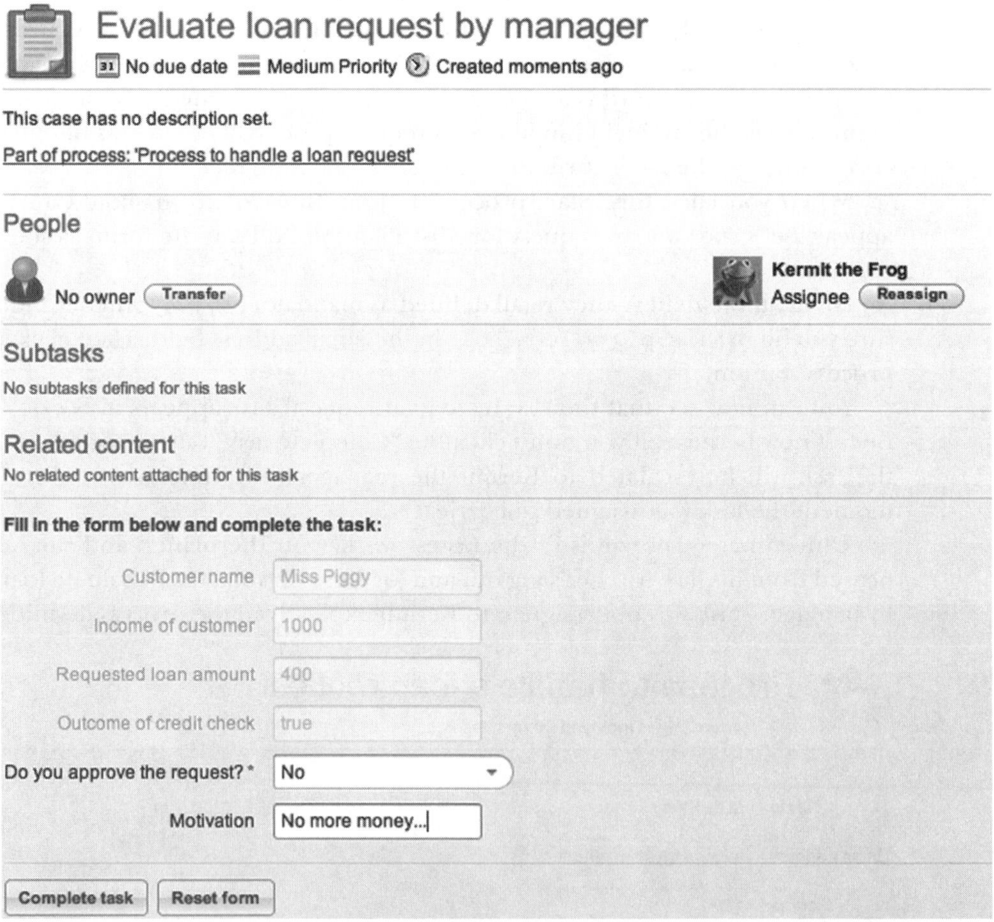

Evaluate loan request by manager

31 No due date ≡ Medium Priority ⊙ Created moments ago

This case has no description set.

Part of process: 'Process to handle a loan request'

People

No owner (Transfer)   **Kermit the Frog**
                                                Assignee (Reassign)

Subtasks

No subtasks defined for this task

Related content

No related content attached for this task

Fill in the form below and complete the task:

Customer name	Miss Piggy
Income of customer	1000
Requested loan amount	400
Outcome of credit check	true
Do you approve the request? *	No
Motivation	No more money...

(Complete task) (Reset form)

Figure 5.10   Denying Miss Piggy's loan request with a user task form in the Activiti Explorer

5.7 Summary

A complete business process has been implemented in this chapter. You've seen how script tasks and Java service tasks can perform the logic that's needed to handle a loan request. We also covered the exclusive gateway, which controls the path of execution in a process. You also saw how Activiti extends the BPMN 2.0 functionality with an email service task.

We also examined how to apply workflows in Activiti with user tasks and forms and, by using a timer boundary event, to escalate a task to another employee. In addition, we covered the deployment options for getting the process running on the Activiti Engine and testing it with the Activiti Explorer application.

You already know a lot about implementing BPMN 2.0 business processes, from the abstract model to concrete code, and you're ready to create your own processes. In chapter 6, we'll take a look at the more advanced BPMN 2.0 constructs like the parallel gateway and subprocesses and Activiti extensions like event listeners. We'll take it one step further to a real-life business process!

Applying advanced
BPMN 2.0 and extensions

This chapter covers

- Using subprocesses
- Working with parallel gateways
- Persistency with JPA
- Learning about execution and task listeners

In the previous chapter, we implemented a full business process from start to finish using a subset of the BPMN 2.0 constructs. When you want to build your own business process, you'll likely find that you need more advanced functionality in your processes. On the following pages, you'll learn all about developing processes with Activiti that use subprocesses, parallel execution, database integration and execution, and task listeners.

In this chapter, we'll approach each advanced construct separately so we can focus on that piece of process logic and learn all the nitty-gritty details. First, you'll see how to structure business processes using subprocesses and learn about the differences between embedded and standalone subprocesses. Then we'll go on with parallel gateways and discuss the consequences of parallel execution in a business process.

In addition, we'll explain the use of JPA to access various databases transparently in Activiti. Together with execution and task listeners, the functionality of JPA is offered via Activiti extensions on top of the BPMN 2.0 specification. These powerful parts of the Activiti toolbox aren't standardized by OMG, but they provide additional functionality to process developers.

We're going to take off on our Activiti trip and progress into the more advanced features of the process engine. Fasten your seatbelts and enjoy the flight while you read about subprocesses and work with the examples.

6.1 Using BPMN 2.0 subprocesses

Business processes that consist of dozens or even hundreds of activities aren't rare in large organizations. For example, a business process for ordering a complex product like an airplane or even a car consists of several steps: order part A, test part B, and so on. To make a large business process more readable and better structured, it can be a good idea to divide parts of the business process into smaller subprocesses. Another advantage of using subprocesses is that they can be reused by other business processes, resulting in standardization.

6.1.1 Background to BPMN subprocesses

When an organization has multiple ordering business processes that each consist of a number of common activities and a small number of process-specific activities, it would be a nightmare to maintain each order process definition separately. It would be better to define subprocesses that can be shared by each business process and then add the process-specific activities.

Subprocesses have a number of advantages from a business and modeling perspective, but what are your choices for implementing such subprocesses? The first choice that has to be made is between embedded (inline) and standalone subprocesses.

An embedded subprocess is part of the main process but defines its own scope in the process. The embedded subprocess shown in figure 6.1 is collapsed so that the activities in the subprocess aren't shown. You can imagine that, for large processes, a model with collapsed subprocesses can make the process definition more readable. And, when you want to see the activities inside the subprocess, you can expand it.

A standalone subprocess is a business process that can also be used as a main process when this is applicable. This means that the subprocess has its own versioning life

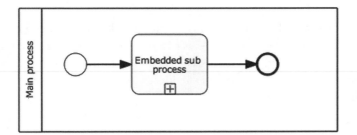

Figure 6.1 An embedded subprocess is an integral part of the main process and introduces a new scope for the whole subprocess in the main process.

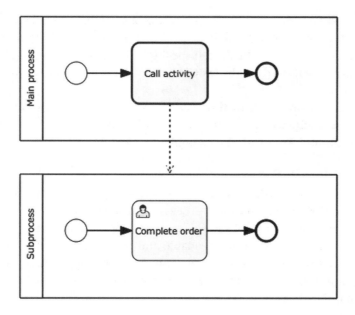

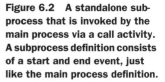

Figure 6.2 A standalone sub-process that is invoked by the main process via a call activity. A subprocess definition consists of a start and end event, just like the main process definition.

cycle in contrast to an embedded subprocess. A standalone subprocess can be invoked from a main process by using a call activity. In the call activity, the unique identifier of the subprocess is defined so a process engine can retrieve and start it. Figure 6.2 shows an overview of a standalone subprocess.

In the case of a standalone subprocess, the main process starts a new process instance of the subprocess definition and waits until the subprocess completes. The subprocess can just as easily be started by another main process or be started as a main process itself.

That's enough about the theory of subprocesses; let's implement the embedded and standalone subprocess types in Activiti.

6.1.2   *Implementing embedded subprocesses*

Real-life process definitions often don't consist of just a few activities—they can be so enormous that they don't fit on A3 pages. Embedded subprocesses can provide a great help for these process definitions by structuring them into smaller parts. When each embedded subprocess is collapsed, the process definition is readable as a series of major activities. When you're interested in the details of a specific activity, that one can be expanded.

As we already saw, this same kind of structuring can be achieved by using call activities and standalone subprocess definitions. As is often the case with design decisions, neither standalone nor embedded subprocesses are the best choice all the time. But let's look at some situations where you could decide to go for an embedded subprocess instead of a standalone subprocess:

- The embedded subprocess is an integral part of the main process and needs process context, like the process variables of the main process, to be able to execute its process logic.
- When it's not likely that the subprocess will be reused by other main processes or be used as a main process itself.
- When there's only a need for a separate scope inside the main process and there's no case of reusable logic.

We'll look at reasons to choose standalone subprocesses in the next section. But first, it's time to look at an example featuring embedded subprocesses: the JIRA escalation process.

DEFINING JIRA ESCALATION WITH AN EMBEDDED SUBPROCESS

A popular issue-tracking tool for Java development projects is JIRA from Atlassian. JIRA is well suited for prioritizing issues, but a project manager may want to have additional ways to follow up on specific issues. Let's look at a process definition where a project manager can add an item to the engineering team's task list directing them to work on a specific JIRA issue (see figure 6.3).

In the escalation process definition in figure 6.3, we make use of an embedded process to define a scope for the development and test user tasks. Because we want to define a timer boundary event that fires when the issue isn't resolved within a specific time period, we need these two tasks to be within one scope. An embedded subprocess is the BPMN 2.0 construct used to define such a scope within the main process definition.

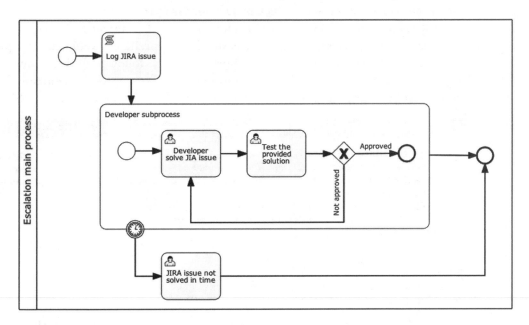

Figure 6.3   An escalation process where a project manager can add a task item for the engineering team to solve an unresolved issue

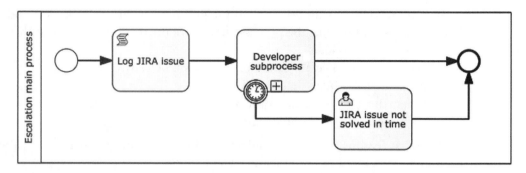

Figure 6.4   The escalation process definition with the embedded subprocess collapsed. This makes the process definition easier to read and to comprehend.

Because the timer boundary event is defined on the embedded subprocess, the timer will fire when the embedded process hasn't ended after the specified time duration. As an added benefit, you can also look at the same escalation process with a collapsed embedded subprocess, shown in figure 6.4.

With the embedded subprocess collapsed, the process definition becomes easy to comprehend. Note that embedded subprocesses can also be used hierarchically; subprocesses can consist of other embedded subprocesses.

With the escalation process defined, let's transform it into an executable BPMN 2.0 process by translating it to XML.

IMPLEMENTING A BPMN 2.0 XML EMBEDDED SUBPROCESS FLOW

The JIRA issue escalation process definition consists of many BPMN 2.0 constructs, so the XML will be verbose. To make it easier to comprehend, we'll start the process implementation with the embedded subprocess in the following listing. Then, in listing 6.2, you'll see the main process definition where the subprocess is embedded. The whole XML process definition can be found in the source code package for this book.

Listing 6.1   The embedded subprocess containing the user tasks

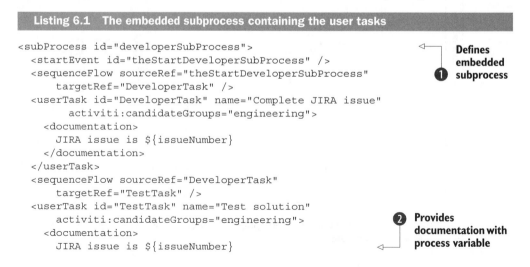

```
<subProcess id="developerSubProcess">                          ◁─┐   Defines
  <startEvent id="theStartDeveloperSubProcess" />                │   embedded
  <sequenceFlow sourceRef="theStartDeveloperSubProcess"        ❶   subprocess
      targetRef="DeveloperTask" />
  <userTask id="DeveloperTask" name="Complete JIRA issue"
      activiti:candidateGroups="engineering">
    <documentation>
      JIRA issue is ${issueNumber}
    </documentation>
  </userTask>
  <sequenceFlow sourceRef="DeveloperTask"
      targetRef="TestTask" />
  <userTask id="TestTask" name="Test solution"
      activiti:candidateGroups="engineering">       ❷   Provides
    <documentation>                                     documentation with
      JIRA issue is ${issueNumber}                      process variable
```

```
    </documentation>
    <extensionElements>
      <activiti:formProperty id="solutionApproved"
          name="Do you approve the solution?"
          required="true"
          type="enum">
        <activiti:value id="true" name="Yes"/>
        <activiti:value id="false" name="No"/>
      </activiti:formProperty>
    </extensionElements>
  </userTask>
  <sequenceFlow sourceRef="TestTask"
      targetRef="TestOK" />
  <exclusiveGateway id="TestOK"/>
  <sequenceFlow sourceRef="TestOK"
      targetRef="DeveloperReady">                    ❸ Checks if tester
    <conditionExpression>                               approved solution
      ${solutionApproved == true}
    </conditionExpression>
  </sequenceFlow>
  <sequenceFlow sourceRef="TestOK"
      targetRef="DeveloperTask">                        Returns to
    <conditionExpression>                            ❹ development task
      ${solutionApproved == false}
    </conditionExpression>
  </sequenceFlow>
    <scriptTask id="DeveloperReady"
        scriptFormat="groovy">
      <script>
        out:println "Developer is ready with JIRA issue "
            + issueNumber
      </script>
    </scriptTask>
    <sequenceFlow sourceRef="DeveloperReady"
        targetRef="theEndDeveloperSubProcess" />      ❺ Leaves embedded
    <endEvent id="theEndDeveloperSubProcess" />          subprocess
  </subProcess>
```

An embedded subprocess is defined with a subProcess element ❶ containing the activities that are executed in the scope of the embedded subprocess. Because you'll test the escalation process with the Activiti Explorer, you add a meaningful documentation element to the user tasks containing the value of the issueNumber process variable ❷.

When the development task is completed, a test task is created to approve the solution. When a tester fills in an approval and completes the user task form, the process continues with the last step in the subprocess ❸. If the tester doesn't approve the solution, the developer task is created again ❹ so a developer can come up with another solution. The embedded subprocess is completed when the end event is reached ❺, as happens in the main process. The difference is that, when the embedded subprocess is completed, the process execution will continue with the next activity attached to the subprocess with a sequence flow.

Now let's look at the main process definition to see how the subprocess from the previous listing is embedded.

Listing 6.2   The jiraIssue.bpmn20.xml file containing the escalation process

```xml
<definitions xmlns="http://www.omg.org/spec/BPMN/20100524/MODEL"
    xmlns:activiti="http://activiti.org/bpmn"
    targetNamespace="http://www.bpmnwithactiviti.org/subprocess">

  <process id="escalationProcess"
      name="Escalation process example">
    <startEvent id="theStart">
      <extensionElements>
        <activiti:formProperty id="issueNumber"
            name="Issue number"
            required="true"
            type="long" />
      </extensionElements>
    </startEvent>
    <sequenceFlow sourceRef="theStart"
        targetRef="LogIssue" />
    <scriptTask id="LogIssue" scriptFormat="groovy">
      <script>
        out:println "Project manager asks developer to
            ➥ complete JIRA issue " + issueNumber
      </script>
    </scriptTask>
    <sequenceFlow sourceRef="LogIssue"
        targetRef="developerSubProcess" />
    <subProcess id="developerSubProcess">
      <!-- see code listing 6.1 -->
    </subProcess>
    <boundaryEvent id="escalationTimerDeveloper"
        cancelActivity="true"
        attachedToRef="developerSubProcess">
      <timerEventDefinition>
        <timeDuration>PT1M</timeDuration>
      </timerEventDefinition>
    </boundaryEvent>
    <sequenceFlow sourceRef="escalationTimerDeveloper"
        targetRef="ProjectManagerEscalationTask" />
    <userTask id="ProjectManagerEscalationTask"
        name="JIRA issue is not completed in time"
        activiti:candidateGroups="management">
      <documentation>
        JIRA issue is ${issueNumber}
      </documentation>
    </userTask>
    <sequenceFlow sourceRef="ProjectManagerEscalationTask"
        targetRef="theEnd" />
    <sequenceFlow sourceRef="developerSubProcess"
        targetRef="theEnd" />
    <endEvent id="theEnd" />
  </process>
</definitions>
```

1 Starts form for issue number

2 Start of embedded subprocess

3 Boundary event attached to subprocess

4 Escalation task

The main process kicks off with a start event containing a task form defined with the formProperty attribute **1**. In the start form, the project manager will specify the issue number. When the issueNumber process variable is logged with the script task, the embedded subprocess of listing 6.1 is executed ➋.

The timer boundary event that's attached to the embedded subprocess is also defined in the main process definition ➌. In this example, the timer will fire when the embedded subprocess hasn't been completed within one minute. When the timer boundary event is executed, a user task is created for the management group ➍.

Before you can test this process in the Activiti Explorer, you'll have to deploy the process definition in a BAR file to the Activiti Engine. Then you can use the Activiti Explorer to work through the various tasks in the issue tracking process.

TESTING THE ISSUE TRACKING PROCESS WITH THE ACTIVITI EXPLORER

First, we'll create a BAR file that contains the BPMN 2.0 XML file for the escalation process. In chapter 5, you created a BAR file with an Ant build file; we'll repeat this to create the BAR file for the escalation process.

The BAR file is created when running the build.xml Ant build file. You can find this build file in src/main/resources/chapter6/embedded_subprocess, and the jiraissue.bar file is created in a dist subdirectory there. You can now start up Activiti Explorer to deploy the escalation deployment artifact. In the Deployments tab, you can upload the jiraissue.bar file.

Now that the escalation process definition is available in the Activiti Engine, it's time to start a new process instance in the Activiti Explorer. Figure 6.5 shows a screenshot of the Activiti Explorer as it starts the escalation process.

When the issue tracking process has started, a new task should be available for the engineering team. Remember that you assigned the first developer task to this candidate group (see listing 6.1). When you click on the Tasks tab in the Activiti Explorer, you should see that a queued task with the name "Complete JIRA issue" has been created in the engineering group. Now, claim and complete this task, and a new "Test solution" task will be created for the same engineering candidate group (see figure 6.6).

When you don't approve the solution, a new developer task will be created. Because you defined a timer boundary event on the embedded subprocess in listing 6.2, an escalation task will be created one minute after the start of the embedded subprocess. Don't approve the test solution and wait a few moments: a new task, "JIRA issue is not completed in time," will be created. When this task is created, you know that the timer boundary event job was executed as you would expect.

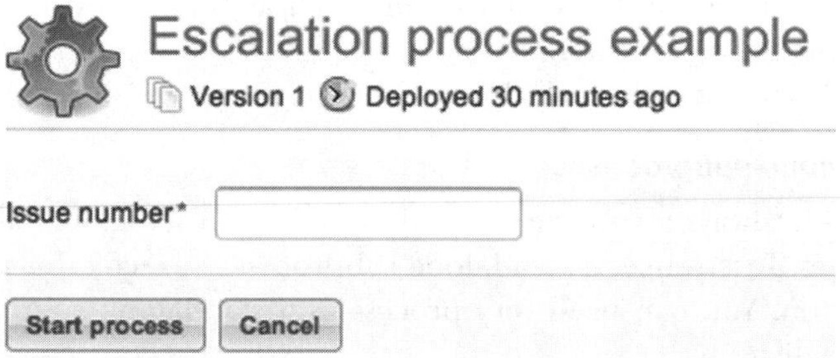

Escalation process example

Version 1 ⊙ Deployed 30 minutes ago

Issue number* [   ]

[**Start process**] [Cancel]

Figure 6.5 The Activiti Explorer showing the start form of the escalation process

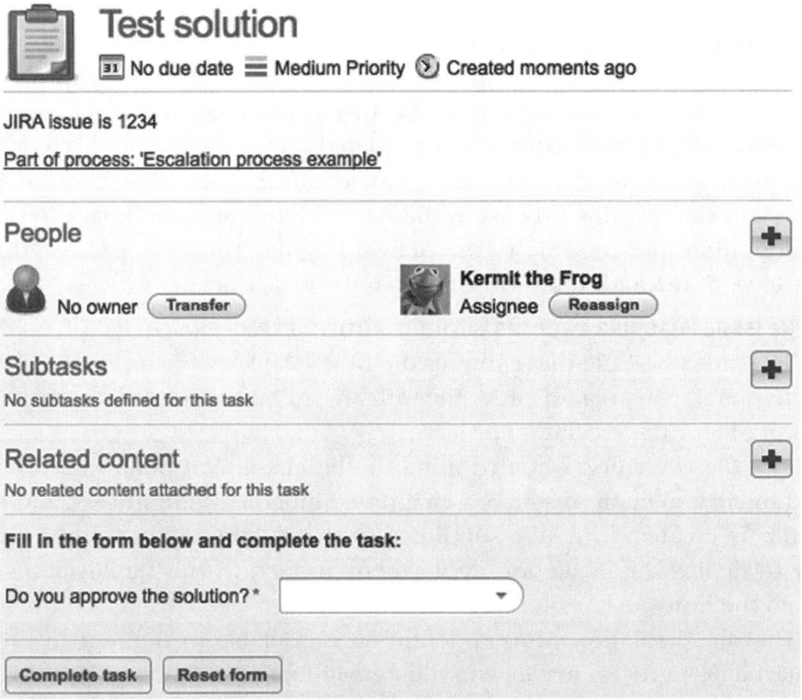

Test solution

31 No due date ≡ Medium Priority ⊘ Created moments ago

JIRA issue is 1234

Part of process: 'Escalation process example'

People   +

No owner (Transfer)

Kermit the Frog
Assignee (Reassign)

Subtasks   +
No subtasks defined for this task

Related content   +
No related content attached for this task

Fill in the form below and complete the task:

Do you approve the solution? *   [▼]

[Complete task] [Reset form]

Figure 6.6   The Test Solution task form in the Activiti Explorer, which is part of the embedded subprocess in the issue tracking process definition

TIP   The timer boundary event only fires when the Activiti Engine's job executor is activated. By default, the job executor is active in the Activiti Engine. This can be overridden by defining a `jobExecutorActivate` property with a value of `false` on the engine configuration. Disabling the job executor can be useful when you have a cluster of Activiti Engines and you only want to execute jobs on specific instances.

As you saw in this issue tracking process example, an embedded subprocess is an integral part of the main process definition. Process variables are shared between the main process and the embedded subprocesses, which introduces no additional complexity to run the process on the Activiti Engine. Embedded subprocesses, first and foremost, provide a way to define scopes in a process definition. And, with the introduction of scopes, you can define boundary events such as timers and errors on a group of activities as you did in the example.

Now let's see how this works with standalone subprocesses using call activities.

6.1.3   *Implementing standalone subprocesses*

An embedded process is always a subprocess by definition, but it's more vague with standalone subprocesses. In essence, a standalone subprocess is exactly the same as a *normal* process definition. You can use every process as a standalone subprocess by invoking it with a call activity.

We already talked about the benefits of using subprocesses in general, but when would a standalone subprocess be a good choice? First of all, it's a choice of design and not of mathematics. But, you should think of using standalone subprocesses in the following situations:

- When a part of a process definition is reusable in other process definitions.
- When process logic inside a subprocess is also used as a main process.
- When a part of a process is expected to change a lot.

A standalone subprocess offers more flexibility than embedded subprocesses because new versions of a subprocess can be deployed without the need to change the parent process. Also, the standalone subprocess can be reused in every process that needs its process logic. Another big difference with an embedded subprocess is that a standalone subprocess can be started as a main process as well.

The downsides of a standalone subprocess are the extra maintenance it requires and the strict separation between the process contexts of a main process and subprocess. While the process context in an embedded subprocess is shared between the main process and the subprocess, it's impossible to share the process context with a standalone subprocess. The only communication that's possible is to add input and output parameters to a call activity configuration. Then the input parameters will be available in the standalone subprocess and the output parameters will be made available to the main process context.

But, enough theory. Let's look at a standalone subprocess definition and see how to implement a call activity to invoke it.

DEFINING A REUSABLE PROCESS

The main benefit of implementing a standalone subprocess is reusability. In the example we'll look at—a mobile telephone contracting process—the focus is on achieving this goal. A mobile telephone company wants to standardize its contract process further for the personal and business market. Although the process steps involved in coming to a contract agreement are different between the personal and business contract processes, the credit check activity is similar in both processes.

Because the credit department handles individual as well as organizational credit check requests, it seems obvious to make this step reusable for other processes. Figure 6.7 shows the credit check process.

First, the customer's credit history is validated. If there's a reason to take a closer look at the customer's current situation, the request is initially disapproved. A credit manager can then make the final decision to approve or disapprove the customer for a new contract. In figure 6.8, this credit check process is used as a standalone subprocess in the personal mobile contract process definition.

The personal mobile contract is simple because a new or existing customer can request a new contract via a website. The customer receives a confirmation or denial via email within seconds based on the outcome of the credit check subprocess. In the remaining part of this section, you'll implement the personal mobile contract process,

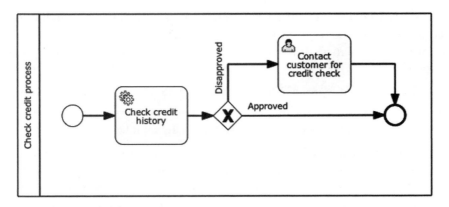

Figure 6.7   A simplified version of a credit check process that's used by both the personal and the business mobile contract processes

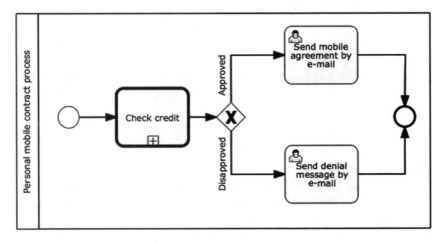

Figure 6.8   The personal mobile contract process definition containing a call activity that invokes the credit check standalone subprocess

but let's take quick look at how the credit check process is also used in the business mobile contract process (see figure 6.9).

As you can see, the business mobile contract process contains more user tasks than the personal process definition. A new business agreement always starts with one or more face-to-face meetings. Then, a sales manager can create a new initial business contract agreement. Before the contract is approved, a credit check is performed, just like in the personal contract process. Eventually, the agreement is approved or disapproved, and this is communicated to the business customer in a meeting.

Because we don't want to repeat ourselves, we'll focus on the personal mobile contract process for the code implementation. Let's see how we can kick off a standalone subprocess with a call activity.

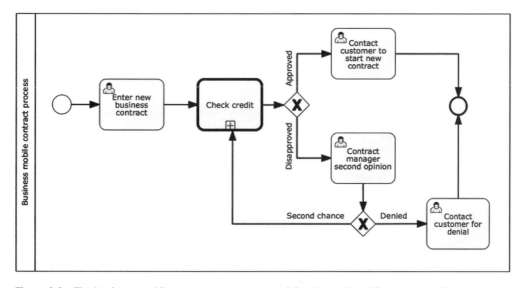

Figure 6.9   The business mobile contract process containing the call activity to the credit check standalone subprocess

CALLING A STANDALONE SUBPROCESS USING A CALL ACTIVITY

To be able to reuse the credit check process, you must be able to provide that process with the necessary customer information—at least a customer number—to perform the credit check. And, when the credit check has been performed, it's important that the approval or disapproval outcome is communicated back to the main process. In the next listing, the implementation of the call activity with input and output parameters is shown.

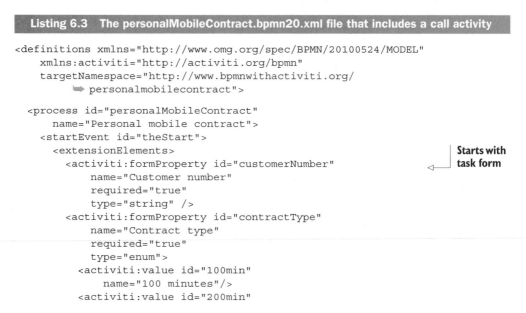

```xml
<definitions xmlns="http://www.omg.org/spec/BPMN/20100524/MODEL"
    xmlns:activiti="http://activiti.org/bpmn"
    targetNamespace="http://www.bpmnwithactiviti.org/
    ➥ personalmobilecontract">

  <process id="personalMobileContract"
     name="Personal mobile contract">
    <startEvent id="theStart">
      <extensionElements>
        <activiti:formProperty id="customerNumber"
           name="Customer number"
           required="true"
           type="string" />
        <activiti:formProperty id="contractType"
           name="Contract type"
           required="true"
           type="enum">
         <activiti:value id="100min"
            name="100 minutes"/>
         <activiti:value id="200min"
```

Listing 6.3   The personalMobileContract.bpmn20.xml file that includes a call activity

> Starts with
> task form

```
                    name="200 minutes"/>
               <activiti:value id="500min"
                    name="500 minutes"/>
             </activiti:formProperty>
          </extensionElements>
        </startEvent>
        <sequenceFlow sourceRef="theStart"
            targetRef="creditCheck" />
        <callActivity id="creditCheck"
            calledElement="creditCheckProcess">
          <extensionElements>
            <activiti:in source="customerNumber"
                target="customerID" />
            <activiti:in source="contractType"
                target="contractType" />
            <activiti:out source="creditCheckApproved"
                target="creditApproved" />
          </extensionElements>
        </callActivity>
        <sequenceFlow sourceRef="creditCheck"
            targetRef="creditApproved" />
        <exclusiveGateway id="creditApproved"/>
        <sequenceFlow sourceRef="creditApproved"
            targetRef="sendMobileAgreement">
          <conditionExpression>
            ${creditApproved == true}
          </conditionExpression>
        </sequenceFlow>
        <sequenceFlow sourceRef="creditApproved"
            targetRef="sendDenial">
          <conditionExpression>
            ${creditApproved == false}
          </conditionExpression>
        </sequenceFlow>
        <userTask id="sendMobileAgreement"
            name="Send mobile contract"
            activiti:candidateGroups="sales"/>
        <sequenceFlow sourceRef="sendMobileAgreement"
            targetRef="theEnd" />
        <userTask id="sendDenial"
            name="Send letter of denial"
            activiti:candidateGroups="sales"/>
        <sequenceFlow sourceRef="sendMobileAgreement"
            targetRef="theEnd" />
        <endEvent id="theEnd" />
      </process>
    </definitions>
```

❶ Invokes credit check process

❷ Defines input parameter

❸ Defines output parameter

❹ Uses credit check outcome

The implementation of a call activity is simple with BPMN 2.0 and Activiti. The identifier of the standalone subprocess is configured in the calledElement attribute ❶. The latest version of the invoked subprocess is always started when the call activity is executed. The call activity waits until the execution of the subprocess is finished.

To communicate with the subprocess, you can define input and output parameters. In this example, a customer number and contract type ❷ are provided as input to the credit check subprocess. As you can see, a mapping defines which variable of the parent process (the source attribute) is copied to which variable of the subprocess (the target attribute).

> **NOTE** The input and output parameter mapping functionality is included in the BPMN 2.0 specification using an ioSpecification element that is very verbose. Therefore, Activiti supports the much simpler to use in and out elements. The Activiti roadmap contains an item to support this BPMN 2.0 compliant way of creating input and output parameters as well.

In addition to the input parameters, the (dis)approval outcome of the credit check process is injected as a creditApproved process variable in the main process context ❸. This process variable is used in the next steps of the personal mobile contract process to decide between emailing a contract agreement or a denial message ❹.

Because the logic of the credit check process is already clear from the definition shown in figure 6.7, the BPMN 2.0 XML isn't shown here. (You can look up the implementation of this subprocess in the book's source code.)

> **NOTE** The credit check process contains an extra script task after the user task to copy the value of the variable that holds the outcome of the user task (creditCheckApprovedForm) to the process variable (creditCheckApproved). The Activiti Engine returns an exception if you use the creditCheckApproved variable directly in the form property definition. This is because the variable is also used in the out parameter definition of the call activity.

Now let's test the process definitions and see if it will work as expected.

TESTING THE PERSONAL MOBILE CONTRACT PROCESS

To test the personal mobile contract process example, you have to deploy two process definitions—the main and the standalone subprocess definition. This isn't a problem because you only have to make sure that both BPMN 2.0 XM files are present in the BAR file you create.

The contract process BAR file is created when running the build.xml Ant build file. In the src/main/resources/chapter6/callactivity directory, you can find this Ant build file and, when executed, the BAR file is created in a dist subdirectory there. Now, deploy the newly created callactivity.bar file to the Activiti Engine using the Activiti Explorer.

Because the credit check process contains a Java service task, you have to perform an additional step to deploy the CreditCheckService Java class to the Activiti Engine classpath. In addition to the BAR file, the Ant build file also created a callactivity.jar file that contains the compiled class file. You need to first stop the running Tomcat instance, for example, by executing the ant tomcat.stop command in the setup directory of your Activiti installation. Then, copy the callactivity.jar file to the webapps/activiti-explorer/WEB-INF/lib directory of the Tomcat instance in the Activiti installation directory. Now, you can start Tomcat again (ant tomcat.start) and the CreditCheckService class will be available on the Activiti Engine classpath.

With the personal mobile contract and credit check processes fully deployed, you can now go to the Activiti Explorer to start a new process instance. Note that both processes are available to start in the process instance list in the Activiti Explorer. But, you want to start the personal mobile contract process—you can do that as shown in figure 6.10.

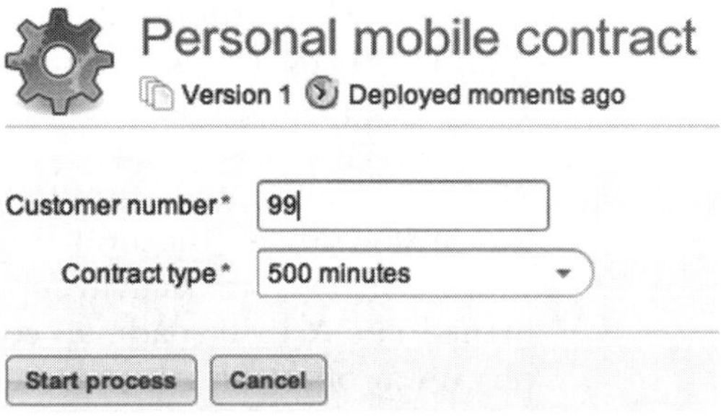

When the process is started, a customer number and a contract type value have to be provided. Note that

Personal mobile contract
Version 1 · Deployed moments ago

Customer number* `99`

Contract type* `500 minutes`

[Start process] [Cancel]

Figure 6.10   Screenshot of starting the personal mobile contract process within the Activiti Explorer

the credit history service task in the credit check subprocess automatically approves processes for customer numbers between 1,000 and 10,000. If you fill in a customer number of 99, a new user task named "Personal credit check" will be created to perform an extra validation on the credit of the customer. When you complete that user task, you can choose to approve or disapprove the request, and you should see a corresponding user task created from the personal contract main process.

We've talked about subprocesses in a lot of detail. A subprocess is an essential and powerful construct in BPMN because it can provide a scope definition with an embedded subprocess and reusability and flexibility with a standalone subprocesses and call activity. Our next topic is the parallel gateway construct, which provides functionality to perform activities simultaneously.

6.2   *Working with BPMN 2.0 parallel gateways*

You already used an exclusive gateway in a number of examples in the previous chapters. An exclusive gateway is a simple but powerful construct for controlling the flow throughout a process definition. A parallel gateway is part of the same gateway construct family, but it can be considered a more advanced BPMN element.

It's a common requirement for parts of process logic to be executed at the same time. If there are multiple tasks to perform, it would be inefficient to place the activities in a waiting line. A parallel gateway makes it possible to perform multiple activities simultaneously.

In addition, when a parallel gateway is placed after multiple incoming sequence flows, it will make sure that all activities are finished before the process execution goes further. A parallel gateway executes all outgoing sequence flows leaving the gateway and waits for all incoming sequence flows to complete.

With a simplified example process, the functionality of a parallel gateway becomes easier to comprehend. Let's look at a fictional day in the life of a multitasking developer in figure 6.11. The first parallel gateway is called a fork because it makes the process execution fork into two parallel executions. The second parallel gateway is a join because it makes the process execution wait until all the activities between the fork and join gateways are executed.

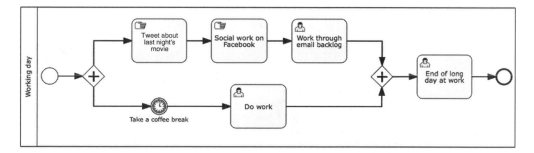

Figure 6.11 A multitasking process definition with a fork and join parallel gateway. All activities must be executed before the process will end with the last activity after the join parallel gateway.

In the following sections, we'll implement the multitasking process in a BPMN 2.0 XML file.

6.2.1 *Implementing a process with a parallel gateway*

Parallel gateways aren't hard to implement in a BPMN 2.0 process definition. But the runtime behavior is more difficult to grasp. As you'll discover, the different outgoing sequence flows aren't really executed in parallel but are still running one after another.

> **HINT** Real parallel execution with multiple threads running at the same time isn't the result of using a parallel gateway. The activity sequences that are modeled after the fork construct run after each other. The first sequence of activities is executed until a wait state is encountered. This can be a receive or user task or a parallel gateway join when there are no wait state activities in the sequence. After the first sequence of activities has come into a wait state, the second sequence of activities will be executed, and so on. There are good reasons why the Activiti framework decided to implement the parallel gateway this way. If there are multiple threads running at the same time, a need for locking and concurrency checking would come up and that would introduce a lot more complexity and lead to some performance loss.

Let's first look at the implementation of the multitasking example process definition in the next listing.

Listing 6.4 The parallelGateway.bpmn20.xml process with a join and fork gateway

```
<definitions xmlns="http://www.omg.org/spec/BPMN/20100524/MODEL"
    xmlns:activiti="http://activiti.org/bpmn"
    targetNamespace="http://www.bpmnwithactiviti.org/
        ➥ parallelgateway">

  <process id="multitaskingProcess"
      name="Multitasking process">
    <startEvent id="theStart" />
    <sequenceFlow sourceRef="theStart"
        targetRef="fork" />
    <parallelGateway id="fork" />
```

❶ Fork parallel gateway

```
<sequenceFlow sourceRef="fork"
    targetRef="twitterTask" />
<sequenceFlow sourceRef="fork"
    targetRef="coffeebreak" />
<manualTask id="twitterTask" />
<sequenceFlow sourceRef="twitterTask"
    targetRef="facebookTask" />
<manualTask id="facebookTask" />
<sequenceFlow sourceRef="facebookTask"
    targetRef="backlogEmailTask" />
<userTask id="backlogEmailTask"
    name="Read email backlog"
    activiti:assignee="kermit"/>
<sequenceFlow sourceRef="backlogEmailTask"
    targetRef="join" />
<intermediateCatchEvent id="coffeebreak">
  <timerEventDefinition>
    <timeDuration>PT30S</timeDuration>
  </timerEventDefinition>
</intermediateCatchEvent>
<sequenceFlow sourceRef="coffeebreak"
    targetRef="doWorkTask" />
<userTask id="doWorkTask"
    name="Do work"
    activiti:assignee="kermit" />
<sequenceFlow sourceRef="doWorkTask"
    targetRef="join" />
<parallelGateway id="join" />
<sequenceFlow sourceRef="join"
    targetRef="endOfWorkDayTask" />
<userTask id="endOfWorkDayTask"
    name="Finish work day"
    activiti:assignee="kermit"/>
<sequenceFlow sourceRef="endOfWorkDayTask"
    targetRef="theEnd" />
<endEvent id="theEnd" />
  </process>
</definitions>
```

2 First activity of
first sequence

3 First activity of
second sequence

4 Join parallel
gateway

As you already saw, the BPMN 2.0 XML definition of a parallel gateway isn't difficult. The runtime behavior is another thing. For example, how does the Activiti Engine know the first defined parallel gateway **1** is a fork? It doesn't know that. The parallel gateway acts as a join *and* fork. First, the Activiti Engine waits until all incoming sequence flows have been executed; then, it will fork into all outgoing sequence flows. For your fork parallel gateway, there's only one incoming sequence flow, so the process will immediately perform the fork behavior.

> **NOTE** The parallel gateway won't evaluate any condition expression on an outgoing sequence flow; if a condition expression is present on one of the sequence flows out of a fork parallel gateway, it's ignored.

In this example process, the first sequence of activities that's executed starts with a Twitter task **2**. For the sake of showing the functionality of a parallel gateway, this is a manual task. A manual task can be regarded as a kind of pass-through activity so the process *immediately continues*. Because the first two tasks in the first sequence of activities are pass-through activities, the first sequence doesn't stop until it reaches the `backlogEmailTask` user task, which is a wait state. Then execution continues in the second sequence where the `coffeebreak` intermediate timer event ❸ is executed. Be aware that the activities in the second outgoing sequence flow of the fork parallel gateway aren't executed before the first sequence flow reaches the `backlogEmailTask` user task.

Eventually, all the activities in both sequence flows will be executed and the `join` parallel gateway ❹ progresses the process execution to the `endOfWorkDayTask` user task. Note that the `join` parallel gateway makes sure that both incoming sequence flows have been completed before the process continues.

> **TIP** If you had implemented the backlog email user task as an automatic task, all the activities in the first outgoing sequence flow of the fork parallel gateway would be executed before the second outgoing sequence flow was executed. In that case, the parallel gateways in the multitasking process definition could be removed, the activities of the second outgoing sequence flow could be added after the backlog email user task, and the process execution would be exactly the same.

With the parallel process implementation in place, you can test the multitasking process with the Activiti Explorer to get a better understanding of the process execution flow.

6.2.2 *Testing a process with a parallel gateway*

The challenge in testing the process definition with a parallel gateway is that some parts of the process execution aren't visible in the process instance and task details. You'll, therefore, need to switch to the database view in the Activiti Explorer a few times. But first, you have to create the BAR file using the Ant build file build.xml in the src/main/resources/chapter6/parallel directory. Then you can deploy the created BAR file to the Activiti Engine using Activiti Explorer like you did before.

When you've deployed the process definition and started a new process instance in the Activiti Explorer, you should see one user task appearing (when logged in as *kermit*), as shown in figure 6.12.

Take a look back at the multitasking process definition in listing 6.4 and you'll see that the backlog email user task is the third activity in the first outgoing sequence flow of the parallel gateway. The first two activities, Twitter and Facebook, have already been executed because they're implemented as manual tasks.

In the Activiti Explorer, you can look in the database view to check whether the Twitter and Facebook manual tasks really have been executed. Click on the ACT_HI_ACTINST table, and you should see a similar overview to that shown in figure 6.13.

As you can see in figure 6.13, these activities have been executed as expected. You can now complete the email backlog user task. Notice that the "end workday" user task isn't yet created. Remember that you first have to complete the "do work" user

Read email backlog

[31] No due date ≡ Medium Priority ⊙ Created moments ago

This case has no description set.

Part of process: 'Multitasking process'

People

➕

No owner [Transfer]

Kermit the Frog
Assignee [Reassign]

Subtasks

➕

No subtasks defined for this task

Related content

➕

No related content attached for this task

[Complete task]

Figure 6.12   The Activiti Explorer showing the user task that will be created when you start a new instance of the multitasking process definition

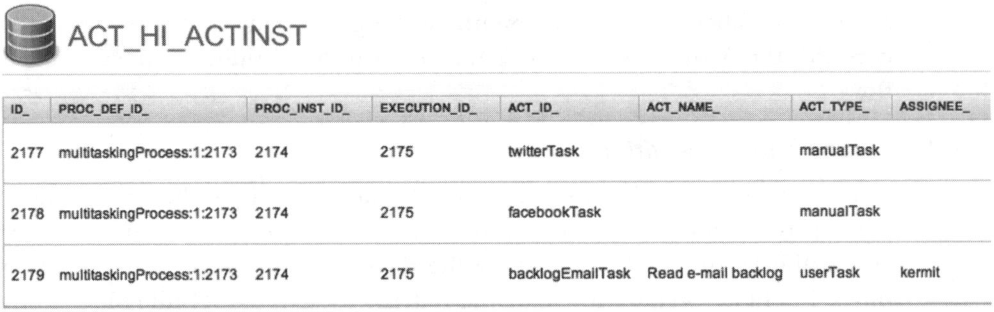

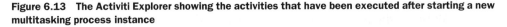

ACT_HI_ACTINST

ID_	PROC_DEF_ID_	PROC_INST_ID_	EXECUTION_ID_	ACT_ID_	ACT_NAME_	ACT_TYPE_	ASSIGNEE_
2177	multitaskingProcess:1:2173	2174	2175	twitterTask		manualTask	
2178	multitaskingProcess:1:2173	2174	2175	facebookTask		manualTask	
2179	multitaskingProcess:1:2173	2174	2175	backlogEmailTask	Read e-mail backlog	userTask	kermit

Figure 6.13   The Activiti Explorer showing the activities that have been executed after starting a new multitasking process instance

task before the second parallel gateway continues the process execution. And because there's first a "coffee break" intermediate timer of 30 seconds, you have to wait a bit. When the 30 seconds have passed, the "do work" user task can be completed and the "end workday" user task appears.

With the multitasking process tested, you can now move on to a piece of functionality that's not part of the BPMN 2.0 specification but that can certainly provide great value: the Java Persistence API (JPA) integration. This powerful feature helps to retrieve database entities within a process instance without the need to write database logic.

6.3   *Adding a JPA extension to your process*

The Java Persistence API (JPA) is an important specification for implementing persistency within Java. JPA is also widely adopted, not only by the JEE application server vendors but also by open source frameworks like Hibernate and Apache OpenJPA. If you aren't yet familiar with JPA, you can read about all of its details on the Hibernate and Apache OpenJPA websites or in a book like *Java Persistence with Hibernate* by Christian Bauer and Gavin King (Manning, 2006).

What's the use case for using the JPA extension in your process definition? When you have a business process that needs a database entity like "customer" or "address" from a relational database, you can write the data access logic yourself in a Java service task and add this to the process definition. But, with the JPA extension, this isn't necessary. You can create a process variable implemented with a JPA annotated JavaBean and use the database entity in your process definition like a normal process variable.

To really grasp the JPA extension functionality, we'll take a look at a small example so we can discuss in detail the use of JPA in Activiti and note some caveats.

6.3.1 Modeling a process with a database entity

When a publisher signs a book contract, one of the first tasks is to create a title and ISBN for the book. More interestingly, with regard to the JPA extension, the book's information must be entered into the publisher's database. In the process definition of figure 6.14, the start of a new book project is modeled.

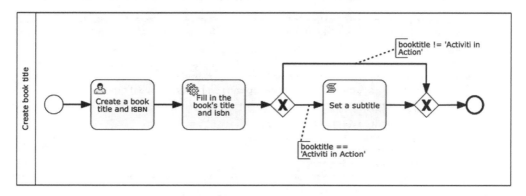

Figure 6.14   When a new book project is started, the initial available book information is stored in the publisher's database. Then the publisher adds the necessary title and ISBN information and, optionally, a subtitle.

As you can see, the process definition is centered on the book object. You need to make sure that the title, ISBN, author list, and optional subtitle are available in the publisher's book database—to do so, you can use the JPA extension. The book object is simple because it contains the four already mentioned attributes. Let's look at the book entity object in the following code snippet:

```
@Entity
public class Book {

    @Id
    @GeneratedValue
```

```
    private int id;
    private String title;
    private String subTitle;
    private String isbn;

    @ElementCollection(fetch=FetchType.EAGER)
    private List<String> authors;

    // getters and setters
}
```

Notice that Java's `Book` object uses the `ElementCollection` annotation that's part of JPA 2.0. With this handy annotation, you can use collection attributes inside an entity object without needing any additional coding. You'll now use the `Book` object to create, update, and retrieve a book entity object with the JPA extension in the implementation of the new book project process definition.

6.3.2 Implementing a process with JPA extensions

Starting with the process model in figure 6.14, you can define a BPMN 2.0 XML definition, including the database persistency logic. For this example, you'll use Activiti inside a Spring container because the Spring framework makes the transaction handling and `EntityManager` injection easy. The BPMN 2.0 XML is shown in the next listing.

Listing 6.5   Implementation of processWithJPA.bpmn2.0.xml using JPA extension

```
<definitions xmlns="http://www.omg.org/spec/BPMN/20100524/MODEL"
    xmlns:xsi="http://www.w3.org/2001/XMLSchema-instance"
    xmlns:activiti="http://activiti.org/bpmn"
    targetNamespace="http://www.bpmnwithactiviti.org/jpa">

  <process id="jpaTest">
    <startEvent id="theStart" />
    <sequenceFlow sourceRef="theStart"
        targetRef="createBook" />
    <serviceTask id="createBook"
        activiti:expression="${bookService.createBook(
            ➥ authorList)}"
        activiti:resultVariableName="book"/>            ◁─┘  ❶ Creates and
    <sequenceFlow sourceRef="createBook"                       persist book
        targetRef="fillBookInfo" />                            object
    <userTask id="fillBookInfo"
        activiti:assignee="kermit">
      <extensionElements>
        <activiti:formProperty id="booktitle"
            name="Book title"
            expression="#{book.title}"                  ❷ Updates
            required="true" />                              book title
        <activiti:formProperty id="isbn"
            name="Isbn"
            expression="#{book.isbn}"
            required="true" />
      </extensionElements>
    </userTask>
    <sequenceFlow sourceRef="fillBookInfo"
```

```
                targetRef="makeSubtitle" />
    <exclusiveGateway id="makeSubtitle"/>
    <sequenceFlow id="makeSubtitleYes"
        sourceRef="makeSubtitle"
        targetRef="createSubtitle">
      <conditionExpression>
        ${book.title == 'Activiti in Action'}
      </conditionExpression>
    </sequenceFlow>
    <sequenceFlow id="makeSubtitleNo"
        sourceRef="makeSubtitle"
        targetRef="makeSubtitleReady">
      <conditionExpression>
        ${book.title != 'Activiti in Action'}
      </conditionExpression>
    </sequenceFlow>
    <scriptTask id="createSubtitle"
        scriptFormat="groovy">
      <script>
        book.subTitle = "Executable business
            ➥ processes in BPMN 2.0";
        out:println "book subTitle is set to " +
            book.subTitle;
      </script>
    </scriptTask>
    <sequenceFlow sourceRef="createSubtitle"
        targetRef="makeSubtitleReady" />
    <exclusiveGateway id="makeSubtitleReady"/>
    <sequenceFlow id="toEnd"
        sourceRef="makeSubtitleReady"
        targetRef="theEnd" />
    <endEvent id="theEnd" />
  </process>
</definitions>
```

3 Checks book title

4 Updates book subtitle

Notice that you can't tell from the BPMN 2.0 XML that the JPA extension is being used for this process definition. The XML definition only mentions the book process variable, and this could just as well be implemented with a normal JavaBean.

In the first step of the process, you use a Java service task to create and persist a Book entity object **1**. As you can see in the Java service task definition, the result of the createBook method will be set as a new process variable, book. The book service itself is a Spring bean, which we'll discuss in the listing 6.7.

After the Book object is persisted, you use a user task to let the publisher fill in the title and ISBN for the book. With the form properties and JPA functionality of Activiti, you can use the task form to update the book process variable, which is also automatically saved into the database. The booktitle form property will, for example, update the title attribute of the Book entity object **2**.

Because the Book entity object is available through the book process variable, it can be used in other parts of the process like a conditional expression on a sequence flow **3**. If the book title is equal to this book's title, the subTitle attribute is set in a script task **4**. In JPA terms, the persisted Book object is updated with a subTitle value.

With the BPMN 2.0 XML definition in place, you can now glue things together with the Spring configuration. Because it would be repetitious to include the whole Spring configuration, the following listing only shows the JPA-specific differences. In chapter 4 and in the source code of the book, you can find the details about the rest of the Spring configuration.

Listing 6.6 JPA-specific parts of the jpa-application-context.xml Spring configuration

```
<bean id="transactionManager"                                          ◄┐
    class="org.springframework.orm.jpa.JpaTransactionManager">          │
  <property name="entityManagerFactory"                                 │
           ref="entityManagerFactory"/>                    JPA transaction
</bean>                                                          manager ❶

<bean id="persistenceUnitManager"
    class="org.springframework.orm.jpa.persistenceunit.
        ➥ DefaultPersistenceUnitManager">
  <property name="persistenceXmlLocation">
    <value>                                              ❷ JPA persistence
       classpath:chapter6/jpa/jpa-persistence.xml  ◄┘    unit configuration
    </value>
  </property>
</bean>

<bean id="entityManagerFactory"                     ◄┐   Defines an
    class="org.springframework.orm.jpa.              ❸   EntityManagerFactory
        ➥ LocalContainerEntityManagerFactoryBean">
  <property name="persistenceUnitManager"
     ref="persistenceUnitManager"/>
</bean>

<bean id="processEngineConfiguration"
    class="org.activiti.spring.SpringProcessEngineConfiguration">
  <property name="databaseType" value="h2" />
  <property name="dataSource" ref="activitiDataSource" />
  <property name="transactionManager"
           ref="transactionManager" />
  <property name="databaseSchemaUpdate" value="true" />  ❹ Injects the entity
  <property name="jpaEntityManagerFactory"          ◄┘     manager factory
           ref="entityManagerFactory" />
  <property name="jpaHandleTransaction" value="true" />
  <property name="jpaCloseEntityManager" value="true" />
  <property name="deploymentResources"
     value="classpath*:chapter6/jpa/processWithJPA.bpmn20.xml" />
  <property name="jobExecutorActivate" value="false" />
</bean>                                               ❺ Spring bean
                                                   ◄┘  with JPA logic
<bean id="bookService"
    class="org.bpmnwithactiviti.chapter6.jpa.BookService"/>
```

The nice thing about using Spring in combination with JPA is that you can use the Spring transaction manager ❶. The transaction manager takes care of creating and committing the transaction necessary to persist the Book entity object, as you'll see in the BookService implementation.

To use JPA, you need an `EntityManagerFactory` definition ❸ that references the persistence unit configuration defined in jpa-persistence.xml ❷. The jpa-persistence.xml JPA configuration file defines a `bookStore` persistence unit with Hibernate as a JPA provider. Note that you could also use another JPA provider like Apache OpenJPA. The jpa-persistence.xml JPA configuration file contains the standard JPA attributes, as you can see in the next code snippet:

```
<persistence xmlns="http://java.sun.com/xml/ns/persistence"
    xmlns:xsi="http://www.w3.org/2001/XMLSchema-instance"
    xsi:schemaLocation="http://java.sun.com/xml/ns/persistence
        http://java.sun.com/xml/ns/persistence/persistence_2_0.xsd"
    version="2.0">

  <persistence-unit name="bookStore" transaction-type="RESOURCE_LOCAL">
    <provider>org.hibernate.ejb.HibernatePersistence</provider>
    <class>org.bpmnwithactiviti.chapter6.jpa.Book</class>
    <exclude-unlisted-classes>true</exclude-unlisted-classes>
    <properties>
      <property name="hibernate.dialect"
                value="org.hibernate.dialect.HSQLDialect"/>
      <property name="hibernate.hbm2ddl.auto" value="create-drop"/>
      <property name="hibernate.connection.url"
          value="jdbc:h2:mem:bookstore;DB_CLOSE_ON_EXIT=FALSE"/>
      <property name="hibernate.connection.driver_class"
          value="org.h2.Driver"/>
      <property name="hibernate.connection.username" value="sa"/>
      <property name="hibernate.connection.password" value=""/>
    </properties>
  </persistence-unit>
</persistence>
```

The `Book` object shown in the previous section is configured here as a JPA entity. In addition, the H2 connection and driver definition are configured and the persistence unit name is set to `bookStore`.

Now back to the Spring configuration from listing 6.6. With the `EntityManagerFactory` defined, you can inject it into the Activiti process engine configuration ❹. This activates the JPA extension in the Activiti Engine, and JPA-annotated classes will be matched against a JPA entity manager. The BPMN 2.0 process definition shown in listing 6.5 is deployed to the engine as well.

The last piece is the Spring bean `bookService` ❺. The Java implementation of this class has to create and persist the JPA book object and return it to the process instance as a new process variable. That sounds like quite a bit of coding to do, but as you can see in the next listing, it's short and easy.

Listing 6.7 Implementation of the Spring bean `bookService`

```
public class BookService {

  @PersistenceContext
  private EntityManager entityManager;

  public Book createBook(List<String> authorList) {
```

```
    Book book = new Book();
    for (String author : authorList) {
      book.getAuthors().add(author);
    }
    entityManager.persist(book);
    return book;
  }
}
```

To persist the Java book object, you need a JPA entity manager. With Spring's dependency injection, it's a simple matter of adding the `@PersistenceContext` annotation to the class to have the Spring container inject it. Note that you don't have to define a `Transactional` annotation, because the Activiti Engine takes care of starting and committing the JPA transaction.

At the start of the process, a list of authors should be provided as a process variable. When you create a new `Book` instance, that list of authors is added and the JPA entity manager persists it to the H2 database defined in the jpa-persistence.xml file.

Now that we've covered all elements of the new book project process implementation, let's move on to validate your implementation with a unit test.

6.3.3   *Testing a process with JPA extensions*

Because you've used the Spring container to glue the Activiti Engine together with the JPA `EntityManagerFactory`, writing a unit test for this process isn't that hard. You just need to start a new process instance, complete the user form, and validate afterward that the book object is stored in the H2 database with the right values (see the next listing).

Listing 6.8   Test to validate the book object in the H2 database

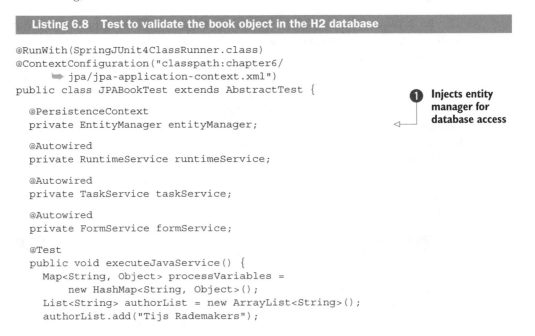

```
@RunWith(SpringJUnit4ClassRunner.class)
@ContextConfiguration("classpath:chapter6/
     ➡ jpa/jpa-application-context.xml")
public class JPABookTest extends AbstractTest {          ❶ Injects entity
                                                            manager for
  @PersistenceContext                                       database access
  private EntityManager entityManager;

  @Autowired
  private RuntimeService runtimeService;

  @Autowired
  private TaskService taskService;

  @Autowired
  private FormService formService;

  @Test
  public void executeJavaService() {
    Map<String, Object> processVariables =
        new HashMap<String, Object>();
    List<String> authorList = new ArrayList<String>();
    authorList.add("Tijs Rademakers");
```

```
        authorList.add("Ron van Liempd");
        processVariables.put("authorList", authorList);

        runtimeService.startProcessInstanceByKey(
            "jpaTest", processVariables);
        Task task = taskService
            .createTaskQuery()
            .singleResult();
        Map<String, String> formProperties =
            new HashMap<String, String>();
        formProperties.put("booktitle", "Activiti in Action");
        formProperties.put("isbn", "123456");
        formService.submitTaskFormData(task.getId(),
            formProperties);

        Book book = (Book) entityManager.createQuery(
            "from Book b where b.title = ?")
                .setParameter(1, "Activiti in Action")
                .getSingleResult();
        assertNotNull(book);
        assertEquals("Activiti in Action", book.getTitle());
        assertEquals("Executable business " +
            "processes in BPMN 2.0", book.getSubTitle());
        assertEquals(2, book.getAuthors().size());
        assertEquals("Tijs Rademakers",
            book.getAuthors().get(0));
    }
}
```

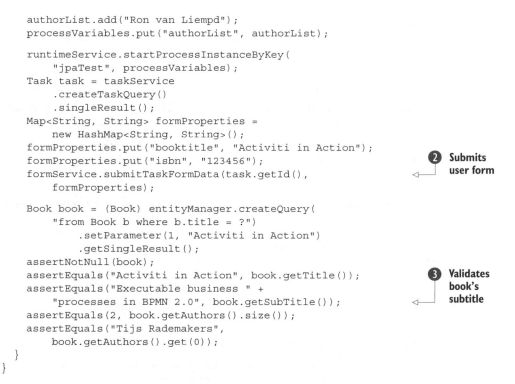

2 Submits
user form

3 Validates
book's
subtitle

To be able to validate the Book entity object after the process instance has ended, you need an EntityManager to access the database via JPA **1**. After the process instance is started with a list of authors, the user task is retrieved and the book title and ISBN user form values are submitted using the FormService **2**. The FormService is a handy interface to simulate a user filling in a user task form.

After the process instance has ended, you can check whether the Book entity object was created and persisted in the H2 database. Because you're testing with this book's name, the subTitle attribute should be filled **3**.

> **NOTE** There is an important requirement to using the Activiti JPA extension. All JPA entity objects should have an @Id-annotated primary key. @EmbeddedId and @IdClass aren't supported. This is something to be aware of when using the JPA extension.

This simplified new book project process definition example gave a good overview of the possibilities of the JPA extension. With a checkbox at the JPA extension, there's another interesting and powerful Activiti extension to explore: the event listener.

6.4 Using execution and task listeners

When the process engine executes a process, several things happen in the background that you won't necessarily be aware of. Automatic activities are executed, transitions are performed, and user tasks are created and assigned to the configured users and groups. When you want to get more information out of the process execution, Activiti provides an extension on top of the BPMN 2.0 specification, referred to as execution and task listeners.

Execution listeners can be configured on the process itself, on activities, and on transitions. Task listeners can only be configured on user tasks. These listeners provide great hooks into the process execution, and they can be used for things like business process monitoring and simpler things like flexibly assigning a group of candidate users to a user task. Table 6.1 provides an overview of the BPMN 2.0 constructs and event types that can be monitored using the Activiti execution and task listeners extension.

Table 6.1 An overview of the event types that can be configured in a BPMN 2.0 XML process definition using the Activiti execution and task listeners extension

BPMN 2.0 construct	Event types	Description
Process	start, end	A start and end event of a process instance can be captured with a process execution listener
Activity	start, end	A start and end execution listener of an activity can be implemented
Transition	take	A transition execution listener can catch a take transition event
User task	create, assignment, complete	A user task throws events when it's created, when the task assignment has been performed, and when the user task has been completed

As you can see in table 6.1, it's possible to configure execution and task listeners on most elements of the BPMN process definition. But how does this work in practice? Let's start by looking at a short example and then dive into the code to figure it out.

6.4.1 Modeling a process with execution and task listeners

In chapter 14, we'll be discussing business events in-depth with real-life examples. In this section, we'll focus on learning about the implementation of execution and task listeners in Activiti with a simplified and imaginary process. Because execution and task listeners watch and react on the process execution, it works a bit like gossip magazines that follow everything that happens with celebrities and gossip about it. You can make a simple process definition of this, where celebrity Brad goes out for a drink (see figure 6.15).

Because execution and task listeners are an extension provided by the Activiti Engine, you can't make use of standard BPMN 2.0 elements to model the catching of events in figure 6.15. In this model, you use text annotations to point out all the events that will be caught during the execution of the process instance.

This fictitious process definition doesn't need a lot of explaining, so let's start implementing this process definition with BPMN 2.0 XML.

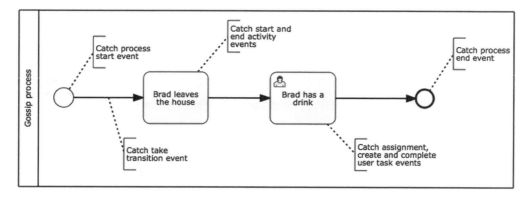

Figure 6.15 An imaginary process definition of gossiping about Brad going out for a drink

6.4.2 *Implementing execution and task listeners*

Activiti supports two types of listeners, the ExecutionListener and the TaskListener. The ExecutionListener can be used to implement a listener for the process, activity, and transition event types. The TaskListener is solely dedicated to the listener implementation of a user task.

Execution and task listeners can be implemented as Java classes but can also be configured with expressions that call JavaBeans. In the gossip process implementation, you'll use all the supported types of listeners, so let's first walk through that BPMN 2.0 XML definition.

Listing 6.9 The processEventListener.bpmn20.xml process with event listeners

```
<definitions xmlns="http://www.omg.org/spec/BPMN/20100524/MODEL"
    xmlns:activiti="http://activiti.org/bpmn"
    targetNamespace="http://www.bpmnwithactiviti.org/
        ➥ processeventlistener">

  <process id="gossipProcess">
    <extensionElements>
      <activiti:executionListener
        class="org.bpmnwithactiviti.chapter6.
            ➥ listener.GossipAboutProcess"
        event="start" />
      <activiti:executionListener
        class="org.bpmnwithactiviti.chapter6.
            ➥ listener.GossipAboutProcess"
        event="end" />
    </extensionElements>
    <startEvent id="theStart" />
    <sequenceFlow sourceRef="theStart"
                  targetRef="bradLeavesHouseTask">
      <extensionElements>
        <activiti:executionListener
          expression="${gossipTransition.gossip(execution)}"/>
      </extensionElements>
    </sequenceFlow>
```

❶ Process start execution listener

❷ Takes transition execution listener

```
<scriptTask id="bradLeavesHouseTask" scriptFormat="groovy">
  <extensionElements>
    <activiti:executionListener
        expression="${gossipActivity.gossipStart(
            ➡ execution)}"
        event="start" />
    <activiti:executionListener
        expression="${gossipActivity.gossipEnd(
            ➡ execution)}"
        event="end" />
  </extensionElements>
  <script>
    out:println "Brad leaves the house";
  </script>
</scriptTask>
<sequenceFlow sourceRef="bradLeavesHouseTask"
            targetRef="bradHasADrinkTask" />
<userTask id="bradHasADrinkTask"
        activiti:assignee="Brad">
  <extensionElements>
    <activiti:taskListener
        expression="${gossipUserTask.gossipTask(
            ➡ task, task.eventName)}"
        event="assignment" />
    <activiti:taskListener
        expression="${gossipUserTask.gossipTask(
            ➡ task, task.eventName)}"
        event="create" />
    <activiti:taskListener
        expression="${execution.setVariable(
            ➡ 'readyDrinking', true)}"
        event="complete"/>
  </extensionElements>
</userTask>
<sequenceFlow sourceRef="bradHasADrinkTask"
            targetRef="theEnd" />
<endEvent id="theEnd" />
  </process>
</definitions>
```

3 Activity start execution listener

4 User task assignment task listener

5 Creates readyDrinking variable on complete task

Because you implement all the available Activiti listeners in this example, it's a long BPMN 2.0 XML definition. In this listing, you use two types of listener implementations: classes and expressions. To show how you can leverage the Spring framework to implement a listener, you run the Activiti Engine inside a Spring container in this example.

The first listener defined in the listing is the start process execution listener **1**. When the process is started, the GossipAboutProcess class is invoked with an execution context as input parameter. An execution listener that's configured with the class attribute is obliged to implement the ExecutionListener interface, as in the following code snippet of the process listener implementation:

```
public class GossipAboutProcess implements ExecutionListener {
  @Override
  public void notify(DelegateExecution execution)
      throws Exception {
```

```
        System.out.println(
            "Did you know the following process event occurred = "
                + execution.getEventName());
        EventUtil.addEvent(execution, "process");
    }
}
```

The `ExecutionListener` interface has one method, `notify`, which must be implemented. The `DelegateExecution` input parameter can be used to retrieve the necessary information about the event and to get information from the process, like process variables. In this case, you print the name of the event that has been fired, which can be `start` or `end` for a process event listener. In addition, you call an `EventUtil` class to add this event to an event stack list that can later be used to test if the events were fired as expected. Let's quickly look at the `EventUtil` class:

```
public class EventUtil {
  @SuppressWarnings("unchecked")
  public static void addEvent(DelegateExecution execution,
      String source) {
    List<String> eventList = (List<String>)
        execution.getVariable("eventList");
    if(eventList == null) {
      eventList = new ArrayList<String>();
    }
    eventList.add(source + ":" + execution.getEventName());
    execution.setVariable("eventList", eventList);
  }
}
```

The `addEvent` method retrieves the `eventList` variable from the process context and adds the event to the event stack list. The `EventUtil` class contains another `addEvent` method to add the task listener event you'll see in a bit because that listener has a process context parameter different from `DelegateExecution`, namely `DelegateTask`.

Back to the BPMN 2.0 XML from listing 6.9. Another execution listener that's implemented for the gossip process is the `take` transition listener ❷. When the transition is executed, this execution listener is fired. The `gossipTransition` part of the expression refers to a Spring bean. On this Spring bean, the gossip method is invoked with the `DelegateExecution` instance as an input parameter. The implementation class is similar to the `GossipAboutProcess` class but without the need to implement the `ExecutionListener` interface. It can be found in the source code of this book.

Another example of an execution listener is the start event listener ❸, which is also configured as a Spring bean. This activity execution listener is similar to the process and transition execution listeners.

The task listeners configured on the user task are a different beast. When the user task is started, the Spring bean corresponding to the `GossipAboutUserTask` class is invoked ❹. To implement a listener on a user task using the `class` attribute, the `TaskListener` interface must be implemented. But, in this example, you use the `expression` attribute instead and pass the `task` and `eventName` variables into the Spring bean yourself. Let's look at the implementation in the next short listing.

Listing 6.10   `TaskListener` interface implementation to listen for user task events

```java
public class GossipAboutUserTask

  public void gossipTask(DelegateTask task,
      String eventName) {

    if(TaskListener.EVENTNAME_CREATE.equals(eventName)) {
      System.out.println(
          "Drink user task is created and assigned to John");
      task.setAssignee("John");                                    ← ❶ Sets a new assignee
    } else if(TaskListener.EVENTNAME_ASSIGNMENT
        .equals(eventName)) {
      System.out.println(
          "Drink user task is assigned to " +
              task.getAssignee());
    }
    EventUtil.addEvent(task, eventName);
  }
}
```

While an execution listener can be used to retrieve information from the process context and set process variables, a task listener can change the assignment of a user task. This gives you great flexibility to implement custom assignment logic when a simple assignment doesn't suit your functional requirements.

First, you need to know which task event type has been fired. In this example, the assignee of the user task is changed to John when the task event type is create ❶. In the task listener implementation, the assignee configuration of the BPMN 2.0 XML definition, Brad, is overridden.

> **TIP**   The order of events for a user task is maybe not what you would expect. The first event that's thrown is the assignment event. After the assignment is handled, the user task create event is fired. When the user task assignment is changed in the task listener, a new assignment event will be thrown. Only change the assignment of the user task in a create event. When it's done inside an assignment event, a StackOverflowError exception is thrown in the Activiti Engine, because the assignment event is then called in a loop.

Enough said about the task listener implementation; let's return for a last comment to the BPMN 2.0 XML definition from listing 6.9. An execution or task listener can also be implemented with an expression that doesn't involve an additional Java class or bean. In the gossip process definition, a new process variable will be created when the user task is completed ❺ and no additional Java class definition is needed to implement this. Now let's see how to test the event stack list to validate the execution of the various listeners.

6.4.3   *Testing the event stack list*

In other examples in this book, we used the HistoryService to get information about the process flow execution after a process instance was ended. Execution and task listeners aren't part of that history information because they aren't process activities.

Therefore, we need another way to validate whether the listeners were executed and if the order of execution was what we expected it to be. In the implementation, we therefore build up an event stack list.

But, as you may recall from the history configuration discussion of chapter 3, process variable information is only stored in the history tables if the history configuration is set to full. In the event listener example, this is done with the history property of the SpringProcessEngineConfiguration in the Spring application context file (gossip-application-context.xml). The Spring configuration file can be found in chapter 6's resources folder in the book's source code.

The test class you have to implement must use the Spring testing functionality to make sure the Spring application context is built up in the right way (see the following listing).

> **Listing 6.11   Test class to validate the execution of the various listeners**

```
@RunWith(SpringJUnit4ClassRunner.class)
@ContextConfiguration("classpath:chapter6/listener
     ➥ gossip-application-context.xml")
public class ProcessListenerTest extends AbstractTest {

  @Autowired
  private RuntimeService runtimeService;

  @Autowired
  private TaskService taskService;

  @Autowired
  private HistoryService historyService;

  @SuppressWarnings("unchecked")
  @Test
  public void gossip() {
    ProcessInstance processInstance = runtimeService
        .startProcessInstanceByKey("gossipProcess");
    assertNotNull(processInstance);
    Task task = taskService
        .createTaskQuery()
        .taskAssignee("John")                          ❶ Task is reassigned
        .singleResult();                                  to John
    taskService.complete(task.getId());
    List<HistoricDetail> historyList = historyService
        .createHistoricDetailQuery()
        .variableUpdates()                             ❷ Queries only
        .list();                                          variable updates

    assertEquals(9, historyList.size());
    HistoricVariableUpdate variableUpdate =
        (HistoricVariableUpdate)
              historyList.get(historyList.size() - 1);
    assertEquals("eventList",
        variableUpdate.getVariableName());
    List<String> variableList =                        ❸ Variable must be
        (List<String>) variableUpdate.getValue();         a list of Strings
```

```
        assertEquals("process:start", variableList.get(0));
        assertEquals("transition:take", variableList.get(1));
        assertEquals("activity:start", variableList.get(2));
        assertEquals("process:end",
            variableList.get(variableList.size() - 1));
        }
}
```

Transition take event should be ❹ second

When a gossip process instance is started, the first wait state is the user task. In the process definition, the user task is assigned to Brad, but in the task listener of listing 6.10 it's reassigned to John. Therefore, you need to query on assignee John ❶ to find the waiting user task.

After the user task is completed, thereby finishing the process instance, you can query the historic information of the ended process instance ❷. Because you want to validate the event stack list, the Activiti Engine should only return the variable updates. Note that in this example you have no form properties and, therefore, the `variableUpdates` method could also be removed to get the same query result.

The event stack list is implemented with the `eventList` process variable, which is a collection of `Strings` ❸.

As you've seen in this example, the use of execution and task listeners can help you to listen for certain events during the process execution. This can provide input to applications, such as business application monitoring applications, which we'll discuss in chapter 14. The task listener provides another layer of flexibility because it provides a way to assign a user task at runtime with custom logic.

6.5   *Summary*

In the previous chapters, we gradually built up the pace to get familiar with the Activiti platform and the BPMN 2.0 specification. But, in this chapter, we stepped it up a bit to introduce you to several more advanced features of Activiti.

Subprocesses can help a lot to increase the readability, flexibility, and reusability of your business processes and, therefore, are first-class citizens of the BPMN 2.0 specification. To run activities in parallel during process execution, the parallel gateway was introduced. The main thing to remember about parallel gateways is that process execution isn't split into multiple threads, but the execution paths are completed until a wait state is reached.

In addition to the subprocess and parallel gateway BPMN 2.0 constructs, two Activiti extensions were highlighted. First, the Activiti Engine provides integration with the JPA persistency standard to make it easy to access database entities from the process instance. Without any additional coding, a customer can be retrieved from a database table based on a customer identifier. Second, execution and task listeners are part of the Activiti Engine implementation. Start and end events can be captured from process, transition, and activity elements of a process definition. And to make it possible to use custom logic at runtime to deal with user tasks, the `create`, `assignment`, and `complete` events can be caught.

With the introduction in the previous chapters and the advanced features introduced in this chapter, you can already implement complex business process can already be implemented. But to be able to implement real-life processes, you need to deal with error handling. That's what we'll talk about in the next chapter.

Dealing with error handling

Having read the first six chapters, you now know a lot about BPMN 2.0 and Activiti. You've been introduced to the tools, taken a good look at the Activiti Engine services API, implemented a real-world business process, and deployed that process on Activiti Engine. In the examples in the previous chapters, we focused on happy flow processes. Now, it's time to start thinking about error handling.

In chapter 5, we implemented a simplified credit check script task, but, if the credit check logic is implemented with a service call to an external component, a lot of errors could occur. Think about "Customer not found" or connection errors; how could they be handled in a BPMN process definition?

There generally are two ways of dealing with errors in a BPMN process definition running on Activiti. The first option is to use the standard BPMN error handling constructs. The second option is to use Java logic and Java service tasks to implement error handling. In section 7.1, we'll discuss the general idea behind both approaches. In section 7.2, we'll look at how you can implement a full business process with the BPMN error handling elements. In the implementation of this example, we'll use the Activiti Designer to speed up the development process. Then, in section 7.3, we'll implement the business process again but, this time, using Java logic to implement the error handling.

To get a good overview of the two approaches to error handling, we'll start by looking at the different ways in which BPMN and Activiti can help you implement error handling logic.

7.1 Choosing between error handling options

Drawing a process model without thinking about possible exceptions or errors is usually not difficult. But, at some point, error handling strategies must be implemented in the process model to make it enterprise ready. What must happen to the process execution when an order fails to be persisted in a database? Must it be handled by a process administrator, or can somebody solve the error using a user task? These kinds of questions need to be answered before the process definition can be regarded as complete.

Implementing error handling in a process model isn't an easy task, but the BPMN standard and the Activiti Engine provide flexible ways to deal with error logic. Section 7.1.1 provides an introduction to error end events and error boundary events as part of the BPMN standard, and, in section 7.1.2, we'll look at using Java logic to implement error handling.

7.1.1 Using error end and boundary events

The first option to think about when implementing error handling is the use of error end events and error boundary events. These constructs are part of the BPMN 2.0 standard and make it possible to design error handling strategies as part of the process model. We already used boundary events in chapters 5 and 6 with the time boundary event. You learned there that you can define a boundary event on a task (often a service task or a user task) and an embedded subprocess.

Error boundary events provide a way to catch errors that occur during process execution; if an error occurs within a subprocess, the error boundary event can be used to catch that error and handle it the way you want it to be handled. To be able to catch an error, you must also be able to throw an error. The need to explicitly throw an error with an error end event is the main difference with the Java exception style of handling errors. Java exceptions occur during Java execution, and they can be caught using standard Java code. Therefore, they can be regarded as technical errors. With error boundary events, the errors need to be explicitly thrown in the process model by using error end events; this type of error is a logical error.

NOTE   Using error boundary events can be regarded as logical error handling because it always requires an error end event for such an error to be fired. Java logic in a service task can be used to implement technical error handling to deal with problems like database connection and web service communication failures.

Because you need an error end event in order to fire an error, an error boundary event must be defined on an embedded subprocess or a call activity. When an error end event is executed in an embedded subprocess or a standalone subprocess, an error boundary event will catch that error. In section 7.2, we'll work through a full example using error end events and error boundary events. For now, let's focus on the basic explanation with a simple process model, shown in figure 7.1.

The symbol for an error end event is the same as a normal end event, but it contains a Z-like icon. The error boundary event contains a similar icon. In the review user task, it's determined whether there are order details lacking. If the necessary order details aren't provided, the error end event is reached. This will throw an error, which is caught by the error boundary event. The error boundary event triggers another user task to complete the order details and executes the embedded subprocess again.

Note that this example only explains the use of the error end event and error boundary event. For this example, you could also leave out the error events and move the "additional order details" user task to the position of the error end event. Then, you could draw the outgoing sequence flow out of the "additional order details" task directly to the "Review order details" user task. But, using the error end event may add

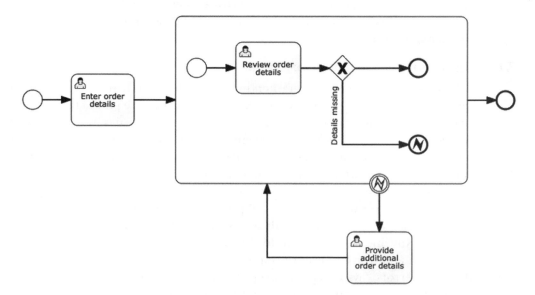

Figure 7.1   Example process showing the use of an error end event and an error boundary event. When there are order details missing, an error end event is thrown and then caught by the error boundary event defined on the embedded subprocess.

more semantics to the process definition to indicate that missing order details should be regarded as a logical error.

How are the error end event and the error boundary event correlated? You can imagine process definitions where there are multiple error end events and error boundary events. The error events contain an error code attribute, which should uniquely define that specific error event. If the error end event and error boundary event each define an error definition with the same error code, they're correlated. You can also define an error boundary event without a reference to an error code to catch all errors that occur within the scope on which the boundary event is defined.

Now that you've been introduced to logical error handling using error end events and error boundary events, let's look at how to deal with technical errors. Using Java logic, you can implement routing logic to choose between outgoing sequence flows to direct the process execution based on the occurrence of an exception.

7.1.2 *Using Java logic for error handling*

It's always good to have a choice in how you implement something like error handling. The Activiti Engine provides this flexibility by supporting both the standard BPMN error handling constructs as well as error handling via Java exceptions. For each error handling implementation, you could choose either one of the two solutions, but there are semantic differences.

With the error end event and error boundary event constructs, you explicitly design the error handling as part of the process model. Choosing the Java logic approach means that the error handling is implemented inside a service task and, therefore, is not part of the process model. Figure 7.2 shows a simplified process model with the Java exception approach.

In figure 7.1, you saw the error handling logic as part of the process model, but, with the Java logic approach, it's not explicitly modeled. Figure 7.2 shows a simplified order-entry process, where the order is persisted in the database via a service task. If you don't implement any error handling logic in the process implementation, the

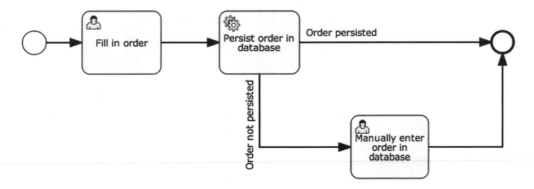

Figure 7.2 Example process model containing error handling with the Java logic approach. In the process model, only multiple outgoing sequence flows are designed out of the service task.

process transaction will roll back when an exception occurs in the persistence logic of the service task. At runtime, this means that the user who fills in the order in a task entry application (like Activiti Explorer) would get an error message when the user task is completed. The transaction of the process is rolled back, and the current state again is the "Fill in order" user task.

This might be good enough for the requirements of the process model, and, in that case, you don't have to implement error handling logic. But, in some cases, you may want to catch the database persistence exception and direct it to a specific administrator user task. With requirements like those, the Java logic approach would fit nicely.

As you can see in figure 7.2, there are two sequence flows going out of the database persistence service task. This means that you can implement decision logic in the service task to choose which sequence flow it should take next. You can implement logic to take sequence flow A if the order is persisted, and to take sequence flow B if a database exception occurred and the order isn't persisted. Let's see how this is implemented in a Java service task.

Listing 7.1   Java service task using Java error handling logic

```java
public class OrderPersistTask implements ActivityBehavior {

  @PersistenceContext
  EntityManager entityManager;

  @Override
  public void execute(ActivityExecution execution)
      throws Exception {
    PvmTransition transition = null;
    try {
      Order order = (Order) execution.getVariable("order");
      entityManager.persist(order);
      transition = execution
          .getActivity()
          .findOutgoingTransition("orderPersisted");
    } catch(Throwable e) {
      transition = execution
          .getActivity()
          .findOutgoingTransition("orderNotPersisted");
    }
    execution.take(transition);
  }
}
```

❶ Get the right sequence flow

❷ Take the retrieved sequence flow

When you want to implement decision logic in a Java service task, the `ActivityBehavior` interface must be implemented instead of the `JavaDelegate` interface. The `Activity-Behavior` interface provides more functionality to control the execution of the process. But, be aware that using the `ActivityBehavior` interface also means that you must explicitly implement logic to leave the service task, as you can see in the last line of the listing with the `take` method invocation ❷. When you use the `JavaDelegate` interface, this isn't necessary because it will take care of leaving the service task when the `execute` method is completed.

Note that you try to persist an `Order` instance via the JPA `EntityManager`. When the database transaction is committed, the sequence flow with an identifier of `order-Persisted` is retrieved ❶. A sequence flow is represented inside the Activiti Engine as a `PvmTransition` instance. When an exception occurs, another sequence flow (with the `orderNotPersisted` identifier) is retrieved.

This approach shows an alternative way of handling errors inside a BPMN process model. Note that this approach is limited to Java service tasks. To complete our overview of error handling patterns in process models running on the Activiti Engine, we'll now take a look at how to use both error handling approaches together in the next section.

7.1.3 *Using both error handling approaches together*

To show that the BPMN error event and Java logic error handling approaches can be used in a flexible manner in the Activiti Engine, we'll use both mechanisms together. This isn't an uncommon way of implementing error handling. With the Java logic approach, you can elegantly handle technical errors in a Java service task. And, by using BPMN error end events and error boundary events, you can make sure that the error handling logic is explicitly designed as part of the process model. That isn't the case when using only the Java logic approach, as you saw in the previous section.

To be able to compare the two options—one using the Java error handling approach and the other combining BPMN error event constructs and Java exceptions—we'll use the same order-entry process example as in figure 7.2. In figure 7.3, there's also a BPMN error end event and an error boundary event.

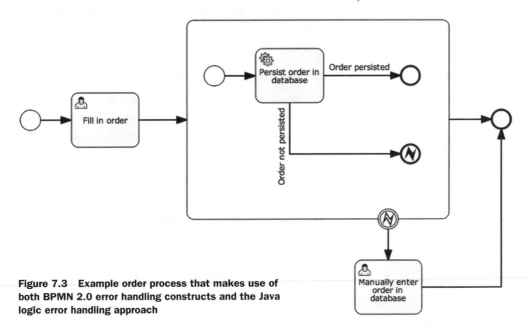

Figure 7.3   Example order process that makes use of both BPMN 2.0 error handling constructs and the Java logic error handling approach

Because we're using the BPMN 2.0 error handling constructs in this sample order process, we must also define a scope with an embedded subprocess to be able to use the error boundary event. When you compare the order processes of figures 7.2 and 7.3, the main difference is that the error handling strategy is explicitly defined in figure 7.3 and implicitly in figure 7.2. The execution flow of both processes is similar, so the differences are more on a semantic level.

In general, it can be said that, if you want to explicitly model the error handling strategies in a process definition, you should use BPMN 2.0 error handling constructs. This approach makes sure that error handling is clearly defined and provides insight to every reader of the process model. If the error handling is technical and it would only clutter the process definition, you could choose the Java logic approach. Remember that this is only possible for Java service tasks.

A third approach is shown in figure 7.3 and combines both error handling approaches. In the combined approach, a technical Java exception is transformed into a logical error with an error end event. This approach is handy if a technical exception is of importance in the process execution flow and therefore should be made explicit with an error end event.

Enough said about the approaches to error handling. Let's get our hands dirty with the implementation of a sales opportunity business processes with error handling.

7.2   Implementing error handling with BPMN 2.0 constructs

To show the usage of the error end event and the error boundary event in a BPMN 2.0 process, we'll implement a sales opportunity process. And, to make the process implementation similar to a real-world project, the service tasks invoke an external service—in this example, a web service—to execute the necessary logic. We have a lot of good stuff coming up, starting with the sample implementation overview.

7.2.1   Designing the sales opportunity process solution

To implement a full sales opportunity process solution, you have to deal with quite a few components. Therefore, we'll start this section off with a high-level design of the solution to give you a good picture of what you'll be implementing in the remainder of this section. Figure 7.4 shows the design of the sales opportunity process implementation and the web service application you'll be invoking.

The `book-sales-app` application shown in figure 7.4 contains a web service that uses a `CustomerDAO` class to retrieve customers and store sales opportunities to an H2 opportunity database instance. It uses Spring to manage the dependencies, Hibernate JPA for persistence, and Apache CXF for the web service implementation. In the book's source code, you can find the full web application.

For the sales opportunity process implementation, you only need to concern yourself with the customer web service because that will be the interface you'll be communicating with from the service tasks. Let's look at the web service operations in a screenshot of the WSDL Design view in Eclipse (see figure 7.5).

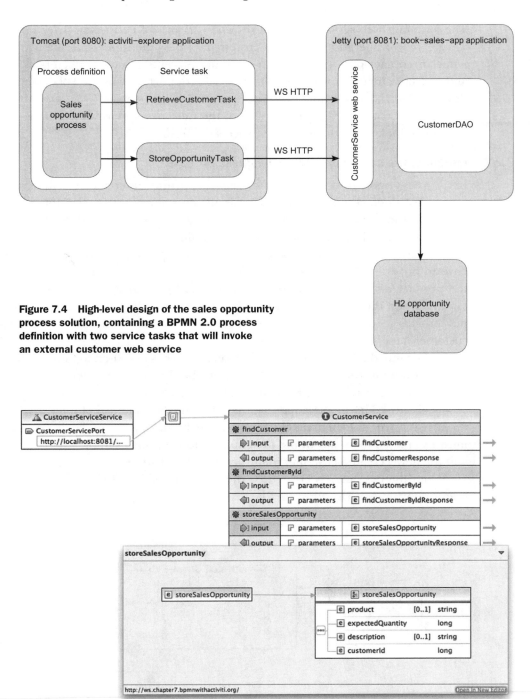

Figure 7.4   High-level design of the sales opportunity process solution, containing a BPMN 2.0 process definition with two service tasks that will invoke an external customer web service

Figure 7.5   The WSDL Design view in Eclipse showing the customer web service interface. The input parameters of the storeSalesOpportunity **operation are highlighted.**

The customer web service interface shown in figure 7.5 consists of three operations. There are two operations to find a customer, one by identifier and one by customer name or contact person. The third operation accepts input parameters as `product` and `customerId` and stores them as a new sales opportunity in the H2 database using the `CustomerDAO` class from figure 7.4.

Now that you have a good overview of the full sales opportunity process solution, it's time to look at the details of the process definition itself.

7.2.2   Modeling the sales opportunity business process

In the sales opportunity process, a new sales opportunity is created for an existing customer. An added complication is that, when a customer isn't yet available in the Customer Relationship Management application, it has to be created. Figure 7.6 shows the process model, created with the Activiti Modeler.

To start a new process instance of the sales opportunity process definition, you have to provide information about the sales opportunity. The input parameters are the product name, expected quantity, a description, and the customer identifier, if known. When the customer identifier isn't known, the first step in the sales opportunity process is to provide additional information about the customer, including the customer name and a contact person.

In the embedded subprocess scope, a service task is executed to find the customer, based on the information provided. This can be the customer identifier or the provided additional customer information. This service task will invoke the customer web service discussed in the previous section. When the customer isn't found, an error end event is thrown and then caught by the error boundary event. Then, the customer must be created manually in the CRM application (in our example, the H2 database) and the newly created customer identifier must be provided.

When the customer is created or the customer is found by the service task, the sales opportunity is stored in the database, again, via the customer web service. The

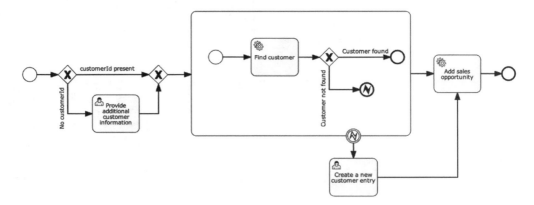

Figure 7.6   A sales opportunity process model that makes use of BPMN error handling constructs. When a customer isn't found, it has to be created, and the customer identifier must be provided via a user task.

process instance is then completed. Now that you have the process model defined, you can implement the process in an executable BPMN 2.0 XML process definition.

7.2.3 *Implementing a BPMN process with the Activiti Designer*

To implement the sales opportunity process definition, you could write the raw BPMN 2.0 XML like you did in the previous chapters and examples. But, when you have already modeled the process definition in the Activiti Modeler (or another BPMN 2.0 compliant process modeler), it's very easy to kick-start the implementation using the Activiti Designer's import functionality. As we look at using the Activiti Designer, we'll also focus on the implementation of the error handling constructs in the sales opportunity process definition.

In chapter 3, we covered how to install the Activiti Designer, so let's start it up. To import the sales opportunity process, you first need to create an Activiti project using Activiti's new project wizard in Eclipse. For this example, name the project `SalesOpportunity`. When the project is created, you can right-click on the project and choose Import BPMN 2.0 file (see figure 7.7).

When you click on the Import BPMN 2.0 file action, a file browser

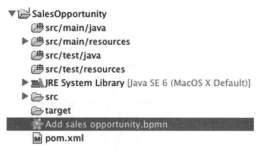

Figure 7.7   The BPMN import command in the Activiti Designer Eclipse plugin

opens so that you can select an XML file for import. When you model a process with the Activiti Modeler and save the diagram, two XML files are created: a signavio.xml file that contains meta-information about the diagram, such as the name of the author and a description, and a bpmn20.xml file that contains the BPMN 2.0 XML and the BPMN Diagram Interchange (DI) information.

BPMN Diagram Interchange (DI)

The Object Management Group (OMG) standardization organization released BPMN 2.0 in January 2011. The main difference from BPMN 1.x was the addition of an executable process definition language using XML. But, in addition to the step forward of being an executable as well as modeling language, the BPMN 2.0 specification added a diagram interchange language.

This diagram interchange language ensures that process diagrams created with one process modeling tool can also be read and maintained by another. They then both have to support the diagram interchange format. The diagram interchange information is also specified in XML and contains the graphical data of the process model; it contains width, height, and x and y position information about the shapes representing the BPMN events, tasks, gateways, and so on. In addition, it contains the graphical information about the sequence flows connecting the different BPMN elements.

> **(continued)**
> The Activiti Modeler adds DI information to the bpmn20.xml file of any process model created with this tool. The Activiti Designer reads BPMN 2.0 process models (both with and without BPMN DI information) and it creates DI information in the bpmn20.xml file.

By default, the signavio.xml and bpmn20.xml files created by the Activiti Modeler can be found in the workspace/activiti-modeler-examples directory in your Activiti installation directory. This directory is a simple file repository, so you can browse it with any file explorer and you can add and delete process models by copying and deleting the files. If you created the process model shown in figure 7.6 with the Activiti Modeler, you can select the bpmn20.xml file in the activiti-modeler-examples directory with the Eclipse file browser. You can also find the process model files in the book's source code examples in the modeler/chapter7 directory of the `bpmn-examples` project. There you can select the Add sales opportunity.bpmn20.xml file.

After selecting the bpmn20.xml file, the Activiti Designer will read the XML file and create a graphical representation of it. Although the process model may not look exactly the same as shown in the Activiti Modeler, after some manual restructuring, the sales opportunity process model should look similar to the screenshot in figure 7.8.

Now you can fill in the missing information in the sales opportunity process definition. First, you need to add conditional logic to the outgoing sequence flows of the first exclusive gateway. When no customer number (identifier) has been provided in the start form, the Provide Additional Customer Information user task must be executed. Click on the incoming sequence flow of this user task and select the Main Config tab in the Properties view. There, you can fill in the conditional logic, as shown in figure 7.9.

When the `customerNumber` process variable is equal to `0`, the "Provide additional customer information" user task will be executed. To complete the conditional logic,

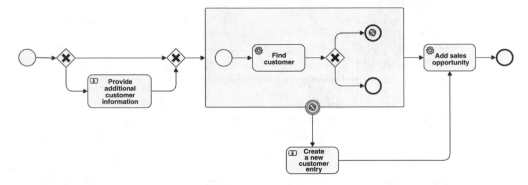

Figure 7.8   The imported sales opportunity process model in the Activiti Designer's canvas

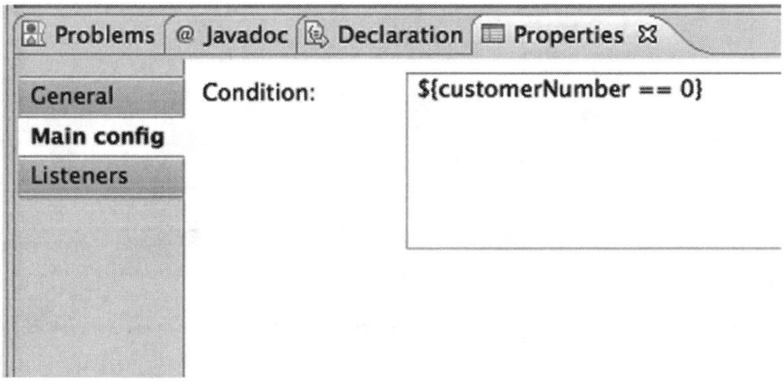

Problems @ Javadoc Declaration Properties ✕

General	Condition:	${customerNumber == 0}
Main config		
Listeners		

Figure 7.9 The Main Config tab in the Properties view of the incoming sequence flow of the "Provide additional customer information" user task

you need to add a condition to the other outgoing sequence flow of the first exclusive gateway as well. There, the conditional logic should be as follows:

```
${customerNumber > 0}
```

The customer number is implemented as a form property that needs to be configured on the start event of the process definition. You can configure the form properties of a start event in its Properties view (see figure 7.10).

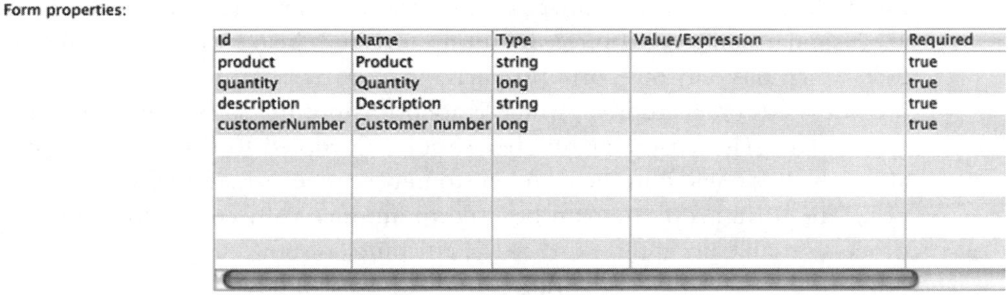

Form properties:

Id	Name	Type	Value/Expression	Required
product	Product	string		true
quantity	Quantity	long		true
description	Description	string		true
customerNumber	Customer number	long		true

Figure 7.10 The Properties view where the form properties of the start event can be configured

When you save the process diagram at this point, you'll notice that the BPMN 2.0 XML hasn't yet been generated due to errors in the process definition. You need to solve these errors (shown in figure 7.11) before the BPMN 2.0 XML will be generated.

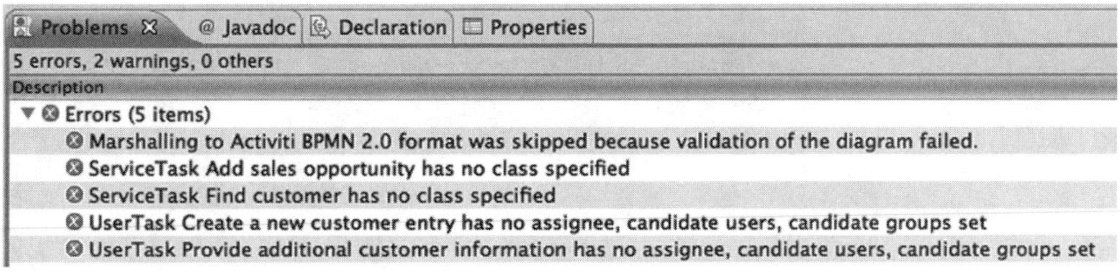

Problems ✕   @ Javadoc Declaration Properties

5 errors, 2 warnings, 0 others

Description

▼ ⊗ Errors (5 items)
  ⊗ Marshalling to Activiti BPMN 2.0 format was skipped because validation of the diagram failed.
  ⊗ ServiceTask Add sales opportunity has no class specified
  ⊗ ServiceTask Find customer has no class specified
  ⊗ UserTask Create a new customer entry has no assignee, candidate users, candidate groups set
  ⊗ UserTask Provide additional customer information has no assignee, candidate users, candidate groups set

Figure 7.11 The Problems view in the Activiti Designer, showing the errors of the sales opportunity process definition

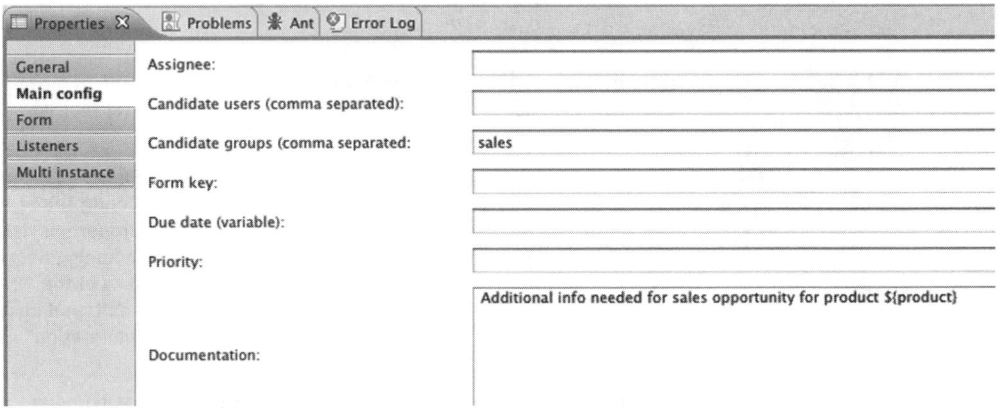

Figure 7.12   The configuration of the additional customer information user task

The service tasks will be implemented in the next section, so we'll focus for now on the user tasks and then the error handling elements. First, you can configure the additional customer information user task to use a `sales` candidate group (see figure 7.12).

You can also configure the form properties for the additional customer information user task with three properties: `customerName`, `contactPerson`, and `customerAddress`.

A similar configuration can be set up for the "Create a new customer entry" user task, which has only one form property, `customerNumber`. In this task form, you must provide a customer number, which is used to store the sales opportunity in the next service task. This customer number should be copied to the customer process variable, which is created in the "Find customer" service task we'll discuss in the next section. The form properties can be used to automatically copy a form field value to a process variable using the `expression` attribute, as shown in figure 7.13.

With the user task configuration in place, we can now focus on the error handling logic. When the "Find customer" service task is unable to retrieve the customer from the CRM application (in our case a web service), the `customerFound` attribute of the `customer` process variable object is set to `false`. We need to add conditional logic to the outgoing sequence flows of the exclusive gateway next to the "Find customer" service task. The sequence flow with the error end event as its target should have the conditional

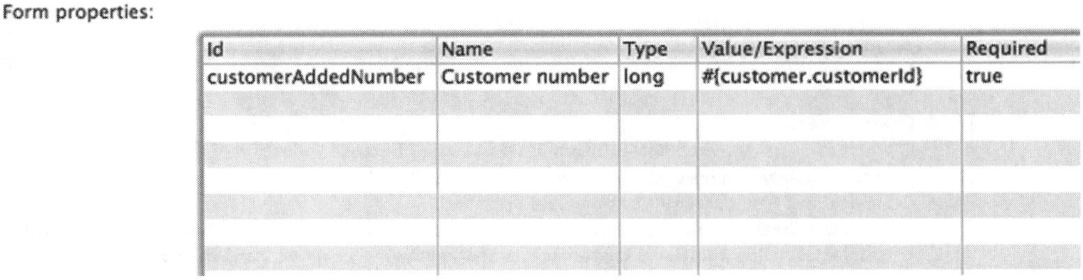

Form properties:

Id	Name	Type	Value/Expression	Required
customerAddedNumber	Customer number	long	#{customer.customerId}	true

Figure 7.13   The Properties tab of the "Create a new customer entry" user task, showing the form property configuration

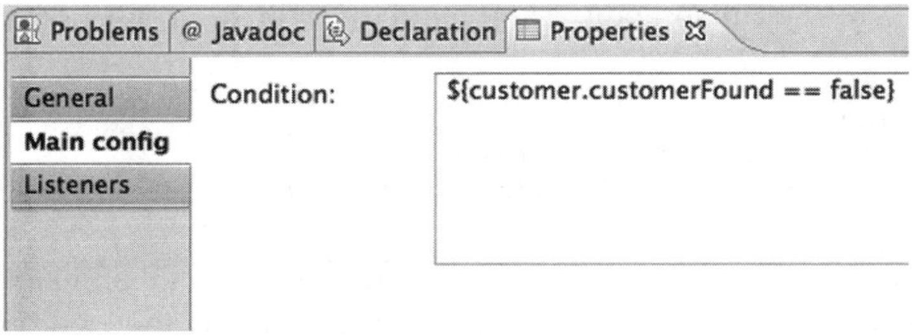

Figure 7.14 The conditional logic of the incoming sequence flow of the error end event

logic configured as shown in figure 7.14. The other sequence flow should have a similar conditional logic configuration with a customerFound validation set to true.

That brings us to the configuration of the error end event and the error boundary error event. These events should be correlated with an error code. The error end event should always have an error definition, so let's configure a customerNotFound error code for this event, as shown in figure 7.15.

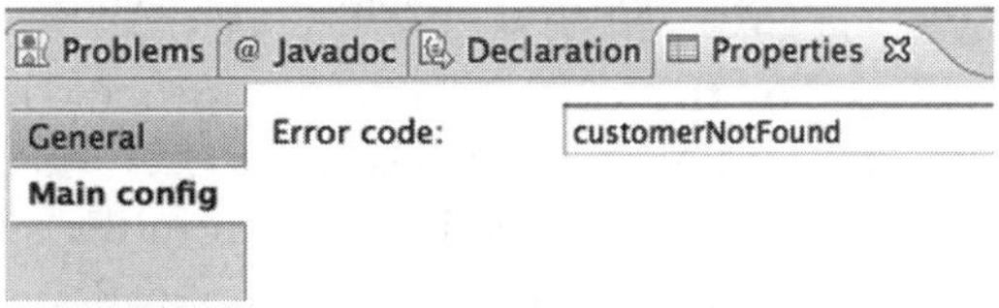

Figure 7.15 The error code configuration of the error end event

For the error boundary event, you can choose not to define an error code at all or to define the same error code as the error end event. If you leave the error code blank, every error that occurs inside the subprocess will be caught by the error boundary event. In this example, only one error end event is defined, so that would work. To make the process definition clearer for another developer, it would be better to define the same error code for the error boundary event.

Although you're not yet able to generate the BPMN 2.0 XML because of the missing implementation configuration of the two service tasks, you can already have a sneak preview of the XML configuration of the error end event and the error boundary event. It's not groundbreaking but it's good to understand the underlying details. The error end event configuration looks like this:

```
<endEvent id="errorendevent1">
  <errorEventDefinition errorRef="customerNotFound" />
</endEvent>
```

The errorRef attribute can be used in two ways. In this example, it's used to define an error code value of customerNotFound. But, you can also use it as a reference to an error definition in the process definition. Such an error definition would look like the following:

```
<error id="customerNotFound" errorCode="123" />
```

The Activiti Designer always generates the errorRef attribute as a plain error code definition without an additional error definition. But, there's no reason to not use the error definition way of configuration. The boundary error event uses similar error definition syntax:

```
<boundaryEvent id="boundaryerror1"
               attachedToRef="subprocess1">
  <errorEventDefinition errorRef="customerNotFound" />
</boundaryEvent>
```

As you saw in previous examples using a timer boundary event, a boundary event is attached to another BPMN element. In the preceding example, the error boundary event is attached to the subprocess. In addition, the error boundary event uses the exact same error event definition element to configure the error that it will handle.

Now we have filled in most of the missing process logic. There are two important pieces missing, namely the two service task implementations.

7.2.4 *Implementing service tasks that invoke a web service*

For the sales opportunity process implementation, we're in need of a CRM application. As you saw in section 7.2.1, we created a web application with a customer web service that can be invoked from the sales opportunity process. Let's use this simple web application as our CRM application for now.

We could use a web service task that's part of the BPMN 2.0 specification to invoke the customer web service, but we'll discuss that option in chapter 11. In this chapter, we'll be using a Java service task with a generated web service client using the Apache CXF framework to invoke the customer web service. The generated web service client code is also part of the bpmn-examples project in the book's source code, but we now need to add it to the Activiti Designer project.

The following plugin configuration should be added to the Maven pom.xml file of the SalesOpportunity project:

```
<build>
  <plugins>
    <plugin>
      <groupId>org.apache.cxf</groupId>
      <artifactId>cxf-codegen-plugin</artifactId>
      <version>2.3.4</version>
      <executions>
        <execution>
          <id>generate-sources</id>
          <phase>generate-sources</phase>
          <configuration>
            <sourceRoot>generated/cxf</sourceRoot>
            <wsdlOptions>
              <wsdlOption>
                <wsdl>src/main/resources/chapter7/errorevent/
                   ➥ wsdl/customerService.wsdl</wsdl>
                <wsdlLocation>http://localhost:8081/book-sales-app/
                   ➥ services/customer?wsdl</wsdlLocation>
              </wsdlOption>
            </wsdlOptions>
          </configuration>
```

```
        <goals>
          <goal>wsdl2java</goal>
        </goals>
      </execution>
    </executions>
  </plugin>
</plugins>
</build>
```

As you can see, the plugin expects a WSDL file in the src/main/resources/chapter7/ errorevent/wsdl folder. The WSDL can be copied from the same location in the bpmn-examples project to your Designer project.

Make sure that the web service client code is generated when executing the mvn eclipse:eclipse command. The web service client code is generated into the generated/cxf folder inside the Designer project. The CustomerServiceService class (the additional Service postfix is generated by the CXF framework) is the main web service client interface for communicating with the customer web service.

Now let's create the RetrieveCustomerTask class (see the following listing) that you'll use for the "Find customer" service task in the Activiti Designer. The class needs to be created in the org.bpmnwithactiviti.chapter7.errorevent package.

Listing 7.2 The RetrieveCustomerTask class that invokes the customer web service

```
public class RetrieveCustomerTask implements JavaDelegate {

  private CustomerServiceService customerService =       ◁— ❶ Instantiates web
      new CustomerServiceService();                              service client

  @Override
  public void execute(DelegateExecution execution)
      throws Exception {
    Long customerId = (Long) execution.getVariable(       ❷ Gets customer number
        "customerNumber");                                    process variable
    Customer customer = null;
    if(customerId > 0) {
      customer = customerService
        .getCustomerServicePort()
        .findCustomerById(customerId);
    } else {
      String customerName = (String) execution.getVariable(
          "customerName");
      String contactPerson = (String) execution.getVariable(
          "contactPerson");
      customer = customerService                          ❸ Invokes
        .getCustomerServicePort()                            findCustomer
        .findCustomer(customerName, contactPerson);   ◁—      operation
    }
    CustomerVariable variable = new CustomerVariable();
    if(customer != null) {
      variable.setCustomerFound(true);
      variable.setCustomerId(customer.getCustomerId());
      variable.setCustomerName(customer.getCustomerName());
      variable.setContactPerson(customer.getContactPerson());
```

```
      variable.setCustomerAddress(
         customer.getCustomerAddress());
   } else {
      variable.setCustomerFound(false);
   }
   execution.setVariable("customer", variable);
  }
}
```

4 Sets customer process variable

To be able to invoke the customer web service, you need an instance of the `Customer-erServiceService` web service client class that you generated with the Apache CXF code generation plugin ❶. And, because you can find customers both on customer identifier as well as customer name and contact person name, you first need to determine if the `customerNumber` process variable ❷ is greater than 0. Then, you can invoke the web service via the web service client class with the `findCustomerById` or the `findCustomer` ❸ operations.

When the response is received from the customer web service, the `CustomerVariable` process variable object is filled with the response parameters when a customer is found. When no customer is found, there's still a `CustomerVariable` instance set as a process variable ❹ but the `customerFound` attribute is set to `false`.

As you can see in the implementation of this service task, it's quite simple to invoke a web service with a generated web service client. We'll discuss the standard BPMN 2.0 web service task in chapter 11, but this way of dealing with web services remains an interesting option.

The `RetrieveCustomerTask` class uses the `CustomerVariable` class, which you haven't created yet. But, this class can be copied from the bpmn-examples project (see the `org.bpmnwithactiviti.chapter7.errorevent` package). Now that you've created the `RetrieveCustomerTask` class, you can configure it to be used on the "Find customer" service task, as shown in figure 7.16.

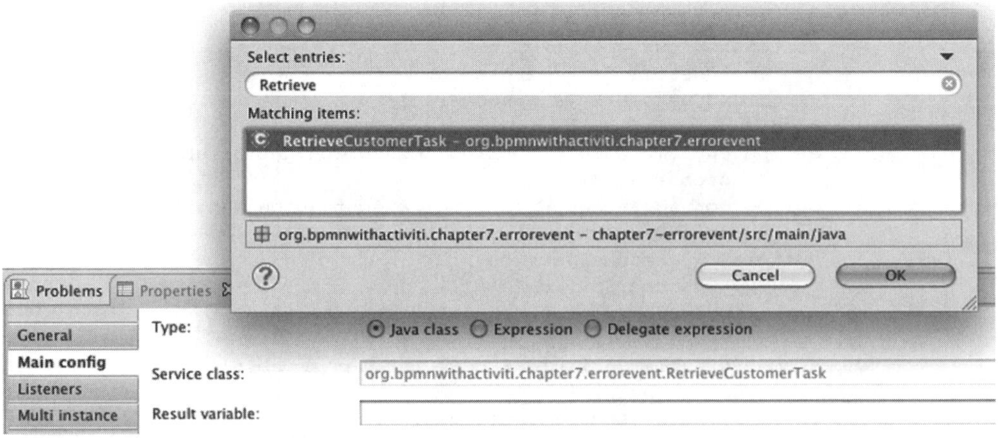

Figure 7.16 The configuration of the find customer service task, which uses the `RetrieveCustomerTask`

Now, there's one Java service task configuration missing, which is the "Add sales opportunity" service task. You need an additional service task class implementation for this: `StoreOpportunityTask`.

Listing 7.3 The `StoreOpportunityTask` class that stores an sales opportunity

```
public class StoreOpportunityTask implements JavaDelegate {

  private CustomerServiceService customerService =
    new CustomerServiceService();

  @Override
  public void execute(DelegateExecution execution)
      throws Exception {
    CustomerVariable customer = (CustomerVariable)        ❶ Gets customer
      execution.getVariable("customer");                     process variable
    String product = (String)
      execution.getVariable("product");
    Long expectedQuantity = (Long)
      execution.getVariable("quantity");
    String description = (String)
      execution.getVariable("description");
    customerService.getCustomerServicePort()
      .storeSalesOpportunity(product, expectedQuantity,   ❷ Stores sales
        description, customer.getCustomerId());               opportunity
  }
}
```

In the `StoreOpportunityTask` class, you store the opportunity information like `product` and `quantity` with a reference to the `customer`. You retrieve the necessary customer ❶ and opportunity information from the process variables. Then, you use the generated web service client to store the sales opportunity in the CRM application ❷.

The last bit of work left is to configure this `JavaDelegate` class on the "new customer entry" Java service task, like you did in figure 7.15.

This completes our design work for the sales opportunity process definition, so let's take it to the next level and start deploying and testing the solution.

7.2.5 *Testing the sales opportunity process solution*

To be able to test the sales opportunity example, you need to start the customer web service application and deploy the sales opportunity process artifacts.

First, start the web service with the `book-sales-app` application, which is part of the book's source code. The web application uses an H2 database running on `localhost`, so make sure the Activiti H2 database is running (with the `ant h2.start` command).

To build and run the web application in Jetty, go to the project's root directory and run the `mvn clean install jetty:run` command. The web application should now be running inside the Jetty web container on port 8081.

The customer web service is now running and ready to be invoked from the sales opportunity process. To test whether the web service is running, you can open a web browser on http://localhost:8081/book-sales-app/services/customer?wsdl.

In the Activiti Designer, it's easy to create the deployment artifacts for your process definition. From within the Activiti perspective, right-click on the Activiti project and choose Create Deployment Artifacts from the menu (see figure 7.17).

When the Create Deployment Artifacts menu option is selected, a deployment directory is created with a BAR file and a JAR file inside it. The BAR file contains the BPMN 2.0 XML file of the sales opportunity process and the three user task forms that you've implemented. The JAR file contains the class files of the service tasks (`RetrieveCustomerTask`, `StoreOpportunityTask`) and the web service client classes.

Run As	▶
Debug As	▶
Validate	
Team	▶
Compare With	▶
Restore from Local History...	
Configure	▶
Properties	⌘I

✉ Create deployment artifacts

Figure 7.17 The pop-up menu that's shown when you right-click on an Activiti project. The option to create the deployment artifacts, like the BAR and JAR files, is highlighted.

To be able to execute the sales opportunity process using the Activiti Explorer, you must make sure that the JAR file is published to the classpath of the Activiti Explorer web application. Copy the JAR file to the WEB-INF/lib directory of the Activiti Explorer web application. The Tomcat instance should then be stopped (`ant tomcat.stop`) if it's already running and started again (`ant tomcat.start`).

You're almost ready with the deployment steps; only the BAR deployment remains. This can be done using the Deployment tab in the Activiti Explorer. Select the BAR file, which was created by the Activiti Designer in the deployment directory of the Activiti Eclipse project.

When the sales opportunity BAR file is deployed on the Activiti Engine via the Activiti Explorer, you can start a new process instance like before. The start form of the sales opportunity process definition is shown in figure 7.18.

In order to use the unit test we'll discuss later on, you should fill the Product field exactly as shown in figure 7.18. When the customer number isn't known, a value of 0

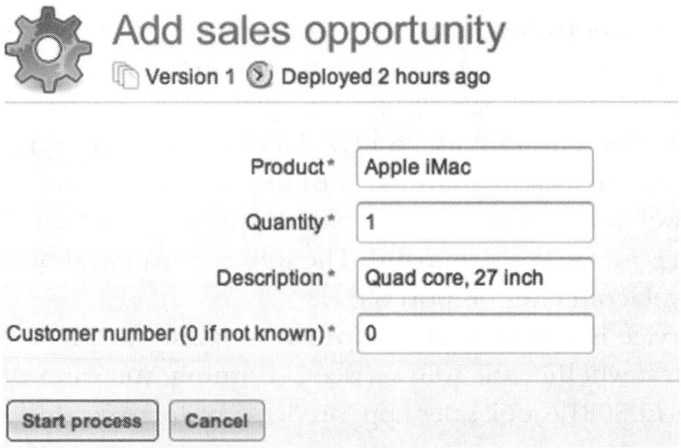

Add sales opportunity
📋 Version 1 ⊙ Deployed 2 hours ago

Product*	Apple iMac
Quantity*	1
Description*	Quad core, 27 inch
Customer number (0 if not known)*	0

[Start process] [Cancel]

Figure 7.18 Activiti Explorer showing the start form of the sales opportunity process

must be filled in. In this case, a new user task is created for the sales group to fill in additional information about the customer. If you fill in a customer number in the start form, this step is skipped. Find out if a user task has been created by logging in to the Activiti Explorer with the Kermit user. Then, fill in some values for the customer name, contact person, and customer address.

Next, the service task that retrieves the customer by invoking the customer web service is executed. In this case, the customer can't be found, because the H2 database doesn't contain any customers yet. Then, the error event is executed, and the boundary error event should catch this error and create a new user task to add a new customer entry. Make sure that this user task is created for the sales candidate group.

In this new customer entry user task form, a valid customer identifier must be provided because, in the next service task, the sales opportunity will be stored in the H2 database with a reference to the customer table. In the book-sales-app project, you've provided a TestData class in the main source tree. By executing this class, a new customer entry is created in the H2 database and the customer identifier is printed in the Eclipse console. Fill in the printed customer identifier and complete the user task.

Then, you can perform the final test and validate whether the sales opportunity indeed is created in the H2 database for the provided customer identifier. This test is implemented in the OpportunityTest unit test, which can also be found in the main source tree of the book-sales-app project.

We've now covered in detail how to implement a process definition using an error end event and an error boundary event. In the next section, we'll spend some more time on error handling in process definitions using Activiti as we discuss the use of Java exceptions.

7.3 Implementing error handling using Java logic

In section 7.1, you saw that implementing error handling without error end events and error boundary events is possible using Java service tasks with logic to choose between different outgoing sequence flows. To be able to compare the use of this type of error handling to the BPMN 2.0 style using error end and boundary events, we'll implement the sales opportunity process from section 7.2 again in this section.

We already went through all the activities of the sales opportunity process in the previous section, so we'll focus on the differences related to the Java logic error handling here. To get a good picture of the differences, let's start with the process model shown in figure 7.19.

As you can see in figure 7.19, the process model is easy to comprehend because you don't need a subprocess scope for the error handling constructs. The error handling logic isn't expressed in the process diagram but instead is implemented inside the "Find customer" service task.

Let's look at the revised implementation of the RetrieveCustomerTask class, which still is the implementation of the "Find customer" service task.

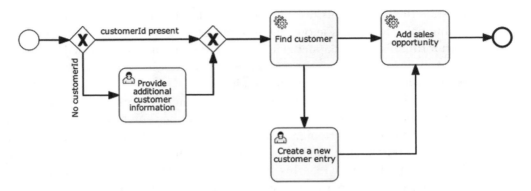

Figure 7.19   Process model of the sales opportunity process using Java service logic to implement error handling

Listing 7.4   Revised version of `RetrieveCustomerTask` that implements error handling

```java
public class RetrieveCustomerTask
    implements ActivityBehavior {
```
◁── **Implements ActivityBehavior interface** ❶

```java
    private CustomerServiceService customerService =
        new CustomerServiceService();

    @Override
    public void execute(ActivityExecution execution)
        throws Exception {
```
◁── **Defines input parameter as ActivityExecution instance** ❷

```java
      Long customerId = (Long)
          execution.getVariable("customerNumber");
      Customer customer = null;
      if(customerId > 0) {
        customer = customerService
            .getCustomerServicePort()
            .findCustomerById(customerId);
      } else {
        String customerName = (String)
            execution.getVariable("customerName");
        String contactPerson = (String)
            execution.getVariable("contactPerson");
        customer = customerService
            .getCustomerServicePort()
            .findCustomer(customerName, contactPerson);
      }
      CustomerVariable variable = new CustomerVariable();
      if(customer != null && customer.getCustomerId() > 0) {
        variable.setCustomerFound(true);
        variable.setCustomerId(customer.getCustomerId());
        variable.setCustomerName(
            customer.getCustomerName());
        variable.setContactPerson(
            customer.getContactPerson());
        variable.setCustomerAddress(
            customer.getCustomerAddress());
      } else {
```

```
      variable.setCustomerFound(false);
    }
    execution.setVariable("customer", variable);
    PvmTransition transition = null;
    if(variable.isCustomerFound() == true) {
      transition = execution
          .getActivity()
          .findOutgoingTransition("customerFound");
    } else {
      transition = execution
          .getActivity()
          .findOutgoingTransition("customerNotFound");
    }
    execution.take(transition);
  }
}
```

❸ **Finds outgoing sequence flow by ID**

❹ **Takes right transition**

When you want to implement a Java service task with logic that chooses between different outgoing sequence flows, make sure you implement the `ActivityBehavior` interface ❶ instead of the `JavaDelegate` interface you'd normally use. The `ActivitiBehavior` interface provides an `ActivityExecution` instance parameter ❷, which can be used to choose a specific outgoing sequence flow.

With the `findOutgoingTransition` method, you can retrieve an outgoing sequence flow by identifier ❸. If the customer can be found by the customer web service, the `customerFound` sequence flow is retrieved.

Look at the BPMN 2.0 XML snippet of the revised sales opportunity process with a focus on the outgoing sequence flows of the Java service task:

```
<serviceTask id="RetrieveCustomerTask"
    activiti:class="org.bpmnwithactiviti.chapter7.
      ➥ errorjava.RetrieveCustomerTask" />
<sequenceFlow id="customerNotFound"
    sourceRef="RetrieveCustomerTask"
    targetRef="HandleCustomerNotFoundTask" />
<sequenceFlow id="customerFound"
    sourceRef="RetrieveCustomerTask"
    targetRef="StoreOpportunityTask" />
```

Here, you can see that there are two outgoing sequence flows defined for the "Find customer" Java service task. When the right outgoing sequence flow is retrieved, the `take` method is invoked ❹ to execute this sequence flow. Be aware that, if you don't `take` an outgoing sequence flow in the `execute` method implementation, the process instance execution will stop at the current Java service task. The `JavaDelegate` interface makes sure that a default outgoing sequence flow is executed when the `execute` method is completed.

The rest of the BPMN 2.0 XML remains the same as the process implementation from the previous section. To test the revised solution using the Java logic for error handling, run the Ant build file build.xml that you can find in the src/main/resources/chaper7/errorjava folder. This creates a dist folder containing a BAR and a JAR file, which you can deploy in the same manner as in the previous section. The JAR file must be copied to the WEB-INF/lib directory of the `activiti-explorer` application, and the BAR file can de deployed using Activiti Explorer.

The tests here are exactly the same as the one performed in section 7.2.5. This completes our discussion about ways to implement error handling in process definitions for the Activiti Engine.

7.4 Summary

Although most people think about process definitions in a happy flow manner (that is, without error and transaction handling and other detailed process modeling), the exceptions and errors that can occur during process execution are equally important. Thinking about all paths that handle possible errors during process execution is difficult, so it's important to understand the different ways you can implement error handling.

Luckily, the BPMN 2.0 specification provides specific constructs for dealing with errors, with the error end event and the error boundary event as the best examples. Using the BPMN error handling constructs enhances the process definition because it clearly shows the way errors are handled during process execution. But, when you think of all the errors that could occur during process execution, a lot of them are related to connectivity problems, database connections, and other technical errors. When you model these error paths in a process definition using the BPMN error constructs, the diagram becomes unreadable.

For both technical and other types of errors, you have the option of using Java logic in Java service tasks to deal with the errors. With multiple sequence flows going out of a service task, you can choose the right process path based on Java logic. This approach can be used to terminate a process if a web service call fails and to proceed with the normal process execution if the call succeeds. In this case, the error handling logic is implemented in the Java service task and, therefore, is not readable in the process model.

When dealing with error handling, it's important to choose between explicitly modeling the error paths and implicitly implementing it in a Java service task. You can also mix both ways of handling errors in a process definition when needed.

We've talked a lot about the API for the Activiti Engine and implementing BPMN 2.0 processes to run on it. But, to run the Activiti Engine in your enterprise, you'll have to understand the different ways you can install and deploy the Activiti tool stack, and mainly the Activiti Engine, in your environment. That's what we'll cover in the next chapter.

Deploying and configuring the Activiti Engine

8

This chapter covers

- Choosing between deployment options with the Activiti Engine
- Exploring transaction management with Activiti and Spring
- Configuring the Activiti Engine
- Communicating with the Activiti Engine using the Activiti REST API

In the last two chapters, you were introduced to advanced BPMN constructs, including error boundary events and embedded subprocesses. That's all great—but how can you install and deploy these advanced BPMN process definitions in your environment? Now, it's time to take a step back and see how Activiti fits into the big picture of your application landscape.

First, we'll discuss the two common deployment scenarios for the Activiti Engine: the embedded and the standalone options. In addition, we'll take a look at how you can use the Spring container for transaction management. With the standalone option, I'll show how you can use the Activiti REST web application as a foundation for implementing the Activiti Engine in your organization. Then, I'll show you how to configure the Activiti Engine. Finally, you'll see how to communicate with the Activiti Engine using the REST API and learn how to add a new Activiti REST service.

First things first: let's take a look at the deployment options you have with the Activiti Engine and discuss why you would choose one configuration over the other.

8.1   Choosing between deployment options

There are two common ways to set up your application environment with an Activiti Engine.

- *Embedded*—Embed the Activiti Engine instance in your application and use the Activiti Java API to communicate with the Activiti Engine. This involves copying the necessary Activiti JARs into your project and starting up the Activiti Engine from within your application using a default Activiti configuration file.
- *Standalone*—Set up a standalone Activiti Engine instance and have multiple applications access the Activiti Engine via the REST API. This option is created when you run the Activiti installation script. The Activiti Engine runs on the provided Apache Tomcat instance in the Activiti Explorer and the REST web application.

As you can see, the main options are embedded and standalone deployments. In addition, you'll have to choose whether you want to use a Spring container.

In this section, we'll examine these two deployment options from an architectural point of view. We'll also look at options to think about when setting up your Activiti Engine application, such as required library dependencies.

First, let's talk about the details of the embedded deployment option.

8.1.1   Embedding the Activiti Engine in a Java application

One way to use the Activiti Engine is to embed it in your application. This application can be a web application deployed on an application server or even a Java client application. To embed the Activiti Engine in your application, you only have to include the Activiti Engine and its dependent JARs. Then you can start the process engine and you're good to go from the application's perspective.

You also need a database server to host the Activiti Engine database. In the previous chapters, we used the H2 database a lot, but you can use other database servers like MySQL, PostgreSQL, and Oracle.

Before we explore things a bit further, take a look at figure 8.1, which outlines the embedded deployment option.

The main idea of the embedded deployment option is that the Activiti Engine runs in the same JVM as your own application code. This can be a good choice if

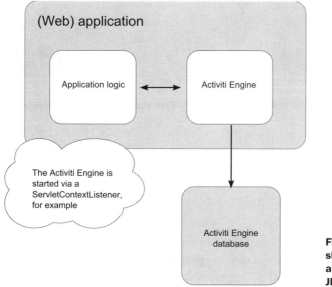

Figure 8.1 Deployment diagram showing Activiti Engine embedded in a Java application using the standard JEE ServletContextListener

there's an application that needs workflow or process logic and there's no central process engine available.

The first thing to consider is how to handle the process engine startup and shutdown.

STARTING AND STOPPING THE ACTIVITI ENGINE

The easiest way to build a new `ProcessEngine` instance is to use the `org.activiti .engine.ProcessEngines` management class. The following snippet starts the process engine and returns the default process engine instance:

```
ProcessEngine processEngine = ProcessEngines.getDefaultProcessEngine();
```

The `getDefaultProcessEngine` method will first invoke the `init` method of the `ProcessEngines` class, which will scan the classpath and look for an activiti.cfg.xml or an activiti-context.xml Spring configuration file. Based on the configuration files found, the process engine is configured. We used a number of different configuration files in the previous chapters, so you have at least a basic understanding of the contents of such a configuration file. We'll discuss configuration files in more detail in section 8.2.

When you're developing a web application, a good place for the `ProcessEngines` `getDefaultProcessEngine` method call is a standard JEE `ServletContextListener`; this ensures the Activiti Engine is started when the web application is started. A sample implementation of such a listener class is shown in the next listing.

Listing 8.1   Initializing the Activiti Engine with a `ServletContextListener`

```
public class ActivitiServletContextListener implements
    ServletContextListener {

  private static final Logger logger =
```

```
      Logger.getLogger(ActivitiServletContextListener.class);

  @Override
  public void contextInitialized(ServletContextEvent
      servletContextEvent){
    ProcessEngine processEngine =
        ProcessEngines.getDefaultProcessEngine();
    if (processEngine == null) {
      logger.error("Could not start the Activiti Engine");
    }
  }

  @Override
  public void contextDestroyed(ServletContextEvent
      servletContextEvent){
    ProcessEngines.destroy();
  }
}
```

❶ Initializes, configures, and builds engine

❷ Destroys process engine

That's not hard, is it? The ProcessEngines management class provides a getDefault-ProcessEngine ❶ and a destroy convenience method ❷ to take care of starting and destroying the Activiti Engine. The ProcessEngine class provides an easy access to the Activiti Engine from within your Java (web) application. You can, for example, start new process instances via the ProcessEngine getRuntimeService method.

Another option is to use the Activiti Engine as a standalone application and communicate via the Activiti REST API or the Activiti Explorer. Let's explore that option in more detail.

8.1.2 *Using a standalone Activiti Engine instance*

In the previous section, you saw how you can embed the Activiti Engine in an application. The communication between the application and the Activiti Engine is implemented using the Java API. In this section, we'll look at how to set up a so-called standalone Activiti Engine. The main difference is the use of the Activiti REST API in the standalone deployment setup of the Activiti Engine.

> **What is REST?**
>
> REST is an acronym for Representational State Transfer, a popular style of software architecture for distributed systems. Applications providing a REST interface, such as Activiti, are often referred to as *Restful* applications. REST is based on the standard HTTP operations, like GET, PUT, and POST, and makes use of those operations to provide CRUD (create, read, update, and delete) functionality.
>
> For Activiti, this means you can retrieve process instances using a GET operation or deploy a new process definition using a PUT operation. For more information about REST in general and how to work with a REST framework called Restlet, you can read the book *Restlet in Action* by Jerome Louvel, Thierry Templier, and Thierry Boileau (Manning, 2009). In addition, we'll talk about the Activiti REST API in more detail in section 8.4.

Activiti provides an out-of-the-box REST component, which can be used to communicate with the Activiti Engine from any remote location. Mobile, Groovy, and other applications leverage this communication layer because of REST's simple communication protocol. Figure 8.2 provides an overview of the standalone Activiti Engine deployment setup.

Notice that the Activiti REST API is implemented in a separate web application named `activiti-rest`. In the previous section about the embedded deployment option, you saw that you can use a `ServletContextListener` to manage starting and destroying the Activiti Engine. In the Activiti REST web application, starting the Activiti Engine is implemented in exactly the same way.

In figure 8.2, three applications (A, B, and C) have been included to show how you can communicate with the Activiti Engine from another application. As you can see, it doesn't matter whether an application is deployed on the same application server or even on a mobile phone; all communication is via the Activiti REST API.

The `activiti-rest` web application is an important component if you want to use the Activiti Engine in a standalone deployment option, so let's look at one of the REST service implementations to get a better idea of its functionality.

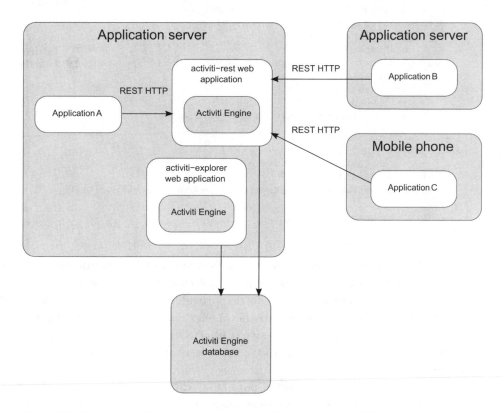

Figure 8.2   Deployment diagram showing the Activiti Engine in a standalone setup

INTRODUCING THE ACTIVITI REST WEB APPLICATION

When you download the Activiti distribution and run the Ant `demo.start` task, the Activiti REST application is installed together with all the other Activiti applications. Activiti uses the Restlet framework (www.restlet.org) for the implementation of the REST services.

> **NOTE**   All the Activiti REST services are described in the Activiti user guide. It's a good source if you're looking for a service overview.

Let's look at one of the REST service implementations to get an idea of the implementation logic. The REST service class that's invoked when you need to collect details about a certain task instance is the `TaskResource` class. The next listing shows the implementation of this class.

Listing 8.2   Implementation of the Activiti REST service class `TaskGet`

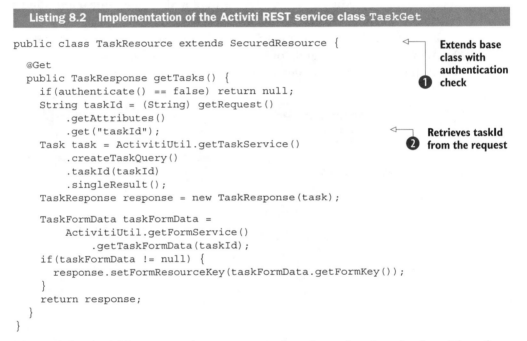

```
public class TaskResource extends SecuredResource {          ◁─┐  Extends base
                                                               │  class with
  @Get                                                         │  authentication
  public TaskResponse getTasks() {                           ❶ │  check
    if(authenticate() == false) return null;
    String taskId = (String) getRequest()
       .getAttributes()
       .get("taskId");                                         ◁─┐  Retrieves taskId
    Task task = ActivitiUtil.getTaskService()              ❷ │  from the request
       .createTaskQuery()
       .taskId(taskId)
       .singleResult();
    TaskResponse response = new TaskResponse(task);

    TaskFormData taskFormData =
        ActivitiUtil.getFormService()
            .getTaskFormData(taskId);
    if(taskFormData != null) {
      response.setFormResourceKey(taskFormData.getFormKey());
    }
    return response;
  }
}
```

Most of the Activiti REST services are secured and need authentication. Therefore, most REST service classes extend the `SecuredResource` base class ❶, which provides an `authenticate` method to validate the provided username and password. When no group parameter is provided to the `authenticate` method, all registered users are allowed to access the REST service. Otherwise, only members of the group can access the REST service, in which case the admin or system administrators group is typically used.

In the REST service, the `taskId` parameter can be easily retrieved ❷. Then, the task query is executed, and a response object that will be transformed to JSON automatically by Restlet framework's Jackson plugin is created.

Now that you understand the purpose of the `activiti-rest` application, let's take a step back and discuss the standalone deployment option shown in figure 8.2 in a bit more detail.

GO FOR THE STANDALONE DEPLOYMENT OPTION

In the default Tomcat setup created when you install Activiti, there are two web applications deployed (the Activiti Explorer and Activiti REST). An important thing to be aware of is that each web application contains its own process engine instance but they share the same H2 database (see figure 8.2).

If you want to run your processes with Java service tasks or listeners on both the Activiti Explorer and the Activiti REST web application, you'll have to make sure that the Java service task and listener classes are available on both classpaths. It's perfectly fine to run more than one Activiti Engine on the same database. Activiti is designed to run well in this kind of deployment scenario, and there are no specific issues that you have to take into account.

Another solution could be to merge the Activiti Explorer and Activiti REST web applications into a single web application. That would eliminate the need to deploy the service task and listener classes to more than one web application. The Activiti REST web application can be easily merged with any web application that supports the use of the Restlet framework. In section 8.4, we'll discuss how to create a new web application out of the Activiti REST subproject.

Now let's recap the two deployment options.

8.1.3 Choosing between the deployment options

Your choice of deployment option will generally depend on the application you are working with. Table 8.1 identifies some application characteristics that can help you choose between the embedded and standalone deployment options.

Now that we've taken a look at the different ways you can deploy the Activiti Engine, let's dive a bit deeper and consider the choice of whether to run the Activiti Engine within a Spring container or not.

Table 8.1 Choosing a deployment option based on application characteristics

Application characteristics	Deployment option	Explanation
More than one application needs to access the Activiti Engine instance	Standalone	To communicate with the Activiti Engine from multiple applications, you need the REST API, so your choice should be the standalone setup.
You need specific workflow or process capabilities in a single web application	Embedded	Because you only need the Activiti Engine for one application, the embedded setup will work well.
You need to communicate with the Activiti Engine from a non-Java platform	Standalone	The Activiti REST API is the obvious communication layer for non-Java applications.
You want to use Activiti Explorer	Standalone	When you want to use the Activiti Explorer to manage the process engine, the standalone deployment is the obvious choice.

8.2   *Using a Spring-managed Activiti Engine*

In chapter 4, we discussed the use of Spring beans with the Activiti Engine. As you know, the Activiti Engine uses a Spring-based configuration file. But, in addition to the configuration, you can also choose to run the Activiti Engine inside a Spring-managed container. In this section, we'll first look at running the Activiti Engine with only a Spring-based configuration, and then we'll look at additional benefits of using a Spring-managed container.

8.2.1   *Creating a process engine from a config file or Java*

An Activiti Engine can be configured in multiple ways. In this section, we'll look at two options, starting with the XML configuration in an activiti.cfg.xml configuration file:

```
<beans xmlns="http://www.springframework.org/schema/beans"
    xmlns:xsi="http://www.w3.org/2001/XMLSchema-instance"
    xsi:schemaLocation="http://www.springframework.org/schema/beans
        http://www.springframework.org/schema/beans/spring-beans.xsd">

  <bean id="processEngineConfiguration"
      class="org.activiti.engine.impl.cfg.
          StandaloneProcessEngineConfiguration" />
</beans>
```

This configuration starts an Activiti Engine that connects by default to a H2 database. The Activiti Engine will manage the database transactions in isolation, so there's no way to integrate your own service task implementation logic with the Activiti Engine transaction manager.

If you don't want to use a Spring configuration at all, that's also possible. But, then, the ProcessEngines init method will not start the Activiti Engine because no activiti.cxf.xml or activiti-context.xml file will be present. Let's change the example from listing 8.1 and refactor it to remove the need for a (Spring) configuration file.

> ### Listing 8.3   Servlet context listener managing the Activiti Engine without Spring

```
public class ActivitiJavaServletContextListener implements
    ServletContextListener {

  @Override
  public void contextInitialized(ServletContextEvent event) {
    ProcessEngines.init();
    ProcessEngine processEngine = ProcessEngineConfiguration
        .createStandaloneProcessEngineConfiguration()          ◁──┐  Creates
        .setJdbcUrl("jdbc:mysql://localhost:3306/                  │  Activiti Engine
            activiti?autoReconnect=true")                       ❶ configuration
        .setJdbcDriver("com.mysql.jdbc.Driver")
        .setJdbcUsername("activiti")
        .setJdbcPassword("test")
        .setJobExecutorActivate(true)
        .buildProcessEngine();
                                                              ❷  Registers
    ProcessEngines.registerProcessEngine(processEngine);    ◁──   engine
  }
```

```
  @Override
  public void contextDestroyed(ServletContextEvent event) {
    ProcessEngines.destroy();
  }
}
```

As you can see, the `init` method is invoked in the `ProcessEngines` class to initialize it. Because no activiti.cfg.xml or activiti-context.xml file is implemented in this case, no process engine is yet created. But you still need to run the `init` method to make sure some internal class attributes are initialized correctly.

No problem; you can create a new `ProcessEngine` instance by using the `Process-EngineConfiguration` class. In the first method, you create a default process engine ❶ that uses the default H2 database configuration. As you can see, it's easy to choose your own database—in this case, a MySQL database. When the `buildProcessEngine` method is invoked, the Activiti process engine is created and started.

Because you still want to use the `ProcessEngines` class to manage the available process engine instances, you register the newly created engine in that class ❷. Considering the engine is registered, you can still use the `destroy` method of the `ProcessEngines` class to stop the Activiti Engine.

Now, let's look at how you can run the Activiti Engine in a Spring-managed container.

8.2.2 Creating a process engine from a Spring configuration

When you do want to make use of a Spring container's transaction management, Activiti also makes that easy. You can define an activiti-context.xml file containing the Activiti Spring configuration. Then, you can reuse the `ServletContextListener` from listing 8.1.

Another way would be to use a context listener provided by the Spring framework, as shown in the following web.xml code snippet:

```
<context-param>
  <param-name>contextConfigLocation</param-name>
  <param-value>/WEB-INF/activiti-context.xml</param-value>
</context-param>

<listener>
  <listener-class>
    org.springframework.web.context.ContextLoaderListener
  </listener-class>
</listener>
```

When this snippet is included in the web.xml file of your web application, the activiti-context.xml Spring configuration file will be loaded. In that file, you can define an Activiti Engine. This means that the Activiti Engine is started within the Spring container. Now, you can use Spring beans in a BPMN 2.0 XML process implementation but also use the Spring transaction manager to manage both the Activiti data source and Java service task implementations with a `@Transaction` annotation.

Let's finish this section with a recap of how such a Spring configuration file can be implemented.

Listing 8.4 A Spring configuration file defining an Activiti Engine

```
<bean id="dataSource"
      class="org.springframework.jdbc.datasource.
           ➥ SimpleDriverDataSource">
  <property name="driverClass"
      value="org.h2.Driver" />
  <property name="url"
      value="jdbc:h2:tcp://localhost/activiti" />
  <property name="username" value="sa" />
  <property name="password" value="" />
</bean>

<bean id="transactionManager"
      class="org.springframework.jdbc.datasource.
           ➥ DataSourceTransactionManager">
  <property name="dataSource" ref="dataSource" />
</bean>

<bean id="processEngineConfiguration"
      class="org.activiti.spring.
           ➥ SpringProcessEngineConfiguration">
  <property name="databaseType" value="h2" />
  <property name="dataSource" ref="dataSource" />
  <property name="transactionManager"
      ref="transactionManager" />
</bean>

<bean id="processEngine"
      class="org.activiti.spring.ProcessEngineFactoryBean">
  <property name="processEngineConfiguration"
      ref="processEngineConfiguration" />
</bean>

<tx:annotation-driven
      transaction-manager="transactionManager" />

<bean id="historyService"
      factory-bean="processEngine"
      factory-method="getHistoryService" />

<bean id="runtimeService"
      factory-bean="processEngine"
      factory-method="getRuntimeService" />
```

① Identifies Activiti database configuration

② Defines transaction manager

③ Defines Activiti engine config

④ Creates process engine

⑤ Defines manager for @Transactional annotation

In the Spring configuration, you do the same sorts of things that you did in listing 8.3. You define the Activiti data source **①**, create an Activiti Engine configuration **③**, and build a new `ProcessEngine` instance **④**. The difference is that you define a Spring transaction manager **②**, which will manage the Activiti database transactions. In addition, you can use the transaction manager to coordinate multiple Activiti API invocations in the same transaction using the `@Transactional` annotation **⑤**.

Let's look at an example where you start two process instances in the same transaction.

Listing 8.5 Example Spring bean that uses the `@Transactional` annotation

```
public class TransactionalBean {

    @Autowired
    private RuntimeService runtimeService;

    @Transactional
    public void execute(boolean throwError)
        throws Exception {

        runtimeService.startProcessInstanceByKey(
            "transactionTest");

        Map<String, Object> variableMap =
            new HashMap<String, Object>();
        variableMap.put("throwError", throwError);

        runtimeService.startProcessInstanceByKey(
            "transactionTest", variableMap);
    }
}
```

① Execute method in a transaction

In this transactional example, a `RuntimeService` is used to start two new process instances of a simple process definition with only start and end events and in between a service task. The `execute` method is annotated with the `@Transactional` annotation **①**, which means that a transaction is started before the execution of the method, and the transaction is committed when the method is completed, unless a `RuntimeException` is thrown. The Activiti Engine will use the transaction to start the process instance. If the process execution throws an error, the whole transaction will be rolled back and no process instance will run or be stored in the Activiti database.

And, that's exactly what you do if the input parameter `throwError` is equal to `true`. When a process instance is started with a `throwError` variable set to `true`, the service task within the process definition will throw an `IllegalArgumentException`, as you can see here:

```
public class ErrorServiceTask implements JavaDelegate {

    @Override
    public void execute(DelegateExecution execution) throws Exception {
        if(execution.hasVariable("throwError") &&
           Boolean.valueOf(execution.getVariable("throwError").toString())) {

            throw new IllegalArgumentException("Rollback!!");
        }
    }
}
```

This shows how easy it is to wrap two Activiti transactions in one Spring transaction to prevent the first process instance from being persisted when the second process instance fails.

Let's complete this example with a unit test, as shown in the next listing.

Listing 8.6   Unit test for testing the Spring transaction example

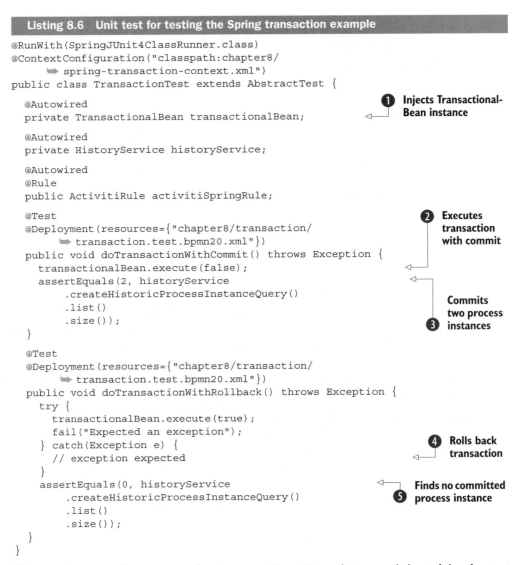

```
@RunWith(SpringJUnit4ClassRunner.class)
@ContextConfiguration("classpath:chapter8/
    ➥ spring-transaction-context.xml")
public class TransactionTest extends AbstractTest {

  @Autowired                                                ❶ Injects Transactional-
  private TransactionalBean transactionalBean;                Bean instance

  @Autowired
  private HistoryService historyService;

  @Autowired
  @Rule
  public ActivitiRule activitiSpringRule;

  @Test                                                     ❷ Executes
  @Deployment(resources={"chapter8/transaction/               transaction
      ➥ transaction.test.bpmn20.xml"})                       with commit
  public void doTransactionWithCommit() throws Exception {
    transactionalBean.execute(false);
    assertEquals(2, historyService
      .createHistoricProcessInstanceQuery()
      .list()                                               ❸ Commits
      .size());                                               two process
  }                                                           instances

  @Test
  @Deployment(resources={"chapter8/transaction/
      ➥ transaction.test.bpmn20.xml"})
  public void doTransactionWithRollback() throws Exception {
    try {
      transactionalBean.execute(true);
      fail("Expected an exception");
    } catch(Exception e) {                                  ❹ Rolls back
      // exception expected                                   transaction
    }
    assertEquals(0, historyService
      .createHistoricProcessInstanceQuery()                 ❺ Finds no committed
      .list()                                                 process instance
      .size());
  }
}
```

To test the example, you need a `TransactionalBean` instance injected in the test class ❶. In the first method, you test whether the transaction is committed when you don't throw an error ❷. To test this, you query the Activiti Engine to see if you can find two committed process instances ❸.

In the second method, you let the second process instance throw an `Illegal-ArgumentException` ❹. In that case, the transaction should be rolled back, so no committed process instance should be found ❺.

To be thorough, you can remove the `@Transactional` annotation from the `execute` method of `TransactionalBean` and make sure that the second test method fails in that case. The first process instance should be committed to the database, in this case, but not the second.

Now that we've explored the options for running the Activiti Engine inside a Spring container, we can look in more detail at the different configuration options for the Activiti Engine. These configuration options are independent of whether you use a Spring container or not.

8.3 Configuring the Activiti Engine

We looked at the differences between using the embedded and standalone deployment options and the choices for using a Spring container, but configuring the Activiti Engine is necessary regardless of how you deploy it. To fully optimize the process engine for your needs, it's good to have an overview of the configuration options. And that overview is what you'll get in this section.

8.3.1 Basic configuration overview of the Activiti Engine

Remember that, when the Activiti Engine is started, the `ProcessEngines` singleton class scans the classpath for an activiti.cfg.xml or activiti-context.xml configuration file. Let's start with a simple configuration example of the activiti.cfg.xml file:

```
<beans xmlns="http://www.springframework.org/schema/beans"
  xmlns:xsi="http://www.w3.org/2001/XMLSchema-instance"
  xsi:schemaLocation="http://www.springframework.org/schema/beans
      http://www.springframework.org/schema/beans/spring-beans.xsd">

  <bean id="processEngineConfiguration"
      class="org.activiti.engine.impl.cfg.
          ➥ StandaloneProcessEngineConfiguration">
  </bean>
</beans>
```

The configuration must contain a bean with ID `processEngineConfiguration`. This bean is used to construct the `ProcessEngine` class instance that's equivalent to an Activiti Engine instance.

There are multiple convenience classes that can be used to define the `processEngineConfiguration`; in this code snippet, the `StandaloneProcessEngineConfiguration` is used. Each of these convenience classes represents a different environment and sets default configuration options accordingly. The following classes extend the `ProcessEngineConfiguration` class:

- `org.activiti.engine.impl.cfg.StandaloneProcessEngineConfiguration`
  This is the implementation you need in a regular Activiti environment when you aren't using Spring. With this class, the process engine is started by default with a standalone H2 database, and Activiti will take care of the database transactions.
- `org.activiti.spring.SpringProcessEngineConfiguration`
  This class is used in a Spring environment. This enables the use of Spring beans in the Activiti Engine and BPMN 2.0 XML process definitions. By default, this configuration class also uses a standalone H2 database.

- `org.activiti.engine.impl.cfg.StandaloneInMemProcessEngineConfiguration`
  This is a convenience class used for unit testing purposes. An in-memory H2 database is used by default and will be created and dropped when the engine boots and shuts down.

- `org.activiti.engine.impl.cfg.JtaProcessEngineConfiguration`
  This class is to be used when the Activiti Engine runs on an application server and there's a need for participating in JTA transactions.

For illustration purposes, let's look at how you can create a complete `ProcessEngine-Configuration` object programmatically, instead of configuring Activiti with a configuration file. In this way, you can choose not to use a configuration file at all. Take a look at the following code line:

```
ProcessEngineConfiguration.createStandaloneProcessEngineConfiguration();
```

After the `createStandaloneProcessEngineConfiguration` method returns, you have a `ProcessEngineConfiguration` that can be further configured if the defaults don't fit your needs.

To give you an idea about what you can do to configure your engine instance, check out this snippet:

```
ProcessEngine processEngine = ProcessEngineConfiguration
    .createStandaloneProcessEngineConfiguration()
    .setJdbcUrl("jdbc:h2:tcp://localhost/activiti")
    .setJobExecutorActivate(true)
    .buildProcessEngine();
```

You can also set all the options that are available in the configuration file programmatically.

Now, let's explore the different configuration options in more detail, starting with the database configuration options.

8.3.2 *Configuring the Activiti Engine database options*

Because the Activiti Engine is implemented with the MyBatis database framework (for more information, see www.mybatis.org), the process engine data model can be deployed on several databases. The MyBatis framework abstracts the database logic from the specific database implementation, like other popular object-relational mapping (ORM) frameworks, such as Hibernate and OpenJPA. Activiti supports the databases listed in table 8.2.

Database	Version tested
H2	1.2.132
MySQL	5.1.11
Oracle	10.2.0
PostgreSQL	8.4
DB2	9.7
Microsoft SQL Server	2008

Table 8.2 Databases supported by Activiti

You can configure the database in the Activiti configuration file in three different ways:

- Define JDBC properties, such as the database driver and the JDBC URL location.
- Use a `javax.sql.DataSource` implementation and refer to the defined data source in the `ProcessEngineConfiguration` bean.
- Use a JNDI reference to a database resource, so you can leverage the application server configuration capabilities.

In order to configure a database to be used by the Activiti Engine, you need to define the database location URL and driver; also, to be able to login, you need to define the `jdbcUsername` and `jdbcPassword` properties:

```
<property name="jdbcUrl"
    value="jdbc:postgresql://localhost:5432/activiti" />
<property name="jdbcDriver" value="org.postgresql.Driver" />
<property name="jdbcUsername" value="activiti" />
<property name="jdbcPassword" value="activiti" />
```

A data source is constructed by interpreting the defined properties and a default MyBatis connection pool is created. Optionally, the values of the following properties can be changed:

- `jdbcMaxActiveConnections`—The number of active connections that the connection pool can hold at any given moment. The default value is 10.
- `jdbcMaxIdleConnections`—The number of idle connections that the connection pool can hold at any given moment. The default value is 5.
- `jdbcMaxCheckoutTime`—The amount of time in milliseconds that a connection can be "checked out" from the connection pool before it's forcefully returned. The default is 20,000 milliseconds (20 seconds).
- `jdbcMaxWaitTime`—A low-level setting that gives the pool a chance to print a log status and re-attempt to acquire a connection if it's taking unusually long. The default value is 20,000 milliseconds (20 seconds).

There's one last database property that deserves some special attention: the `database-SchemaUpdate` property. It defines the strategy for handling the update to a new Activiti database schema when the process engine boots up. It can have one of the following three values:

- `false`—This is the default value. It checks the version of the database schema against the Activiti Engine library when the process engine is being created and throws an exception if the database version doesn't match the version of the engine.
- `true`—When the process engine is being built, a check is done. When an update of the schema is necessary, it will be performed, and, if the schema doesn't exist yet, it will be created.
- `create-drop`—This option creates the database schema when the process engine is being created and drops it when the engine shuts down.

With these database configuration options in mind, let's look at other options you can use to configure the Activiti Engine, such as options to configure a mail server or define history settings.

8.3.3   *Exploring other configuration options*

Let's start with the `jobExecutorActivate` property. The job executor is a component that manages threads that fire timers and asynchronous tasks. You saw its use in the loan request example in chapter 5, where the timer boundary event was introduced to escalate a user task. Figure 8.3 shows an example with a timer boundary event.

When the Activiti Engine encounters a BPMN element with a boundary timer, a new job is created in the job executor to handle the timer event; so, the job execu-

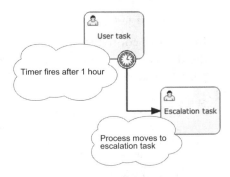

Figure 8.3   A simple example of a timer boundary event, showing the result of the job execution of a timer boundary event.

tor can be regarded as a management component that handles all of the scheduled events. By default, the job executor is turned on when the process engine boots, but you can define its activation in the Activiti Engine configuration like this:

```
<property name="jobExecutorActivate" value="false" />
```

When you need timer support, such as a timer boundary event in your process definitions, keep in mind that you don't switch off the job executor.

It's also possible to override the default job executor settings, like the number of jobs to retrieve and execute in one batch and the wait time in milliseconds that's used when a job has failed during execution. The following code snippet shows how you can override the default job executor settings in an Activiti Engine configuration:

```
<bean id="processEngineConfiguration"
 class="org.activiti.engine.impl.cfg.StandaloneProcessEngineConfiguration">

  <property name="jobExecutor" ref="jobExecutorBean" />
</bean>

<bean id="jobExecutorBean"
    class="org.activiti.engine.impl.jobexecutor.JobExecutor">

  <property name="maxJobsPerAcquisition" value="10" />
  <property name="waitTimeInMillis" value="10000" />
</bean>
```

Another set of configuration options defines the mail server settings. Next to the `mailServerPort` and `mailServerHost` attributes, you can set the mail server username (`mailServerUsername`), the password (`mailServerPassword`), and the default from address (`mailServerDefaultFrom`). If you don't set the default from address, noreply@activiti.org will be used instead.

The last configuration parameter concerns the amount of history information the Activiti Engine will write to the history tables of the Activiti database. It's configured with the `history` property:

```
<property name="history" value="audit" />
```

Using the `history` property gives you options in configuring how much history you want to store in the history tables. There are four options, listed in ascending order of information that's written:

1 `none`—After a process instance is finished, there's no historical information available.
2 `activity`—This option archives all process and activity instances; no additional details will be persisted.
3 `audit`—This is the default history parameter. It archives all process and activity instances and all form properties that are submitted so that all user interaction through forms is auditable.
4 `full`—This is the highest and, therefore, the slowest archiving configuration. This option archives the audit level data as well as all process variable updates.

That concludes our trip through the configuration options. You're now ready to use the Activiti Engine in your projects. In the next section, we'll check out more details about the Activiti Engine REST API and take a look at how you can use and extend it.

8.4 REST communication with the Activiti Engine

In this section, we'll take a look at how you can communicate with the Activiti Engine in a distributed manner using the Activiti REST API. Because the amount of REST language and framework support is enormous, you can use the REST API from all kinds of devices, implemented with the language of your choice. Let's meet the Activiti REST API.

8.4.1 Introducing the Activiti REST API

The Activiti REST web application `activiti-rest` is installed by default, so you can use the REST API right away. The REST services are organized around similar names, like the `TaskService` and `RepositoryService` core interface classes you saw in chapter 4. For example, the `TaskService` logic is available at activiti-rest/service/task.

Let's take a closer look at one of the REST services. In order to list all of the installed process definitions, you can call the API using the following URI:

```
http://localhost:8080/activiti-rest/service/process-definitions
```

This REST service is equivalent to the following Java code snippet:

```
repositoryService.createProcessDefinitionQuery().list();
```

You can also use the process query options that are available in the Java API. If, for example, you want to limit the result set of the call to two definitions and receive the list in descending order, you would use this call:

```
http://localhost:8080/activiti-rest/service/process-definitions?
    size=2&order=desc
```

The same functionality can be implemented with the following code snippet:

```
repositoryService.createProcessDefinitionQuery()
    .desc()
    .listPage(0, 2);
```

Starting process instances using the REST API is also possible. You can do this, for example, with a REST client plugin available for Firefox, RESTClient.

In the previous query for all process definitions, we retrieved a list of all of the deployed process definitions, including a key and a unique identifier. You have two ways to start a new process instance via the REST API. The first option is to use the key parameter, which corresponds to the id attribute of the process element in the BPMN 2.0 XML file. For the ad hoc expense process that's part of the Activiti out-of-the-box examples, the following POST request can be used to start a new process instance:

```
URI: http://localhost:8080/activiti-rest/service/process-instance
Request body: { "processDefinitionKey":"fixSystemFailure" }
```

You can do the same with a POST request using the process definition identifier you can look up in the process definition query:

```
URI: http://localhost:8080/activiti-rest/service/process-instance
Request body: { "processDefinitionId":"fixSystemFailure:1:24" }
```

With the RESTClient Firefox plugin, you can make this POST request as shown in figure 8.4. Don't forget to log in first using the Login button for the RESTClient Firefox plugin.

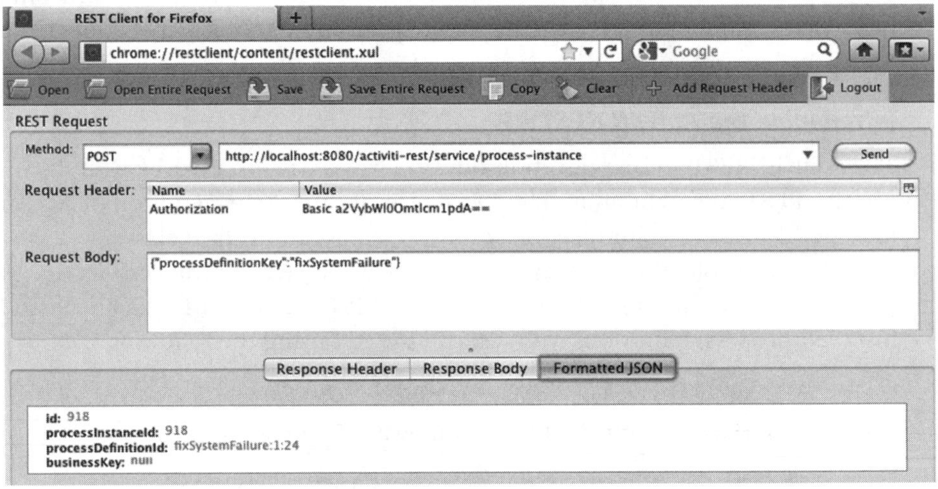

Figure 8.4   The RESTClient Firefox plugin after having invoked a REST POST request to start a new ad hoc expense process instance

Regardless of which way you start a new process instance, you should receive the same response from the Activiti Engine. As you can see in figure 8.4, the response should be something like this:

```
{
  "id": "918",
  "processInstanceId": "918",
  "processDefinitionId": "fixSystemFailure:1:24",
  "businessKey": null
}
```

You now have an id value that corresponds to the unique identifier of the newly created process instance. This process instance identifier can be used to communicate with the running process instance on the Activiti Engine.

In the next section, you'll see how you can enhance the REST API to do just that!

8.4.2 *Implementing a new Activiti REST service*

Although the Activiti REST API already contains a range of services, you may have a reason to create an additional REST service, for example, a REST service that returns details of a specific process instance regardless of whether it's still running or already archived. Such a REST service is not available by default, so it would provide a nice addition to the set of available REST services.

Before you begin the task of adding a new REST service, you need to create a copy of the `activiti-rest` project so you have a project environment to work in. In the source code accompanying this book, you can find a project named `book-rest-app`, which contains a copy of the `activiti-rest` project.

With the source code of the Activiti REST application in place, you can start adding the new detailed process instance REST service. Before we go through the different steps that are needed to get your custom history service up and running, take a look at an overview of the steps involved:

1 Implement a REST service class with the desired history logic.
2 Configure that service class and URI in the Activiti REST root class `Activiti-RestApplication`.
3 Fire up the revised Activiti REST application.

Let's get started with the first step. The REST service you implement will return all the details about a process instance, including the open user tasks and process variables. Let's look at the main part of the REST service implementation.

> **Listing 8.7   Implementation of the `HistoryInstanceDetailsResource` REST service**

```
public class HistoryInstanceDetailsResource
    extends SecuredResource {

  @Get
  public ObjectNode getProcessInfo() {                    ❶ Creates JSON
    ObjectNode responseJSON = new ObjectMapper()             response
```

```
          .createObjectNode();
      String processInstanceId = null;
      try {
        if(authenticate() == false) return null;

        processInstanceId = (String) getRequest()
            .getAttributes()
            .get("processInstanceId");

        HistoricProcessInstance instance =
            ActivitiUtil.getHistoryService()
                .createHistoricProcessInstanceQuery()
                .processInstanceId(processInstanceId)
                .singleResult();

      if(instance == null) return null;

      responseJSON.put("processInstanceId",
          instance.getId());
      responseJSON.put("businessKey",
          instance.getBusinessKey() != null ?
              instance.getBusinessKey() : "null");
      responseJSON.put("processDefinitionId",
          instance.getProcessDefinitionId());
      responseJSON.put("startTime",
          RequestUtil.dateToString(instance.getStartTime()));
        if(instance.getEndTime() == null) {
          responseJSON.put("completed", false);
        } else {
          responseJSON.put("completed", true);
          responseJSON.put("endTime",
              RequestUtil.dateToString(instance.getEndTime()));
          responseJSON.put("duration",
              instance.getDurationInMillis());
        }

        addTaskList(processInstanceId, responseJSON);
        addActivityList(processInstanceId, responseJSON);
        addVariableList(processInstanceId, responseJSON);
      } catch (Exception e) {
        throw new ActivitiException(
            "Failed to retrieve the process instance" +
                " details for id " + processInstanceId, e);
      }
      return responseJSON;
    }
}
```

2 Gets process instance ID

3 Queries for requested process

4 Determines if process has completed

5 Adds all open user tasks

All Activiti REST services work with JSON messages, so first you create a JSON response object **1** that you can fill with the process instance detail information. To be able to query the Activiti Engine, you need to retrieve the process instance ID from the REST service call **2**. There are two common ways to provide variables to a REST service. In this case, we expect the process instance ID to be part of the URL, like this:

```
http://localhost:8080/activiti-rest/service/process-instance/562
```

Another way to pass variables to a REST service is to use request parameters like this:

```
http://localhost:8080/activiti-rest/service/process-instance?id=562
```

The id request parameter can be easily retrieved using the API provided by the Restlet framework getQuery().getValues("id"). With the process instance ID retrieved, you can query the process engine for its details ❸. As you can see, you use the History-Service to get both running and completed process instances.

You can now fill the JSON response object with the basic information about the retrieved process instance. You check whether the end time is filled to see if the process instance is already completed ❹. But only returning the basic information about the process instance wouldn't give a full overview of the state of the instance, so you also retrieve the user tasks ❺, executed activities, and process variables related to the process instance.

In the source code (the book-rest-app project), you can find the full implementation of the REST service, but here we'll focus on retrieving the user task information because the other parts are similar to the history REST service we saw in listing 8.7. Let's look at the addTaskList method in the next listing.

Listing 8.8   Retrieving user tasks related to a specific process instance

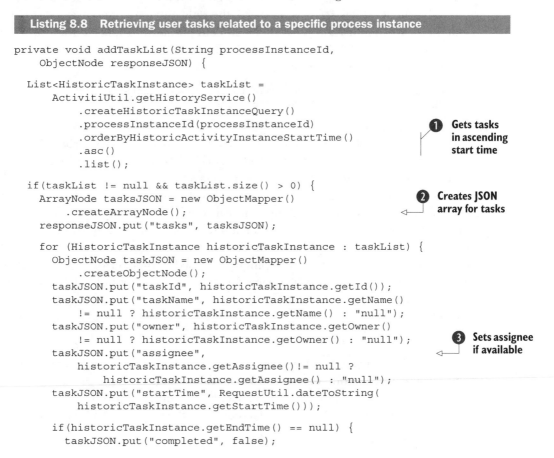

```
private void addTaskList(String processInstanceId,
    ObjectNode responseJSON) {

  List<HistoricTaskInstance> taskList =
      ActivitiUtil.getHistoryService()
          .createHistoricTaskInstanceQuery()
          .processInstanceId(processInstanceId)          ❶ Gets tasks
          .orderByHistoricActivityInstanceStartTime()       in ascending
          .asc()                                             start time
          .list();

  if(taskList != null && taskList.size() > 0) {
    ArrayNode tasksJSON = new ObjectMapper()              ❷ Creates JSON
        .createArrayNode();                                  array for tasks
    responseJSON.put("tasks", tasksJSON);

    for (HistoricTaskInstance historicTaskInstance : taskList) {
      ObjectNode taskJSON = new ObjectMapper()
          .createObjectNode();
      taskJSON.put("taskId", historicTaskInstance.getId());
      taskJSON.put("taskName", historicTaskInstance.getName()
          != null ? historicTaskInstance.getName() : "null");
      taskJSON.put("owner", historicTaskInstance.getOwner()
          != null ? historicTaskInstance.getOwner() : "null");   ❸ Sets assignee
      taskJSON.put("assignee",                                      if available
          historicTaskInstance.getAssignee()!= null ?
              historicTaskInstance.getAssignee() : "null");
      taskJSON.put("startTime", RequestUtil.dateToString(
          historicTaskInstance.getStartTime()));

      if(historicTaskInstance.getEndTime() == null) {
        taskJSON.put("completed", false);
```

```
        } else {
          taskJSON.put("completed", true);
          taskJSON.put("endTime", RequestUtil.dateToString(
              historicTaskInstance.getEndTime()));
          taskJSON.put("duration", historicTaskInstance
              .getDurationInMillis());
        }
        tasksJSON.add(taskJSON);
      }
    }
}
```

With the same `HistoryService` you used in the previous listing, you can retrieve all user tasks, open or completed, related to a specific process instance. To produce a nicely ordered list, the user tasks are retrieved in the order of start time ❶. If there are user tasks available, you create a JSON array ❷ that you'll fill with the retrieved list of tasks.

For every task instance, you can now get the details, such as the assignee allocated to the user task ❸. Note that you can't add `null` values to a JSON object (otherwise, you'll get a `NullPointerException`); therefore, you need the additional if/else logic.

With the REST service class in place, the only implementation step needed to start the REST web application is to add a URI configuration to specify where the REST service can be invoked. You can do this in the `ActivitiRestApplication` class, as shown in the following code snippet:

```
router.attach("/history/processInstance/{processInstanceId}",
    HistoryInstanceDetailsResource.class);
```

The preceding code snippet shows the line you need to add to make the REST service class from listing 8.7 available on http://localhost:8081/history/processInstance/562 for a process instance with an ID of 562. This line is added to the `createInboundRoot` method of the `ActivitiRestApplication` class.

Now that you've finished the new process instance details REST service, you're ready to deploy and test it. When you run the `mvn clean install jetty:run` command on the `book-rest-app` project, a Jetty servlet container is started on port 8081 with the Activiti REST application deployed.

With the RESTClient Firefox plugin you used earlier on in this chapter, you can now easily test your new REST service. First, you need to get hold of a process instance ID that you can use for the REST service call. Let's send the following URI request (see also figure 8.5):

```
http://localhost:8081/book-rest-app/service/process-instances
```

This should return a list of process instances that are stored on your Activiti Engine. Now you can select one of these process instances and use the process instance ID to invoke the newly developed REST service. For example, if you select the expense process shown in figure 8.5, you'll send a request to the following URI (see also figure 8.6):

```
http://localhost:8081/book-rest-app/service/history/processInstance/441
```

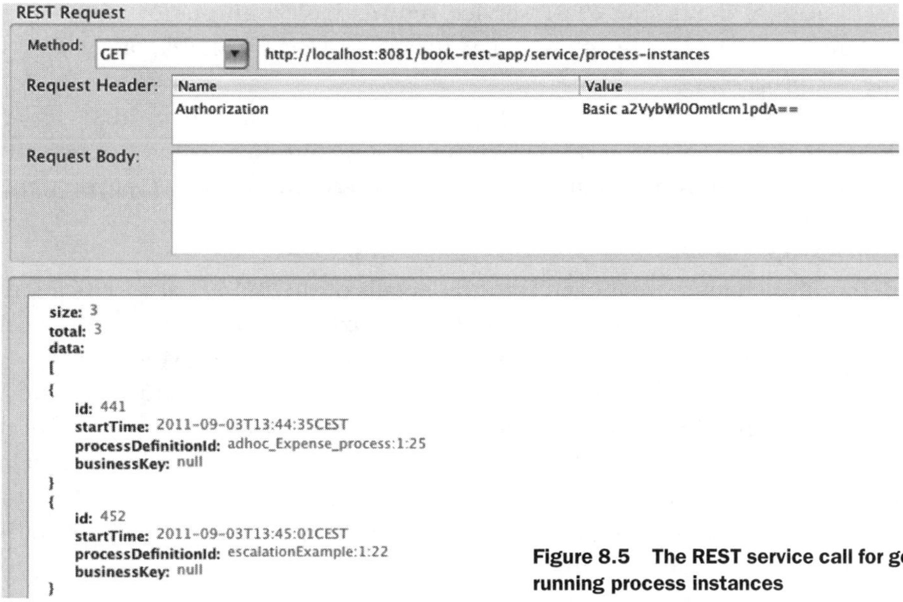

REST Request

Method: GET   `http://localhost:8081/book-rest-app/service/process-instances`

Request Header:

Name	Value
Authorization	Basic a2VybWl0Omtlcm1pdA==

Request Body:

```
size: 3
total: 3
data:
[
{
    id: 441
    startTime: 2011-09-03T13:44:35CEST
    processDefinitionId: adhoc_Expense_process:1:25
    businessKey: null
}
{
    id: 452
    startTime: 2011-09-03T13:45:01CEST
    processDefinitionId: escalationExample:1:22
    businessKey: null
}
```

Figure 8.5 The REST service call for getting all running process instances

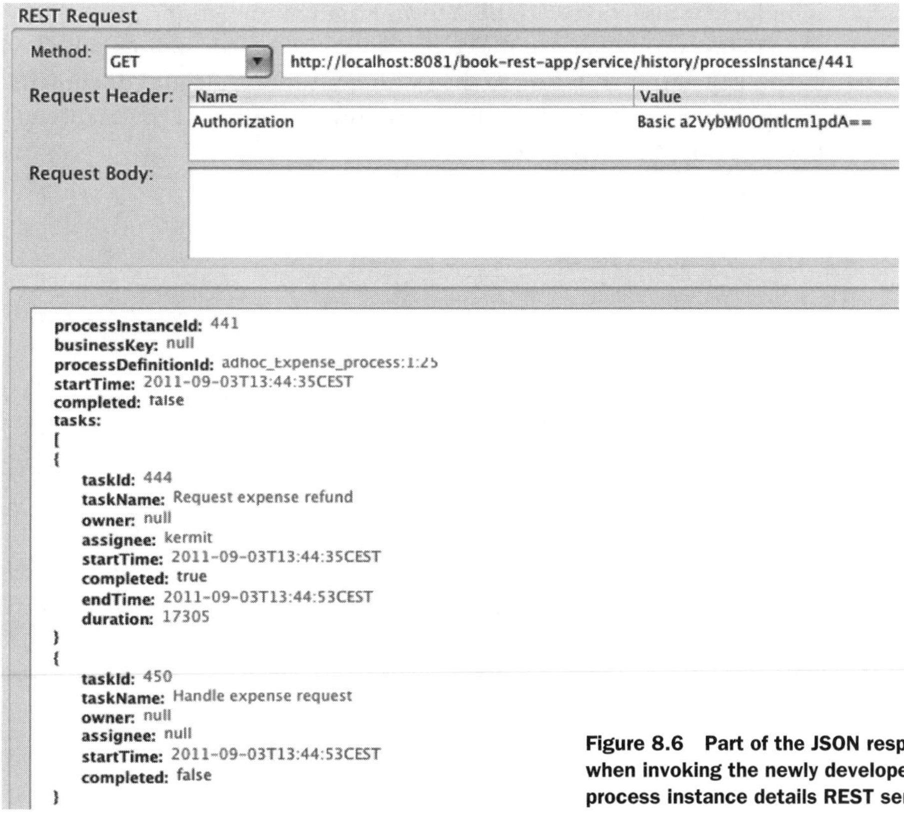

REST Request

Method: GET   `http://localhost:8081/book-rest-app/service/history/processInstance/441`

Request Header:

Name	Value
Authorization	Basic a2VybWl0Omtlcm1pdA==

Request Body:

```
processInstanceId: 441
businessKey: null
processDefinitionId: adhoc_Expense_process:1:25
startTime: 2011-09-03T13:44:35CEST
completed: false
tasks:
[
{
    taskId: 444
    taskName: Request expense refund
    owner: null
    assignee: kermit
    startTime: 2011-09-03T13:44:35CEST
    completed: true
    endTime: 2011-09-03T13:44:53CEST
    duration: 17305
}
{
    taskId: 450
    taskName: Handle expense request
    owner: null
    assignee: null
    startTime: 2011-09-03T13:44:53CEST
    completed: false
}
```

Figure 8.6 Part of the JSON response when invoking the newly developed process instance details REST service

As figure 8.6 shows, the REST service returns basic information about the process instance along with a list of tasks, activities, and process variables associated with that specific process.

With this detailed example of implementing a new Activiti REST service, we've completed this chapter. You now certainly know your way around the Activiti configuration and setup. You should now able to set up Activiti any way that you want.

8.5   Summary

Before this chapter, we looked into the details of the BPMN 2.0 specification and the Activiti Engine. In this chapter, we took a step back and saw how you can position the Activiti Engine and the other applications in your application landscape.

There are two different ways of deploying Activiti in your environment. With the embedded approach, the Java API is used, as in all of the examples we've discussed since the beginning of the book. In contrast, deploying Activiti in a standalone fashion, such as on Tomcat, implies using the Activiti REST API. You saw how to use the REST services, and we even took a shot at extending the available services by introducing a new process instance details service.

In addition, you saw how transaction management can be done with Activiti's Spring integration features. This provides powerful integration options between your application logic transaction and the Activiti Engine transactions.

In the chapters to come, we'll explore more advanced options, like hooking up Activiti to an ESB and integrating Activiti with a business rule and document management system. But, first, we'll take a deep dive into a number of powerful Activiti modules: Activiti Spring, CDI, and OSGi.

Exploring additional
Activiti modules

9

This chapter covers

- Introducing new Spring features
- Developing a JEE 6 application with Activiti CDI
- Learning about Activiti OSGi

We've already covered a lot of the core Activiti functionality and become familiar with the BPMN 2.0 industry standard. You're already able to design and implement complex business processes using advanced BPMN 2.0 constructs, like the parallel gateway and error boundary events. We also covered how to set up a production environment for Activiti Engine using the embedded and standalone approaches.

We haven't yet discussed the full range of possibilities for the Activiti Spring module. In this chapter, I'll introduce you to a method annotation that starts new processes and to the use of process-scoped variables. This provides a good warm-up for the Activiti CDI and OSGi module sections because they also provide this functionality, among a lot of additional possibilities.

You can do a lot more with Activiti than just embedding it or deploying it to a servlet container. In this chapter, you'll see how you can develop full-fledged JEE 6 applications using the Contexts and Dependency Injection (CDI) specification (JSR 299). You'll make use of the Activiti CDI module and see how to deploy this application on JBoss and GlassFish application servers.

Another interesting approach to using the Activiti Engine is by deploying it to an OSGi container so you can make use of all the OSGi versioning and dependency management capabilities. The Activiti OSGi module enables you to deploy the Activiti Engine to an OSGi container, like the Apache Karaf framework that we'll use in the examples.

We'll begin with an overview of the additional Spring annotations available when using the Spring container approach. You already saw how to make use of Spring beans in the process definition, but there's more to see. Let's get started!

9.1 Spring annotations

We'll start this chapter with a short introduction to a number of Spring annotations that can ease the development of an Activiti Spring application. In addition to the use of Spring beans for service tasks, there are a couple of additional Spring annotations that you can use.

First, the `@StartProcess` annotation can be used to start a new process instance when the method is invoked. The following listing shows the implementation of a `ProcessInitiator` class that uses this annotation.

> **Listing 9.1 A class that uses the `@StartProcess` annotation**

```
public class ProcessInitiator {

  @StartProcess(processKey="bookorder",
      returnProcessInstanceId=true)
  public String startBookOrder(@ProcessVariable("isbn")
      String isbn, @ProcessVariable("amount") int amount) {

    return null;
  }
}
```

When you use the `@StartProcess` annotation, it's required to define a `processKey` that matches a deployed process definition. In addition, you can specify whether you want the process instance identifier to be returned by the method (the default is no). For the method attributes, you can implement `@ProcessVariable` annotations to expose these values as new process variables in the newly created process instance.

Because a Spring interceptor will enhance this method, you don't have to return anything, and, if you do return a value, it will be ignored. As I said before, a process instance identifier can be returned, but that's specified with the `returnProcessInstanceId` attribute. When you invoke the `startBookOrder` method, a new process instance of the `bookorder` process definition will be created, and the `isbn` and `amount` values will be available as process variables.

Another feature that you can use is a process-scoped object instance. You can define a Spring bean as process scoped, which means that it will be automatically tied to the execution lifetime of a process instance. Defining a Spring bean as a process-scoped object is easy to do in a Spring configuration, as you can see in this snippet:

```
<bean id="bookOrder"
      class="org.bpmnwithactiviti.chapter9.BookOrder"
      scope="process"/>
```

You can autowire such a process-scoped object in a service task, as you can see in the ValidateOrderTask implementation in the next listing.

Listing 9.2 A service task class using a process-scoped object

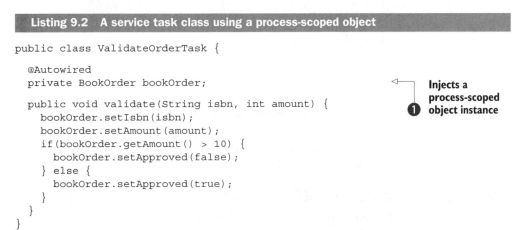

```
public class ValidateOrderTask {

  @Autowired
  private BookOrder bookOrder;                         Injects a
                                                       process-scoped
  public void validate(String isbn, int amount) {    ❶ object instance
    bookOrder.setIsbn(isbn);
    bookOrder.setAmount(amount);
    if(bookOrder.getAmount() > 10) {
      bookOrder.setApproved(false);
    } else {
      bookOrder.setApproved(true);
    }
  }
}
```

A process-scoped object can be injected using the @Autowired annotation ❶. This makes the BookOrder instance available for use without additional coding. When you pass along the isbn and amount process variables exposed in listing 9.1, you can use the BookOrder object as a process instance object.

In the following snippet, you can see how the process variables are passed to the ValidateOrderTask:

```
<process id="bookorder" name="bookorder">
  <startEvent id="startEvent" name="Start" />
  <sequenceFlow sourceRef="startEvent"
      targetRef="validateOrder"/>
  <serviceTask id="validateOrder"
      activiti:expression="#{validateTask.validate(isbn, amount)}" />
  <sequenceFlow sourceRef="validateOrder"
      targetRef="scriptOutput"/>
  <scriptTask id="scriptOutput" scriptFormat="groovy">
    <script>
        out:println "order for isbn " + bookOrder.isbn + " and amount " +
          bookOrder.amount + " is approved? " + bookOrder.approved + "\n";
    </script>
  </scriptTask>
  <sequenceFlow sourceRef="scriptOutput"
      targetRef="endEvent"/>
  <endEvent id="endEvent" name="End"/>
</process>
```

The process-scoped `BookOrder` variable can also be used in a script task by using the `bookOrder` process variable name. Using these additional Activiti Spring capabilities makes the code even cleaner, as you can see in the following unit test:

```
@RunWith(SpringJUnit4ClassRunner.class)
@ContextConfiguration("classpath:chapter9/spring-application-context.xml")
public class SpringAnnotationTest extends AbstractTest {

  @Autowired
  ProcessInitiator initiator;

  @Test
  public void simpleProcessTest() {
    String instanceID = initiator.startBookOrder("123456", 3);
    assertNotNull(instanceID);
  }
}
```

You don't need any more Activiti API classes because the `@StartProcess` abstracts that for you.

Now that you're warmed up, let's explore the possibilities of deploying the Activiti Engine on a JEE application server, leveraging technologies such as CDI and EJB.

9.2   *Building an Activiti JEE 6 application*

The Activiti Engine can be easily embedded into a web or enterprise application and, therefore, is also easily embeddable in a JEE (Java Enterprise Edition) application. But, it would also be cool to use EJBs or CDI beans for Java service task implementations and make use of the hot deployment features of an application server. In this section, we'll cover how to deploy the Activiti Engine in a JBoss Application Server 7 (JBoss AS 7) and make use of CDI and EJB beans. Figure 9.1 illustrates the JBoss AS 7 infrastructure we'll be using.

In this section, we'll be using the Activiti CDI module that's part of the Activiti project and that implements the logic needed to use the Activiti Engine with CDI. In addition,

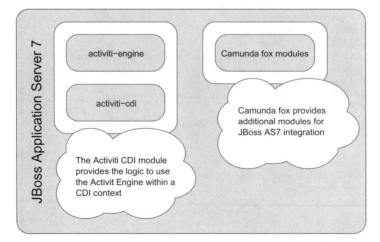

Figure 9.1   An overview of the JBOSS AS 7 environment we'll be using in this section. We'll make use of the Activiti CDI module and the open source camunda fox product.

we'll be using the camunda fox distribution of JBoss AS 7 with the Activiti Engine installed by default. Camunda (www.camunda.com) is a German company that's part of the Activiti community and employs committers of the Activiti Engine. They provide an open source product called camunda fox (www.camunda.com/fox) that provides a version of Activiti with support and additional functionality. An example of this additional functionality is the JBoss AS 7 integration that we'll use to implement a process definition that uses an EJB service task to implement the process logic.

9.2.1 Implementing EJB service tasks

Although we use camunda fox in this example, the source code isn't dependent on this product and solely makes use of the Activiti framework. What camunda fox provides us with is a JBoss AS 7 environment with the Activiti Engine installed by default; when you start the JBoss AS 7 server, the Activiti Engine is also started and is available via JNDI. In addition, when you deploy a new module to the JBoss AS 7 container (a JAR, WAR, or EAR file), this module is scanned for process definitions that will be deployed automatically on the Activiti Engine. (If you're interested in the source code of the deployer, you can look at https://bitbucket.org/camunda.) This means that you don't have to worry about installing Activiti anymore; it's already available out of the box.

In this section, we'll develop three modules. The first module contains the process definition and a Java delegate class that's called from a service task inside the process. The second module contains an EJB that will be called by the Java delegate class. This EJB holds the service task logic. The third module contains the EJB interface that's injected in the Java delegate class and is implemented by the EJB. Figure 9.2 provides a quick overview of this example.

We'll split the process definition from the service task logic to make it possible to deploy new versions of the service task logic (the EJB) without needing to deploy a new process definition. You could also deploy the process definition with the service task logic in one deployment artifact. If you were to redeploy a new version of the service task logic together with an unchanged process definition in one deployment artifact,

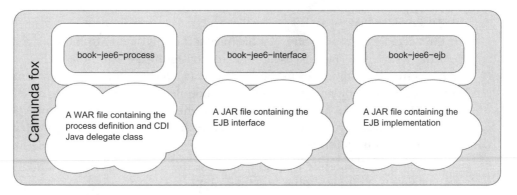

Figure 9.2   An overview of the EJB example we'll implement in this section. Note that we're also making use of a CDI-enabled Java delegate class.

the process definition wouldn't be redeployed because it remained the same. There's logic in the camunda fox deployer module that takes care of this.

We're going to implement the service task logic in an EJB. In addition to EJB goodies such as transactions and security, there's an additional benefit of deploying the EJB on another server than the Activiti Engine. It opens up new possibilities for scaling.

But, because we can't invoke an EJB directly from a service task in a process definition, we need an additional Java delegate to inject the EJB. This Java delegate needs to be implemented in the same module as the process definition (the `book-jee6-pro-cess` module that you can find in the book's source code). Let's look at the implementation of this Java delegate.

Listing 9.3   Java delegate implementation using CDI and showing an EJB injection

```java
@Named
public class HelloDelegate implements JavaDelegate {

    @EJB(lookup="java:global/book-jee6-ejb/HelloBean")
    private Hello helloBean;

    @Override
    public void execute(DelegateExecution execution)
        throws Exception {

      helloBean.sayHello((String)
          execution.getVariable("name"));
    }
}
```

Although the `HelloDelegate` implementation contains just a few lines, a lot is happening. First, you annotate the delegate class with the `@Named` annotation. This is a CDI annotation that you can use in the process definition you'll see in listing 9.4. The `@Named` annotation makes the `helloDelegate` name available to be used in a `delegateExpression`.

This example uses the Java delegate only as a gateway to the `HelloBean` EJB, which is injected using the `@EJB` annotation. The lookup value is constructed in the following way:

```
java:global/module-name/EJB-class-name
```

In the execute method, you can now invoke the EJB `sayHello` method. As you can see, the `Hello` interface is used here to communicate with the `HelloBean`. This removes the dependency from the Java delegate to the EJB and thereby removes the dependency from the `book-jee6-process` module to the `book-jee6-ejb` module.

But both modules need a dependency to the `Hello` interface. Because you don't want a dependency from the `book-jee6-process` module to the `book-jee6-ejb` module, you have two options:

- Add a third module that only includes the `Hello` interface and add a dependency from the two other modules to it.
- Include the `Hello` interface in the `book-jee6-process` module and add a dependency to it from the `book-jee6-ejb` module.

In this example, we'll go for the first option because that's a lot cleaner implementation and really separates the EJB logic from the process definition.

Now let's look at the process definition for this example. We're implementing a simple process here because we want to focus on the CDI Java delegate and the EJB service task approach. In the next listing, you can see how you can invoke the CDI Java delegate from the process definition.

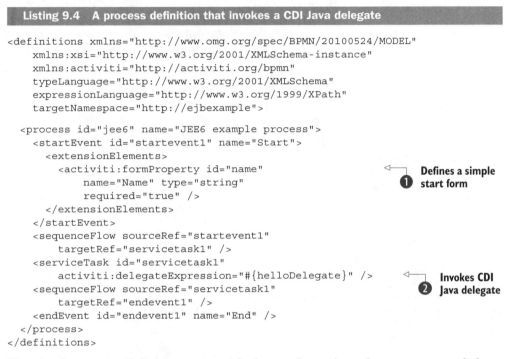

Listing 9.4 A process definition that invokes a CDI Java delegate

```xml
<definitions xmlns="http://www.omg.org/spec/BPMN/20100524/MODEL"
    xmlns:xsi="http://www.w3.org/2001/XMLSchema-instance"
    xmlns:activiti="http://activiti.org/bpmn"
    typeLanguage="http://www.w3.org/2001/XMLSchema"
    expressionLanguage="http://www.w3.org/1999/XPath"
    targetNamespace="http://ejbexample">

  <process id="jee6" name="JEE6 example process">
    <startEvent id="startevent1" name="Start">
      <extensionElements>
        <activiti:formProperty id="name"
            name="Name" type="string"
            required="true" />
      </extensionElements>
    </startEvent>
    <sequenceFlow sourceRef="startevent1"
        targetRef="servicetask1" />
    <serviceTask id="servicetask1"
        activiti:delegateExpression="#{helloDelegate}" />
    <sequenceFlow sourceRef="servicetask1"
        targetRef="endevent1" />
    <endEvent id="endevent1" name="End" />
  </process>
</definitions>
```

❶ Defines a simple start form

❷ Invokes CDI Java delegate

The simple process definition starts with the configuration of a start event task form containing one form property, name ❶. You'll be passing this form value along to the EJB bean from the service task. The Java delegate can be invoked using the delegate-Expression ❷. Because the @Named annotation is added to the HelloDelegate (see listing 9.3), you can invoke it with the helloDelegate value.

You now have the process definition and the Java delegate class in place in the book-jee6-process module. There are still two files that you need to add to the book-jee6-process project to make it complete: an empty WEB-INF/beans.xml file to enable CDI and the META-INF/processes.xml file to configure the process engine deployment of the process definition. This second file is specific to the camunda fox implementation and looks like this:

```xml
<processArchive>
  <configuration>
    <undeployment delete="false" />
  </configuration>
</processArchive>
```

You can configure whether you want to delete the process definition when the WAR file is undeployed.

You can also use an empty META-INF/processes.xml file if you want to accept the defaults. The default value when undeploying the WAR file is `false`—so, by default, the process definition remains installed.

When we deploy the WAR file later on in this section, the process definition from listing 9.4 should be deployed on the Activiti process engine running on the camunda fox JBoss server. At the time of this writing, the process definition is always deployed to the default Activiti process engine that's installed with camunda fox. In the near future, this will be made configurable via the META-INF/processes.xml file.

The process definition is deployed to the Activiti Engine using a camunda fox client library. When the WAR file is deployed and started, this client library is activated. The camunda fox client library looks for process definition files in the WAR file and deploys them to the default Activiti engine. All you have to do is include the client library dependency in your pom.xml file, as shown in the following code snippet:

```xml
<properties>
  <fox.version>1.18.4.CR</fox.version>
</properties>

<dependencies>
  <dependency>
    <groupId>org.bpmnwithactiviti</groupId>
    <artifactId>book-jee6-interface</artifactId>
    <scope>provided</scope>
  </dependency>
  <dependency>
    <groupId>com.camunda.fox</groupId>
    <artifactId>fox-platform-client</artifactId>
    <version>${fox.version}</version>
  </dependency>
  <dependency>
    <groupId>javax</groupId>
    <artifactId>javaee-api</artifactId>
  </dependency>
</dependencies>

<repositories>
  <repository>
    <id>camunda-fox</id>
    <name>camunda fox Maven Repository</name>
    <url>http://fox.camunda.com/mvn/</url>
  </repository>
</repositories>
```

The `book-jee6-process` module is now complete. The implementation of the `book-jee6-ejb` module is simple. First, you have the `HelloBean` EJB implementation:

```java
@Stateless
public class HelloBean implements Hello {

  public void sayHello(String name) {
    System.out.println("hello " + name);
  }
}
```

You define a standard stateless EJB bean here.

There's only one thing left before you can deploy both modules to the JBoss AS 7 container. You need to define a dependency from the `book-jee6-ejb` module to the `book-jee6-interface` module so you can resolve the `Hello` interface. The dependency needs to be added to the MANIFEST.MF file in the JAR file. With the Maven JAR plugin, you can configure this in the pom.xml file of the `book-jee6-ejb` project:

```
<build>
  <finalName>book-jee6-ejb</finalName>
  <plugins>
    <plugin>
      <groupId>org.apache.maven.plugins</groupId>
      <artifactId>maven-jar-plugin</artifactId>
      <configuration>
        <archive>
          <manifestEntries>
            <Dependencies>deployment.book-jee6-interface.jar</Dependencies>
          </manifestEntries>
        </archive>
      </configuration>
    </plugin>
  </plugins>
</build>
```

The `Dependencies` entry in the manifest file adds a direct dependency to the JAR file with `deployment.` as a prefix. You can now build the three modules by running the `mvn clean install` command from the `book-jee6-parent` project.

But before you can deploy the WAR and two JAR files, you need to get the camunda fox distribution of the JBoss AS 7 server. You can download the server from the following website: www.camunda.com/fox/community/download. Unzip the download to a directory of your choice and run it by executing the appropriate command from the root directory:

- For Linux or Mac OS X:
  ```
  ./server/jboss-as-7.1.0.Final/bin/standalone.sh
  ```
- For Windows:
  ```
  server\jboss-as-7.1.0.Final\bin\standalone.bat
  ```

You can check that the Activiti Engine is running by opening the Activiti Explorer on http://localhost:8080/explorer. Note that this URI is different from the Activiti Explorer installed on the default Tomcat server. This Activiti Explorer is connected to the default Activiti Engine started within the JBoss AS 7 server. The Activiti Engine uses an in-memory H2 database by default.

Now let's deploy the three modules you developed in this section. First, copy the book-jee6-interface.jar module you can find in the book-jee6-interface/target directory to the standalone/deployments directory in the JBoss AS 7 server. Then deploy the book-jee6-process.war file to deploy the process definition from listing 9.4. Next, copy the book-jee6-ejb.jar file to the same directory.

You can now start a new instance of the example process using the Activiti Explorer deployed on the JBoss AS 7 server. Figure 9.3 shows the start form you'll need

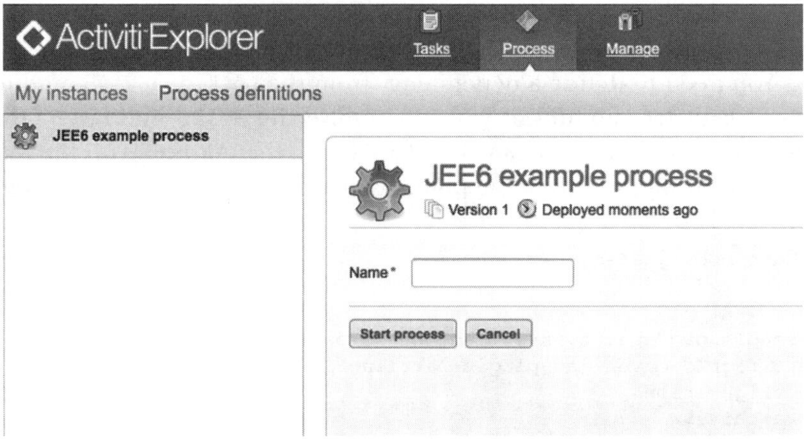

Figure 9.3   Activiti Explorer showing the start form of the EJB example process

to fill in when starting a new process instance. You can now start a new process instance, and you should see a hello message in the JBoss console.

It's also easy to test the flexibility of introducing a new implementation of the Hello-Bean EJB. Change the System.out message and run the mvn clean install command again. Then, delete the book-jee6-ejb.jar file from the standalone/deployments directory in the JBoss AS 7 server and the newly generated book-jee6-ejb.jar.undeployed file. Now, copy the newly built book-jee6-ejb.jar file to the standalone/deployments directory, start a new process instance via the Activiti Explorer, and watch the JBoss console for the changed hello message.

Now that you're familiar with CDI and using EJB service tasks, we can go ahead and extend our use of the Activiti CDI module when developing a JSF process application using CDI.

9.2.2   *Implementing a JSF process application using CDI*

One of the uses of CDI is to provide easy integration of bean logic and JSF pages. The Activiti CDI module enables you to use the Activiti API and process variables directly from a JSF page. This makes it easy to develop custom task list applications and even full process applications yourself.

In this section, we're going to implement a simple JSF book order application (see book-cdi-app in the book's source code) using several CDI beans and an Activiti process definition. Figure 9.4 gives a general overview of the book order process.

Let's start with the process model at the center of figure 9.4. First, we'll validate an ISBN number that's provided via a JSF start form page. The validation is implemented in a CDI bean named BookOrderTask. Next, a user task is created to complete the order, which means that somebody has to approve the order. Finally, the outcome of the approval step is processed via the CDI bean. We'll add the order to an approved or disapproved list of book orders in this step.

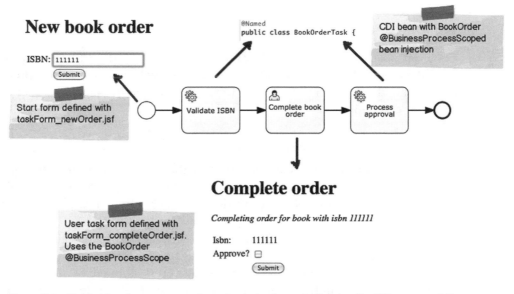

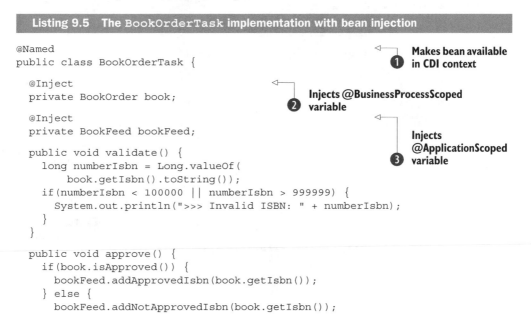

Figure 9.4 The book order process we're going to implement, showing the JSF pages and the `BookOrderTask` CDI bean

We're also going to create a `BookOrder` bean that has a `@BusinessProcessScoped` annotation. This annotation is also part of the Activiti CDI module and tells the application server to bind that bean to a process instance for its whole execution.

Let's first look at the implementation of the `BookOrderTask` to understand the main functionality of the book order process.

Listing 9.5 The `BookOrderTask` implementation with bean injection

```
@Named                                              ◁─┐  Makes bean available
public class BookOrderTask {                        ❶  in CDI context

  @Inject                                           ◁─┐
  private BookOrder book;                           ❷  Injects @BusinessProcessScoped
                                                       variable
  @Inject                                           ◁─┐
  private BookFeed bookFeed;                            Injects
                                                       @ApplicationScoped
  public void validate() {                          ❸  variable
    long numberIsbn = Long.valueOf(
        book.getIsbn().toString());
    if(numberIsbn < 100000 || numberIsbn > 999999) {
      System.out.println(">>> Invalid ISBN: " + numberIsbn);
    }
  }

  public void approve() {
    if(book.isApproved()) {
      bookFeed.addApprovedIsbn(book.getIsbn());
    } else {
      bookFeed.addNotApprovedIsbn(book.getIsbn());
```

```
        }
      }
    }
}
```

First, you need to make the `BookOrderTask` available in the CDI context using the `@Named` annotation ❶. Once that's done, you can invoke the class from a process definition using the following expression, which comes from the validate task of the book order process definition:

```
<serviceTask id="validateTask"
    activiti:expression="#{bookOrderTask.validate()}" />
```

In addition, you can inject beans that are available in the CDI context into the service task class. First, you inject the `BookOrder` instance attached to the current process instance ❷. You use this object to retrieve the ISBN number and the approval outcome variables in the `validate` and `approve` methods.

The second bean you inject is the `BookFeed` instance, which is an `@Application-Scoped` bean ❸. This means that there's exactly one instance of this object during the lifetime of the CDI application; when the server is stopped or the application is restarted, the bean will be initialized again. You use this bean to store approved and disapproved book orders so that you can display them via a JSF page. Let's take a look the bean implementation.

> **Listing 9.6 Implementation of the application scoped `BookFeed` bean**

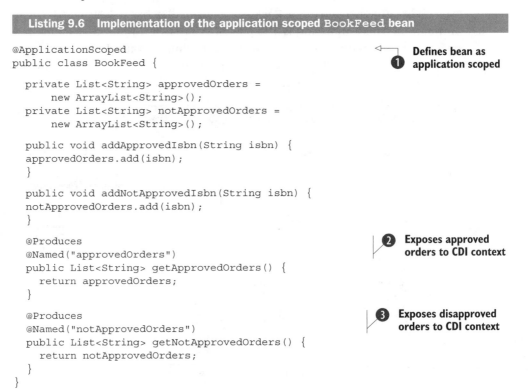

```
@ApplicationScoped                                          Defines bean as
public class BookFeed {                                 ❶  application scoped

  private List<String> approvedOrders =
      new ArrayList<String>();
  private List<String> notApprovedOrders =
      new ArrayList<String>();

  public void addApprovedIsbn(String isbn) {
  approvedOrders.add(isbn);
  }

  public void addNotApprovedIsbn(String isbn) {
  notApprovedOrders.add(isbn);
  }

  @Produces                                             ❷  Exposes approved
  @Named("approvedOrders")                                  orders to CDI context
  public List<String> getApprovedOrders() {
    return approvedOrders;
  }

  @Produces                                             ❸  Exposes disapproved
  @Named("notApprovedOrders")                               orders to CDI context
  public List<String> getNotApprovedOrders() {
    return notApprovedOrders;
  }
}
```

A bean can be defined as application scoped using the @ApplicationScoped annotation ❶. The BookFeed class is used as a convenience class to expose the approved order ❷ and disapproved order ❸ lists to the CDI context for use in a JSF page. You use these exposed entries in the template.xhtml page, which you can find in the src/main/webapp/WEB-INF/templates directory of the book-cdi-app project. The following code snippet shows the definition of a JSF table listing the approved orders:

```
<h1>Approved orders:</h1>
<h:dataTable value="#{approvedOrders}" var="v_isbn">
  <h:column>#{v_isbn}</h:column>
</h:dataTable>
```

Now that you're familiar with the logic of the book order process definition, let's go back to the beginning of the process and look at the start form defined in the start event. The start event contains the following configuration of the form key:

```
<startEvent id="startEvent" name="Start"
    activiti:formKey="taskForm_newOrder.jsf" />
```

You can retrieve the form key definition directly from JSF. In the main screen of the JSF book order application, you're presented with a list of deployed process definitions (see figure 9.5).

In the example shown in figure 9.5, there are two versions of the book order process definition deployed. To generate the HTML link (see the Action column in figure 9.5) that leads to the JSF start form,

List of deployed processes

Key	Name	Version	Action
bookorder	bookorder	1	Start
bookorder	bookorder	2	Start

Figure 9.5 The JSF book order application showing a list of deployed process definitions

you need a bit of logic. The following code snippet generates the data table and the link from the processList.xhtml page:

```
<h:dataTable value="#{processDefinitionList}" var="v_process"
  <h:column>
    <f:facet name="header">Key</f:facet>
    #{v_process.key}
  </h:column>
  <h:column>
    <f:facet name="header">Name</f:facet>
    #{v_process.name}
  </h:column>
  <h:column>
    <f:facet name="header">Version</f:facet>
    #{v_process.version}
  </h:column>
  <h:column>
    <f:facet name="header">Action</f:facet>
    <h:outputLink
        value="#{formService.getStartFormData(v_process.id).formKey}">
      Start
      <f:param name="processDefinitionKey"
```

```
                        value="#{v_process.key}" />
      </h:outputLink>
    </h:column>
</h:dataTable>
```

In the table, you list all the items found in the `processDefinitionList` variable. This variable is produced by the `ProcessList` class, which abstracts the JSF page from the process definition query, as you can see in the next snippet:

```
public class ProcessList {

  @Inject
  private RepositoryService repositoryService;

  @Produces
  @Named("processDefinitionList")
  public List<ProcessDefinition> getProcessDefinitionList() {
    return repositoryService.createProcessDefinitionQuery()
            .list();
  }
}
```

The key, name, and version attributes of the process definition are shown in the first three columns of the JSF table. In the fourth column, the form key is retrieved via the `FormService` and the process definition identifier. As you can see, the Activiti CDI module enables the use of Activiti API interfaces directly in the JSF page. The link will send you to the form key value (taskForm_newOrder.jsf) with the process definition key as a request parameter.

Let's look at the form definition in the taskForm_newOrder.xhtml page:

```
<h:form>
  <table>
    <tr>
      <td>ISBN:</td>
      <td><h:inputText value="#{bookOrder.isbn}" /></td>
    </tr>
    <tr>
      <td></td>
      <td><h:commandButton value="Submit"
          action="#{businessProcess.startProcessByKey(
              ➥ processDefinitionKey)}" />
      </td>
    </tr>
  </table>
</h:form>
```

In addition to using the Activiti API interfaces in a JSF page, the Activiti CDI module also offers a `businessProcess` context variable that corresponds to the `BusinessProcess` bean. This bean provides a lot of convenience methods to start new process instances, complete tasks, and get process variables, for example. In this snippet, you use it to start a new process instance for a specific process definition key.

In addition, you use the `BookOrder` `@BusinessProcessScoped` bean to couple the ISBN form field to the `isbn` attribute of that bean. When the process instance is started, the value entered in the ISBN form field will be available in the BookOrder bean instance in listing 9.5.

You now have a good overview of the possibilities provided by the Activiti CDI module when it's used in a JSF application like the book-cdi-app project. But, before you deploy that application to a JBoss AS 7 server, there's an additional interesting function to discuss; you can listen to process events without defining process event listeners in a process definition. The next listing gives an idea of how this works.

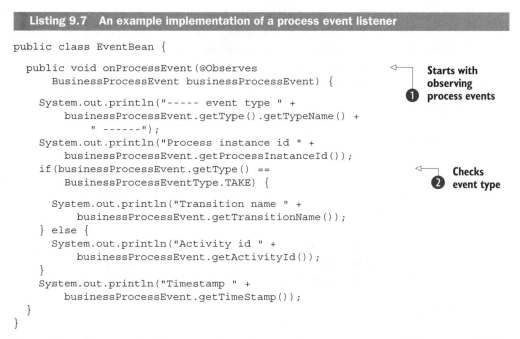

Listing 9.7   An example implementation of a process event listener

```
public class EventBean {

  public void onProcessEvent(@Observes
      BusinessProcessEvent businessProcessEvent) {          ◁─┐  Starts with
                                                              │  observing
    System.out.println("----- event type " +              ❶  process events
        businessProcessEvent.getType().getTypeName() +
          " ------");
    System.out.println("Process instance id " +
        businessProcessEvent.getProcessInstanceId());
    if(businessProcessEvent.getType() ==                   ◁─┐  Checks
        BusinessProcessEventType.TAKE) {                    ❷  event type

      System.out.println("Transition name " +
          businessProcessEvent.getTransitionName());
    } else {
      System.out.println("Activity id " +
          businessProcessEvent.getActivityId());
    }
    System.out.println("Timestamp " +
        businessProcessEvent.getTimeStamp());
  }
}
```

To enable a bean method to start observing process events, you only have to add the @Observes annotation to a method parameter with a type of BusinessProcessEvent ❶. Once you've added this annotation, you get every start and end event of an activity and the take event when a sequence flow is executed. In this example, you only print the various attributes of a BusinessProcessEvent to the console. When the event type is a sequence flow take event ❷, you print the transition name; otherwise, you print the activity identifier.

To enable the process event listening capabilities of the Activiti CDI module, you have to add an additional bean in the Activiti process engine configuration. The following snippet shows the engine configuration as you can find it in the src/main/resources/activiti.cfg.xml file:

```
<bean id="processEngineConfiguration"
    class="org.activiti.cdi.CdiJtaProcessEngineConfiguration">
  <property name="dataSourceJndiName"
      value="java:jboss/datasources/ExampleDS" />
  <property name="databaseType" value="h2" />
  <property name="transactionManager" ref="transactionManager" />
```

```
    <property name="transactionsExternallyManaged" value="true" />
    <property name="databaseSchemaUpdate" value="true" />
    <property name="customPostBPMNParseListeners">
      <list>
        <bean
      class="org.activiti.cdi.impl.event.CdiEventSupportBpmnParseListener"/>
      </list>
    </property>
  </bean>
```

You need to add a custom BPMN parse listener to enable the process event listener. With this in place, you only have to add a couple of boilerplate configurations. First, you need to enable the start process instance and complete task capabilities of the Apache CDI module by defining the following beans.xml file in the src/main/webapp/WEB-INF directory:

```
<beans xmlns="http://java.sun.com/xml/ns/javaee"
       xmlns:xsi="http://www.w3.org/2001/XMLSchema-instance"
       xsi:schemaLocation="http://java.sun.com/xml/ns/javaee
           http://java.sun.com/xml/ns/javaee/beans_1_0.xsd">

  <interceptors>
    <class>org.activiti.cdi.impl.annotation.StartProcessInterceptor</class>
    <class>org.activiti.cdi.impl.annotation.CompleteTaskInterceptor</class>
  </interceptors>
</beans>
```

Next, you have to deploy the diagrams/bookorder.bpmn20.xml process definition when the JSF application is installed and started. You can define the process files you want to deploy in the processes.xml file in the src/main/resources folder:

```
<processes>
  <process resource="diagrams/bookorder.bpmn20.xml" />
</processes>
```

There's only one piece remaining now: the Activiti CDI module needs a way to get a reference to the Activiti Engine. In this example, you extend the LocalProcess-EngineLookup class, which means that the process engine is configured locally in the application using an activiti.cfg.xml file or an activiti-context.xml file. You implement the following simple class:

```
public class ProcessEngineConfiguration extends LocalProcessEngineLookup {
}
```

This makes this application deployable on every JEE application server with support for JSF 2.0. You could also make use of the process engine installed in the camunda fox server by making a JNDI reference:

```
public class ProcessEngineConfiguration extends JndiProcessEngineLookup {
  @Override
  protected void initJndiName() {
    jndiName = "java:global/processEngine/default";
  }
}
```

If you use this JNDI-based configuration, you don't need an additional activiti.cfg.xml file anymore.

But, let's focus on the first version with the local process engine configuration. You can build the WAR file by running a `mvn clean package` command from the book-cdi-app project directory. This generates a WAR file in the target directory, which you can copy to the standalone/deployments folder of a JBoss application server. But, you could also deploy this WAR on any other application server like GlassFish.

The application can be tested by opening a web browser with the following location: http://localhost:8080/book-cdi-app-1.0. You can now start a new process instance by clicking on the list of processes link and filling in the start form.

Take your time to look through the full source code of the `book-cdi-app` application because we haven't discussed all the files in detail.

Now that you understand how to use the Activiti Engine on a JEE application server using CDI and EJBs, it's time to look at another deployment option. With the Activiti OSGi module you're able to work with Activiti using OSGi bundles. This opens up new opportunities for hot deployment and modular process applications.

9.3   Deploying Activiti to an OSGi container

You're already able to use the Activiti Engine on a JEE 6 application server like JBoss or GlassFish. But, there's another interesting deployment approach available with the Activiti OSGi module. In this section, we'll start with a short introduction to OSGi, and then we'll quickly move on and use the Activiti Engine on the Apache Karaf OSGi container.

9.3.1   Introducing the OSGi standard

The OSGi standard has been available for quite some time now. It was founded by the OSGi Alliance (www.osgi.org) in 1999. It provides a framework for a modular and dynamic component model, mainly to overcome the classloading and versioning issues on the Java platform. OSGi is a standard solely available for the Java platform.

The deployment environment for the OSGi framework is often referred to as an OSGi container. Probably the most famous OSGi container is the Eclipse platform, where the full platform and all plugins are implemented with OSGi *bundles*. As a developer, you'll be developing these OSGi bundles to implement logic in an OSGi container.

That may sound a bit complex, but an OSGi bundle is often no more than a JAR file produced by a Java project. The great thing about OSGi is that you divide an application, or even multiple applications, into multiple bundles. When you want to change a specific part of an application, you only have to change one or two bundles and redeploy them, and the application will automatically (without restarting) make use of these new bundles.

An OSGi bundle typically provides a component implementation that exposes certain classes to other OSGi bundles. It can also import interfaces that are implemented by other OSGi bundles, which are required to be available in the OSGi container.

A bundle follows a defined life cycle, as shown in figure 9.6. This life cycle is implemented by the OSGi container to handle an OSGi bundle. First, the bundle has the state installed, which means the bundle is deployed on the OSGi container but is not yet available to be used by other bundles. Then, the OSGi container looks to find out if the required dependencies specified by the bundle meta information can be resolved. If the required dependencies can be found, the life cycle will move to the resolved state. From there, the states are pretty self-explanatory. When the bundle is active, it needs to be in the started state.

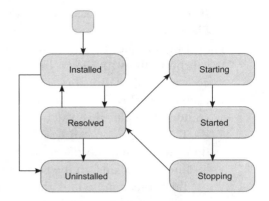

Figure 9.6   An overview of an OSGi bundle life cycle, starting with installed state and ending with the uninstalled state

I know this is a short introduction to OSGi, but there's a lot of material about it available on the internet, and you can read a lot more in the book *OSGi in Action*, by Richard S. Hall, Karl Pauls, Stuart McCulloch, and David Savage (Manning, 2011).

Later on in this section, we'll be deploying the Activiti Engine as an OSGi bundle to an OSGi container. In addition, we'll deploy a process definition and a Java service task class in separate bundles to the OSGi Activiti Engine. But first, we need an OSGi container to work with. Let's introduce Apache Karaf.

9.3.2   Using Apache Karaf as an OSGi container

Apache Karaf is an OSGi runtime environment and it uses Apache Felix as its default OSGi container. It's also possible to run the Activiti Engine on Apache Felix, but Apache Karaf provides a nice administration console, integration with Maven, and an OSGi Blueprint implementation. These additions make the development and deployment of OSGi bundles a lot easier, so that's why we'll use Apache Karaf here.

Take a look at the simplified architectural overview of the Apache Karaf framework in figure 9.7.

All of the Apache Karaf components are built on an OSGi container foundation. By default, Karaf uses the Apache Felix implementation, but you can also use the Equinox

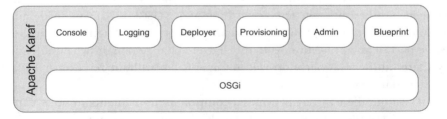

Figure 9.7   An architectural overview of Apache Karaf showing its main components, which are built on an OSGi container like Apache Felix or Equinox

OSGi container (the Eclipse implementation) by changing one property file. We'll be using the console component quite a lot in the remainder of this section. By using the console, we can deploy new OSGi bundles, for example, from a Maven repository.

Another component that's important for the Activiti Engine implementation is the Blueprint component. The OSGi Enterprise Specification contains the definition of a blueprint container. The goal of the Blueprint container is to integrate the OSGi specification with JEE technologies like JTA and JNDI. Another benefit is that it's easy to define exposed and referenced services to and from other bundles using an XML definition or annotations. We'll be using the Blueprint XML definition in some examples here shortly.

First, let's get the Apache Karaf framework installed and started. Installing is easy: Download the latest version from the http://karaf.apache.org website. (Note that version 2.2.3 is used in the examples in this chapter.) Unpack the distribution to your location of choice, and open a command console or terminal. Then, go to the unpacked directory and start the Karaf container:

- Linux, Mac OS X:
  ```
  ./bin/karaf
  ```
- Windows:
  ```
  bin\karaf.bat
  ```

When the Karaf container is started, you should see a console similar to what's shown in figure 9.8.

The Karaf console has a lot of available commands when you press Tab, as shown in the welcome text in figure 9.8. One of the commands shows which bundles are installed and running on the Apache Karaf container: the `osgi:list` command. If you run this command, you'll notice that by

```
C02FN23JDF93:apache-karaf-2.2.3 trademakers$ ./bin/karaf
```

Apache Karaf (2.2.3)

```
Hit '<tab>' for a list of available commands
and '[cmd] --help' for help on a specific command.
Hit '<ctrl-d>' or 'osgi:shutdown' to shutdown Karaf.

karaf@root> ▌
```

Figure 9.8   The Apache Karaf console, shown when you start the Karaf container with default settings

default you have an empty container. Let's change that and install the Activiti Engine.

9.3.3   *Installing the Activiti OSGi bundle*

To make the Activiti Engine available in an OSGi container, you need additional logic that's provided by the Activiti OSGi module. The Activiti OSGi module will scan every OSGi bundle in the OSGI-INF/activiti folder for process definitions. When a new process definition is found, it will deploy the definition on the Activiti Engine that's exposed via the `org.activiti.engine.ProcessEngine` interface. Figure 9.9 shows the bundles that we'll be deploying to the Apache Karaf container.

The Activiti Engine and Activiti OSGI modules are provided out of the box by the Activiti framework. The `book-osgi-engine` module is provided with the `book-osgi-app` project that you can find in the book's source code.

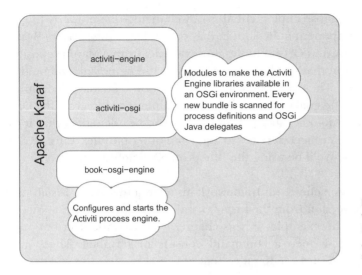

Figure 9.9 The OSGi bundles we'll be deploying on the Apache Karaf container to get the Activiti Engine available and started

The `book-osgi-engine` project contains a context.xml file in the src/main/resources/OSGI-INF/blueprint folder that will create a new instance of the Activiti Engine in the Apache Karaf container. The context.xml file is the OSGi Blueprint XML definition introduced in section 9.3.2. As you can see in the next listing, it contains a lot of XML elements, but you're already familiar with most of them because the configuration is similar to the Activiti Engine Spring configuration. Note that I left out some bits that we'll discuss in section 9.3.4.

Listing 9.8 Blueprint configuration of the Activiti Engine

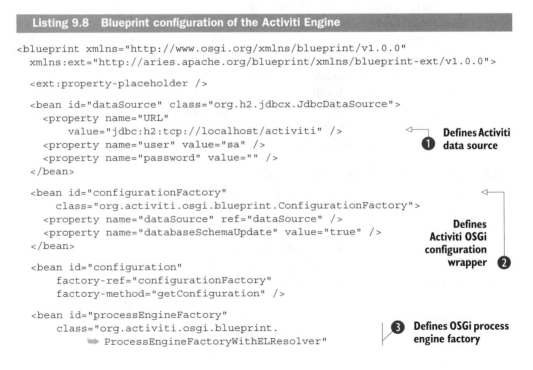

```
<blueprint xmlns="http://www.osgi.org/xmlns/blueprint/v1.0.0"
  xmlns:ext="http://aries.apache.org/blueprint/xmlns/blueprint-ext/v1.0.0">

  <ext:property-placeholder />

  <bean id="dataSource" class="org.h2.jdbcx.JdbcDataSource">
    <property name="URL"
        value="jdbc:h2:tcp://localhost/activiti" />              ◁──  Defines Activiti
    <property name="user" value="sa" />                           ❶    data source
    <property name="password" value="" />
  </bean>

  <bean id="configurationFactory"
      class="org.activiti.osgi.blueprint.ConfigurationFactory">   ◁─
    <property name="dataSource" ref="dataSource" />                    Defines
    <property name="databaseSchemaUpdate" value="true" />             Activiti OSGi
  </bean>                                                             configuration
                                                                      wrapper  ❷
  <bean id="configuration"
      factory-ref="configurationFactory"
      factory-method="getConfiguration" />

  <bean id="processEngineFactory"
      class="org.activiti.osgi.blueprint.                        ❸  Defines OSGi process
          ProcessEngineFactoryWithELResolver"                         engine factory
```

```
        init-method="init"
        destroy-method="destroy">

    <property name="processEngineConfiguration"
        ref="configuration" />
    <property name="bundle" ref="blueprintBundle" />
    <property name="blueprintELResolver"
        ref="blueprintELResolver" />
  </bean>

  <bean id="processEngine" factory-ref="processEngineFactory"
    factory-method="getObject" />

  <bean id="runtimeService" factory-ref="processEngine"
    factory-method="getRuntimeService" />
  <bean id="repositoryService" factory-ref="processEngine"
    factory-method="getRepositoryService" />

  <bean id="blueprintELResolver"
      class="org.activiti.osgi.blueprint.BlueprintELResolver" />

  <service ref="processEngine"
      interface="org.activiti.engine.ProcessEngine" />
  <service ref="runtimeService"
      interface="org.activiti.engine.RuntimeService" />
  <service ref="repositoryService"
      interface="org.activiti.engine.RepositoryService" />
</blueprint>
```

4 Injects Blueprint bundle context

Defines process engine 5 OSGi service

You start the Activiti Engine configuration with the definition of the data source ❶. Then you need a new `ProcessEngineConfiguration` definition ❷ because the Blueprint container can't work with the default ones. The `ConfigurationFactory` class is just a wrapper around a `StandaloneProcessEngineConfiguration`, and you can inject a data source into it.

Then you arrive at the main part of the process engine configuration, which is the `ProcessEngineFactory` subclass `ProcessEngineFactoryWithELResolver` definition ❸. Because you can't use the default bean classloading logic implemented in the standard Activiti Engine process engine factories, an OSGi-specific subclass is needed. The Activiti OSGi module provides this subclass with the `ProcessEngine-FactoryWithELResolver` class to deal with the OSGi classloading.

You inject the OSGi bundle context by referring to the `blueprintBundle` ❹. What the Activiti OSGi module adds in the `ProcessEngineFactoryELResolver` class is the resolving of expressions used in a process definition.

For example, consider an Activiti service task configuration with an attribute like `activiti:delegateExpression="${myBean}"`. By default, this expression is resolved with Java classloading logic, but that doesn't work in an OSGi container like Apache Karaf. Therefore, you can use the Activiti OSGi-specific process engine factory to search in the OSGi service registry, create a new process engine instance, and expose it as an OSGi service ❺. The process engine OSGi service can now be resolved by the Activiti OSGi bundle to deploy new process definitions.

Now let's get this package ready to be deployed on Apache Karaf. To make the installation easy, you've created a features project named book-osgi-features. This project contains a features.xml file in the src/main/resources folder that contains all the dependencies necessary to get the Activiti Engine and OSGi modules installed. You've also added the book-osgi-engine module so that the process engine will get created. The following code snippet shows the part in the features.xml file where you need to add the book-osgi-engine module:

```
<features name="book-osgi-${project.version}">
  <feature name="book-osgi" version="${project.version}">
    <feature version="${activiti.version}">activiti</feature>
    <bundle>
      mvn:org.bpmnwithactiviti/book-osgi-engine/${project.version}
    </bundle>
  </feature>
</features>
```

As you can see, this defines a new feature named book-osgi, consisting of an OSGi bundle book-osgi-engine and a nested activiti feature, which contains the Activiti Engine and OSGi modules and dependencies. Now you can build the OSGi bundle and feature projects by running mvn clean install from the book-osgi-app root directory.

Now that you have the OSGi bundles and the feature definitions available in your Maven repository, it's time to go back to the Apache Karaf console started in the previous section. Apache Karaf can install new bundles and features directly from a Maven repository. To use your bundles, you first have to make the Maven repository location of the book-osgi-features project available to Apache Karaf by executing the following command in the Apache Karaf console:

```
features:addurl mvn:org.bpmnwithactiviti/book-osgi-features/
    ➥ 1.0.0/xml/features
```

The features are now read by the Apache Karaf container, and you can view them by executing the features:list command in the Karaf console.

Next, you can install and start the Activiti Engine in the Karaf container by executing the following command, but first make sure the H2 database in the Activiti distribution is running (ant h2.start from the setup folder):

```
features:install book-osgi
```

The Activiti Engine and OSGi modules and their dependencies are now installed, and the book-osgi-engine module will create a new process engine instance and make it available in the OSGi registry. In figure 9.10, you can see that these modules are installed by running the features:list command.

To check that the Activiti Engine is started, you can run the log:tail command in the Karaf console. You should see a log statement like this:

```
ProcessEngine default created
```

```
karaf@root> features:list
State          Version            Name              Repository
[installed  ] [3.0.5.RELEASE  ] spring            book-osgi-1.0.0
[installed  ] [5.9            ] activiti          book-osgi-1.0.0
[installed  ] [1.0.0          ] book-osgi         book-osgi-1.0.0
```

Figure 9.10 The Apache Karaf console showing that the Activiti Engine and the `book-osgi` features have been installed

That's great, but how can you use this running OSGi process engine? Let's begin by adding a new custom command to the Apache Karaf console that lists all deployed process definitions on the Activiti Engine. That will give you a first view of this OSGi process engine.

9.3.4 *Getting a list of process definitions in Apache Karaf*

When we use Apache Karaf as our OSGi container and manager, it would be nice to be able to communicate with the Activiti Engine from the Karaf console. It turns out that this is quite easy to do by using the Karaf console extensibility points and plugging new commands into the container.

First, you need to define a new `OsgiCommandSupport` subclass that implements the logic you want to use in the Karaf console. The following listing shows a command implementation that will list all deployed process definitions (you can find it in the `book-osgi-karaf` module of the `book-osgi-app` project).

Listing 9.9 A Karaf console command class showing all deployed process definitions

```
@Command(scope="activiti", name="list-definitions",           ❶ Defines console
    description="List all process definitions")                  command text
public class ListDefinitionsCommand
    extends OsgiCommandSupport {

  private RepositoryService repositoryService;                 ❷ Injects RepositoryService
                                                                  instance
  @Override
  protected Object doExecute() throws Exception {
    List<ProcessDefinition> definitionList =
        repositoryService                                      ❸ Queries
            .createProcessDefinitionQuery()                       Activiti
            .list();                                              Engine
    if(definitionList != null && definitionList.size() > 0) {
      System.out.println("-------------------------------");
      System.out.println("--Activiti process definitions--");
      System.out.println("-------------------------------");
      for (ProcessDefinition processDefinition : definitionList) {
        System.out.println("");
        System.out.println("------------------------------");
        System.out.println("Name\t\t\t\t" +
            processDefinition.getName());
        System.out.println("Key\t\t\t\t" +
            processDefinition.getKey());
        System.out.println("Id\t\t\t\t" +
```

```
            processDefinition.getId());
        System.out.println("-------------------------------");
        System.out.println("");
      }
    }
    return null;
  }

  public void setRepositoryService(RepositoryService
        repositoryService) {
    this.repositoryService = repositoryService;
  }
}
```

As you can see, defining a new Karaf console command is quite easy. You start by defining the command text, which in this case, is `activiti:list-definitions` ❶. To be able to query the Activiti Engine for deployed process definitions, you need an instance of the `RepositoryService` interface ❷. In listing 9.10, you'll see that the Karaf container will inject this instance. Finally, in the `doExecute` method, you can query the Activiti Engine using the `RepositoryService` interface ❸ as you've done before (for example, in chapter 4).

To get this new command installed on the Karaf container, you need to define a Blueprint XML definition like you did in the previous section. In the next listing, the OSGi-INF/blueprint/context.xml file of the `book-osgi-karaf` project is shown.

Listing 9.10   Blueprint definition of the newly created process definition list command

```
<blueprint xmlns="http://www.osgi.org/xmlns/blueprint/v1.0.0">

  <command-bundle
      xmlns="http://karaf.apache.org/xmlns/shell/v1.0.0">
    <command name="activiti/list-definitions">          ⟵  Defines Karaf
      <action class="org.bpmnwithactiviti.karaf.        ❶  console command
        ⮕ ListDefinitionsCommand">
        <property name="repositoryService"
            ref="repositoryService"/>
      </action>
    </command>
  </command-bundle>
                                                            ❷ References
  <reference id="repositoryService"                            RepositoryService
      interface="org.activiti.engine.RepositoryService" />  ⟵  OSGi service

</blueprint>
```

This context.xml file is read by the Karaf container when you deploy the `book-osgi-karaf` OSGi module. You first need to define the name of the command, which often corresponds to the scope and name annotations in the command class ❶. To inject an instance of the `RepositoryService`, you need to reference the OSGi service published in the OSGi registry with the `org.activiti.engine.RepositoryService` interface ❷.

Remember that you defined this OSGi service in listing 9.8. This shows the power of the OSGi container's modular architecture. You can register services in the OSGi registry that you can use from other OSGi modules. Without the Blueprint container,

```
karaf@root> osgi:install -s mvn:org.bpmnwithactiviti/book-osgi-karaf/1.0.0
Bundle ID: 74
karaf@root> activiti:list-definitions
-----------------------------------------
--Activiti process definitions--
-----------------------------------------


-----------------------------------------
Name                              Vacation request
Key                               vacationRequest
Id                                vacationRequest:1:21
-----------------------------------------


-----------------------------------------
Name                              Helpdesk process
Key                               escalationExample
Id                                escalationExample:1:22
-----------------------------------------
```

Figure 9.11 The Karaf console output when running the `activiti:list-definitions` **command**

you'd need a lot of additional configuration to export and import packages to and from the OSGi modules. But, with the Blueprint container, it's as easy as defining a `service` and a `reference` element in a context.xml configuration.

Now that you have the configuration in place, you can install the new command on the Karaf container. If you haven't already executed an `mvn clean install` in the book-osgi-app directory, you should do this now to get the book-osgi-karaf bundle installed in the Maven repository. Next, you can run the following command in the Karaf console to make the new command class available:

```
osgi:install -s mvn:org.bpmnwithactiviti/book-osgi-karaf/1.0.0
```

It's as simple as that. Now you can execute the `activiti:list-definitions` command and you'll see an output similar to what's shown in figure 9.11.

Now that you can communicate with the Activiti Engine from the Karaf console, it's time to get your first process running and to deploy it in an OSGi bundle.

9.3.5 *Building a process and task OSGi bundle*

Developing process and service task OSGi bundles is quite easy. First, look at figure 9.12 to get an idea of the bundles you will have deployed at the end of this section.

As you can see in figure 9.12, you'll deploy two additional OSGi bundles in this subsection: the book-osgi-process and the book-osgi-task bundle.

First, you'll implement the process bundle. This means you have to create a pom.xml file (at least if you take the Maven approach) with contents similar to the following:

```
<groupId>org.bpmnwithactiviti</groupId>
<artifactId>book-osgi-process</artifactId>
<name>Activiti in Action OSGi process</name>
<packaging>bundle</packaging>
<version>1.0.0</version>
```

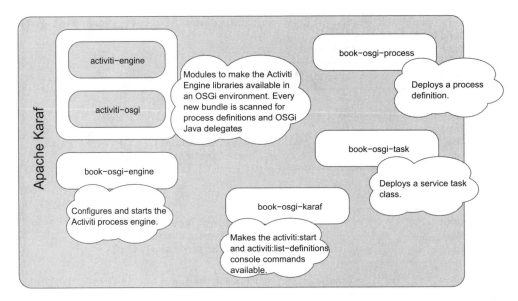

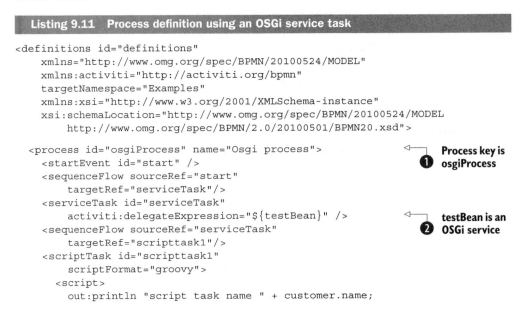

Figure 9.12   An overview of all the OSGi bundles that will have been deployed at the end of the Activiti OSGi examples

The only element that's different from normal Maven build files is the packaging type of `bundle`.

The only thing left to do is define a process definition XML file in the OSGi-INF/ activiti folder, because this folder is scanned by the Activiti OSGi module for new process definitions. Let's take a quick look at the example.bpmn20.xml file you need to create there.

Listing 9.11   Process definition using an OSGi service task

```
<definitions id="definitions"
    xmlns="http://www.omg.org/spec/BPMN/20100524/MODEL"
    xmlns:activiti="http://activiti.org/bpmn"
    targetNamespace="Examples"
    xmlns:xsi="http://www.w3.org/2001/XMLSchema-instance"
    xsi:schemaLocation="http://www.omg.org/spec/BPMN/20100524/MODEL
        http://www.omg.org/spec/BPMN/2.0/20100501/BPMN20.xsd">

  <process id="osgiProcess" name="Osgi process">          ❶ Process key is
    <startEvent id="start" />                                osgiProcess
    <sequenceFlow sourceRef="start"
        targetRef="serviceTask"/>
    <serviceTask id="serviceTask"
        activiti:delegateExpression="${testBean}" />        ❷ testBean is an
    <sequenceFlow sourceRef="serviceTask"                     OSGi service
        targetRef="scripttask1"/>
    <scriptTask id="scripttask1"
        scriptFormat="groovy">
      <script>
      out:println "script task name " + customer.name;
```

```
        </script>
      </scriptTask>
      <sequenceFlow sourceRef="scripttask1"
          targetRef="end"/>
    <endEvent id="end"/>
  </process>
</definitions>
```

There's nothing special about this process definition. You can start a new process instance using the key osgiProcess ❶, like you'll do in a few moments. But the interesting part is the service task definition ❷. You're using a delegateExpression definition of testBean, which references an OSGi service. And, finally, you print the name of a customer process variable object to the console using a script task.

You define the testBean OSGi service in a separate OSGi bundle in the book-osgi-task project. In this project, you need to implement a service task class and define a Blueprint configuration in the OSGi-INF/blueprint folder (see the following listing).

Listing 9.12   Blueprint definition of a service task class

```
<blueprint xmlns="http://www.osgi.org/xmlns/blueprint/v1.0.0">

  <bean id="testBean"
      class="org.bpmnwithactiviti.osgi.TestBean" />

  <service ref="testBean"
      interface="org.activiti.engine.delegate.
          ➥ JavaDelegate" />

</blueprint>
```

The service task implementation TestBean is simple. What's important is that the service task implements the JavaDelegate interface because this interface will be used to reference the service task from the BlueprintELResolver, as you'll see in listing 9.13. For the sake of completeness, here's the TestBean implementation:

```
public class TestBean implements JavaDelegate {

  @Override
  public void execute(DelegateExecution execution) throws Exception {
    System.out.println("invoked TestBean !!!!!!!!!!!!!!!!!!!!!!");
    Customer customer = new Customer();
    customer.setName("test");
    execution.setVariable("customer", customer);
  }
}
```

Because you implement the JavaDelegate interface you've been using a lot in the previous chapters, you don't have to do anything special in the service task class implementation.

Let's take a quick look back at figure 9.12 and see what's left to develop. As you can see, you've implemented all OSGi bundles, so what's missing? We haven't discussed the BlueprintELResolver configuration yet. This configuration makes sure that the test-Bean OSGi service is available to be used in a process instance in the Activiti Engine.

You already saw that a `BlueprintELResolver` instance was injected into the process engine configuration (see listing 9.8). But you need to add a few lines to the same process engine configuration file of the `book-osgi-engine` project to make your service task bean available in the Activiti Engine (see the next listing).

Listing 9.13   Additional lines added to the context.xml file of the Blueprint project

```
<reference-list id="activityProviders"
    availability="optional"
    interface="org.activiti.engine.delegate.JavaDelegate"
    activation="eager">

  <reference-listener ref="blueprintELResolver"
      bind-method="bindService"
      unbind-method="unbindService"/>
</reference-list>
```

You already saw that you can define a reference to an OSGi service from another bundle. Here, you see that you can also define a reference list of all OSGi services implementing the `ActivityBehavior` interface. With the `optional` value in the `availability` attribute, you tell the Blueprint container that the list can be empty.

Then you make use of a neat feature of the Blueprint container. When something changes in the reference list, the `blueprintELResolver` bean will be invoked. The `bindService` method will be invoked when a new reference is found, and the `unbindService` will be invoked only if a reference is removed.

Now you're all set. You can deploy the `book-osgi-task` and `book-osgi-process` bundles to the Karaf container. Run the following two commands:

```
osgi:install -s mvn:org.bpmnwithactiviti/book-osgi-task/1.0.0
osgi:install -s mvn:org.bpmnwithactiviti/book-osgi-process/1.0.0
```

After the first command is executed, you should see the following message appear in the Apache Karaf logging (`log:tail`):

```
added Activiti service to delegate cache testBean
```

This tells you that the service task class has been added to the cache discussed in listing 9.13. When you run the `log:tail` command, you should see a message saying that the example process definition has been processed:

```
Processing resource OSGI-INF/activiti/example.bpmn20.xml
```

Now you know the service task has been added to the cache and the process definition has been parsed. Try running the `activiti:list-definitions` command now. You should see the new process definition in the list with the key `osgiProcess`.

But now you need a way to start a new process instance. You already installed the `activiti:start` command as part of the `book-osgi-karaf` module. If you want to look at the implementation code for this command, you can look for the `StartInstanceCommand` class in this project. You can now run the following command to start a new process instance:

```
activiti:start osgiProcess
```

You should now see output that matches the screenshot in figure 9.13.

The `invoked` message is produced by the service task class `TestBean` in the `book-osgi-task` bundle. The rest of the console output shows the output of the script task: the process instance ID and a Boolean value of the process end status. That's great, but wouldn't it be cool if we

```
karaf@root> activiti:start osgiProcess
invoked TestBean !!!!!!!!!!!!!!!!!!!!!!!!
script task name test
-------------------------------------
--Activiti start process instance--
-------------------------------------
Instance id                      11629
Ended?                    true
```

Figure 9.13 The Karaf console output after starting a new process instance

could redeploy the `book-osgi-task` bundle without changing the process definition?

First, change the `TestBean` class in the book-osgi-task project and edit the `System.out` call to `invoked2`. Next, build the module by running `mvn clean install` in the project directory. Now, look up the bundle ID of the old `book-osgi-task` bundle by running the `osgi:list` command.

In the following lines, which should execute to redeploy the new `book-osgi-task` bundle, we assume a bundle ID of 68:

```
osgi:uninstall 68
osgi:refresh mvn:org.bpmnwithactiviti/book-osgi-task/1.0.0
osgi:install mvn:org.bpmnwithactiviti/book-osgi-task/1.0.0
activiti:start osgiProcess
```

You can see that the `invoked` message has changed to `invoked2`.

This example shows no production-like code, but it does show the possibilities available when using the Karaf container to deploy the Activiti Engine and how you can make the service task classes hot deployable.

We've covered a lot of interesting stuff in this chapter; if you want more, take a moment to rethink the possibilities shown in the examples. You can take this one step further and do some experimenting with the chapter's source code.

9.4 *Summary*

In the previous chapter, you learned how to run the process engine either embedded in the application or on its own in the out-of-the-box Tomcat installation. But, for enterprise deployments, the possibilities don't stop there.

First, you saw that the Activiti Spring module provides some useful additional functionality. You can use a simple annotation to start a new process instance, and you can use process-scoped variables.

Then, we moved to a more complicated topic and installed the Activiti Engine as a service in a JBoss application server to use it in a JEE 6 application. We also looked at combining Activiti with CDI and at how you can develop web applications that can communicate with processes via simple expressions and beans.

Then, you saw how to run the Activiti Engine in an OSGi container with Apache Karaf. By developing OSGi bundles, you can separate the process definitions from the service task implementations. You also learned how to communicate with the Activiti Engine from the Karaf console by implementing custom command classes.

In the next chapter, we'll approach the Activiti Engine from another angle as we focus on the workflow, or human task functionality. You're already familiar with the Activiti Explorer's default workflow and task management capabilities, but, in the next chapter, you'll discover the possibilities of integrating an LDAP server with Activiti and implementing custom forms.

Part 3

Enhancing
BPMN 2.0 processes

We've covered how to implement complex business or technical processes with Activiti. But, how can you leverage additional components like a rule engine, a document management system, and an ESB? In this part of the book, we'll be exploring possibilities for extending the Activiti process engine with other great open source components. Note that, if you already want to create your first process in a real-life project and learn about important Activiti Engine administration knowledge, you can jump ahead to part 4.

First up in chapter 10, we'll discuss how to enhance the standard workflow functionality with the four-eye principle, LDAP integration, and the BPMN 2.0 multi-instance construct. Then, in chapter 11, we'll move on to communicating with external services and applications using Mule and Apache Camel. Chapter 12 covers the usage of the Drools rule engine via the BPMN 2.0 business rule task element. In chapter 13, we'll discuss the functionality Activiti provides to the Alfresco document and records management system and explore how to use CMIS to communicate with the Alfresco repository from a process definition. Finally, in chapter 14, we'll cover the integration with Activiti listeners and Esper to produce a business activity monitoring dashboard.

Implementing
advanced workflow

This chapter covers

- Learning about new workflow features, including delegation and subtasks
- Integrating Activiti with an LDAP server
- Using the multi-instance BPMN construct for workflow
- Advanced usage of Activiti forms

In the previous chapters, we implemented a lot of user tasks to deal with manual or workflow functionality in a business process. By now, you're also already familiar with the technique of defining form properties to create forms in the Activiti Explorer web application. But there's a lot more to explore.

When you're dealing with tasks like "Organize a developer conference," you want to be able to structure tasks into subtasks. Imagine that you have that exact task. You could break the work up into multiple subtasks like "Book venue," "Invite speakers," and "Organize catering." Activiti provides an API to create such subtasks.

In addition, you'll want to be able to assign a task or subtask to another person and be informed when the task is completed. Activiti provides task delegation functionality that allows you to delegate a task to another person, and when this person completes the task, the task will be placed in your inbox again.

Activiti also provides support for more complex workflow functionality like the *four-eye principle*. Think of a process where there are two user tasks, "Develop" and "Test," that should be executed by the same group of people, like the engineers group. The four-eye principle ensures that the person who performs the "Develop" task isn't allowed to perform the "Test" task. There should be at least four eyes (two people) involved in the execution of the two user tasks.

In this chapter, we'll go beyond the definition of a simple user task and make your processes ready for more complex workflow requirements. First, we'll look at several additional workflow features around user tasks that are supported by the Activiti Engine out of the box. We'll introduce you to creating subtasks, delegating tasks to a colleague, and implementing the four-eye principle.

Then we'll move on to managing the user identities outside of the Activiti Engine database. In a lot of organizations, identity management is implemented in an LDAP server. We'll take a look at integrating the Activiti identity management functionality with the Apache Directory Server (an LDAP server).

In the third section, we'll take a look at a new BPMN 2.0 construct called multi-instance. By defining a user task with a multi-instance configuration, you can assign multiple related user tasks to users or groups. This can be handy for review or approval tasks where more than one person has to perform the user task.

Finally, we'll look at ways to enhance the task form handling for a user task in the Activiti Explorer or a custom web application. In the previous chapters, we were restricted in the simple form field types like `string`, `date`, and `long`. In this chapter, you'll see how to extend the form types for more complex form field requirements.

That's a lot of ground to cover. Let's start with a number of workflow features implemented in the Activiti user task element that are waiting to be used in the process applications.

10.1 Going beyond a simple user task

The workflow functionality surrounding a user task doesn't stop with claiming and completing tasks in the Activiti Engine. In this section, we'll be looking at more advanced workflow patterns to support use cases where, for example, we need hierarchical tasks or want to delegate a specific task to another person. First, we'll discuss the concept of creating subtasks. Then, we'll introduce a common management skill called delegation. Finally, we'll look at an implementation of the four-eye workflow pattern using a task listener.

10.1.1 Working with subtasks

In a process definition, we can define a flat user task. BPMN 2.0 doesn't talk about grouping user tasks into a parent task with multiple subtasks, but there are a lot of cases where there's a need for hierarchies in tasks. For example, when you're planning a wedding, there are a lot of subtasks related to this large parent task, such as inviting the guests, hiring a wedding location, choosing the dinner menu, and so on.

The Activiti Engine provides functionality to create a subtask for a specific user task. The next listing presents a unit test that uses the `TaskService` interface to create subtasks.

Listing 10.1 A unit test showing the functionality to create subtasks

```
public class SubTaskTest extends AbstractTest {

  @Rule
  public ActivitiRule activitiRule = new ActivitiRule(
      "activiti.cfg-mem.xml");

  @Test
  public void completeSubTasks() {
    TaskService taskService = activitiRule.getTaskService();
    Task parentTask = taskService.newTask();
    parentTask.setAssignee("kermit");
    taskService.saveTask(parentTask);
    createSubTask("fozzie", parentTask.getId());
    createSubTask("gonzo", parentTask.getId());
    List<Task> taskList = taskService.getSubTasks(
        parentTask.getId());
    assertEquals(2, taskList.size());
    taskService.complete(taskList.get(0).getId());
    taskService.complete(taskList.get(1).getId());
    taskList = taskService.getSubTasks(parentTask.getId());
    assertEquals(0, taskList.size());

    List<HistoricTaskInstance> historicTaskList =
        activitiRule.getHistoryService()
            .createHistoricTaskInstanceQuery()
            .finished()
            .list();
    assertEquals(2, historicTaskList.size());

    taskService.complete(parentTask.getId());

    historicTaskList = activitiRule.getHistoryService()
            .createHistoricTaskInstanceQuery()
            .finished()
            .list();
    assertEquals(3, historicTaskList.size());

    cleanUpTaskHistory();
  }

  private void cleanUpTaskHistory() {
    List<HistoricTaskInstance> historicTaskList =
        activitiRule.getHistoryService()
            .createHistoricTaskInstanceQuery()
            .finished()
            .list();

    List<String> taskIds = new ArrayList<String>();
    for (HistoricTaskInstance historicTaskInstance :
        historicTaskList) {
```

① Creates parent user task

② Creates subtask

③ Gets all subtasks

④ Completes second subtask

⑤ Completes parent task

⑥ All tasks are completed now

```
        assertNotNull(historicTaskInstance.getEndTime());
        taskIds.add(historicTaskInstance.getId());
    }

    for(String taskId : taskIds) {
        activitiRule.getHistoryService()
            .deleteHistoricTaskInstance(taskId);
    }
}
private void createSubTask(String assignee,
    String parentTaskId) {

    TaskService taskService = activitiRule.getTaskService();
    Task subTask = taskService.newTask();
    subTask.setAssignee(assignee);
    subTask.setParentTaskId(parentTaskId);
    taskService.saveTask(subTask);
    }
}
```

> **Cleans up created user tasks** (points to `.deleteHistoricTaskInstance(taskId);`)

> **Sets parent task identifier** (points to `subTask.setParentTaskId(parentTaskId);`)

In this example, you don't use a process definition. You can easily create user tasks without the need for a process definition, and doing so makes it easier to show the use of subtasks.

The first step in the unit test is to create a parent user task ❶. The Activiti Engine has created a user task assigned to Kermit.

Then, you can use the identifier of this parent task to create a subtask ❷. Two subtasks are created and assigned to Fozzie and Gonzo. To retrieve the subtasks of a specific user task, you can now use the getSubTasks method on the TaskService with the parent task identifier as an input parameter ❸.

The subtasks are created like normal user tasks, but they have a parent task identifier pointing to the parent user task. Despite this difference, you can complete the individual subtasks just like you do with a standard user task ❹.

> **NOTE** When the subtasks of a parent user task are all completed, the parent user task will not be automatically completed. You'll have to explicitly complete the parent user task as well.

With the subtasks completed, you now need to complete the parent user task ❺. When you query the history tables of the Activiti Engine for finished user tasks, you should see that all three user tasks (the parent task and the two subtasks) have been completed ❻.

The unit test in listing 10.1 showed the default way of dealing with subtasks. First, the subtasks are completed, and then the parent user task. In the next listing, you'll see that you can also complete a parent user task without the subtasks being completed.

Listing 10.2 Completing a parent user task before the subtasks have been completed

```
@Test
public void completeSubTasksViaParentTask() {
    TaskService taskService = activitiRule.getTaskService();
```

```
Task parentTask = taskService.newTask();
parentTask.setAssignee("kermit");
taskService.saveTask(parentTask);
createSubTask("fozzie", parentTask.getId());
createSubTask("gonzo", parentTask.getId());
List<Task> taskList = taskService.getSubTasks(
    parentTask.getId());
assertEquals(2, taskList.size());
taskService.complete(parentTask.getId());
taskList = taskService.getSubTasks(parentTask.getId());
assertEquals(0, taskList.size());
List<HistoricTaskInstance> historicTaskList =
    activitiRule.getHistoryService()
        .createHistoricTaskInstanceQuery()
        .finished()
        .list();
assertEquals(3, historicTaskList.size());
cleanUpTaskHistory();
}
```

1 Creates subtask

2 Completes parent task

3 Retrieves all subtasks

This unit test method is implemented in the same `SubTaskTest` unit test class discussed in listing 10.1. The first part of the unit test is very similar to that listing. You start with creating a parent user task and two subtasks **1**. But, here, you complete the parent user task **2** before the subtasks.

In this listing, when you query the Activiti Engine for subtasks of the completed parent user task, you get zero tasks back **3**. This is the result of completing the parent user task. When a parent user task is completed, the subtasks are automatically completed as well, so when you query the Activiti Engine for finished task instances, you get three results: the parent user task and the two subtasks.

As you saw in the previous examples, it's easy to create subtasks on a parent user task. For a user task in a process definition, you could automate creating subtasks by implementing a task listener on the user task. This task listener could create a specified number of subtasks when the user task is created. The following code snippet shows how you can implement this:

```
public class SubTaskListener implements TaskListener {

  private Expression subTaskList;

  @Override
  public void notify(DelegateTask delegateTask) {
    ProcessEngine processEngine = ProcessEngines.getProcessEngines()
        .get(ProcessEngines.NAME_DEFAULT);
    TaskService taskService = processEngine.getTaskService();
    @SuppressWarnings("unchecked")
    List<String> subTaskNames = (List<String>)
        subTaskList.getValue(delegateTask.getExecution());
    for(String subTaskName : subTaskNames) {

      Task subTask = taskService.newTask();
      subTask.setName(subTaskName);
      subTask.setAssignee("kermit");
```

```
        subTask.setParentTaskId(delegateTask.getId());
        taskService.saveTask(subTask);
    }
  }
  public void setSubTaskList(Expression subTaskList) {
    this.subTaskList = subTaskList;
  }
}
```

When a user task is created in a process definition that has a task listener configuration on a create task event, this `TaskListener` will be invoked. Then, the Activiti Engine retrieves a process variable containing a list of subtask names from the process context and create a subtask for every name in that list. This example needs some polishing before you could use it in an enterprise context, but it shows that you can create subtasks in a process instance without lots of coding.

Another way to create subtasks in a parent user task is by using the Activiti Explorer. For example, when a process instance has created a user task, you can use the Activiti Explorer to create a number of subtasks on the fly. Figure 10.1 shows an example of a user task where a subtask called "Expense analysis" has been created.

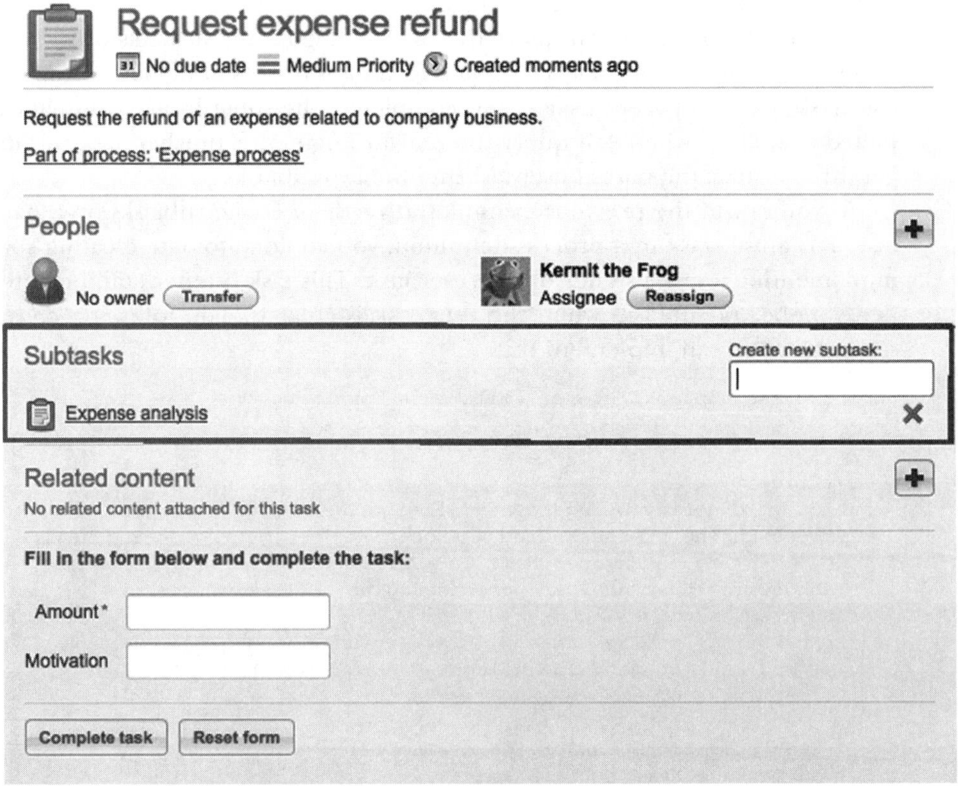

Figure 10.1   The Activiti Explorer, highlighting the functionality that creates subtasks

By defining a name for the subtask, a new subtask is created and you can click through to that subtask to assign it to a user or group.

Let's move on to the next workflow feature we want to discuss—delegation.

10.1.2 Delegating tasks

Delegating a task means transferring the task to another person; then, once it's done, the user task will be assigned back to the person who delegated the task so it can be reviewed and completed. Figure 10.2 outlines the default sequence of steps that are involved when delegating a user task.

When a user task is created in a process instance or as an ad hoc user task, it first only has a name and a unique identifier. In the example shown in figure 10.2, there's a user task named Process Sales Order. When you want to delegate a user task in Activiti, it's important that the user task has an owner. In this example, the owner is set to Kermit. Then Kermit can delegate the task to another user, such as Fozzie. At that point, the user task has an assignee named Fozzie and an owner named Kermit. This means that when you query the Activiti Engine for user tasks assigned to Kermit, you won't retrieve this task anymore. Only Fozzie can work on it.

Then, the most interesting step of delegating a user task is executed. When Fozzie completes the task, the assignee of the user task will be set to Kermit because he's the one

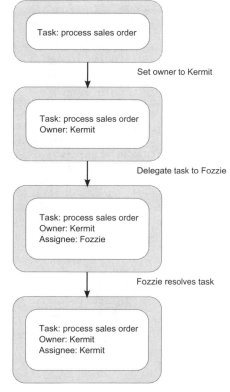

Figure 10.2 The default flow of steps when delegating a user task. In this example, Kermit delegates a task to Fozzie.

who delegated the task and is the owner. So the user task will not be completed; the assignee value is just changed to the value of the user task owner.

NOTE *Resolving* a user task is something other than *completing* a user task, and it's implemented via another `TaskService` method, as you'll soon see in listing 10.3.

Let's look at a unit test example in the next listing, which shows how you can use the task delegation features of the Activiti Engine using the `TaskService` interface.

Listing 10.3 Unit test example showing the task delegation functionality

```
public class DelegateTaskTest extends AbstractTest {

    @Rule
    public ActivitiRule activitiRule = new ActivitiRule(
```

```
        "activiti.cfg-mem.xml");
```

Kermit is ❶
task owner

```
@Test
public void delegateTask() {
  TaskService taskService = activitiRule.getTaskService();
  Task delegateTask = taskService.newTask();
  delegateTask.setOwner("kermit");
  taskService.saveTask(delegateTask);
  Task queryTask = taskService.createTaskQuery()
      .singleResult();
  assertEquals("kermit", queryTask.getOwner());
  assertNull(queryTask.getAssignee());
  taskService.delegateTask(
      delegateTask.getId(), "fonzie");
  queryTask = taskService.createTaskQuery().singleResult();
  assertEquals("fonzie", queryTask.getAssignee());
  assertEquals(DelegationState.PENDING,
      queryTask.getDelegationState());
  taskService.resolveTask(delegateTask.getId());
  queryTask = taskService.createTaskQuery().singleResult();
  assertEquals("kermit", queryTask.getAssignee());
  assertEquals(DelegationState.RESOLVED,
      queryTask.getDelegationState());
  taskService.complete(delegateTask.getId());
  List<HistoricTaskInstance> historicTaskList =
      activitiRule.getHistoryService()
          .createHistoricTaskInstanceQuery()
          .list();
  assertEquals(1, historicTaskList.size());
  for (HistoricTaskInstance historicTaskInstance :
      historicTaskList) {

    assertNotNull(historicTaskInstance.getEndTime());
  }
 }
}
```

❷ **Kermit delegates**
task to Fozzie

❸ **Fozzie**
resolves task

Kermit
becomes
assignee ❹

In this example, you first create a user task and set the task owner to Kermit ❶. Then you delegate the user task to Fozzie using the `delegateTask` method ❷. Now the user task has an assignee value of `Fozzie` and the Activiti Engine also maintains a `DelegationState` value, which is `PENDING` at first. `PENDING` means that the person to whom the task is delegated to still has to complete the work.

When Fozzie has finished his work, the user task is resolved using the `resolveTask` method ❸. When this method is invoked, the Activiti Engine processes the delegation logic and sets the assignee to the task owner, which is Kermit in this example ❹. The `DelegationState` is also changed to `RESOLVED` at that point.

Kermit can now complete the user task when he chooses to.

Task delegation is an interesting workflow feature that you can use for ad hoc tasks, but also for user tasks in process definitions. In the previous subsection about subtasks, you saw that you can use a task listener to implement additional workflow features in a process definition; that would also work well for task delegation.

Because task delegation isn't implemented in the Activiti Explorer, this completes our delegation discussion. We'll now move on to implementing the four-eye principle, which isn't supported by the Activiti Engine out of the box.

10.1.3 Implementing the four-eye principle

A commonly used workflow pattern is the four-eye principle. Imagine you have two user tasks, "Develop solution" and "Review solution" in a process, and both tasks are assigned to the same engineering group. Kermit claims and completes the first user task, and then Kermit also wants to claim the review user task. The four-eye principle prohibits Kermit from claiming the "Review solution" user task because he also completed the first user task. According to the four-eye principle, the Review Solution user task must be performed by a second pair of eyes, which explains the name of the principle.

The Activiti Engine doesn't support the four-eye principle pattern by default, but you can implement this functionality without a lot of coding. What you need is a piece of logic that checks that the person who claims the second user task isn't the person who claimed and completed the first user task.

You can implement a task listener that's executed when someone claims the user task. Let's look at the task listener implementation in the following listing.

Listing 10.4 Task listener that implements the four-eye principle

```java
public class FourEyesListener implements TaskListener {

  private FixedValue otherTaskId;
  private FixedValue processEngineName;

  @Override
  public void notify(DelegateTask delegateTask) {
    String name = null;
    if(processEngineName != null) {

      name = processEngineName.getExpressionText();
    } else {
      name = ProcessEngines.NAME_DEFAULT;
    }
    ProcessEngine processEngine =
        ProcessEngines.getProcessEngines().get(name);
    HistoryService historyService =
        processEngine.getHistoryService();
    HistoricTaskInstance historicTask = historyService
        .createHistoricTaskInstanceQuery()
        .processInstanceId(delegateTask.getProcessInstanceId())
        .taskDefinitionKey(
            otherTaskId.getExpressionText())
        .singleResult();

    if(historicTask == null) {
      throw new ActivitiException("The previous task " +
          otherTaskId.getExpressionText() +
              " could not be found");
```

❶ Sets the default process engine name

❷ Retrieves process engine

❸ Retrieves other task instance

```
      }

      String claimer = delegateTask.getAssignee();
      String previousAssigneee = historicTask.getAssignee();

      if(claimer.equalsIgnoreCase(previousAssigneee)) {
        throw new ActivitiException("Assignee of task " +
            otherTaskId.getExpressionText() +
                " is not allowed to claim this task");
      }
    }
  }
  public void setOtherTaskId(FixedValue otherTaskId) {
    this.otherTaskId = otherTaskId;
  }
  public void setProcessEngineName(
      FixedValue processEngineName) {
    this.processEngineName = processEngineName;
  }
}
```

❹ **Checks if assignee isn't the same**

This task listener implementation is designed to be reusable in your process definitions, so the process engine name can be overridden in the task listener configuration in the process definition. If you don't override the name, the default value is used ❶ to retrieve the process engine from the cache ❷. When a process engine is created in the Activiti Explorer or by using the Java API, it's registered in the cache of the `ProcessEngines` singleton.

With the process engine instance available, you can implement the four-eye principle logic. First, you have to retrieve the previous user task completed by some user. The task identifier of the previous user task needs to be set as a field property in the Activiti listener configuration, as you'll see in listing 10.5. Then this task identifier is used to retrieve the user task via the `HistoryService` ❸.

Then, you can check whether the person who tries to claim the second user task is the same as the assignee of the first user task ❹. If the values are the same, an `ActivitiException` is thrown and the user task will not be claimed.

The next listing shows how you can use this newly created task listener. This small process definition example configures this task listener on the second user task.

Listing 10.5   Example process definition using the four-eye task listener

```
<definitions xmlns="http://www.omg.org/spec/BPMN/20100524/MODEL"
    xmlns:activiti="http://activiti.org/bpmn"
    targetNamespace="http://www.bpmnwithactiviti.org/foureyes">

  <process id="fourEyesProcess">
    <startEvent id="theStart" />
    <sequenceFlow sourceRef="theStart"
        targetRef="firstTask" />
    <userTask id="firstTask"
        activiti:candidateGroups="sales" />
    <sequenceFlow sourceRef="firstTask"
        targetRef="secondTask" />
```

❶ **Assigns to candidate group sales**

```
            <userTask id="secondTask"
                activiti:candidateGroups="sales">
              <extensionElements>
                <activiti:taskListener
                    class="org.bpmnwithactiviti.chapter10.
                        ➡ foureyes.FourEyesListener"
                    event="assignment">
                  <activiti:field name="otherTaskId"
                      stringValue="firstTask" />
                </activiti:taskListener>
              </extensionElements>
            </userTask>
            <sequenceFlow sourceRef="secondTask"
                targetRef="theEnd" />
            <endEvent id="theEnd" />
          </process>
        </definitions>
```

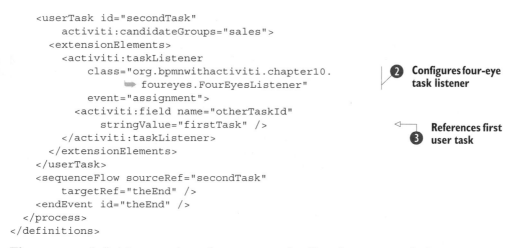

2 Configures four-eye task listener

3 References first user task

The process definition consists of two user tasks directly connected via a sequence flow. Both user tasks have the sales group defined as their candidate group **1**. The second user task, to which you want to apply the four-eye principle, has a task listener configured **2** so that it corresponds to the implementation in listing 10.4. The otherTaskId field property is set to reference the first user task **3**.

With the task listener implementation and process definition in place, you can now easily create a unit test to test the solution. Because you want to use the default process engine configuration, you need to initialize the process engine without the help of the Activiti test classes. The ActivitiRule test class initializes the process engine without registering it in the ProcessEngines cache. The following listing shows the unit test implementation.

Listing 10.6 Testing the four-eye task listener implementation

```
public class FourEyesTest extends AbstractTest {

  @Test
  public void validateFourEyes() {
    ProcessEngine processEngine = ProcessEngineConfiguration
        .createProcessEngineConfigurationFromResource(
            "activiti.cfg-mem.xml")
        .setProcessEngineName(
            ProcessEngines.NAME_DEFAULT)
        .buildProcessEngine();

    processEngine.getRepositoryService().createDeployment()
        .addClasspathResource(
            "chapter10/foureyes/fourEyes.bpmn20.xml")
        .name("fourEyes")
        .deploy();

    processEngine.getRuntimeService()
        .startProcessInstanceByKey("fourEyesProcess");

    TaskService taskService = processEngine.getTaskService();
    Task firstTask = taskService
```

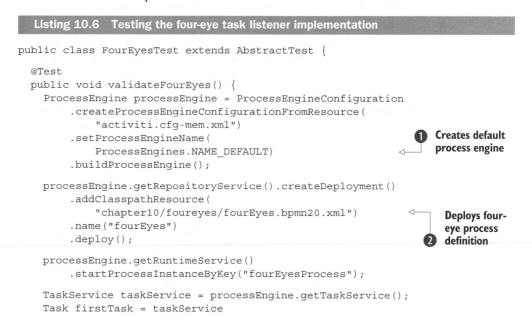

1 Creates default process engine

Deploys four-eye process **2** definition

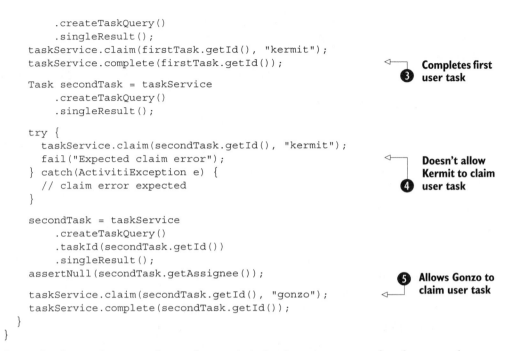

```
    .createTaskQuery()
    .singleResult();
taskService.claim(firstTask.getId(), "kermit");
taskService.complete(firstTask.getId());

Task secondTask = taskService
    .createTaskQuery()
    .singleResult();

try {
  taskService.claim(secondTask.getId(), "kermit");
  fail("Expected claim error");
} catch(ActivitiException e) {
  // claim error expected
}

secondTask = taskService
    .createTaskQuery()
    .taskId(secondTask.getId())
    .singleResult();
assertNull(secondTask.getAssignee());

taskService.claim(secondTask.getId(), "gonzo");
taskService.complete(secondTask.getId());
  }
}
```

❸ Completes first user task

❹ Doesn't allow Kermit to claim user task

❺ Allows Gonzo to claim user task

As you've learned, you can't use the `ActivitiRule` test support class because the process engine is registered in the cache being used in the listener implementation (see listing 10.4), so you must build the process engine with a default process name yourself ❶. Then you deploy the process definition discussed in listing 10.5 to the process engine ❷.

When the process instance is started, the first user task is created and claimed and completed by Kermit ❸. The process instance then creates the second user task. First, you try to claim the user task with the Kermit user. But, because Kermit also has claimed and completed the first user task, the four-eye task listener throws an `Activiti-Exception` ❹. Then, you claim and complete the user task using the user Gonzo ❺ because he's allowed to claim the user task.

Task listeners provide nice integration points in the Activiti Engine and user tasks in particular, which helps to implement workflow patterns without a lot of additional coding. The four-eye principle is just one example that demonstrates this. Now let's move on to the topic of managing user and group identities. In the next section, we'll take a look at how to integrate an LDAP server with the Activiti Engine.

10.2 Managing the user identities in an LDAP server

By default, the Activiti Engine uses a couple of database tables to manage the user and group identities. We've worked with the demo users Kermit and Fozzie in the previous examples. But a typical organization has a centralized solution for managing the user and group identities for all the applications in the organization. In many cases, an LDAP server is chosen as the identity management solution.

In this section, you'll learn how to use an LDAP server for managing the user and group identities available to the Activiti Engine. You'll use the open source Apache Directory Server to implement the examples. Let's first install the Apache Directory Server before we dive into Activiti's user and group management classes.

10.2.1 *Installing Apache Directory Server*

The Apache Directory Server project provides you with an LDAP server, an Eclipse plugin to manage the LDAP server, and an LDAP client API framework. We'll use all these products in this section.

First, you can install the LDAP server by selecting the latest ApacheDS release from http://directory.apache.org. In the examples in this book, I've used ApacheDS 1.5.7. Go through the installation screens and accept the default options. Once it's installed, you'll have an LDAP server running on port 10389.

Next, you can install the latest version of the Apache Directory Studio from the same website. This will install an Eclipse product with the Apache Directory Studio plugins preinstalled. The studio eases the administration of the LDAP server a lot, so let's start it up.

First you need to add a new connection in the Apache Directory Studio to the ApacheDS LDAP server. Choose File > New from the toolbar, go to LDAP Browser > LDAP Connection, and click Next. There, you can fill in the connection settings for the ApacheDS LDAP server you installed (see figure 10.3).

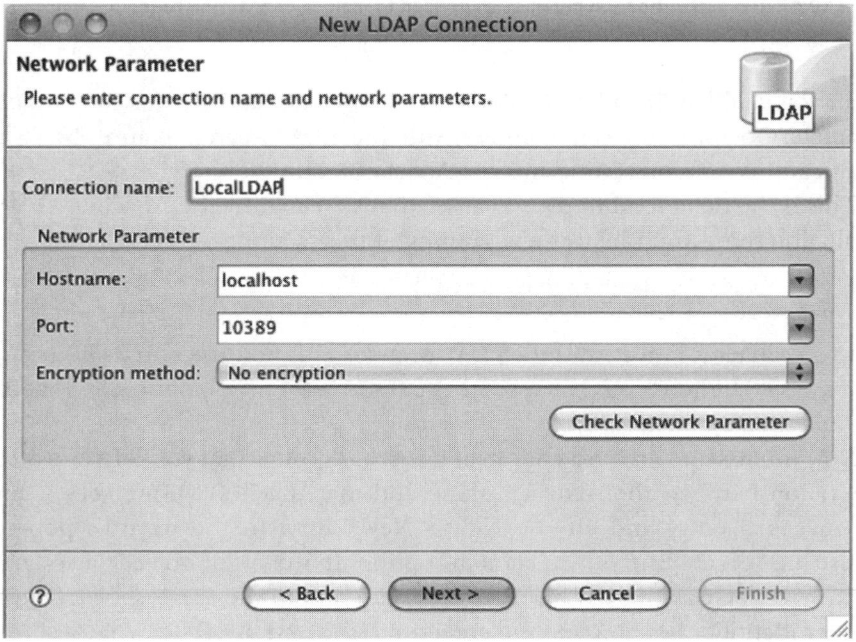

Figure 10.3   The wizard that creates a new LDAP connection in the Apache Directory Studio, showing the connection settings

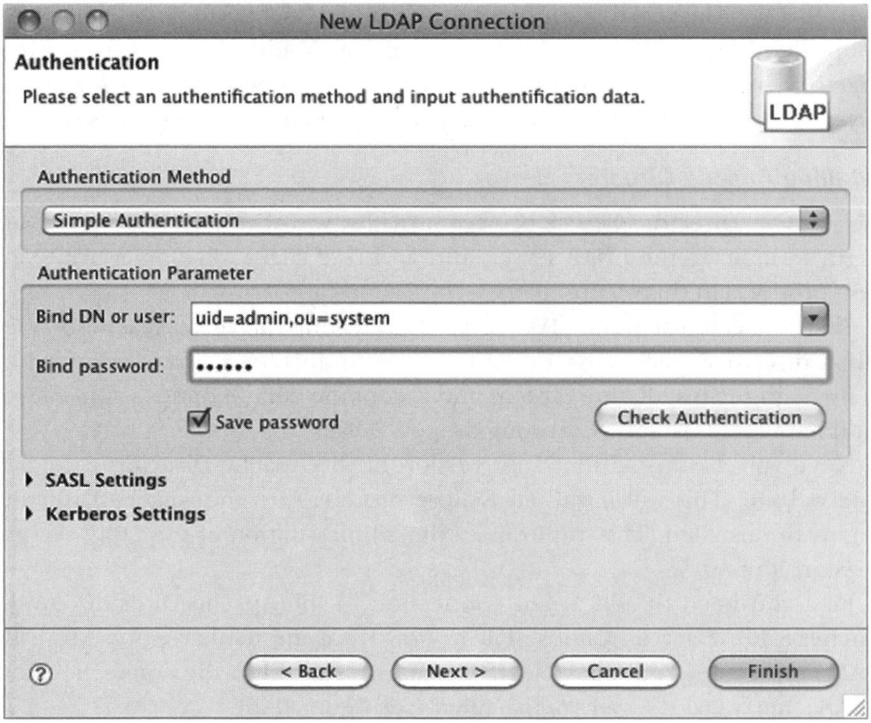

Figure 10.4 The authentication parameters needed to make a connection to the ApacheDS LDAP server using the default administrator user

When you've filled in the connection settings, you need to enter the authentication parameters before you can connect with the LDAP server. Figure 10.4 shows the default authentication settings for the ApacheDS LDAP server.

This is the default administrator user that's created by the ApacheDS LDAP server installation script you ran at the beginning of this section:

```
Bind DN or user: uid=admin,ou=system
Bind password: secret
```

Now you can click Finish, and the LDAP browser will show the entries in the ApacheDS LDAP server. When you collapse the ou=system entry, you'll see that there's a uid=admin entry.

Now you need to create a couple of users and groups that you'll later use to test the integration between the Activiti Engine and the ApacheDS LDAP server. Right-click the ou=users entry and choose New > New Entry. In the wizard's pop-up menu, choose the "Create Entry from Scratch" option. In the list of object classes, choose the inetOrgPerson class, which represents a user entry in the LDAP server. Then, choose the user identifier to complete the creation of the new user.

In figure 10.5, you add a user with a unique identifier, uid, of Kermit. When you click Next, you'll see the last page of the wizard, where you have to fill in the sn (surname)

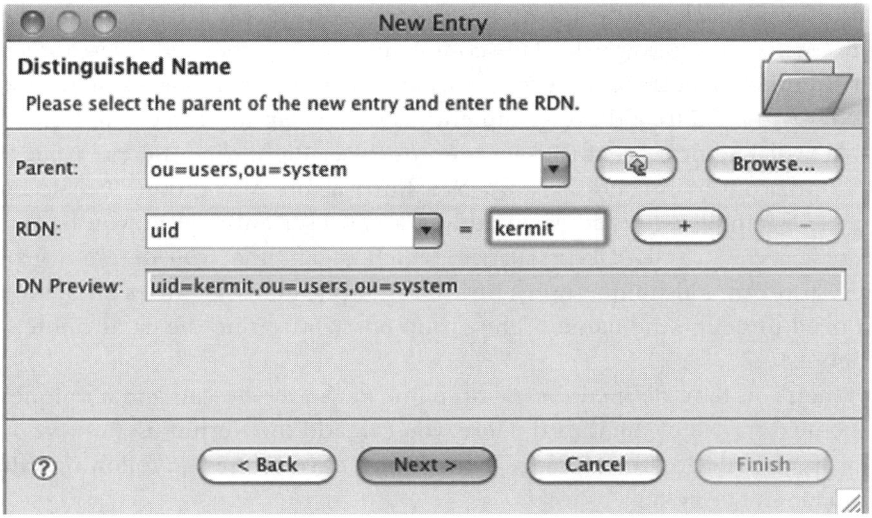

Figure 10.5   The New Entry wizard showing a new user entry for the user Kermit

and cn (complete name) attributes. When you click Finish, the user entry is created in the ApacheDS LDAP server.

If you also want to store the password value for the Kermit user in the LDAP server, you need to add an additional attribute to the uid=kermit entry. When you click the newly created user entry in the LDAP browser, you get an overview of the attributes in the main panel of the Apache Directory Studio. When you right-click in the Attributes view, you can choose New Attribute. Then you can select the userPassword attribute from the list, as shown in figure 10.6.

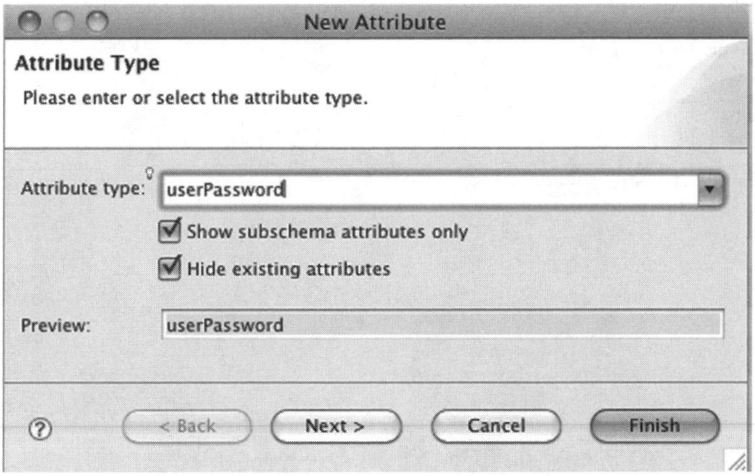

Figure 10.6   Adding a new userPassword attribute to complete the credentials for the newly created user entry

Then you can click Finish and enter a password of your choice. (In the examples, I've used *kermit* as the password.) This completes the steps needed to create a new user entry in the ApacheDS LDAP server. You can add additional users using the same steps.

Now you need to add two group entries so you can test the group functionality of the Activiti Engine's `IdentityService` interface. Right-click the `ou=groups` entry in the LDAP browser and choose New > New Entry again. Also choose "Create Entry from Scratch" again, like you did when adding a new user entry. Next, you have to choose the object class `groupOfUniqueNames`, which means that you define a group entry where you can add unique user entries; no duplicate user entries are allowed. Then you need to define the name of the group entry by setting the `cn` attribute, as shown in figure 10.7.

When you have defined the group name `manager`, you can add a unique member in the next screen of the wizard. Here, you can add the Kermit user entry you created a few moments ago. To reference Kermit, you have to use the following value in the unique member field:

```
uid=kermit,ou=users,ou=system
```

If there are more users available, you can add them by creating a new `uniqueMember` attribute in the group entry.

To complete the group setup, create a group named `sales` by following the same steps you did for the `manager` group entry. You're all set up now to implement the logic needed to integrate the Activiti Engine with the ApacheDS LDAP server. You've

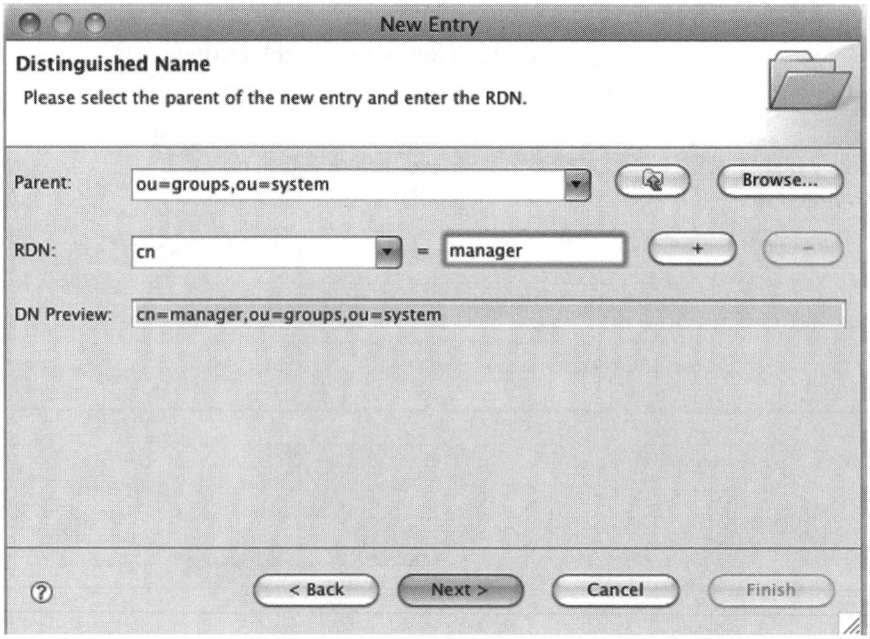

Figure 10.7   Defining the group name by setting the `cn` attribute in the New Entry wizard

created a Kermit user and two groups, manager and sales, where you added the Kermit user entry. Let's implement the LDAP query logic and configure the Activiti Engine to use the new user and group manager classes.

10.2.2 *Writing LDAP query logic for the Activiti Engine*

Implementing a different identity management solution for the Activiti Engine isn't hard. The Activiti Engine provides integration points that you can implement to access an identity management solution of your choice. The integration points are separated in a user manager and a group manager class. We'll start with the user manager, which provides capabilities to query the Activiti Engine for users and validates the user's credentials.

First, you have to implement the Activiti Engine `SessionFactory` interface to create a factory class for the user manager.

> **Listing 10.7 Implement the `SessionFactory` interface to create a new user manager**

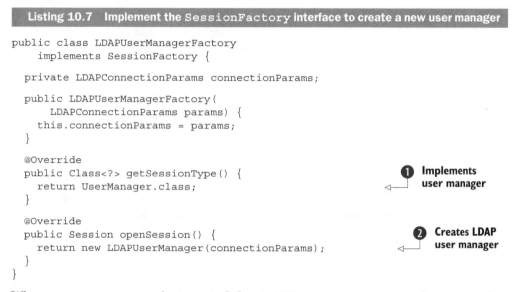

```
public class LDAPUserManagerFactory
    implements SessionFactory {

  private LDAPConnectionParams connectionParams;

  public LDAPUserManagerFactory(
      LDAPConnectionParams params) {
    this.connectionParams = params;
  }

  @Override
  public Class<?> getSessionType() {        ❶ Implements
    return UserManager.class;                   user manager
  }

  @Override
  public Session openSession() {            ❷ Creates LDAP
    return new LDAPUserManager(connectionParams);   user manager
  }
}
```

When you create a new instance of the `LDAPUserManagerFactory`, the connection parameters needed to communicate with the ApacheDS LDAP server are provided. You'll see the definition of these parameters in the Spring configuration later on, in listing 10.10. The `LDAPConnectionParams` class is simple and is just a container for the connection parameters:

```
public class LDAPConnectionParams {

  private String ldapServer;
  private int ldapPort;
  private String ldapUser;
  private String ldapPassword;

  // getters and setters
}
```

The Activiti Engine needs to know what kind of manager will be created with this factory class, so you have to implement the getSessionType method and specify that you'll implement a UserManager type **①**. And, finally, you have to implement the openSession method to create a new instance of the LDAPUserManager **②** that contains the LDAP query logic needed for the user manager.

That brings us immediately to the user manager class that contains the communication and query logic for the ApacheDS LDAP server: the LDAPUserManager. We'll look at this class in two parts because it's a larger class as a result of the LDAP query logic.

Listing 10.8 Part 1 of the LDAP user manager implementation

```
public class LDAPUserManager extends UserManager {        ◁──┐  Subclass of Activiti
                                                           ① UserManager
  private static final String USER_GROUP =
    "ou=users,ou=system";

  private LDAPConnectionParams connectionParams;

  public LDAPUserManager(LDAPConnectionParams params) {
    this.connectionParams = params;
  }

  @Override                                                ② Overrides
  public User createNewUser(String userId) {        ◁──────  default methods
    throw new ActivitiException(
      "LDAP user manager doesn't support creating a new user");
  }

  @Override
  public Boolean checkPassword(String userId,
      String password) {

    boolean credentialsValid = false;                      ③ Opens connection
    LdapConnection connection = new LdapConnection(  ◁──────  to LDAP server
        connectionParams.getLdapServer(),
        connectionParams.getLdapPort());
    try {
      BindResponse response = connection.bind(       ◁──┐  Authenticates
          "uid=" + userId + "," + USER_GROUP, password);  ④ to LDAP server
      if(response.getLdapResult().getResultCode() ==
         ResultCodeEnum.SUCCESS) {

        credentialsValid = true;
      }
    } catch (Exception e) {
      throw new ActivitiException(
          "LDAP connection bind failure", e);
    }
    LDAPConnectionUtil.closeConnection(connection);
    return credentialsValid;
  }
}
```

In this first part of the LDAPUserManager implementation, you can see that it's implemented as a subclass of the Activiti UserManager class **①**. The UserManager class is the default implementation used to query for users in the Activiti database. That's also why you have to override several methods that deal with creating, deleting, and updating a user entry, as you see here with the createNewUser method ❷. Because you're managing the user identities in an LDAP server, you don't want the Activiti Engine to modify it; that's only allowed by LDAP administrators who manage the identities using, for example, the Apache Directory Studio. Therefore, you throw an ActivitiException when these methods are invoked. This listing only includes the createNewUser method, but, in the book's source code you can see that more of these methods are overridden.

The checkPassword method is invoked when the Activiti Engine wants to validate the user credentials. This is done when a user logs in to the Activiti Explorer and the Activiti REST API. To be able to validate the credentials, you need to open a connection to the ApacheDS LDAP server ❸. Then you can authenticate with the user identifier and the provided password ❹. The outcome of the authentication request is the result of the checkPassword method.

But you don't only want to check a user's credentials. You also want to be able to query the Activiti Engine for users. That's done via the findUserByQueryCriteria method, which is shown in part 2 of the LDAPUserManager class.

Listing 10.9 Part 2 of the LDAP user manager implementation

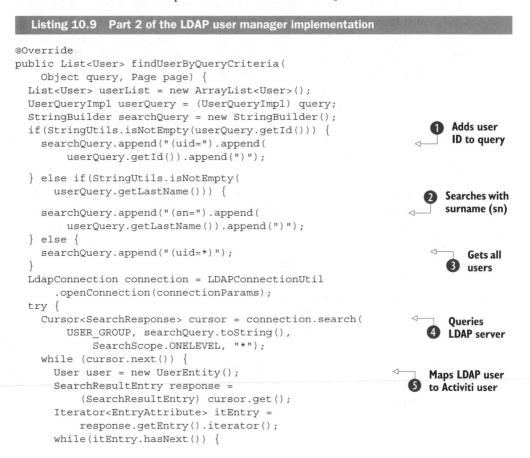

```
@Override
public List<User> findUserByQueryCriteria(
    Object query, Page page) {
  List<User> userList = new ArrayList<User>();
  UserQueryImpl userQuery = (UserQueryImpl) query;
  StringBuilder searchQuery = new StringBuilder();
  if(StringUtils.isNotEmpty(userQuery.getId())) {        ❶ Adds user
    searchQuery.append("(uid=").append(                     ID to query
        userQuery.getId()).append(")");

  } else if(StringUtils.isNotEmpty(
      userQuery.getLastName())) {
                                                           ❷ Searches with
    searchQuery.append("(sn=").append(                        surname (sn)
        userQuery.getLastName()).append(")");
  } else {
    searchQuery.append("(uid=*)");                            Gets all
  }                                                        ❸ users
  LdapConnection connection = LDAPConnectionUtil
    .openConnection(connectionParams);
  try {
    Cursor<SearchResponse> cursor = connection.search(       Queries
      USER_GROUP, searchQuery.toString(),                ❹ LDAP server
          SearchScope.ONELEVEL, "*");
    while (cursor.next()) {
      User user = new UserEntity();                         Maps LDAP user
      SearchResultEntry response =                        ❺ to Activiti user
          (SearchResultEntry) cursor.get();
      Iterator<EntryAttribute> itEntry =
          response.getEntry().iterator();
      while(itEntry.hasNext()) {
```

```
        EntryAttribute attribute = itEntry.next();
        String key = attribute.getId();
        if("uid".equalsIgnoreCase(key)) {
          user.setId(attribute.getString());
        } else if("sn".equalsIgnoreCase(key)) {
          user.setLastName(attribute.getString());
        } else if("cn".equalsIgnoreCase(key)) {
          user.setFirstName(attribute.getString().substring(
              0, attribute.getString().indexOf(" ")));
        }
      }
      userList.add(user);
    }
    cursor.close();
  } catch (Exception e) {
    throw new ActivitiException(
        "LDAP connection search failure", e);
  }
  LDAPConnectionUtil.closeConnection(connection);
  return userList;
}
```

This second part of the LDAPUserManager class contains a bit more logic related to
the implementation of the LDAP user query. You have to be able to define an LDAP
query matching the values provided by the UserQueryImpl input parameter. In this
example, you can use the user identifier ❶ and the last name ❷ set in the query
parameter instance. There are also other query parameters that you can set when
using the createUserQuery method of the Activiti Engine IdentityService. You
may want to support all of these query parameters, and that's possible by adding
more attributes to the user entry attributes in the LDAP server. But, for this example, you stop with supporting the user identifier and last name parameters. In addition, when no query parameter is set in the UserQueryImpl instance, you query the
LDAP server for all users ❸.

When the query is defined, you can connect to the ApacheDS LDAP server and
query it using the query string ❹. Note that you also use the USER_GROUP class attribute that tells the LDAP server to only look in the ou=users,ou=system entry. When
you get a response from the LDAP server, you map every retrieved user entry to an
Activiti Engine User instance ❺.

In the book's source code, you can find an implementation similar to listings 10.7
to 10.9 for the LDAP group manager: one queries for users belonging to a specific
group and the other gets all available groups. In the book's source code, you can look
at the LDAPGroupManagerFactory and LDAPGroupManager classes for the implementation details.

Now that you have the implementation classes, you still need to register them in
the Activiti Engine configuration. The following listing shows a sample Activiti Engine
configuration using an in-memory database and the LDAP user and group manager.

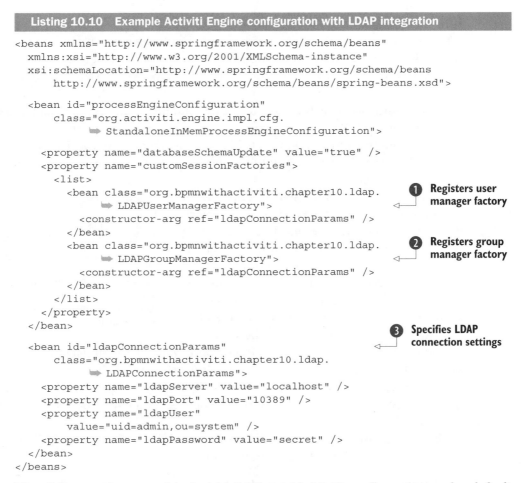

Listing 10.10 Example Activiti Engine configuration with LDAP integration

```
<beans xmlns="http://www.springframework.org/schema/beans"
  xmlns:xsi="http://www.w3.org/2001/XMLSchema-instance"
  xsi:schemaLocation="http://www.springframework.org/schema/beans
      http://www.springframework.org/schema/beans/spring-beans.xsd">

  <bean id="processEngineConfiguration"
      class="org.activiti.engine.impl.cfg.
            ➥ StandaloneInMemProcessEngineConfiguration">

    <property name="databaseSchemaUpdate" value="true" />
    <property name="customSessionFactories">
      <list>
        <bean class="org.bpmnwithactiviti.chapter10.ldap.
              ➥ LDAPUserManagerFactory">
          <constructor-arg ref="ldapConnectionParams" />
        </bean>
        <bean class="org.bpmnwithactiviti.chapter10.ldap.
              ➥ LDAPGroupManagerFactory">
          <constructor-arg ref="ldapConnectionParams" />
        </bean>
      </list>
    </property>
  </bean>

  <bean id="ldapConnectionParams"
      class="org.bpmnwithactiviti.chapter10.ldap.
            ➥ LDAPConnectionParams">
    <property name="ldapServer" value="localhost" />
    <property name="ldapPort" value="10389" />
    <property name="ldapUser"
        value="uid=admin,ou=system" />
    <property name="ldapPassword" value="secret" />
  </bean>
</beans>
```

❶ **Registers user manager factory**

❷ **Registers group manager factory**

❸ **Specifies LDAP connection settings**

The difference between this Activiti Engine with LDAP configuration and a default Activiti Engine configuration is the use of the customSessionFactories property. This property allows you to override the default user and group managers by defining the factory classes ❶ ❷. As you can see, you can use Spring bean injection to pass along the LDAP connection parameters ❸ to the constructor of the factory classes.

In the book's source code, you can find two unit tests, LDAPUserTest and LDAP-GroupTest, that use this example Activiti Engine configuration and fire a couple of tests using the IdentityService interface.

You now have a good overview of what needs to be done to integrate Activiti with an LDAP server or another identity management solution. It's time to move on to another workflow feature of the Activiti Engine. We'll be looking at a whole new BPMN 2.0 element that we haven't used before: the multi-instance construct.

10.3   *Implementing the BPMN 2.0 multi-instance activity*

When you want to implement a review process with Activiti, you need a way to add a user task for every reviewer. And, suppose you want at least 75 percent of the reviewers to complete the user task before the review can be considered finished. This kind of functionality is what the multi-instance construct adds to the BPMN 2.0 palette.

A multi-instance activity is used to create multiple instances of an activity like in a for-each construct. You can configure all task activities (like service and user task), embedded subprocesses, and call activities to be a multi-instance activity. For example, if you define a service task as a multi-instance activity, the same service task will be executed multiple times.

You can define a multi-instance activity to run sequentially or in parallel. Furthermore, you can define how many instances must be created. Figure 10.8 shows a parallel multi-instance user task and a sequential multi-instance service task.

You can see that a parallel multi-instance activity (user task) has a different icon than the sequential multi-instance activity (service task). Also note that, for a service task, there's techni-

Figure 10.8   Multi-instance examples showing a parallel multi-instance user task and a sequential multi-instance service task

cally no difference between a parallel and sequential multi-instance definition because the instances are always executed after each other. But, for a user task and also for an embedded subprocess, there's a big difference. For a parallel user task, the user task instances are created all at once, whereas, for a sequential user task, they are created after each other .

Before you implement a workflow example using a multi-instance definition, let's take a look at the different configuration options.

10.3.1   *Configuring a multi-instance activity*

Let's start with a simple multi-instance definition for a user task that creates three parallel instances of the review user task:

```
<userTask id="reviewTask">
  <multiInstanceLoopCharacteristics isSequential="false">
    <loopCardinality>3</loopCardinality>
  </ multiInstanceLoopCharacteristics>
</userTask>
```

The multi-instance definition is a child element of a task activity, embedded subprocess, or call activity. You have to set the attribute `isSequential` to `true` or `false` for sequential or parallel multi-instance activities. The number of instances can be defined using the `loopCardinality` element. In this example, you set a static value of 3, but you can also use process variables to define the number of instances:

```
<loopCardinality>${nrOfReviewers}</loopCardinality>
```

NOTE The loop cardinality value is processed only once, when the multi-instance activity is created. When the process variable value changes during the multi-instance activity execution, this doesn't result in another number of instances.

This is nice, but it gets more interesting if you pass a process variable containing a collection and use the values of the collection for the user task assignment:

```
<userTask id="reviewTask"
    name="Review task ${loopCounter}"
    activiti:assignee="${reviewer}">
  <multiInstanceLoopCharacteristics isSequential="false">
    <loopDataInputRef>reviewersList</loopDataInputRef>
    <inputDataItem name="reviewer"/>
  </ multiInstanceLoopCharacteristics>
</userTask>
```

In this example, you have a process variable named `reviewersList`, which consists of an array of string values. For every string value in the reviewers list, a new process variable named `reviewer` is created in the context of the multi-instance user task. You can use this `reviewer` process variable in the assignment definition (as you can see in the code snippet). Implicit process variables are also created. For every instance of the user task, a unique `loopCounter` value corresponding to an instance number is available. The `loopCounter` value ranges from 1 to the number of instances.

The review task example has a list of reviewers that consists of an array of string values. But more often, you would have a piece of Java logic to retrieve the reviewers from a database, for example. This can be implemented with the following Activiti extension attributes:

```
<userTask id="reviewTask"
    name="Review task ${loopCounter}"
    activiti:assignee="${reviewer}">
  <multiInstanceLoopCharacteristics isSequential="false"
      activiti:collection="${userService.getReviewers()}"
      activiti:elementVariable="reviewer"/>
</userTask>
```

In this example, you have a `userService` process variable or Spring bean on which you can invoke the `getReviewers` method.

Another use of the multi-instance definition is a decision-making process. Because you need multiple persons to vote for a decision, a multi-instance definition can help to create a user task for every voter. In the next section, we'll discuss an example showing a simple decision process.

10.3.2 *Implementing a multi-instance embedded process*

A typical workflow requirement is to have review or decision functionality in a process definition. And when multiple people are involved in the review or decision process, a multi-instance definition can help to ease the complexity of the process definition. In this section, we'll implement a decision process where multiple people can vote for a

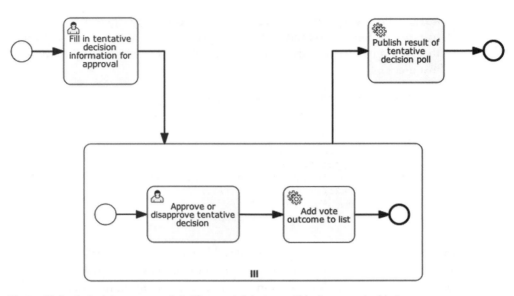

Figure 10.9   A decision process definition containing a multi-instance embedded subprocess to allow multiple people to vote for the final decision

preliminary decision to be made final. Figure 10.9 shows the decision process definition, as modeled with the Activiti Modeler.

In the first user task of the process, you have to provide information about the preliminary decision and the participants. Then, multiple instances of the embedded subprocess are created to allow each of the participants to vote for the final decision. To make it easy to gather all votes, you add the vote to a process variable containing all the votes. Finally, the outcome of the decision process is published.

To implement this process definition in the Activiti Engine, you need a BPMN 2.0 XML definition, but also a number of Java service tasks. Let's start with the BPMN 2.0 XML definition in the next listing. Don't be distracted by the length of the listing; it contains a lot of familiar constructs.

Listing 10.11   BPMN 2.0 XML definition of the decision process

```
<definitions xmlns="http://www.omg.org/spec/BPMN/20100524/MODEL"
    xmlns:activiti="http://activiti.org/bpmn"
    targetNamespace="http://www.bpmnwithactiviti.org/multiinstance">

  <process id="decisionProcess" name="Decision making process">
    <startEvent id="theStart">
      <extensionElements>
        <activiti:formProperty id="decisionInfo"
            name="Decision info"
            required="true"
            type="string" />
        <activiti:formProperty id="participants"
            name="Participants (comma separated)"
            required="true"
            type="string" />
```

① **Provides comma-separated participants**

```
        </extensionElements>
      </startEvent>
      <sequenceFlow sourceRef="theStart"
          targetRef="createAssigneeList" />
      <serviceTask id="createAssigneeList"
          activiti:class="org.bpmnwithactiviti.chapter10.
              ➥ multiinstance.CreateAssigneeList" />
      <sequenceFlow sourceRef="createAssigneeList"
          targetRef="decisionSubProcess"/>
      <subProcess id="decisionSubProcess">
        <multiInstanceLoopCharacteristics
            isSequential="false">
          <loopDataInputRef>assigneeList</loopDataInputRef>
          <inputDataItem name="assignee"/>
          <completionCondition>
            ${nrOfCompletedInstances/nrOfInstances > 0.5 }
          </completionCondition>
        </multiInstanceLoopCharacteristics>
        <startEvent id="theStartSubProcess" />
        <sequenceFlow sourceRef="theStartSubProcess"
            targetRef="decisionTask" />
        <userTask id="decisionTask" name="Decision task"
            activiti:assignee="${assignee}">
          <extensionElements>
            <activiti:formProperty id="decisionInfo"
                name="Decision info"
                expression="${decisionInfo}"
                writable="false"/>
            <activiti:formProperty id="vote"
                name="Do you approve the preliminary decision"
                required="true"
                type="enum">
              <activiti:value id="true" name="Yes"/>
              <activiti:value id="false" name="No"/>
            </activiti:formProperty>
          </extensionElements>
        </userTask>
        <sequenceFlow sourceRef="decisionTask"
            targetRef="gatherDecisionVote" />
        <serviceTask id="gatherDecisionVote"
            activiti:class="org.bpmnwithactiviti.chapter10.
                ➥ multiinstance.AddDecisionVote" />
        <sequenceFlow sourceRef="gatherDecisionVote"
            targetRef="theEndSubProcess" />
        <endEvent id="theEndSubProcess" />
      </subProcess>
      <sequenceFlow sourceRef="decisionSubProcess"
          targetRef="outcomeTask" />
      <serviceTask id="outcomeTask"
          activiti:class="org.bpmnwithactiviti.chapter10.
              ➥ multiinstance.PublishVotePoll" />
      <sequenceFlow sourceRef="outcomeTask"
          targetRef="theEnd" />
      <endEvent id="theEnd" />
  </process>
</definitions>
```

2 Creates list of participants

3 Creates a multi-instance subprocess

4 Defines completion condition

5 Provides participant vote

6 Publishes result of votes

As you can see, BPMN 2.0 XML gets quite verbose when implementing a decision process. You can also use the Activiti Designer to abstract you from the XML, because the multi-instance definition is supported there also. But to learn about all the details, it's good to start with the XML definition as in this process example.

When the process instance is started, a form property containing the participants as a comma-separated string must be provided ❶. Because the multi-instance construct doesn't support a comma-separated string, you first must transform it to a java.util.List and add it as an assigneeList process variable ❷.

Then you define multi-instance characteristics on the embedded subprocess using the assigneeList ❸. You add a new configuration option to the multi-instance definition by defining a completion condition ❹. In a completion condition, you can define an expression that completes the multi-instance activity before all instances have completed. In this example, you use the implicit process variables nrOfCompletedInstances (the number of instances of the multi-instance activity that have already been completed) and nrOfInstances (the total number of instances calculated when creating the multi-instance activity). When more than half of the instances have been completed, the multi-instance embedded subprocess will complete and progress to the next activity; in this example, outcomeTask.

As part of the multi-instance embedded subprocess, you define a vote user task where a participant can enter a vote for the preliminary decision ❺. After the vote is entered, the vote is added to a global list of votes in the gatherDecisionVote service task. At the end of the process definition, the outcomeTask service task ❻ prints the vote outcome to the console.

The implementation logic of the Java service task classes isn't hard to understand. The CreateAssigneeList transforms the comma-separated string into a list. The AddDecisionVote class is quite simple, too, but it contains an important piece of logic concerning the process context, as you can see in the next listing.

Listing 10.12   Implementation of the AddDecisionVote service task class

```java
public class AddDecisionVote implements JavaDelegate {

  public void execute(DelegateExecution execution) {
    String assignee = (String)
        execution.getVariableLocal("assignee");              // ❶ Gets assignee
    String voteOutcome = (String)                            //   from local context
        execution.getVariable("vote");
    Vote vote = new Vote();
    vote.setName(assignee);
    vote.setApproved(Boolean.valueOf(voteOutcome));
    DecisionVoting voting = (DecisionVoting)
        execution.getVariable("voteOutcome");
    voting.addVote(vote);
    execution.setVariable("voteOutcome", voting);
  }
}
```

The AddDecisionVote class is executed after the participant enters the vote. You can retrieve the assignee of the previous user task from the local context ❶. Because the assignee is different for every instance of the multi-instance embedded subprocess, it's important that you can retrieve it from the local process context because the local process context is unique for every instance. The assignee variable is available in the local context of the Java service task.

Note that the vote outcome of the previous user task isn't available in the local context of the Java service task. This means you have to retrieve it from the global process context using the getVariable method.

> **NOTE** In a multi-instance subprocess, the form properties of a user task are set to the global process context and not to the multi-instance local context. This means that when you have multiple user tasks in a multi-instance subprocess, the values of the form properties mapped to process variables are overwritten by the last user task. In this example, you use one user task, and then it's no problem because the service task is executed in the same transaction as the complete action of the user task.

At the end of the execute method of the AddDecisionVote class, you explicitly set the DecisionVoting instance as a variable again after adding the vote outcome. You do this so the new value of the voteOutcome process variable is added to the historic variable update list.

In the last service task class of the decision process definition, PublishVotePoll, the outcome of the voting is printed to the console. You can look at the details in the book's source code.

Now, let's execute the decision process definition using a unit test.

Listing 10.13 A unit test that runs the decision process definition

```java
public class MultiInstanceTest extends AbstractTest {

  @Rule
  public ActivitiRule activitiRule = new ActivitiRule(
      "activiti.cfg-mem-fullhistory.xml");

  @Test
  @Deployment(resources={"chapter10/multiinstance/" +
      "multiinstance.bpmn20.xml"})
  public void doMultiTasking() {
    String processDefinitionId = activitiRule
        .getRepositoryService()
        .createProcessDefinitionQuery()
        .singleResult()
        .getId();
    Map<String, String> variableMap =
        new HashMap<String, String>();
    variableMap.put("decisionInfo", "test");
    variableMap.put("participants",
        "kermit,fonzie,gonzo");                        ❶ Enters three
    ProcessInstance processInstance = activitiRule       participants for
                                                         decision process
```

```
            .getFormService()
            .submitStartFormData(
                processDefinitionId, variableMap);
    assertNotNull(processInstance);
    List<Task> taskList = activitiRule
        .getTaskService()
        .createTaskQuery()
        .list();                                              ❷ Creates three
    assertEquals(3, taskList.size());                           user tasks
    for (Task task : taskList) {
      if (activitiRule.getTaskService()
            .createTaskQuery().taskId(task.getId()).count() > 0 ) {
        Map<String, String> taskMap =
            new HashMap<String, String>();
        taskMap.put("vote", "true");
        activitiRule.getFormService()
            .submitTaskFormData(task.getId(), taskMap);       Completes
      }                                                       two of three
    }                                                       ❸ user tasks

    boolean voteOutcomeTested = false;
    List<HistoricDetail> historicVariableUpdateList =
        activitiRule
            .getHistoryService()
            .createHistoricDetailQuery()
            .variableUpdates()
            .orderByTime()
            .desc()                                           ❹ Gets all process
            .list();                                              variables
    for (HistoricDetail historicDetail :
        historicVariableUpdateList) {

      HistoricVariableUpdate historicVariableUpdate =
          (HistoricVariableUpdate) historicDetail;
      if("voteOutcome".equals(
          historicVariableUpdate.getVariableName())) {

        voteOutcomeTested = true;
        DecisionVoting voting = (DecisionVoting)
            historicVariableUpdate.getValue();
        assertTrue(voting.isDecisionVotingOutcome());         ❺ Makes sure there
        assertEquals(2, voting.getVotes().size());               are two votes
        for (Vote vote : voting.getVotes()) {
          assertTrue(vote.isApproved());
        }
        break;
      }
    }
    assertTrue(voteOutcomeTested);
  }
}
```

To test the decision process definition, you start a new process instance with three participants ❶. When the process instance is started, three instances of the embedded subprocess should be created, so three user tasks should be found when retrieving all the user tasks ❷. Then you complete the user tasks with a vote equal to `true` ❸.

When the second user task is completed, the completion condition that more than half of the instances should be completed is true, and, therefore, the multi-instance embedded subprocess will finish. This also implies that the third task is deleted before it can be completed, and, therefore, the unit test implementation validates whether a task still exists before it is completed. Then the vote results are published via the PublishVotePoll service task class.

To validate the process variables, you use the HistoryService interface to retrieve all process variable updates ordered by update time in descending order ❹; you'll get the latest process variable updates at the top of the list. You're interested in the vote-Outcome process variable to test whether the decision outcome equals true, as expected. In addition, you test whether there are two votes in the list ❺ that also have a value of true.

As you've seen in this example, the multi-instance definition can be handy when you want to implement review, approval, or decision-like logic in your process definition. In this decision process example, we used form properties again to define the user forms that interact with the process. But we're restricted to the form types supported by the Activiti Engine. In the next section, we'll explore defining new form types and using another type of form rendering.

10.4 Custom form types and external form rendering

We've been defining user task forms using the start event and user task form properties in this chapter's examples as well as in previous chapters. But the number of default form types supported by the Activiti Engine and Activiti Explorer is pretty limited when you want to implement complex user forms.

10.4.1 Implementing a custom form type

One example of a more complex form type is the UserFormType that you can find in the Activiti Explorer classes. The UserFormType can be used to select a user from the list of users in the Activiti Engine IdentityService. Figure 10.10 shows a screenshot of a sample process definition that requires selecting an approver using the UserFormType.

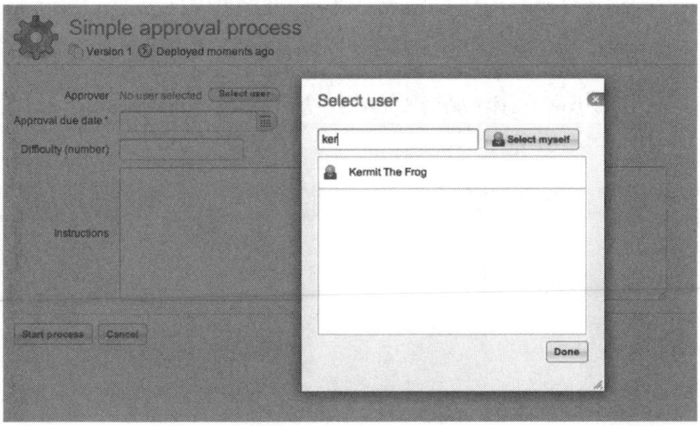

Figure 10.10 An example approval process using the UserFormType to select an approver for the approval process

As you can see, the `UserFormType` contains a lot more logic than the simple `String` or `Date` form types. It's implemented with a pop-up menu that searches in the user list while you are typing the search characters. It's possible to implement more complex form types of this sort using the Vaadin framework (the web framework that is used to implement the Activiti Explorer). In this section, we'll take a look at how to implement a simple custom form type.

The first step in implementing a custom form type is to check out the source code of the Activiti Explorer. This has been done for you, as you can see in the `book-explorer-form` project in the book's source code. There, you can start defining a new form type by extending the `AbstractFormType` class, as shown in the next listing.

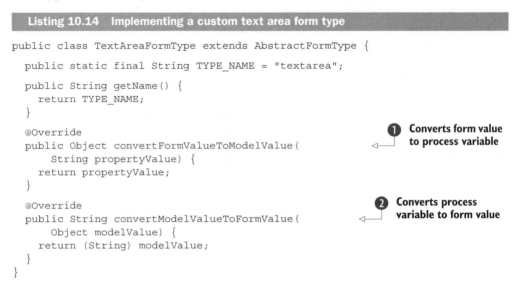

Listing 10.14   Implementing a custom text area form type

```
public class TextAreaFormType extends AbstractFormType {

  public static final String TYPE_NAME = "textarea";

  public String getName() {
    return TYPE_NAME;
  }

  @Override
  public Object convertFormValueToModelValue(                    ❶ Converts form value
      String propertyValue) {                                       to process variable
    return propertyValue;
  }

  @Override
  public String convertModelValueToFormValue(                    ❷ Converts process
      Object modelValue) {                                          variable to form value
    return (String) modelValue;
  }
}
```

Because the text area contains text, you don't have to do a lot to implement the new form type. You have to define a name that can be used to uniquely reference the form type in the form properties definition. Then you need to implement logic to convert the `String` value of the form field into a process variable ❶, in this case, also a `String` value. You also need to convert the process variable object into a form field `String` ❷.

In addition to the form type definition, you also need to implement the form field user interface. Because the Activiti Explorer is implemented in Vaadin, the form field UI logic also has to be implemented using Vaadin. Let's see how we can implement a text area in Vaadin in the following listing.

Listing 10.15   Implementing a custom text area form field UI using Vaadin

```
public class TextAreaFormPropertyRenderer extends
    AbstractFormPropertyRenderer {

  public TextAreaFormPropertyRenderer() {                        ❶ Sets form
    super(TextAreaFormType.class);                                  type class
  }

  @Override
```

```
public Field getPropertyField(FormProperty formProperty) {
  TextArea textArea = new TextArea(
      getPropertyLabel(formProperty));
  textArea.setRequired(formProperty.isRequired());
  textArea.setEnabled(formProperty.isWritable());
  textArea.setRows(10);
  textArea.setColumns(50);
  textArea.setRequiredError(getMessage(
      Messages.FORM_FIELD_REQUIRED,
          getPropertyLabel(formProperty)));
  if (formProperty.getValue() != null) {
    textArea.setValue(formProperty.getValue());
  }
  return textArea;
}
}
```

2 Defines field label

3 Sets text area value

When you want to implement the UI for a new custom form field, it's best to start with extending the AbstractFormPropertyRenderer class. The UI implementation is coupled to the form type definition class by calling the superclass with the TextAreaForm-Type class **1**. The form renderer of the Activiti Explorer expects a Field instance to display on the screen. A TextArea is also a subclass of Field, so you can return a TextArea as the result of the getPropertyField method. The AbstractFormProperty-Renderer provides a number of convenience class already, like the getPropertyLabel method to retrieve the label text from a form property **2**. Eventually, the value defined in the form property is set to fill the text area **3**.

With the form type definition and the form field UI classes implemented, you have to configure the new form type in two Spring configuration files in the Activiti Explorer source code (or book-explorer-form, for this example). First, you have to add a custom form type to the process engine configuration in the src/main/webapp/WEB-INF/applicationContext.xml file:

```
<bean id="processEngineConfiguration"
    class="org.activiti.spring.SpringProcessEngineConfiguration">
  <property name="dataSource" ref="dataSource" />
  <property name="transactionManager" ref="transactionManager" />
  <property name="databaseSchemaUpdate" value="true" />
  <property name="jobExecutorActivate" value="true" />
  <property name="customFormTypes">
    <list>
      <ref bean="userFormType"/>
      <ref bean="textAreaFormType"/>
    </list>
  </property>
</bean>

<bean id="textAreaFormType"
    class="org.bpmnwithactiviti.explorer.form.TextAreaFormType"/>
```

The second configuration file is the src/main/webapp/WEB-INF/activiti-ui-context.xml definition of UI-related classes. There you need to register the form property renderer class, TextAreaFormPropertyRenderer:

```
<property name="propertyRenderers">
  <list>
    <bean
      class="org.activiti.explorer.ui.form.StringFormPropertyRenderer" />
    <bean class="org.activiti.explorer.ui.form.EnumFormPropertyRenderer" />
    <bean class="org.activiti.explorer.ui.form.LongFormPropertyRenderer" />
    <bean class="org.activiti.explorer.ui.form.DateFormPropertyRenderer" />
    <bean class="org.activiti.explorer.ui.form.UserFormPropertyRenderer" />
    <bean
      class="org.activiti.explorer.ui.form.BooleanFormPropertyRenderer" />
    <bean
      class="org.bpmnwithactiviti.explorer.form.
        ➥ TextAreaFormPropertyRenderer" />
  </list>
</property>
```

Now you can start using the text area form type in the form property definition of a BPMN 2.0 XML file. In the `book-explorer-form` project, the approval process contains a start event form with a text area for the instructions form property. Start the `book-explorer-form` application by running `mvn clean install jetty:run` in the root directory of the project. Next, open a web browser to http://localhost:8080/book-explorer and start a new approval process. The instructions form field should now contain the text area form field you defined in the custom form type classes (see figure 10.11).

You can implement a lot of different form types to support all kinds of form fields. But, you may not want to invest in a Vaadin-based web application because your organization may have standardized on another UI technology. In the next section, we'll look into the external form rendering support in the Activiti Engine so that you can use other UI technologies.

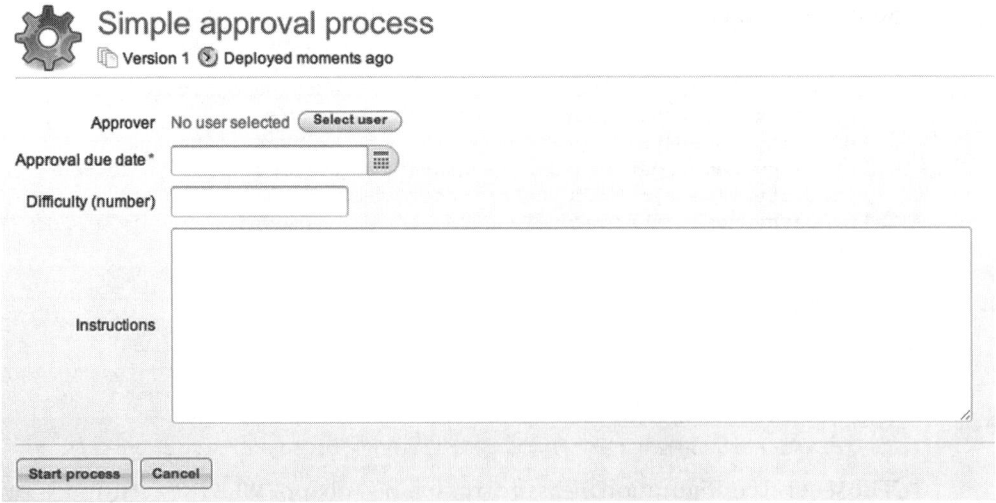

Figure 10.11   A sample process using the new text area custom form type

10.4.2 *Using external form rendering*

When you don't want to use the already existing form rendering infrastructure of the Activiti Explorer written in Vaadin, there's the option of external form rendering. With external form rendering, you're writing the user forms with your technology of choice, but that also means you're pretty much on your own when writing the logic.

There are two ways to go ahead with external form rendering:

- Use the form properties infrastructure and build a form-rendering engine in the UI technology of your choice.
- Only use the form key attribute in the start event or user task definition and develop a web application pretty much the way you're used to. The main difference is that the navigation will be partially dominated by the process definition.

When you go for the first option, your best reference is the Activiti Explorer code— look at how the form rendering is implemented there. We looked at how the form types and the field form rendering is implemented and configured in section 10.4.1.

But it may be better to go for the second option because you can then leverage the UI technology in a more default way. In chapter 9, we looked at how you can use JSF 2 in combination with CDI to build a custom workflow and process application. In the remainder of this section, we'll focus on the form rendering implementation of the book-cdi-app project you built in chapter 9.

Let's go back to the book order process definition implemented in the book-cdi-app project. You start the process definition with a start event for which you configured a form key attribute:

```
<startEvent id="startEvent" name="Start"
    activiti:formKey="taskForm_newOrder.jsf" />
```

The form key corresponds directly to a JSF page that you want to use to present the start form of the book order process. You could also use a logical name for the form key and add a navigation rule in the faces-config.xml file.

When you want to open the start form of a process definition, you can use the default JSF output link component. In the processList.xhtml file of the book-cdi-app project, you list all the process definitions deployed on the Activiti Engine and, for every process, you can go to the start form page using the following output link configuration:

```
<h:outputLink
    value="#{formService.getStartFormData(v_process.id).formKey}">
  Start
  <f:param name="processDefinitionKey" value="#{v_process.key}"></f:param>
</h:outputLink>
```

In this example, you use the Activiti CDI module to get the form service interface. Then you retrieve the start form data using the process definition identifier, and you can access the form key attribute. You also pass along the process definition key as a request parameter to be used in the taskForm_newOrder.jsf page.

In this start form page, you can now implement a user form using standard JSF tags. Let's look at the main part of the `taskForm_newOrder.xhtml` page to see how this is done:

```
<ui:define name="content">
  <f:metadata>
    <!-- bind the key of the process to be started -->
    <f:viewParam id="processDefinitionKey" name="processDefinitionKey" />
  </f:metadata>

  <h1>New book order</h1>
  <h:form>
    <table>
      <tr>
        <td>ISBN:</td>
        <td><h:inputText value="#{bookOrder.isbn}" /></td>
      </tr>
      <tr>
        <td></td>
        <td><h:commandButton value="Submit"
        action="#{businessProcess.startProcessByKey(processDefinitionKey)}"/>
        </td>
      </tr>
    </table>
  </h:form>
</ui:define>
```

As you can see, this page contains only standard JSF tags. But, you also leverage the Activiti CDI module for convenience. First, the process-scoped `bookOrder` variable is available in the JSF page context, so you can inject the value of the ISBN form field directly into the `isbn` attribute of the `bookOrder` process variable. You don't use any form property definition because you define the user form directly using JSF tags. But you can directly set a form field value in a process variable by using the process-scoped beans functionality of the Activiti CDI module.

In addition, you need a way to start a new process instance when you click Submit in the user form. The Activiti CDI module helps here by offering a `businessProcess` bean that you can invoke directly from a command button. But when you can't or don't want to use the Activiti CDI module, you can still implement this logic easily in a JSF managed bean.

As you can see, it's not hard to implement your own form rendering logic. You can utilize your UI technology of choice and Activiti can help with the form key attribute to do basic page navigation for the user forms.

We've come to the end of a long chapter. We took a look at a good number of workflow features you can implement on the Activiti Engine by utilizing the out-of-the-box functionality or by developing small pieces of logic and configuring them in the process engine configuration. You're now ready to develop your own workflow application!

10.5 *Summary*

Workflow is an important part of developing business process applications. In many cases, not all tasks in a process can be executed automatically by invoking web services or other external resources. For example, people must provide information in the process, and they're needed to review and approve specific parts of the process execution. In this chapter, you saw that Activiti supports a wide range of workflow features.

We started with an introduction to subtasks and task delegation features that are supported via the Activiti API and, in part, via the Activiti Explorer. Then we saw that it's not hard to implement a workflow pattern like the four-eye principle using a task listener.

Then we moved on to integrating an LDAP server with the Activiti Engine for identity management. In a lot of organizations, you don't want to add a separate store of identities like the default Activiti Engine database, but you want to leverage the existing identity management solution. Activiti is pluggable and can integrate with another identity management solution using custom user and group managers.

We also looked at the configuration options of the new BPMN 2.0 multi-instance construct and implemented an example process definition using a multi-instance embedded subprocess. Multi-instance activities like user tasks and embedded subprocesses can be handy when implementing review and approval logic involving multiple people.

Finally, we looked at how to extend and customize the form rendering capabilities of the Activiti Engine. You can extend the set of supported form types by implementing a new form type using the Vaadin UI framework. But, it's also possible to use a UI technology of your choice, like JSF (see chapter 9).

In the next chapter, we'll start looking outside the Activiti Engine. Often, you need to communicate with external resources such as ERP, CRM, and billing applications from a business process. We'll look at how you can leverage integration frameworks like Mule and Camel to communicate with applications outside the Activiti Engine.

Integrating services
with a BPMN 2.0 process

11

This chapter covers

- Providing a clean separation between processes and integration logic
- Explaining the BPMN 2.0 web services support
- Using Apache Camel to implement integration logic
- Using Mule ESB to implement integration logic

Up to now, we've been focusing on the Activiti process engine running BPMN 2.0 process definitions. But let's think about a use case where we'd want an order process accessing an order or enterprise resource planning (ERP) application, like SAP. Using what we've covered so far, we could implement a service task with a Java class or a Spring bean. In chapter 7, we saw that we can invoke a web service using a Java service task, so that could be a good approach.

But, if we want to send a message to a queue or communicate with a legacy system that only supports COBOL copybooks, this gets harder and harder. Wouldn't it be nice to leverage an integration platform like an enterprise service bus (ESB) or something similar to implement this integration functionality? The Activiti project contains integration with Mule ESB (from MuleSoft) and Apache Camel without the need for glue coding.

This chapter will show you how to communicate with external services and applications, starting with the BPMN 2.0 web service support in section 11.2. Then, we'll discuss the Camel integration of the Activiti framework in section 11.3 and use the Mule ESB from a BPMN process in section 11.4. Because Camel and Mule provide similar capabilities, we'll implement comparable code examples, so you can decide which coding style you like most.

But, first, let's start with an introduction to communicating with external services and applications from a process instance.

11.1 Invoking services from a BPMN 2.0 process

Activiti provides a flexible and extendable API to implement custom logic in BPMN processes, for example, by implementing a Java service task or an event listener. You can use plain Java to code your logic, or you can leverage the wide set of functionality offered by the Spring framework and use expressions or delegate expressions in a service task. This paves the way to also implement integration logic to invoke external services or applications from a BPMN process.

But is the process engine the right place to implement this integration logic? If you want to invoke a simple web service, it could be the right place. In section 11.2, you'll see that the BPMN palette includes a web service task to invoke web services. But, what if the web service interface contains a data model that's very different from the process data model? Then you would need to implement transformation logic to be able to invoke this web service.

Let's look at two ways to communicate with services from a process, starting with communicating via the service tasks.

11.1.1 Calling services via a service task

With the Java service task and the web service task (implementing a web service task is explained in section 11.2), all the options are open to implement integration logic in the BPMN process definition itself. Let's imagine a use case where an order process needs to communicate with a customer relationship management (CRM) application to retrieve credit rating details about a specific customer and communicate with the ERP application to store order information.

To be able to communicate with these applications, you'll have to implement quite a bit of integration logic. First, you'll need to transform the process variables into a format that the CRM application and the ERP application can understand. If the ERP application only communicates via, for example, a COBOL copybook format, this can be quite cumbersome.

In addition, you'll have to interface with the communication protocol of these applications, whether message queuing, FTP, file, or something else. You'd have to implement this kind of interfacing logic as well. You could use a framework to provide

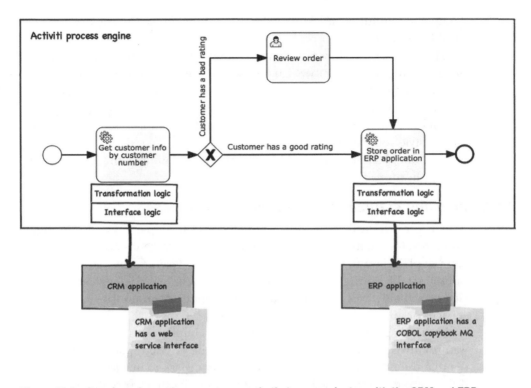

Figure 11.1 Overview of an order process example that communicates with the CRM and ERP applications. Because these applications use a different data model, transformation logic is needed in addition to the interfacing logic to communicate via web services and a message queue.

message queuing capabilities, like Apache ActiveMQ, but this would still mean additional coding. Figure 11.1 provides an overview of this use case.

As figure 11.1 shows, you'll have to enhance the service tasks with transformation and interface logic. Why not use a framework that provides tools to create integration logic? That would clearly separate the process logic from the integration logic and keep the Activiti process engine dedicated to managing processes. Activiti provides out-of-the-box integration with Apache Camel and Mule ESB to let these frameworks (or ESBs, if you prefer) handle the integration logic details.

Let's look at an architecture that clearly separates process logic (BPM) from integration logic (ESB).

11.1.2 Separating process logic from integration logic

Although the Activiti Engine has a flexible and extendable foundation, it's important to keep in mind that it's a process engine. Everything that closely relates to process logic, like workflow people assignment, handling process events, or working with process variables, has its place on the Activiti Engine. Even simple database logic with the JPA extension and straightforward web service invocations using the web service task or a Java service task with CXF client code (like we used in chapter 7) is fine.

But, when you run into requirements where you have to communicate with a service or application, and you need to apply data transformation or implement logic to communicate via message queuing or a file interface, you may want to consider using an additional integration framework (like Apache Camel or Mule ESB) to implement the integration logic. Let's look at the same order process example as in the previous section, but now with an integration framework or ESB added to the architecture (see figure 11.2).

The addition of an ESB or integration framework to the architecture provides a clear separation between the process definition and instances on the one side and the logic to communicate with the CRM and ERP applications on the other side. Adding an integration framework causes an additional learning curve and maintenance requirements, but, as you'll see in sections 11.3 and 11.4, it's easy to leverage Apache Camel and Mule ESB functionality without a lot of additional knowledge.

NOTE   If you do want to know more about Camel and Mule, you can learn all about them in *Camel in Action* by Claus Ibsen and Jonathan Anstey (Manning, 2010) and *Mule in Action* by David Dossot and John D'Emic (Manning, 2009).

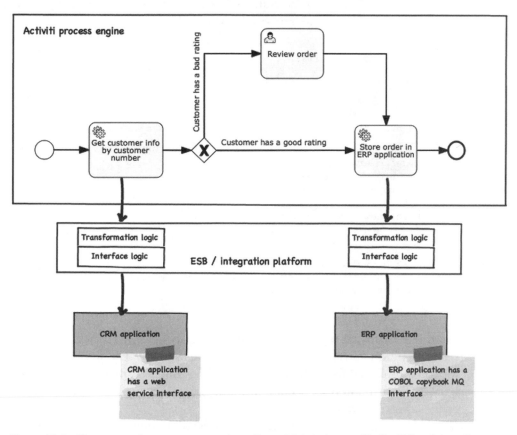

Figure 11.2   The same order process example as figure 11.1, but now with the ESB or integration framework added as an additional layer in the architecture

But, before we dive into the integration frameworks, we'll first look at the BPMN web service task. For simple web service invocations, this BPMN 2.0 task element provides you with all the functionality you need.

11.2   *Using the BPMN 2.0 web service task*

SOAP web service communication between applications is common in a lot of organizations. In the BPMN 2.0 specification, a special task element to support web service communication was added to facilitate this common way of communicating. In chapter 7, we saw that it's quite easy to implement a web service client in a Java service task using a web service framework like Apache CXF. In this section, we'll explore how you can implement a web service invocation in a BPMN 2.0 process definition without the need for additional Java coding.

As you'll see in a moment, the configuration of the web service task is far from easy. Remember that there's an alternative: implementing a web service client using a Java service task (see chapter 7). In the example implemented in this section, you'll invoke a simple web service, which will look up the address of a customer based on its name. We'll reuse some of the code we used in chapter 7 in the book-sales-app web application. The address web service looks like this:

```
@WebService
public class AddressService {

  private CustomerDAO customerDAO;

  @WebResult(name="address")
  public String findCustomerAddress(
      @WebParam(name="customerName") String customerName) {

    Customer customer = customerDAO.getCustomerByNameOrContactPerson(
        customerName, null);
    if (customer != null) {
      return customer.getCustomerAddress();
    } else {
      throw new RuntimeException("Customer not found!");
    }
  }

  @WebMethod(exclude=true)
  public void setCustomerDAO(CustomerDAO customerDAO) {
    this.customerDAO = customerDAO;
  }
}
```

From the BPMN 2.0 process definition, you'll invoke the findCustomerAddress web service method and provide a customer name as input. The web service will respond with a customer address when the provided customer name can be found in the database. To start the web service application, execute mvn jetty:run in the root of the book-sales-app web application project.

Now let's move on to the BPMN 2.0 process definition. Because we want to focus on the web service invocation, we'll keep the rest of the process definition simple. The process definition contains quite a lot of XML elements, so the BPMN 2.0 XML is divided into two sections, starting with the web service definition in the next listing.

Listing 11.1 BPMN 2.0 process definition part 1 with the web service import

```
<definitions xmlns="http://www.omg.org/spec/BPMN/20100524/MODEL"
    targetNamespace="http://www.bpmnwithactiviti.org"
    xmlns:tns="http://www.bpmnwithactiviti.org"
    xmlns:activiti="http://activiti.org/bpmn"
    xmlns:sales="http://ws.chapter11.bpmnwithactiviti.org/">         ❶ Imports
                                                                          web
                                                                          service
  <import importType="http://schemas.xmlsoap.org/wsdl/"
      location="http://localhost:8081/book-sales-app/
          ➥ services/address?wsdl"
      namespace="http://ws.chapter11.bpmnwithactiviti.org/" />        ❷ Defines
                                                                         request
                                                                         message
  <message id="findCustomerAddressRequestMessage"
      itemRef="tns:findCustomerAddressRequestItem" />
  <message id="findCustomerAddressResponseMessage"
      itemRef="tns:findCustomerAddressResponseItem" />               ❸ References
                                                                        WSDL input
                                                                        message
  <itemDefinition id="findCustomerAddressRequestItem"
      structureRef="sales:findCustomerAddress" />
  <itemDefinition id="findCustomerAddressResponseItem"
      structureRef="sales:findCustomerAddressResponse" />            ❹ References
                                                                        WSDL port
                                                                        type
  <interface name="Find customer address"
      implementationRef="sales:AddressService">
    <operation id="findCustomerAddressOperation"
       name="Find customer address operation"
       implementationRef="sales:findCustomerAddress">               ❺ References
      <inMessageRef>                                                   WSDL
        tns:findCustomerAddressRequestMessage                         operation
      </inMessageRef>
      <outMessageRef>
        tns:findCustomerAddressResponseMessage
      </outMessageRef>
    </operation>
  </interface>

  <itemDefinition id="name"
      structureRef="string" />
  <itemDefinition id="customerName"
      structureRef="string" />                                       Input element
  <itemDefinition id="address"                                       as defined in
      structureRef="string" />                                     ❻ WSDL
  <itemDefinition id="webserviceResponse"
      structureRef="string" />

  <!-- remaining, see code listing 11.2 -->

</definitions>
```

To be able to invoke a web service from a web service task, you first have to import the web service definition ❶. The location of the WSDL file must be defined and the target namespace of the imported WSDL must be configured. Then the input and output messages for the web service invocation must be defined ❷. These messages use an item definition with a reference to the input and output messages defined in the WSDL ❸. This makes the structure of the input and output message of the web service operation available in the BPMN 2.0 process definition.

With the message structure defined, you can define the interface of the web service invocation with a reference to the WSDL port type AddressService ❹. In the interface, the web service operation you want to invoke, findCustomerAddress, is defined ❺. In the web service operation, the input and output message definitions are referenced.

Finally, the input and output element variables are defined. The customerName item definition ❻ references the XSD element name of the input message defined in the WSDL of the address web service. The name item definition will be used in the next listing to fill the customerName item definition from the name process variable. The same goes for the address item definition, which matches the output XSD element in the WSDL, and the webserviceResponse item definition that will be used as the new process variable containing the web service result.

With the web service definition imported, you can now implement the web service task and the rest of the process definition.

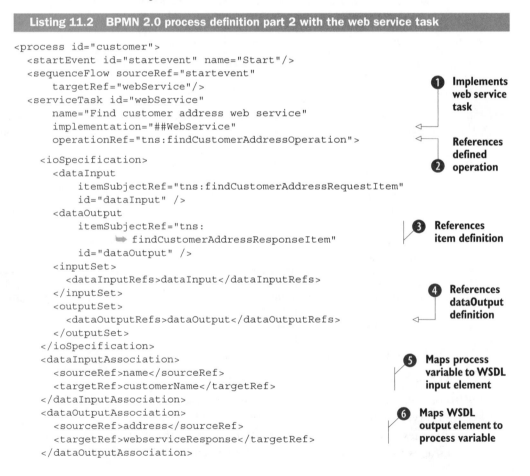

Listing 11.2   BPMN 2.0 process definition part 2 with the web service task

```
<process id="customer">
  <startEvent id="startevent" name="Start"/>
  <sequenceFlow sourceRef="startevent"
      targetRef="webService"/>
  <serviceTask id="webService"
      name="Find customer address web service"
      implementation="##WebService"
      operationRef="tns:findCustomerAddressOperation">

    <ioSpecification>
      <dataInput
          itemSubjectRef="tns:findCustomerAddressRequestItem"
          id="dataInput" />
      <dataOutput
          itemSubjectRef="tns:
              ➦ findCustomerAddressResponseItem"
          id="dataOutput" />
      <inputSet>
        <dataInputRefs>dataInput</dataInputRefs>
      </inputSet>
      <outputSet>
        <dataOutputRefs>dataOutput</dataOutputRefs>
      </outputSet>
    </ioSpecification>
    <dataInputAssociation>
      <sourceRef>name</sourceRef>
      <targetRef>customerName</targetRef>
    </dataInputAssociation>
    <dataOutputAssociation>
      <sourceRef>address</sourceRef>
      <targetRef>webserviceResponse</targetRef>
    </dataOutputAssociation>
```

❶ Implements web service task

❷ References defined operation

❸ References item definition

❹ References dataOutput definition

❺ Maps process variable to WSDL input element

❻ Maps WSDL output element to process variable

```
        </serviceTask>
        <sequenceFlow sourceRef="webService"
            targetRef="waitState"/>
        <receiveTask id="waitState" />
        <sequenceFlow sourceRef="waitState"
            targetRef="endevent" />
        <endEvent id="endevent" name="End"/>
</process>
```

A web service task can be defined by using the `implementation` attribute value of `##WebService` ❶. In addition, the web service operation that should be invoked must be defined ❷. This is a reference to the operation definition you implemented in the first part of this process definition, in listing 11.1.

To fill in the customer name as an input variable for the web service and handle the web service result, an `ioSpecification` and an input and output `dataAssociation` must be defined. The `ioSpecification` references the item definitions of the input and output ❸ messages defined in listing 11.1. This is completed with `inputSet` and `outputSet` ❹ definitions.

Next, the input and output element values must be defined. The `dataInput-Association` contains a `sourceRef` value with the process variable that will be used as input and a `targetRef` value that matches the XSD element of the input message ❺. The `dataOutputAssociation` contains a `sourceRef` value that matches the XSD element of the output message and a `targetRef` value with the name of the new process variable that will contain the web service result ❻.

This example has only one input XSD element and one output XSD element, but you can add as many input and output elements as needed. But, as you can see, the number of XML elements needed to implement a web service invocation is quite large. To test this web service example, you can run the `WebServiceTest` unit test available in the `bpmn-examples` project:

```java
public class WebServiceTest extends AbstractTest {

  @Rule
  public ActivitiRule activitiRule =
      new ActivitiRule("activiti.cfg-mem.xml");

  @Test
  @Deployment(resources={"chapter11/webservice/customer.bpmn20.xml"})
  public void queryTask() {
    Map<String, Object> variableMap = new HashMap<String, Object>();
    variableMap.put("name", "Alfresco");
    variableMap.put("contactperson", "Tom Baeyens");
    ProcessInstance processInstance = activitiRule
        .getRuntimeService()
        .startProcessInstanceByKey("customer", variableMap);
    Object responseValue = activitiRule
        .getRuntimeService()
        .getVariable(processInstance.getProcessInstanceId(),
            "webserviceResponse");
    assertEquals("Highlands 343", responseValue);
  }
}
```

This unit test should run green when the web service is available and the `TestData` class in the `book-sales-app` is executed to fill the database with test data. Combined with the web service client example from chapter 7, this example gives a good picture of the possibilities for communicating with web services from a BPMN 2.0 process in Activiti.

Using a web service task

Activiti's web service task is implemented in a separate module named Activiti CXF. Make sure that the dependency is on the classpath when using the web service task functionality. The Activiti CXF module isn't, for example, installed in the WEB-INF/lib directory of the Activiti Explorer. We've added the following dependency to the pom.xml file of the `bpmn-examples` project:

```
<dependency>
  <groupId>org.activiti</groupId>
  <artifactId>activiti-cxf</artifactId>
  <version>${activiti-version}</version>
</dependency>
```

But, there are usually far more connectivity options needed, like JMS, file, and FTP communication. In the next section, we'll start exploring possibilities for more connectivity options by using Apache Camel.

11.3   Integrating with Apache Camel

Big books have been written about the Apache Camel framework (such as *Camel in Action*), but to get a clear understanding of the possibilities of integrating the Activiti Engine with Apache Camel, you'll need no more than this section. That's because the Camel integration is simple but powerful, and the Camel framework is quite easy to learn.

Let's start with an introduction into the Apache Camel framework and then look into the Activiti integration.

11.3.1 Introducing Apache Camel

Apache Camel is a powerful open source Java integration framework that can be used by adding some JAR files to your project. There's no need to run Apache Camel in a separate container, although you could do that with Apache ServiceMix. The three main functionalities of Apache Camel are listed below:

- Provides concrete implementations for the enterprise integrations patterns of Hohpe's eponymous book. For example, Apache Camel provides a content-based router, a message filter, and a message transformer.
- Provides a lot of transport and API connectivity options like JMS, file, FTP, and web services.
- Provides a domain-specific language (DSL) for configuring and implementing the integration logic. This makes Apache Camel easy to use.

The Apache Camel framework consists of three basic elements: endpoints, processors, and components, as you can see in figure 11.3.

An endpoint and a component are closely related. An endpoint specifies a location URI from which Camel can send or receive messages. In this URI, a component is used to specify the URI scheme name and thereby tell the Camel engine which connector should be used, as shown in this example of a file endpoint:

```
file://test
```

In this case, the URI scheme is `file`, so the Camel file component will be used. The `test` addition states that it's about the test directory.

Here's another endpoint example, in this case a JMS endpoint:

```
jms:queue:testQueue
```

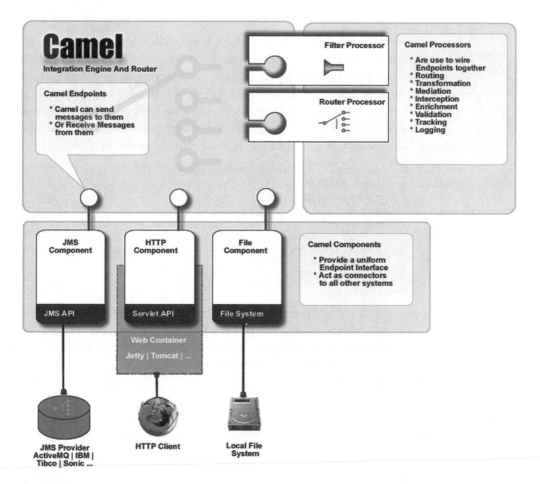

Figure 11.3   The architecture of Apache Camel showing the use of its three basic elements: endpoints, processors, and components

For this endpoint, the URI scheme is jms, so the Camel JMS component will be used. For the JMS component, we have to define whether it's a queue or a topic and also the name of the queue, which is testQueue in this example.

Now let's look at a bigger example that does some integration logic:

```
<route>
  <from uri="jms:queue:orderQueue" />
  <choice>
    <when>
      <xpath>$priority = 'high'</xpath>
      <to uri="jms:queue:processOrder" />
    </when>
    <otherwise>
      <to uri="file://order" />
    </otherwise>
  </choice>
</route>
```

This example already contains quite a bit of logic. When a new message arrives at the orderQueue, it's picked up by Camel and passed on to a content-based router. When the header parameter priority is equal to high, the order message is quickly passed on to another JMS queue named processOrder. When the header parameter priority has another value, the message is written to the order directory and manually processed.

In the previous code snippet, the integration logic is defined using the Spring XML language. But, we can define this logic just as easily using the Java DSL:

```
RouteBuilder routeBuilder = new RouteBuilder() {
  public void configure() {
    from("jms:queue:orderQueue")
        .choice()
            .when(header("priority").isEqualTo("high"))
                .to("jms:queue:processOrder")
            .otherwise()
                .to("file://order");
  }
};
```

As you can see, there's not much difference between the elements in the Spring XML and the Java DSL implementations. The nice thing about the Java DSL is that you have Java code completion, although you can have similar code completion by specifying the XSD schema locations with a decent XML editor.

Before we move on to using Camel with the Activiti Engine, let's first look at a standalone Camel example.

Listing 11.3   Camel `RouteBuilder` example showing content-based routing

```
public class CamelIntroRoute extends RouteBuilder {          Creates
                                                             new Camel
  @Override                                              ➊  route class
  public void configure() throws Exception {

    from("direct:start")
```

```
        .log(LoggingLevel.INFO,
            "Received message ${in.body}")
        .choice()
          .when(xpath("/introduction/text()
              ➥ ='Camel'"))
            .to("file://introduction?fileName=camel-intro-
                ➥ ${in.header.name}-
                ➥ $simple{date:now:yyyyMMdd_HHmmss}.txt")
          .otherwise()
            .to("file://introduction?
                ➥ fileName=other-intro-${in.header.name}-
                ➥ $simple{date:now:yyyyMMdd_HHmmss}.txt");
    }
}
```

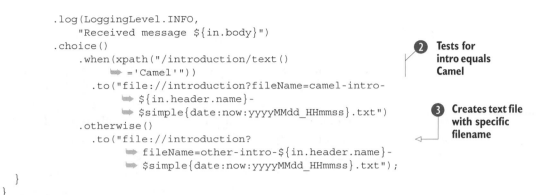

2 Tests for intro equals Camel

3 Creates text file with specific filename

Implementing integrating logic means creating a route in Camel **1**. Think of a route as defining the flow of a message from arrival in the Camel engine until it's passed on to a connector outside the Camel engine. In this example, you use the Camel direct component to make it easy to test this route. The Camel direct component can be used to send a synchronous message to an endpoint in the same Camel context. If you want it to be asynchronous, you can use the Camel SEDA component.

When a message arrives at the start endpoint of the direct component, the message is first logged with Jakarta Commons Logging. As you can see, you can specify the log level and you can use expressions like in.body to select which part of the message you want to log.

After the message is logged, the message is passed on to an endpoint based on the content using an XPath expression **2**. The incoming message is expected to be XML, and the introduction root element should contain a text value that's equal to Camel. Otherwise, the message is passed on to another file endpoint **3**. As you can see, the file component can be instructed to create a file with a specific filename. In this example, the value of the name header parameter is included, and the current date and time are added.

It's quite easy to test this piece of integration logic, as the following listing shows.

Listing 11.4 Testing a Camel route with a simple JUnit class

```
public class CamelIntroTest extends AbstractTest {

  @Test
  public void sendMessages() throws Exception {
    CamelContext camelContext = new DefaultCamelContext();
    camelContext.addRoutes(new CamelIntroRoute());
    camelContext.start();
    ProducerTemplate tpl = camelContext.createProducerTemplate();
    tpl.sendBodyAndHeader("direct:start",
        "<introduction>Camel</introduction>",
            "name", "Rademakers");
    tpl.sendBodyAndHeader("direct:start",
        "<introduction>Mule</introduction>",
            "name", "Rademakers");
```

1 Adds Camel route to context

2 Sends test message

```
    camelContext.stop();
  }
}
```

To test the Camel route in listing 11.3, you have to create a new `CamelContext` and add the `CamelIntroRoute` route class to that context instance ❶. When the context is created, you can start it by invoking the `start` method on the context instance. Then you can start sending messages to endpoints in the Camel engine. In this example, you create an incoming endpoint of `direct:start`, so you can send a simple XML introduction message with a `name` header parameter ❷.

When you run this unit test in the `book-camel` project of the book's source code, you can see that an introduction directory is created and two files are created. You could enhance this test a bit using the Camel test framework to make it standalone testable. But, for now, this should provide you with enough information about the execution of the `CamelIntroRoute` logic.

Now that you've been introduced to Apache Camel, it's time to get back to the topic of this chapter. How can you leverage the Apache Camel framework to communicate with services from a BPMN process? Let's start with an overview of how the Activiti Engine can communicate with Apache Camel.

11.3.2 *Sending and receiving process messages with Apache Camel*

To get a good overview of how Camel and Activiti can be used together, let's look at a hello world example. In the Activiti distribution, you can find a module named `activiti-camel`, which implements the integration between Activiti and Camel. If you add the following dependency to your POM file, you'll have this integration available in your project:

```
<dependency>
  <groupId>org.activiti</groupId>
  <artifactId>activiti-camel</artifactId>
</dependency>
```

The Activiti Camel module uses Spring as a container to bind the Activiti Engine beans with the Camel context beans. You have to set up the Activiti Engine in a Spring configuration like you did several times in the previous chapters. I won't explain it again here, but you can find it in the `camel-book` source code in the src/main/resources/helloworld folder with the filename activiti-application-context.xml.

Let's see how you can set up the Camel context in a Spring configuration in the following listing (camel-application-context.xml).

Listing 11.5   Set up the Camel context with Activiti integration in Spring

```
<beans xmlns="http://www.springframework.org/schema/beans"
    xmlns:xsi="http://www.w3.org/2001/XMLSchema-instance"
    xmlns:camel="http://camel.apache.org/schema/spring"
    xsi:schemaLocation="http://www.springframework.org/schema/beans
        http://www.springframework.org/schema/beans/spring-beans.xsd
```

```
                http://camel.apache.org/schema/spring
                  http://camel.apache.org/schema/spring/camel-spring.xsd">

    <camelContext id="camelProcess"
        xmlns="http://camel.apache.org/schema/spring">
      <packageScan>
        <package>org.bpmnwithactiviti.chapter11.
            ➥ camel.helloworld</package>
      </packageScan>
    </camelContext>

    <bean id="camel"
        class="org.activiti.camel.CamelBehaviour">
      <constructor-arg index="0">
        <list>
          <bean class="org.activiti.camel.
              ➥ SimpleContextProvider">
            <constructor-arg index="0"
                value="helloCamelProcess" />
            <constructor-arg index="1"
                ref="camelProcess" />
          </bean>
        </list>
      </constructor-arg>
    </bean>
</beans>
```

① Defines Camel context

② Scans for RouteBuilders in package

③ Defines the Camel ActivityBehaviour class

④ Couples BPMN process with Camel context

In the Camel configuration, you first define a Camel context where you can add routes **①**. Instead of writing down the route for this example using the Spring language (like you saw in section 11.3.1), you instruct the Camel context to scan the classpath in the helloworld package **②**. In listing 11.6, we'll take a look at the RouteBuilder class that's made available in the Camel context with this package scanning.

This is still plain Camel configuration, but now you have to make this Camel context available to be used in the BPMN process instances of the Activiti Engine. The CamelBehaviour class **③**, which is defined as a Spring bean with an identifier of camel, implements the ActivityBehavior interface, and can, therefore, be used in a Java service task in a BPMN process.

This is a good time to look at the process definition of our hello world process (helloworld.bpmn20.xml):

```
<definitions xmlns="http://www.omg.org/spec/BPMN/20100524/MODEL"
    targetNamespace="http://www.bpmnwithactiviti.org"
    xmlns:activiti="http://activiti.org/bpmn">

  <process id="helloCamelProcess">
    <startEvent id="start" />
    <sequenceFlow sourceRef="start"
        targetRef="serviceTask1" />
    <serviceTask id="serviceTask1"
        activiti:delegateExpression="${camel}" />
    <sequenceFlow sourceRef="serviceTask1"
        targetRef="userTask1" />
    <userTask id="userTask1" name="HelloTask"
        activiti:assignee="kermit"/>
```

```
      <sequenceFlow sourceRef="userTask1"
          targetRef="end" />
      <endEvent id="end" />
    </process>
</definitions>
```

This simple process contains one new piece of functionality: the delegateExpression in the Java service task. The camel identifier refers back to the Spring bean definition shown in listing 11.5. When the service task is executed by the Activiti Engine, the execution is delegated to the CamelBehaviour class, which will send a message containing all process variables to an Activiti endpoint defined in the Camel context. We'll look at the RouteBuilder class that defines this Activiti endpoint in a moment, in listing 11.6.

Now you know how to access the Camel context from the Activiti Engine, but how can you access the Activiti Engine from a Camel route? The SimpleContextProvider defined in listing 11.5 couples a BPMN process identifier (helloCamelProcess) to the Camel context identifier (camelProcess) ❹. As you can see, it's possible to define a list of context providers, so each BPMN process can be coupled to a Camel context. This enables you to send messages from the Camel engine to a BPMN process. And, this makes it possible to create a new process instance from the Camel context or to send messages to a process instance that's in a wait state (like the receive BPMN element).

Now let's define a Camel route that creates a new process instance of the hello world process that was shown in the previous code snippet and that can handle the implementation of the service task defined in that process definition.

> **Listing 11.6   Camel RouteBuilder that implements Activiti logic**

```
public class CamelHelloRoute extends RouteBuilder {

  @Override
  public void configure() throws Exception {

    from("activiti:helloCamelProcess:serviceTask1")
        .log(LoggingLevel.INFO,
          "Received message on service task ${property.var1}")
        .setProperty("var2").constant("world")
        .setBody().properties();

    from("direct:start").to("activiti:helloCamelProcess");
  }
}
```

There are two Camel routes defined by this RouteBuilder class. Let's start with the simple, second one. When a message is sent to the synchronous endpoint direct:start, a new process instance of the helloCamelProcess definition is created. You can see that the new Activiti Camel component is used here because of the activiti: prefix in the endpoint definition.

The other route implements the Java service task logic of serviceTask1. Remember that this service task is defined with a delegate expression to the CamelBehaviour class. When the service task is executed, all process variables are passed on to the Camel route as properties. This way, you can easily log a process variable with the name var1 using the Camel log component. In addition, you can define a new property (var2) in the Camel route, and this will be made available in the process instance as a new process variable.

Now let's get this Activiti Camel integration rolling with a unit test implementation.

Listing 11.7 Unit test to start the Activiti Engine and the Camel context

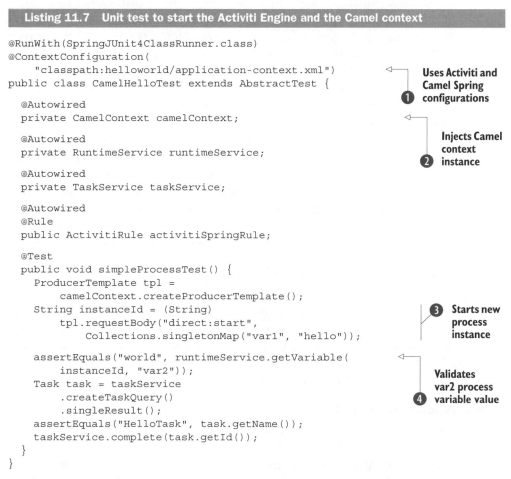

```
@RunWith(SpringJUnit4ClassRunner.class)
@ContextConfiguration(
    "classpath:helloworld/application-context.xml")
public class CamelHelloTest extends AbstractTest {

  @Autowired
  private CamelContext camelContext;

  @Autowired
  private RuntimeService runtimeService;

  @Autowired
  private TaskService taskService;

  @Autowired
  @Rule
  public ActivitiRule activitiSpringRule;

  @Test
  public void simpleProcessTest() {
    ProducerTemplate tpl =
        camelContext.createProducerTemplate();
    String instanceId = (String)
        tpl.requestBody("direct:start",
            Collections.singletonMap("var1", "hello"));

    assertEquals("world", runtimeService.getVariable(
        instanceId, "var2"));
    Task task = taskService
      .createTaskQuery()
      .singleResult();
    assertEquals("HelloTask", task.getName());
    taskService.complete(task.getId());
  }
}
```

Annotations:
- **①** Uses Activiti and Camel Spring configurations
- **②** Injects Camel context instance
- **③** Starts new process instance
- **④** Validates var2 process variable value

To run the Activiti Engine and the Camel context together, you have to define a Spring parent configuration file, which imports both Spring configurations **①**:

```
<beans xmlns="http://www.springframework.org/schema/beans"
    xmlns:xsi="http://www.w3.org/2001/XMLSchema-instance"
    xsi:schemaLocation="http://www.springframework.org/schema/beans
        http://www.springframework.org/schema/beans/spring-beans.xsd">

  <import resource="activiti-application-context.xml" />
  <import resource="camel-application-context.xml" />
</beans>
```

This clearly separates the Activiti Engine configuration from the Camel context configuration and makes them separately maintainable. You can now also use the Spring autowiring mechanism to inject a Camel context in the unit test ❷. Note that you don't have to start and stop it now; that's done for you.

Because there's a Camel route listing on the `direct:start` endpoint, you can send a message that will start a new process instance of the `helloCamelProcess` ❸. Because the message contains a `Map` with a `var1` entry, the Activiti Camel module transforms this into a process variable. Note that Camel returns the process instance ID when the first wait state in the process instance is encountered (in this case, a user task).

The service task in the process instance should have been executed by then, so you can test whether the Camel route that implemented the service task was successful in setting a new process variable `var2` with the value `world` ❹. You also test whether the process instance state is with the `HelloTask` user task and complete it to make sure that the process instance ends.

This completes our introduction to the Activiti Camel integration. Now that you have a good overview of the main capabilities, you can explore more complex capabilities and dive further into Apache Camel by reading the *Camel in Action* book or looking at the documentation on the Apache Camel website (camel.apache.org). In this chapter, though, we'll move on to explore Mule ESB's integration with the Activiti Engine. Note that Apache Camel and Mule ESB provide similar functionality, so we'll show similar examples for Mule ESB to make it easier to compare both options.

11.4   Integrating with Mule ESB

Mule ESB is a widely used and popular open source ESB product that provides a wide range of connectivity options, support for enterprise integration patterns, and an easy to learn flow language. MuleSoft, the company behind Mule ESB, is one the partners of the Activiti project and delivers the web service task implementation we discussed in section 11.2. In this section, we'll focus on how to leverage the Mule ESB functionality from the Activiti Engine, starting with a solid introduction to Mule ESB.

11.4.1 Introducing Mule ESB

Mule ESB is an open source ESB developed by MuleSoft and created by Ross Mason, one of the founders of MuleSoft. Mule ESB was one of the first open source ESBs out there, together with Apache ServiceMix, and it already has far more than a million downloads. Its main difference from Apache Camel, which we discussed in section 11.3, is that Mule ESB typically runs in its own container. This means that Mule ESB runs in a separate JVM and is started with a startup script.

In the next section about the Activiti Mule ESB integration, we'll show that it's possible to run Mule ESB and the Activiti Engine in a shared Spring container. But the easiest way of using Mule ESB is to download the whole package and run it in its own container. Like Apache Camel, Mule ESB provides support for a wide range of connectivity options, like JMS, file, FTP, and web services. Mule ESB also offers support for a wide range of enterprise integration patterns, like content-based routing and a message filter. Figure 11.4 provides an overview of Mule ESB available in its documentation material as well.

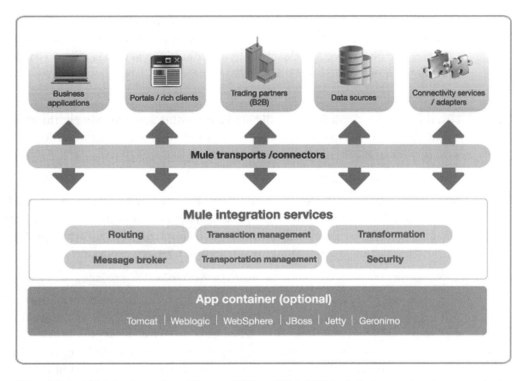

Figure 11.4   A high-level overview of the capabilities of Mule ESB, including connectors to communicate with data sources and business applications

With Mule ESB, you're able to communicate with all kinds of sources, including databases, business applications, and web services. Mule provides services to deal with routing, transformation, message security, and transaction management, and can be run standalone, embedded, and in an application server like Apache Tomcat or JBoss.

But how can we use Mule ESB to implement integration logic? In Mule ESB version 3, everything is centered on the concept of flows. A flow uses Mule building blocks to build a piece of integration logic, starting with the message arrival and continuing until the message is sent to another destination. Figure 11.5 shows the structure of a flow, which consists of a message source and one or more message processors.

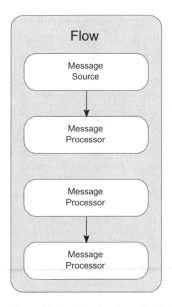

Figure 11.5   The structure of a Mule flow, which is the core concept when using Mule ESB

A message source is an endpoint that Mule ESB will monitor for new messages arriving. The message source can, for example, be a file endpoint, a JMS endpoint, or a web service endpoint. A message source listening for new messages arriving at a JMS endpoint can be defined this way:

```
<jms:inbound-endpoint queue="test" />
```

This message source definition will listen for new messages arriving at the test queue. But just as easily, you can define a message source that listens for new files in a specific directory location:

```
<file:inbound-endpoint path="testDir" />
```

A message processor is a component that processes incoming messages and makes them available to another message processor or an endpoint. A message processor can, for example, be a piece of routing logic or implement transformation functionality. Let's look at an example of a transformation message processor:

```
<xml:xslt-transformer xsl-file="transformation.xsl"/>
```

This message processor will transform a message using the transformation stylesheet and make the outcome available for the next message processor. In addition to a message source and message processors, a flow can also have an exception strategy defined. You can, for example, configure an exception strategy that will be executed when no routing rule matches the message content when using a content-based router.

A flow can also be nested, so a main flow can invoke several subflows. In this way, reusable flow components can be defined, which are reused in a number of main flow definitions.

Enough said about the foundational components of Mule ESB; let's implement a simple piece of integration logic and execute it with a unit test. In the following listing, a Mule flow configuration with content-based routing is shown.

Listing 11.8   Flow configuration using a content-based router and VM and File transports

```
<mule xmlns="http://www.mulesoft.org/schema/mule/core"          ◁──┐   Defines all
  xmlns:xsi="http://www.w3.org/2001/XMLSchema-instance"              │   Mule transport
  xmlns:vm="http://www.mulesoft.org/schema/mule/vm"               ❶ namespaces
  xmlns:file="http://www.mulesoft.org/schema/mule/file"
  xsi:schemaLocation="http://www.mulesoft.org/schema/mule/core
      http://www.mulesoft.org/schema/mule/core/3.1/mule.xsd
    http://www.mulesoft.org/schema/mule/file
      http://www.mulesoft.org/schema/mule/file/3.1/mule-file.xsd
    http://www.mulesoft.org/schema/mule/vm
      http://www.mulesoft.org/schema/mule/vm/3.1/mule-vm.xsd">    ❷   Listens for
                                                                       messages on
  <flow name="MuleIntro">                                              vm queue
    <vm:inbound-endpoint path="in"                               ◁──┘
        exchange-pattern="one-way" />
    <logger message="Received message #[payload]"                ◁──┐   Logs incoming
        level="INFO" />                                          ❸ message
    <choice>
```

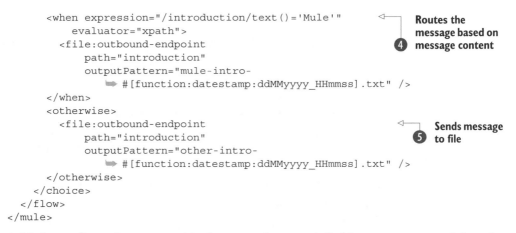

```
      <when expression="/introduction/text()='Mule'"
          evaluator="xpath">
        <file:outbound-endpoint
            path="introduction"
            outputPattern="mule-intro-
              ➥ #[function:datestamp:ddMMyyyy_HHmmss].txt" />
      </when>
      <otherwise>
        <file:outbound-endpoint
            path="introduction"
            outputPattern="other-intro-
              ➥ #[function:datestamp:ddMMyyyy_HHmmss].txt" />
      </otherwise>
    </choice>
  </flow>
</mule>
```

Routes the message based on message content ❹

Sends message to file ❺

A Mule configuration starts with the root element definition `<mule>` containing the namespace definitions of the Mule transports that are used in the flow configuration ❶. In this case, the flow configuration uses the Virtual Machine (VM) and File Mule transports, in addition to the Mule Core component.

In this example, Mule ESB listens for new messages arriving at the in VM queue ❷. The Mule VM component is capable of defining queues within a JVM and even of making them persistent using a file database. In the VM message source definition, you defined that this flow will be `one-way`. This means that no response will be provided by this flow.

After the message is consumed by the VM message source, you log the message payload (content) to the Mule logging file using the `logger` component ❸; `#[payload]` is an expression that is processed by Mule ESB to log the message payload. Mule ESB offers all kinds of expressions to retrieve content from a message, such as header values, message properties, and message payload details.

Once the message is logged, a content-based router makes sure the message is sent to the right outbound endpoint ❹. In this content-based routing rule, you use an XPath expression that checks whether the message payload contains an `introduction` XML element with the value of `Mule`. If this is the case, a mule-intro file is created; otherwise, an other-intro file is created using the Mule File component ❺. The Mule File component offers all kinds of expressions to dynamically add text to the filename. In this case, you use the current date and time value.

Now that you've created a simple flow configuration, how can you test it? Mule provides lots of functionality to write good unit tests. In the unit test shown in the next listing, you start the Mule container in the JVM and send a couple of test messages.

Listing 11.9 A unit test starting the example flow and creating test messages

```
public class MuleIntroTest extends AbstractTest {

  @Test
  public void testSend() throws Exception {
    MuleContext muleContext = new DefaultMuleContextFactory()
```

```
        .createMuleContext("intro/mule-context.xml");
    muleContext.start();
    MuleClient muleClient = new DefaultLocalMuleClient(
        muleContext);
    muleClient.send("vm://in", new DefaultMuleMessage(
        "<introduction>Mule</introduction>", muleContext));
    muleClient.send("vm://in", new DefaultMuleMessage(
        "<introduction>Camel</introduction>", muleContext));
    muleContext.stop();
    muleContext.dispose();
  }
}
```

① Creates client instance

② Sends test message

It's not hard to load a Mule configuration. First, the `DefaultMuleContextFactory` can be used to read the XML file and create a `MuleContext` instance. Then the Mule container can be started by invoking the `start` method on the newly created `MuleContext` instance. The Mule ESB runs within the JVM of the unit test with the flow configuration loaded into it.

To send test messages to the Mule ESB container, you can use all kinds of implementations, depending on the message sources configured in the flow definition. In this case, you've defined a VM queue message source. Mule provides an easy way to send messages to an endpoint with the `MuleClient` class **①**. A Mule client can be local (for Mule ESB running in the same JVM) or remote (when Mule runs standalone or in another JVM). In this unit test, the Mule ESB container runs in the same JVM as the unit test so you can use the local variant with the `DefaultLocalMuleClient` class.

With the Mule client instance available, you can start sending test messages to the Mule container **②**. In this example, you send two messages, one containing a Mule introduction and one with a Camel introduction. Mule provides functionality to validate in a unit test whether a message arrived at a specific endpoint, but to keep it simple, listing 11.9 just looks at the files created in the introduction directory to see if the unit test outcome was successful.

You can run the `MuleIntroTest` unit test in the `book-mule` project that you'll find in the book's source code. After the unit test has executed, you should have two newly created files in the introduction folder, one with mule-intro and another with other-intro as the prefix of the filename.

Now let's move on to integrating Mule ESB with the Activiti Engine.

11.4.2 *Sending and receiving process messages with Mule ESB*

When you want to integrate the Activiti Engine with Mule ESB, you can choose between two configurations. The first is to run them embedded in one Spring configuration, similar to the Apache Camel integration. The other option is to run the Mule ESB container standalone and communicate with the Activiti Engine through the REST API. Both configuration options use the same message processor definition to create a new process, set a process variable, or signal a process instance. The difference between the two options is the Activiti connector configuration that's part of the Mule configuration.

When you use Activiti and Mule in an embedded setup, both engines run in the same Java Virtual Machine (JVM) and they can access each other directly. This means that Mule can access the Activiti process engine beans, and Activiti can send messages to Mule flows using VM queues. In the standalone setup, Mule can access Activiti via the Activiti REST API, and Activiti can send messages to Mule flows via web services.

To make it easier to test the example, we'll implement the embedded integration between the Activiti Engine and Mule ESB, but I'll explain where the standalone configuration would differ.

To add the Mule integration functionality to the Activiti Engine, you'll have to add the following dependency to the project POM file:

```
<dependency>
  <groupId>org.activiti</groupId>
  <artifactId>activiti-mule</artifactId>
</dependency>
```

With this dependency enabled, you can implement the Mule configuration for the example flow definition. This example is similar to the Apache Camel implementation, so it's easy to compare both options. You'll define two flows, one to create a new process instance when a message arrives at a specific VM queue and another that will be invoked from the BPMN process, log the incoming message, and return a simple message back. Let's take a look at the Mule configuration.

Listing 11.10　Mule configuration with an Activiti connector

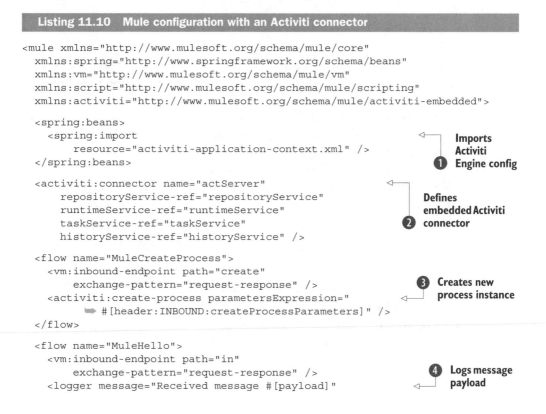

```
<mule xmlns="http://www.mulesoft.org/schema/mule/core"
  xmlns:spring="http://www.springframework.org/schema/beans"
  xmlns:vm="http://www.mulesoft.org/schema/mule/vm"
  xmlns:script="http://www.mulesoft.org/schema/mule/scripting"
  xmlns:activiti="http://www.mulesoft.org/schema/mule/activiti-embedded">

  <spring:beans>
    <spring:import
        resource="activiti-application-context.xml" />
  </spring:beans>

  <activiti:connector name="actServer"
      repositoryService-ref="repositoryService"
      runtimeService-ref="runtimeService"
      taskService-ref="taskService"
      historyService-ref="historyService" />

  <flow name="MuleCreateProcess">
    <vm:inbound-endpoint path="create"
        exchange-pattern="request-response" />
    <activiti:create-process parametersExpression="
        ➥ #[header:INBOUND:createProcessParameters]" />
  </flow>

  <flow name="MuleHello">
    <vm:inbound-endpoint path="in"
        exchange-pattern="request-response" />
    <logger message="Received message #[payload]"
```

① Imports Activiti Engine config

② Defines embedded Activiti connector

③ Creates new process instance

④ Logs message payload

```
        level="INFO" />
    <script:transformer>
      <script:script engine="groovy">
          return 'world'
      </script:script>
    </script:transformer>
  </flow>
</mule>
```

◁─┐ **Sends
   response with
⑤ 'world' string**

Because you want to run the Mule ESB embedded, together with the Activiti Engine, you import the Spring beans that configure the Activiti Engine ❶. The Spring configuration to define the Activiti Engine was already shown a couple of times in the previous chapters, mostly in chapter 4. But to make the Mule ESB context also available in the Activiti Engine, you have to adapt the activiti-application-context.xml file a little bit:

```
<bean id="processEngineConfiguration"
    class="org.activiti.spring.SpringProcessEngineConfiguration">
  <property name="databaseType" value="h2" />
  <property name="dataSource" ref="dataSource" />
  <property name="transactionManager" ref="transactionManager" />
  <property name="databaseSchemaUpdate" value="true" />
  <property name="deploymentResources"
      value="classpath*:helloworld/helloworld.bpmn20.xml" />
  <property name="beans">
    <map>
      <entry key="muleContext" value-ref="_muleContext" />
    </map>
  </property>
</bean>
```

The only difference between this and a normal Spring Activiti Engine configuration is the beans property definition. The Mule context is coupled to the muleContext parameter.

Next up in listing 11.10, the Activiti embedded connector is defined ❷. The Spring Activiti service beans defined in the activiti-application-context.xml are coupled to the Activiti connector. Now the Mule Activiti connector can start a new process instance by using the RuntimeService Spring bean.

When the Mule ESB runs in a JVM separate from the Activiti Engine, this connector definition would change, like this:

```
<activiti:connector name="actServer"
    activitiServerURL="http://localhost:8080/activiti-rest/service/"
    username="kermit"
    password="kermit" />
```

With the remote Activiti connector definition, every call from Mule ESB to the Activiti Engine is performed against the REST service layer, so you have to configure the REST base URL and the username and password.

In the first flow definition of listing 11.10, a new process instance can be started by sending a message to the create VM queue ❸. The parameters needed to start a new process instance, like the process definition key and the process variables, are retrieved from the message header property named `createProcessParameters`. The created process instance is returned as a response of the flow definition.

In the second message flow definition, the incoming message on the `in` queue is logged to the Mule logging component ❹. Then a simple Groovy script is executed and a string with the value of `world` is returned as a response of the flow ❺.

Now let's look how you can send a message to this `in` queue from a BPMN 2.0 process.

Listing 11.11   BPMN process definition with a Mule Send task

```
<definitions xmlns="http://www.omg.org/spec/BPMN/20100524/MODEL"
    xmlns:activiti="http://activiti.org/bpmn"
    targetNamespace="http://www.bpmnwithactiviti.org">

  <process id="helloWorldMule">
    <startEvent id="theStart" />
    <sequenceFlow sourceRef="theStart"
        targetRef="sendMule" />
    <sendTask id="sendMule" activiti:type="mule">
      <extensionElements>
        <activiti:field name="endpointUrl">
          <activiti:string>vm://in</activiti:string>
        </activiti:field>
        <activiti:field name="language">
          <activiti:string>juel</activiti:string>
        </activiti:field>
        <activiti:field name="payloadExpression">
          <activiti:expression>${var1}</activiti:expression>
        </activiti:field>
        <activiti:field name="resultVariable">
          <activiti:string>var2</activiti:string>
        </activiti:field>
      </extensionElements>
    </sendTask>
    <sequenceFlow sourceRef="sendMule"
        targetRef="waitState" />
    <receiveTask id="waitState" />
    <sequenceFlow sourceRef="waitState"
        targetRef="theEnd" />
    <endEvent id="theEnd" />
  </process>
</definitions>
```

❶ BPMN Send task

❷ Targets Mule endpoint

❸ Value of the message payload

❹ Processes variable name for the response

This process definition contains only a few steps. After the process instance has started, a BPMN send task with an Activiti-specific type of `mule` is used to send a message to the Mule ESB container ❶. In the extension fields of the send task, the configuration items needed to send the message are defined. First, the endpoint URI is defined; in this example, the `in` VM queue ❷. Remember that the `in` VM queue was defined as a message source for the second Mule flow definition in listing 11.10.

In addition, the message payload is defined with the `var1` process variable ❸. This means that the value of the `var1` process variable is sent as a message to the `in` VM queue. Finally, the response of the Mule flow execution is set as a new process variable named `var2` ❹.

After the Mule Send task has been completed, the process instance enters a Wait state with the Receive task. This makes it easy to get a hold of the var2 process variable in the unit test, shown in the following listing.

Listing 11.12   Unit test for the Activiti Engine and Mule ESB integration example

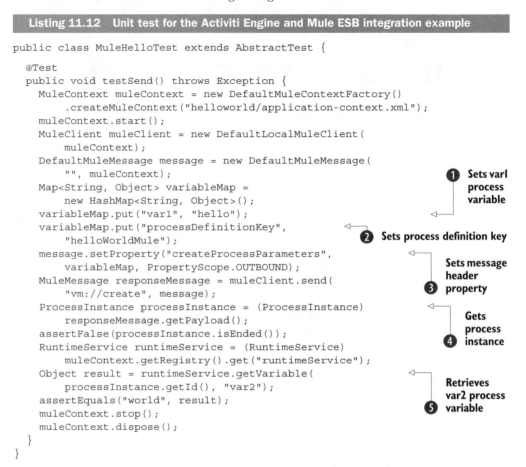

```
public class MuleHelloTest extends AbstractTest {

  @Test
  public void testSend() throws Exception {
    MuleContext muleContext = new DefaultMuleContextFactory()
        .createMuleContext("helloworld/application-context.xml");
    muleContext.start();
    MuleClient muleClient = new DefaultLocalMuleClient(
        muleContext);
    DefaultMuleMessage message = new DefaultMuleMessage(
        "", muleContext);
    Map<String, Object> variableMap =
        new HashMap<String, Object>();
    variableMap.put("var1", "hello");
    variableMap.put("processDefinitionKey",
        "helloWorldMule");
    message.setProperty("createProcessParameters",
        variableMap, PropertyScope.OUTBOUND);
    MuleMessage responseMessage = muleClient.send(
        "vm://create", message);
    ProcessInstance processInstance = (ProcessInstance)
        responseMessage.getPayload();
    assertFalse(processInstance.isEnded());
    RuntimeService runtimeService = (RuntimeService)
        muleContext.getRegistry().get("runtimeService");
    Object result = runtimeService.getVariable(
        processInstance.getId(), "var2");
    assertEquals("world", result);
    muleContext.stop();
    muleContext.dispose();
  }
}
```

1 Sets var1 process variable

2 Sets process definition key

3 Sets message header property

4 Gets process instance

5 Retrieves var2 process variable

This unit test contains quite a bit of logic in just a few lines of code. First, a new Mule context is created for the Mule configuration discussed in listing 11.10. After the Mule ESB instance is started, together with the Activiti Engine, a message is created to start a new process instance. The var1 process variable **1** and the process definition key **2** are set in a Map.

The Map instance is then used to create a message header property named createProcessParameters **3**. Remember that this message header is processed by the Mule Activiti transport (see listing 11.10). Then the Mule message is sent to the create VM queue, and a new process instance of the BPMN process definition shown in listing 11.11 is created in the Activiti Engine. The process instance object is sent back as a response message **4**. Note that this process instance object isn't an Activiti API object, but a Mule Activiti connector API object. The Mule Activiti connector transforms the Activiti process instance to a Mule process instance object.

Finally, the unit test validates whether the `var2` process variable was set and contains the value of `world` **5**. The `RuntimeService` instance is retrieved from the Mule registry, because the Activiti Engine Spring beans are created as part of the Mule configuration.

The Mule ESB website (www.mulesoft.org) and books like *Mule in Action* by David Dossot and John D'Emic (Manning, 2009) and *Open Source ESBs in Action* by Tijs Rademakers and Jos Dirksen (Manning, 2008) contain much more additional information about the functionality of Mule ESB. You now have a good foundation for working on more complex integration logic.

11.5 Summary

Business and application logic is typically scattered across many different applications in an organization. When you're implementing process definitions, there's often a need to communicate with business and application logic, so there's a need to integrate with these applications. And, because these applications are typically not all able to communicate via web services using the same data model, there's generally a need for integration logic like JMS and file connectivity, routing, and transformation.

In this chapter, you saw that the Activiti Engine provides many ways to solve these issues. First, there's a web service task you can leverage to communicate directly with SOAP web services. You saw that you don't need additional Java coding to implement a web service task. But, the amount of XML configuration needed to implement even a simple web service task is quite large, so you can pick your own favorite way of implementing a web service client.

When there's a need for more connectivity options and integration capabilities, you can leverage the Apache Camel and Mule ESB integrations with the Activiti Engine. Both frameworks provide similar functionality, with lots of connectivity options, support for enterprise integration patterns, and an easy to learn flow language or DSL. The main difference between them is that Apache Camel typically runs embedded in your application by adding a couple of Apache Camel JAR files. Mule ESB typically runs standalone in its own container. Again, you can choose your favorite framework here because both options provide similar capabilities. It depends on which coding style you prefer (Camel DSL or Mule flow language) and whether you need a separate container like Mule ESB. In addition, you should know that Apache ServiceMix 4 also provides a separate container and uses Apache Camel to implement the integration logic.

In the next chapter, we'll move on to another interesting topic—adding a business rule engine to the Activiti Engine. By separating business rules from the process definition, the need for new versions of the process definition can be kept to a minimum. And, as you'll see, a business rule engine has great capabilities for implementing business rules using a powerful DSL.

Ruling
the business rule engine

This chapter covers

- Introduction to rules and business rule management
- The BPMN 2.0 business rule task construct
- Introduction to Drools and Drools Expert
- Integrating Drools with Activiti
- Web-based rule editing

Many paths can be taken in the execution of a business process. Often, the path that should be taken in a certain case is determined by specific business decisions. For example, if a customer has spent a certain amount of money in previous purchases, the customer becomes a VIP customer and is routed through the process via an alternative path and rewarded and treated differently. These kinds of flexible decision points in processes are places where business rules can come into play. This chapter is all about how these rules can be applied and integrated with Activiti.

First, we'll take a look at business rule management and see in more detail what kinds of rules you can encounter in a business process. We'll also cover some terminology from the business rule world and link the topic with BPMN 2.0. In section 12.2, you'll learn about an open source business rule management system called Drools and work out a simple example and a more business-friendly one to get familiar with it. In section 12.3, we'll take Drools into Activiti, and you'll see how Drools can be used to bring rules into your processes. We'll look at the integration of Activiti and Drools from an architectural point of view and cover the deployment of rules in the Activiti environment. We'll also pick up the loan request case we covered in chapter 5 and enhance it with business rules to implement business logic. Finally, in section 12.4, we'll take a look at changing rules with a web-based application.

Let's get started. It's time to add some dynamicity and flexibility to our processes. We'll extract the business knowledge from them and take our Activiti processes to the next level!

12.1 Introducing business rule management

Before we dive deep into integrating Activiti with Drools, it's a good idea to get some background on business rule management so we can get our vocabulary aligned. Therefore, this section starts with an introduction to business rules. Then, we'll take a look at a couple of business rule examples and see how the whole environment around business rules becomes a business rule management system. After that, we'll take a look at what type of rules can exist in a business process and see how BPMN 2.0 helps you define rules in business processes.

12.1.1 What's a business rule?

Business rule management is a big topic and many books have been written to cover it. The few terms presented here will introduce you to the field and get you through the chapter. If you want to learn more, a good place to get started is www.businessrules-group.org. You can also search for Ronald Ross online or start at www.ronross.info; he's known as "the father of business rules." Now, back to business; what's a rule, anyway?

Before getting all theoretical with definitions, it's better to look at an example of a business rule:

```
No credit check is to be performed on returning customers
```

This statement tells us something about how that business decided to deal with their customers. It can be written down in some specification to be eventually translated into code, but it can also be a policy that a business applies while communicating with a customer on the phone.

> **DEFINITION** *Business rules* describe initially in plain words how operations, definitions, and constraints are applied by an organization. They can apply to many different things like people, processes, or overall corporate behavior.

While a business rule may be informal or even unwritten and exist only in the heads of people, clarifying, managing, and applying those rules is very valuable. Having a grip on rules like the previous one helps organizations to achieve their goals and avoid mistakes. Take a look at another example:

```
A gold customer gets a 10 percent discount on all book items
```

This rule is a little bit more complex than the first one and illustrates why a company would want their rules to be documented and managed. Customers might belong to a category like regular or silver, indicating their loyalty to the company's products. You see that discounts are given as well. A company might want to give different rates of discount to different categories. Or it may give discounts depending on the type of item a customer wants to purchase—books or DVDs or other product types.

You can see the need for flexibility coming up already! Our fictive company might want to add more categories of customers as sales grow or change their discount rates when time moves on. The need to implement these kinds of rules in a timely fashion can also arise. If the company wants to stay ahead of the competition, it might need to have this rule active right away, preferably to be automated and implemented in a computer system.

Let's say a new book, *Activiti in Action*, is out in the stores and we want to provide Java developers with a discount in the first week:

```
Java developers get a 30 percent discount on Activiti in Action in the
    first week
```

In order to achieve this kind of flexibility and short time to market, business rules need to be documented and managed. We need a business rule management system to do that well.

12.1.2   *Business rule management systems*

Instead of just having a set of policies, rules, or constraints in the heads of employees, hidden in company books, or hardcoded in mainframe systems, we're going to move on to the management of this type of knowledge. Business rule management systems (BRMSs) exist to do just that.

Take a look at figure 12.1 to get an overview of the environment of a typical BRMS.

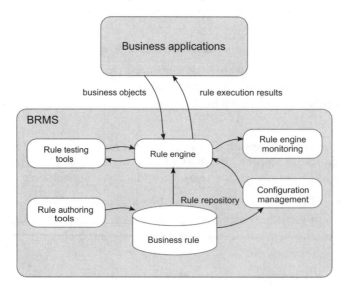

Figure 12.1   Overview of a typical BRMS

To be able to use the full capabilities of a BRMS, you'll need all of the functions shown in figure 12.1. Let's go through them briefly:

- *Rules*—There may be just a few rules concerning a small dynamic part of your organization, or there may be thousands of rules concerning everything a company does, from the maximum amount of money an online customer is allowed to spend to the roles people need to play in order to be allowed to evaluate loan requests.
- *Rule repository*—This is where the rules are stored. This repository is the foundation of a BRMS and contains all the rules available. In the case of IT systems, the repository will contain automated rules, and the repository is typically implemented by a database system with versioning capabilities.
- *Rule engine*—This is another core component of a BRMS. This component loads certain versions of the rules from the repository and runs business objects against those rules, evaluating conditions and executing actions when conditions are met. (For example, If the customer is a gold customer, then the customer gets 10 percent discount.) Rule engines use optimized algorithms to perform this type of logic efficiently and can give quick feedback.
- *Rule authoring tools*—Rule authoring tools are often part of a BRMS as well. These tools help in creating the rules and allow you to manipulate the repository by storing new rules and deleting or changing existing ones. Rule authoring tools come in different types for different users. Some focus on allowing developers to add logic that changes the behavior of the rule engine, others are more business-centric and guide business analysts or users to manipulate rules themselves.
- *Monitor*—Common, but optional, tools can help you monitor rule execution to see what the state of the rule engine is at any given moment or help you determine which rules have fired for a certain input.
- *Configuration management*—This is a vital part of a BRMS. It should be easy to change business rules, and you should be able to find out which rules are currently deployed in production.
- *Test tools*—A good BRMS has test tools for testing rules and promoting rules from development to production.

Now that you have seen what business rules are and how a related system of tools can help to manage those rules, it's time to take a look at how business rule management and business process management fit together.

12.1.3 *Using different types of rules in business processes*

Now, you may be thinking, "This isn't a book about business rule management but business process management!"—and you're right. But one doesn't exclude the other. Business rule management and business process management can easily go hand in hand; they're complementary. Where business process management tells us a lot about *how* a company does its business, business rules tells us about the *what*. Let's look at an example and come back to this in a bit.

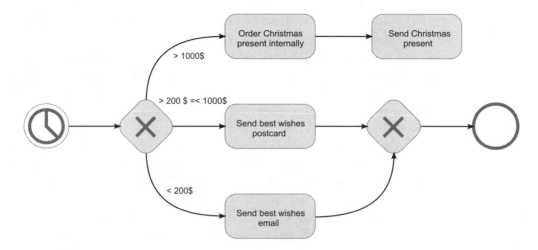

Figure 12.2   **The Christmas wishes business process showing the handling of different customer types**

Let's say that, around Christmas time, a company wants to treat the customers that spent over a thousand dollars to a Christmas gift. Customers that haven't s spent as much—somewhere between two hundred and a thousand dollars—receive a Christmas card. A third type of customer, who spent less than two hundred dollars, receives an email Christmas greeting that also informs them that new stuff is available now. Figure 12.2 shows a process model for this simple process.

The business process model in figure 12.2 expresses *how* our fictive company wants to handle different types of customers when Christmas draws near. Some get a present and others get an email message, depending on their spending behavior. In this model, you can also see *what* a "good" customer is, according to our fictive company. This knowledge, which determines the outcome of the process, is business rule knowledge.

In this case, the type of logic that the rules consist of is decision logic (similar to routing logic). We check how much a customer has spent and then decide which path in the business process to take. You can find another type of logic in a task. Take a look at figure 12.3, which shows a snippet from a process for purchasing a phone subscription.

You can't directly see any business rules in the figure. But, take a closer look at the "Determine contract price" task. If the price were fixed, we wouldn't need that task. It's there because the price that the phone company will charge the customers is determined by some algorithm, such as one based on the customer's loyalty to the firm. The longer the customer does business with the phone company, the lower the price of the contract. This type of logic also consists of business rules, and, again, the rules might be stored in a rule repository and be executed at runtime by a rule engine.

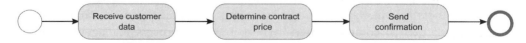

Figure 12.3   **Illustrating business rule logic hidden in tasks**

As you've seen, there are different types of rules in business processes:

- Decision logic rules—These determine process execution paths.
- Business logic rules—These are executed within a certain step of a process execution.

We've seen that the *how* of a business process and the *what* of the rules are a natural fit. Let's take a look at how we can express this connection with a specific BPMN 2.0 construct.

12.1.4 *Business rule management in BPMN 2.0*

Business logic rules and decision logic rules can be modeled in different ways in a BPMN 2.0 process, depending on how the logic is implemented.

Think, for example, about making decisions based on knowledge only available in the heads of company employees. This kind of decision logic is performed by a person and can be modeled in a BPMN 2.0 process as a user task, as you've seen before. Another kind of rule can be based upon knowledge somewhere outside of the system or even outside the company running that system. In this case, the rule logic can be modeled as a send and receive task pair and will rely on messaging to get the job done.

The kinds of rules we're covering in this chapter are automated rules that are executed by a business rule engine. The task construct that the BPMN 2.0 specification defines to model business logic is called the *business rule task.*

A business rule task provides a mechanism for a business process to provide input to a business rule engine and to get the output of calculations or checks that the business rule engine might provide. Because this construct is part of the task family, it has the same familiar shape as the other task types: the rounded rectangle. It has a little graphical marker indicating that the task is a business rule task, which you can see in the process depicted in figure 12.4.

In this small process, the two types of rules we covered before (business logic and decision logic) are implemented with the help of the business rule task construct. In this loan request process, there's first the "Calculate credit score" task, a task containing

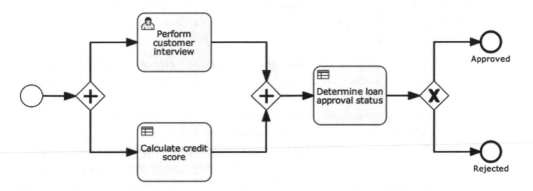

Figure 12.4   A small BPMN 2.0 process model containing multiple business rule task constructs

business logic in the form of rules needed to calculate a credit score. This task is executed in parallel with a user task in which there's personal contact with the loan requester. Both these tasks will produce values for process variables needed for the second business rule task, which determines the status of the loan request. "Determine loan approval status" is a rule task that contains the decision logic that will guide the process execution over either the approved or rejected path.

The BPMN 2.0 specification doesn't define how rule logic should be implemented in business processes. The Activiti project decided not to build their own rule engine and, instead, to integrate with one of the most widely used open source business rule engines available: Drools. Now that you have the rule background and an understanding of the relationship between business rules and process management, it's time to check out Drools and play with it a little to get some rules going!

12.2 *Entering the rule world of Drools*

To enter the rule world of Drools, we'll first discuss the Drools framework. After a brief introduction to the project itself, we'll look at Drools Expert, the Drools rule engine. Then, we'll dive in and get our hands dirty while we work out some rule logic!

12.2.1 *Drools, the business logic integration platform*

Drools is an Apache licensed JBoss project that contains a lot more than just plain business rule functionality. The origin of the project, though, is Drools rules. After a few years, the Drools project became a part of JBoss and grew to the project it is today.

The project is split up into several subprojects. Our focus in this chapter is on the Drools Expert project. Drools Expert contains the business rule engine itself and comes with an Eclipse-based rule authoring environment. There's support for rule testing, rule debugging, and synchronization with the Drools Guvnor rule repository. With domain specific languages (DSLs), Drools Expert supports ways to define *human-friendly* business rules. Guided editors can help you define those DSL rules, and decision tables are supported as well. We'll see more of this later in the chapter.

You can work with Drools Expert without having to use or install any of the other parts of the Drools project. We won't cover the rest of the Drools project in this book, but here's a brief outline of the components, to give you an idea of what they're all about:

- *Drools Guvnor*—A centralized repository for Drools rules and decision tables. It has a web-based user interface, editors, and tools to aid in the management of large numbers of rules. Guvnor also supports rule versioning, deployments, rule authoring, and testing and has the means to synchronize with the Drools rule authoring Eclipse environment.
- *Drools Fusion*—The Drools module responsible for enabling complex event processing capabilities. Complex event processing (CEP), deals with processing and analyzing multiple events to be able to detect patterns to take real-time actions. CEP is used in fraud detection and high volume trade applications, among

others. We'll discuss it in detail in chapter 14, where we'll take a look at the integration of Activiti with the Esper CEP open source framework.

- *Drools Planner*—A module that focuses on optimizing automated planning solutions. Picture use cases such as packing shipping containers: you need to pack goods of different sizes and weights into a minimum number of containers while also spreading that weight evenly and not packing more than the maximum allowed weight in each container.

> ### Drools, Drools Flow, and jBPM 5
>
> Until recently, Drools included a workflow and process component called Drools Flow. Because JBoss already included the jBPM project for workflow and process capabilities, the two projects were merged; jBPM 5 is now a component of the Drools project and supersedes Drools Flow.
>
> As you may know, jBPM 5 offers capabilities similar to the Activiti project. Both implement the BPMN 2.0 specification, offer a web-based modeling and management application, and provide an Eclipse-based Designer plugin. To make it even juicier, the founders of the Activiti project (Tom Baeyens and Joram Barrez) led the jBPM project before they left JBoss to join Alfresco.
>
> jBPM 5 uses an API similar to the one used by Drools Expert, which we'll be discussing in the next section. Therefore, the process and workflow management and rule management capabilities are tightly integrated. Activiti takes another approach. The Activiti platform is solely dedicated to process and workflow management, and it provides integration points to include things like rule capabilities (Drools Expert) and enterprise integration capabilities (Apache Camel and Mule ESB modules).
>
> In summary, Activiti uses Drools Expert to implement the business rule task because it provides a good rule management platform. Drools and jBPM 5 provide a platform for both rule management and process and workflow management, but they use a JBoss-only approach instead of the best-of-breed approach that Activiti adheres to.

Because this chapter is all about business rule management and its integration with Activiti, we'll leave the other modules behind us now and focus on the rules part of the Drools project. On to Drools Expert!

12.2.2 *Introducing Drools Expert*

The underlying idea of a rule engine is to externalize the business logic from your application. Get that rule knowledge clear, remove it from your application, and implement it with a business rule engine that your application calls when needed.

How a business rule engine achieves the goal of executing the defined rules is another topic. From a standardization point of view, the Java Community Process came up with JSR-94, the Java Rule Engine API, about six years ago. That JSR gives rule engine providers a standardized API for executing rules, registering rules, and parsing rules, but it didn't standardize the rule engine itself or the language used to describe rules.

Drools Expert, being JSR-94 compliant, implements a rule engine as a forward-chaining rule engine with a native language, the Drools rule language.

Forward-chaining versus backward-chaining engines

When you hear people talk about rule engines, they often use terms like *forward-chaining engines* and *backward-chaining engines*. What do these terms mean?

Take a look at this example set of rules:

```
If X croaks and eats flies - Then X is a frog
If X chirps and sings - Then X is a canary
If X is a frog - Then X is green
If X is a canary - Then X is yellow
```

Let's say the goal is to determine the color of our Activiti friend Kermit, only knowing that our friend croaks and eats flies. A forward-chaining rule engine is data driven and will select the first rule to fire. The first rule concludes that Kermit is a frog, and the second rule isn't applicable to Kermit. The third rule condition evaluates to true and we get our answer; Kermit is green.

A backward-chaining rule engine tackles the problem differently. It's goal driven and, because the goal is to determine the color of Kermit, it will select the third and fourth rules because those rules match the final goal. The rule engine doesn't know yet if Kermit is a frog or a canary, so it adds the third and fourth rules to the goal list it maintains. Now, the engine processes the first and second rules to determine whether Kermit is a frog or a canary, because the outcome is needed for the final goal to determine the color of Kermit. Because the first rule says that Kermit is a frog, we can now execute the third rule and produce the final result that Kermit is green.

In conclusion, the main difference between forward- and backward-chaining rule engines is that they take different approaches—data versus goal driven—to get to the solution.

Take a look at figure 12.5 to see how the Drools Expert rule engine works and to get familiar with some additional rule engine terminology.

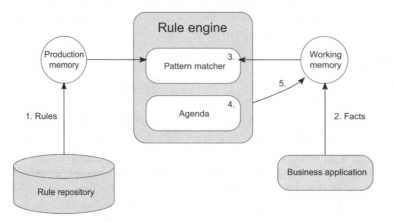

Figure 12.5   The rule engine architecture and its communication partners in the outside world

This layout is pretty much standard in all forward-chaining rule engines. Let's walk through what happens to get the idea behind this architecture:

1   On the left side of the figure, the business rules are loaded from the rule repository into production memory.

2   On the right, business objects (that are often called facts) are loaded into working memory from your application when it calls the engine. These are the business objects you want to apply your rules to. In the sidebar about forward versus backward chaining, rules were written against something called X. In that case, instances of X need to be inserted in the working memory to evaluate against the rules.

3   Now that everything is in place, the engine can do its work and the inserted facts are evaluated against the rule conditions by the pattern matcher.

4   Every time the pattern matcher evaluates a rule condition to true, it puts that rule on the agenda to be fired. This means that it lists the rules in an order, based on priorities attached to the rules or other criteria.

5   Finally, the actions of the rules listed in the agenda are fired, meaning that the then clauses in the eligible rules are executed. This completes the circle, leading to updates, inserts, or removals of facts or objects in the working memory. Think, for example, about an update of a result object containing the verdict about a loan application. Updating that object could set a value to approved or denied.

Now that you know how a rule engine works, let's take a quick look at some Drools specifics before we see things in action. Drools has a native rule format, called the Drools rule language. The rules written in the Drools rule language are saved in a file with a .drl extension. Multiple rules can be written in one file, and the format is pretty straightforward. Take a look at the next snippet to get the idea:

```
rule "name"
    attributes
    when
      X
    then
      Y
end
```

A rule has a name and, optionally, a set of attributes that state its priority, indicate when the rule should become effective or when it should expire, or provide other information. The rule definition uses the keyword when to start a condition description (X, in this case) and uses then to declare the consequence (Y, in this case). The end keyword marks the end of the description.

There are many other options available when writing rules with the Drools rule language, and if you're interested in learning more, you can check out the Drools Expert documentation; it's extensive and well written.

Now that you know how the Drools rule engine works and how to write rules, it's time to see some action. Let's get some hands-on experience with Drools Expert!

12.2.3 *Hands-on with Drools Expert*

We're going to work out some rule examples that we'll later integrate with Activiti in a business process. To get started with Drools Expert and see some of its possibilities up close, you can choose to install the Drools Expert Eclipse environment. In the examples we implement in this chapter, this isn't necessary.

DEFINING RULES

In the loan request process implemented in chapter 5, you used a credit check to determine whether the loan amount requested was too high in relation to the salary of the applicant. Loan Sharks agreed to let a customer pass the credit check when the applicant's income divided by two was bigger than the requested loan amount. Take a look at the following code from listing 5.1 to see the script task used to implement the credit check behavior:

```
<scriptTask id="checkCredit" scriptFormat="groovy">
    <script>
      creditCheckOk = false;
      if((income / 2) > loanAmount) {
        creditCheckOk = true;
      }
    </script>
  </scriptTask>
```

The logic in this task was hardcoded in the BPMN 2.0 XML and, therefore, not very flexible. If you wanted to change the behavior of the script task, you'd have to edit the BPMN 2.0 XML directly. Because you'd have changed the process definition itself, there would be a need for a new deployment and version of the loan request process. As you've probably guessed by now, that isn't the way to go if flexibility is a requirement!

Let's extract that logic now and implement the credit check with a business rule.

RUNNING RULES

As mentioned before, Drools rules are written in the Drools rule language format and saved in a .drl file. You can create a .drl file using the wizard in Eclipse or using a simple text file. The next listing shows the contents of the rule file.

> **Listing 12.1   An example Drools .drl file with the credit check business rule**

```
package org.bpmnwithactiviti.chapter12.rules

import org.bpmnwithactiviti.chapter12.model.LoanApplicant;

rule "CreditCheckRule"
  when
    la: LoanApplicant(income > (2 * loanAmount))
  then
    la.setCheckCreditOk(true);
end
```

Like Java classes, rules can be organized in packages. As you've seen before, facts or objects are pushed into the rule engine's working memory at execution time, and the idea is that rules are written against those objects. The fully qualified class names of the facts are declared in the import statement so you can use the classes while executing rules. You can write multiple rules in one .drl file, and rule definitions start with the rule keyword and a rule name. Because we're starting with an easy example, only one rule is defined in this file. Finally, don't forget to use the end keyword to specify that the rule definition is finished.

With the Drools rule language, you have a lot of options for writing your rules. You can define functions that can be called by rules or introspect the working memory from within rules. This book isn't the place to explain the language, but it's worth checking out the language's syntax in the documentation to get a feel for the possibilities it offers.

Now let's define a CreditCheckRuleRunner class that contains all the code you need to read the rule files and run them with Drools.

Listing 12.2 CreditCheckRuleRunner class needed to run the CreditCheckRule

```
public class CreditCheckRuleRunner {

  public static boolean runRules(LoanApplicant
          loanApplicant) throws Exception {

    KnowledgeBase kbase = readKnowledgeBase();
    StatelessKnowledgeSession ksession =
        kbase.newStatelessKnowledgeSession();
    ksession.execute(loanApplicant);
    return loanApplicant.isCheckCreditOk();
  }
```

First, you need a KnowledgeBase. This is a repository containing all the rules you want to execute. We'll take a detailed look at how to get this repository in the next listing. For now, remember that the KnowledgeBase itself doesn't contain any facts or objects; those are inserted at execution time into the working memory.

Second, you create a StatelessKnowledgeSession that you'll use to communicate with the rule engine. Executing the business rules happens with one simple call.

Finally, after having run the rules, the result of the call to the engine is returned to the application.

Stateless versus stateful knowledge sessions

There are two ways to communicate with Drools to execute rules. You can use the StatelessKnowledgeSession or the StatefulKnowledgeSession. In listing 12.2, you used the StatelessKnowledgeSession to interact with the Drools rule engine.

The two types of sessions are appropriate for different use cases. The Stateless-KnowledgeSession is commonly used in simple use cases. A stateless session can be regarded as a function passing in some data and receiving results back. No session context is created.

(continued)

With the StatefulKnowledgeSession, a session context is created, so objects can be cached in memory. This means you can create intermediate results that can be retrieved from the session context by other rules when needed. While handling the StatefulKnowledgeSession, you must not forget to call the dispose() method to get rid of the session and avoid memory leaks.

Before we get to the next listing, a little warning about KnowledgeBases. As a repository, KnowledgeBases contain the rules and other typical Drools artifacts your application needs. Because the number of rules an application needs can become very large, creating the KnowledgeBase can be a heavy task from a performance perspective. Creating sessions with the engine itself is very light, though, and that's why it's recommended that KnowledgeBases be cached when possible for repeated session creation.

The following listing shows how to create a knowledge base and how to store the rules in it. This listing is part of the same CreditCheckRuleRunner class shown in listing 12.2.

Listing 12.3   Reading rules and creating a KnowledgeBase

```
private static KnowledgeBase readKnowledgeBase()
    throws Exception {

  KnowledgeBuilder kbuilder =
    KnowledgeBuilderFactory.newKnowledgeBuilder();              ❶ Adds rule
                                                                   resources and
  kbuilder.add(ResourceFactory.newClassPathResource             resource type
    ("chapter12" + File.separator + "rules" + File.separator +
      "CreditCheck.drl"), ResourceType.DRL);

  KnowledgeBase kbase =
    KnowledgeBaseFactory.newKnowledgeBase();
  kbase.addKnowledgePackages(
    kbuilder.getKnowledgePackages());
  return kbase;
}
```

Creating a KnowledgeBase isn't a complicated task. You start off by creating a KnowledgeBuilder and feed it the rule resources ❶. You can also add other types of resources, such as .dsl files. These domain specific language files allow you to write rules in a human-friendly fashion. After the resources are read, a KnowledgeBase is instantiated and the knowledge packages are added to the base.

That's it. You're now all set to execute the credit check rule on the Drools rule engine from a unit test. In the source code, you can find the unit test (CreditCheckTest) and associated classes in the bpmn-examples project.

12.2.4   *Using spreadsheets to create Drools decision tables*

The example we used in the previous section was a simple check credit rule. To see how Drools supports more complicated rules and different ways to express them, we'll take a brief look at decision tables.

RuleSet	org.bpmnwithactiviti.chapter12.rules	
Import	org.bpmnwithactiviti.chapter12.model.LoanApplicant	
RuleTable Credit Check		
CONDITION	CONDITION	ACTION
la : LoanApplicant		
income >= $1, income < $2	loanAmount < $1	la.setCheckCreditOk($param);
Applicant's income between:	Requested loan amount:	Credit check passed:
100, 200	30	TRUE
200, 500	100	TRUE
500, 1000	250	TRUE
1000, 2000	500	TRUE

Figure 12.6   Drools spreadsheet decision table representing a more complex credit check

Decision tables are a bunch of rules bundled together. Drools supports decision tables written in a spreadsheet format with spreadsheet programs like Microsoft Excel or OpenOffice Calc (formats XLS and CSV). Drools uses the spreadsheets to generate rules while building the KnowledgeBase. Under the hood, it interprets the spreadsheet file and creates DRL rules for the rows in the sheet that express conditions and actions. Take a look at figure 12.6 to see an example Excel spreadsheet that can be read by Drools.

To give you an idea about what goes on in the spreadsheet, let's look at a few highlights.

When creating the spreadsheet, you can start at any column or row in the sheet you want; the starting point Drools looks for is a cell that uses the RuleSet keyword—that row needs to contain the rule package definition. Directly underneath it, you can add some rule set specific stuff—in this case, the imports you need.

With the RuleTable keyword, the rule definitions part starts. You have to define the RuleTable keyword in the same column that contained the RuleSet keyword.

The keywords Condition and Action follow in the row immediately after the RuleTable row, and the row below that one is where you define optional object types or variables that you can use in the rules, like the definition of the la : LoanApplicant type variable in the figure. If you don't use the row for defining variables, you have to leave it empty.

The next row contains the rule templates. You can use the $param placeholder to indicate where data from the data or rule cells below should be interpolated; for multiple insertions, use $1, $2, and so on, to indicate parameters from a comma-separated list in the cells below. The next row, just before the data, is ignored; it may contain textual descriptions of the column's purpose, and it's there to make the table easier to read. The remaining rows contain the data that forms the rules, one per row.

The conditions and actions themselves are easy to read. They use the attributes of the LoanApplicant class, and both conditions and actions are written to be parameterized. You see, for example, the first condition:

```
income >= $1, income < $2
```

When the engine evaluates this rule, the income attribute of the LoanApplicant class is checked to make sure it's in a certain range defined by the comma-separated values in the columns below. When an applicant's income is in a certain range, a maximum amount can be requested to get approval from the company.

The code needed to invoke this decision table is the same as in listing 12.2. But what's different is the way the `KnowledgeBase` is created, so let's take a look at how it's created using the spreadsheet. The basic idea is the same as what we've seen with the .drl files.

Listing 12.4   Creating the `KnowledgeBase` using Excel and decision tables

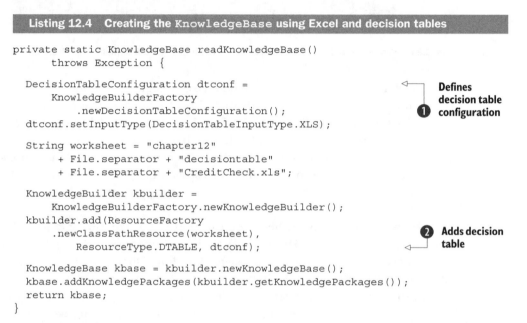

```
private static KnowledgeBase readKnowledgeBase()
    throws Exception {

  DecisionTableConfiguration dtconf =                          Defines
    KnowledgeBuilderFactory                                    decision table
        .newDecisionTableConfiguration();                   ① configuration
  dtconf.setInputType(DecisionTableInputType.XLS);

  String worksheet = "chapter12"
      + File.separator + "decisiontable"
      + File.separator + "CreditCheck.xls";

  KnowledgeBuilder kbuilder =
      KnowledgeBuilderFactory.newKnowledgeBuilder();
  kbuilder.add(ResourceFactory
      .newClassPathResource(worksheet),                     ② Adds decision
          ResourceType.DTABLE, dtconf);                        table

  KnowledgeBase kbase = kbuilder.newKnowledgeBase();
  kbase.addKnowledgePackages(kbuilder.getKnowledgePackages());
  return kbase;
}
```

In the .drl example of listing 12.3, the `KnowledgeBuilder` used the default configuration. In listing 12.4, which uses spreadsheets, you need to define a decision table configuration as an Excel spreadsheet ①. Then, the decision table is added to the repository, and the rules are parsed by Drools and transformed to the structure of the .drl rules ②.

Besides a package's declaration and the imports, four rules are created. To differentiate the different rules, a rule name containing the location in the sheet is generated:

```
...
#From row number: 10
rule "Credit Check_10"
  when
    la : LoanApplicant
      (income >= 100, income < 200, loanAmount < 30)
  then
    la.setCheckCreditOk(true);
end
...
```

You now have a basic idea of the Drools rule engine environment. Besides writing a rule and running it using the Drools API, we've looked at how decision tables can be used with Excel sheets. Now let's move back to the real topic of this book: Activiti. Time to meet the features Activiti developed to extract rule logic from the business process and execute it with Drools!

12.3 Integrating Drools with Activiti

This section will cover the integration of Activiti's features and the Drools Expert rule engine. We'll start off by implementing the credit check task in a small test process. Then we'll look at how rules can be deployed together with the process definition on Activiti Engine, using our loan request process as an example.

12.3.1 Activiti and the business rule task

To execute rules deployed with a BPMN 2.0 process on Activiti, you have to define a few things in the BPMN 2.0 XML. As input for the rules, a comma-separated list of process variables has to be declared. Let's dive in (see the next listing).

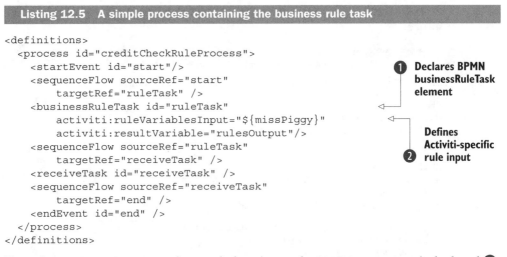

Listing 12.5 A simple process containing the business rule task

```
<definitions>
  <process id="creditCheckRuleProcess">
    <startEvent id="start"/>
    <sequenceFlow sourceRef="start"
        targetRef="ruleTask" />
    <businessRuleTask id="ruleTask"
        activiti:ruleVariablesInput="${missPiggy}"
        activiti:resultVariable="rulesOutput"/>
    <sequenceFlow sourceRef="ruleTask"
        targetRef="receiveTask" />
    <receiveTask id="receiveTask" />
    <sequenceFlow sourceRef="receiveTask"
        targetRef="end" />
    <endEvent id="end" />
  </process>
</definitions>
```

❶ Declares BPMN
businessRuleTask
element

❷ Defines
Activiti-specific
rule input

First, the `businessRuleTask` element belonging to the BPMN namespace is declared ❶. It contains two Activiti-specific attributes: `ruleVariablesInput` ❷ and `resultVariable`.

This little example, which you're about to run in a unit test, only performs the "Credit check" task. You feed the business rule task a process variable of the `LoanApplicant` type. As mentioned, multiple process variables can also be used, as follows:

```
activiti:ruleVariablesInput="${missPiggy}, ${kermit}, ..."
```

After the rule has executed, the results are stored in a single result variable, named `rulesOutput` in this example process. Declaring the name of the result variable in the BPMN 2.0 XML is optional. When it isn't defined, Activiti uses `org.activiti.engine.rules.OUTPUT` as its name. There's only one output variable declared in a business rule task. Therefore, the result variable of the business rule task is always a list of objects.

You'll see in the unit test in listing 12.6 how easy it is to run the creditCheck-RuleProcess. It uses the rule definition implemented earlier:

```
rule "CreditCheckRule"
when
    la: LoanApplicant(income > (2 * loanAmount))
then
    la.setCheckCreditOk(true);
end
```

All the Drools code needed to execute the credit check rule is encapsulated in the Activiti implementation of the business rule task behavior. The business rule task starts by looking for rules deployed together with the process definition, and it creates a StatefulKnowledgeSession that contains the rules it finds. It then looks for the process variables defined as the input of the rules in the BPMN 2.0 XML, executes the rules, and wraps the results in the output variable. After adding the result variable as a process variable on the execution, the business rule task has done its work.

Take a look at the next listing to see what you have to do to start the process instance.

Listing 12.6 Executing the process containing the business rule task

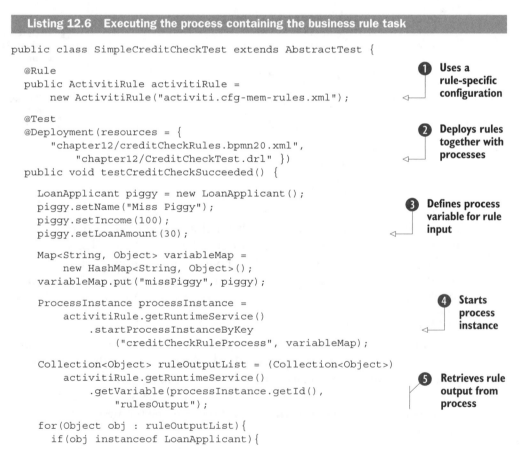

```
public class SimpleCreditCheckTest extends AbstractTest {

    @Rule                                                        ❶ Uses a
    public ActivitiRule activitiRule =                             rule-specific
        new ActivitiRule("activiti.cfg-mem-rules.xml");            configuration

    @Test
    @Deployment(resources = {                                    ❷ Deploys rules
        "chapter12/creditCheckRules.bpmn20.xml",                   together with
            "chapter12/CreditCheckTest.drl" })                     processes
    public void testCreditCheckSucceeded() {

        LoanApplicant piggy = new LoanApplicant();
        piggy.setName("Miss Piggy");                             ❸ Defines process
        piggy.setIncome(100);                                      variable for rule
        piggy.setLoanAmount(30);                                   input

        Map<String, Object> variableMap =
            new HashMap<String, Object>();
        variableMap.put("missPiggy", piggy);

        ProcessInstance processInstance =                        ❹ Starts
            activitiRule.getRuntimeService()                       process
                .startProcessInstanceByKey                         instance
                    ("creditCheckRuleProcess", variableMap);

        Collection<Object> ruleOutputList = (Collection<Object>)
            activitiRule.getRuntimeService()                     ❺ Retrieves rule
                .getVariable(processInstance.getId(),              output from
                    "rulesOutput");                                process

        for(Object obj : ruleOutputList){
            if(obj instanceof LoanApplicant){
```

```
        assertTrue(((LoanApplicant) obj).isCheckCreditOk());
      }
    }
  }
}
```

As before, you use the `ActivitiRule` to configure Activiti Engine ❶. The Activiti Engine configuration is changed to enable the rules functionality as we'll see in the next code snippet. Then, the process is deployed on the engine, together with the rule file ❷.

You then define a `LoanApplicant` object with the loan request information for Miss Piggy ❸. Then, a new process instance is started ❹ and the business rule task is executed. Finally, the process variable that contains the rule output is retrieved from the execution using the variable name defined in the process definition ❺.

Now that you've defined the unit test, we'll take a look at the Activiti configuration. In order to configure the Activiti Engine, you need to configure something we haven't seen before in the Activiti configuration file: the `RulesDeployer`. The following code snippet shows how this is done:

```
<beans>
  <bean id="processEngineConfiguration"
      class="org.activiti.engine.impl.cfg.
          ➥ StandaloneInMemProcessEngineConfiguration">
    <property name="databaseSchemaUpdate" value="true" />
    <property name="customPostDeployers">
     <list>
      <bean class="org.activiti.engine.impl.rules.RulesDeployer" />
     </list>
    </property>
  </bean>
</beans>
```

Activiti defines a `Deployer` interface with a `deploy()` method to be implemented. Implementers of that interface can be configured in the Activiti configuration, and, in this case, because you're deploying rules, you need the `RulesDeployer`.

What the `RulesDeployer` does is build and cache the `KnowledgeBase` at deployment time. When a business rule task is executed, the Activiti implementation will start looking in the cache to look up the `KnowledgeBase` and execute the rules.

Now that you've implemented a simple example process with a business rule task, let's go ahead with a full-blown process example.

12.3.2 *Using business rules in a process definition*

Let's go back to the loan request process definition from chapter 5 and replace the simple script logic with a couple of business rules. Figure 12.7 shows the loan request process definition, enhanced with two business rule tasks.

You can see the Check Credit task in the modeled process. We saw in section 12.1 that there are two types of business logic you can implement with rules. The "Check credit" task is a business rule task that implements a piece of business logic with

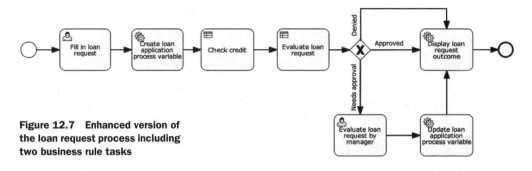

Figure 12.7   Enhanced version of the loan request process including two business rule tasks

rules. The second type of rule functionality is decision logic that's used for routing purposes.

A decision rule is implemented with the "Evaluate loan request" business rule task, which replaces the previous user task. Previously, this task was performed by an employee of Loan Sharks. In your new process, on the other hand, this task is automated with help of the business rule task construct. The task will evaluate the loan application with a couple of business rules, and the outcome of the rule logic will determine which path the process execution will follow.

Based on the business rule outcome, the request will be approved, denied, or marked as in need of management approval when the requested loan amount is above a certain limit. For brevity, the steps that need to be performed by the process after choosing an execution path have been left out; we'll focus on the business rule part of the process.

Before we move on to the changed BPMN 2.0 XML code, let's first take a look at the business rules concerning the loan request evaluation:

```
rule "LoanApplicationEvaluationRule_1"
  when
    la: LoanApplication((applicant.isCheckCreditOk == true)
        && (applicant.getLoanAmount < 100000))
  then
    la.setStatus("approved");
end

rule "LoanApplicationEvaluationRule_2"
  when
    la: LoanApplication((applicant.isCheckCreditOk == true)
        && (applicant.getLoanAmount >= 100000))
  then
    la.setStatus("needs manager approval");
end

rule "LoanApplicationEvaluationRule_3"
  when
    la: LoanApplication(applicant.isCheckCreditOk == false)
  then
    la.setStatus("denied");
end
```

These three rules are stored in the same file as the credit check rule defined earlier. This isn't necessary; you can deploy multiple .drl files within the same BAR file. The rules act on a `LoanApplication` object that's created and set as a process variable in the "Create loan application" process variable service task after the credit check has been performed. They also use a `LoanApplicant` object which is created in the "Create loan request application" task.

Now that the rules are defined, let's take a look at the process definition. Quite a few things have changed since you automated some behavior and got rid of the Groovy script task that implemented the check credit logic. The next listing shows the important parts of the BPMN 2.0 XML (the whole process definition is available in the source code examples accompanying this book).

Listing 12.7 Enhanced loan request process with the two business rule tasks

```xml
<definitions>
  <process id="loanrequestWithRules">
    <startEvent id="theStart">
      ...
    </startEvent>
    <sequenceFlow sourceRef="theStart"
        targetRef="createApplication" />
    <serviceTask id="createApplication"
        activiti:class="org.bpmnwithactiviti.chapter12.
            ➥ ruletask.ApplicationCreator" />
    <sequenceFlow sourceRef="createApplication"
        targetRef="checkCredit" />
    <businessRuleTask id="checkCredit"
        activiti:ruleVariablesInput="${loanApplicant}"
        activiti:resultVariable="rulesOutput"
        activiti:rules="CreditCheckRule" />
    <sequenceFlow sourceRef="checkCredit"
        targetRef="evaluateLoanRequest" />
    <businessRuleTask id="evaluateLoanRequest"
      activiti:ruleVariablesInput="${loanApplication}"
      activiti:resultVariable="rulesOutput"
      activiti:rules="CreditCheckRule"
      exclude="true" />
    <sequenceFlow sourceRef="evaluateLoanRequest"
      targetRef="approvalGateway" />
    <exclusiveGateway id="approvalGateway" />
    <sequenceFlow sourceRef="approvalGateway"
        targetRef="displayResult">
      <conditionExpression xsi:type="tFormalExpression">
        ${loanApplication.status == 'denied'}
      </conditionExpression>
    </sequenceFlow>
    <sequenceFlow sourceRef="approvalGateway"
        targetRef="evaluateRequestByManager">
      <conditionExpression xsi:type="tFormalExpression">
        ${loanApplication.status == 'needs manager approval'}
      </conditionExpression>
    </sequenceFlow>
```

❶ Defines checkCredit business rule task

❷ Only executes CreditCheckRule

❸ Defines evaluateLoan-Request task

❹ Executes all rules except CreditCheckRule

❺ Uses results to determine execution path

```
<sequenceFlow sourceRef="approvalGateway"
    targetRef="displayResult">
  <conditionExpression xsi:type="tFormalExpression">
    ${loanApplication.status == 'approved'}
  </conditionExpression>
</sequenceFlow>
...
  </process>
</definitions>
```

First, you define the `checkCredit` rule task ❶. The task definition contains an Activiti-specific attribute that explicitly states which rules need to be executed in that task ❷. The input of the `checkCredit` rule task is a `LoanApplicant` instance, which is created by the `createApplication` service task based on the values entered in the start form (which aren't shown in listing 12.7).

In the `evaluateLoanRequest` business rule task ❸, you can again see the `activiti:rules` attribute. It contains the same rule name and indicates with the `exclude="true"` statement that all of the rules but that one need to be executed ❹. Finally, the rule result of the `evaluateLoanRequest` business rule task is used to determine which path in the execution to take ❺.

Now let's go ahead and deploy the loan request process to the Activiti Engine. This takes a few steps.

1 Make sure the Activiti H2 database is running. Remember that you can start the H2 database by running `ant h2.start` from the setup directory of your Activiti installation.

2 Make sure the Activiti Tomcat instance is stopped. Run the `ant tomcat.stop` command to do this.

3 Run the `build.xml` Ant script available in the `bpmn-examples` project in the src/main/resources/chapter12/ruletask directory. This will create a dist/enginelibs directory containing the JARs to be copied to the Activiti Engine and a dist/deploy directory containing the BAR file.

4 Copy the JARs in the dist/enginelibs directory to the webapps/activiti-explorer/WEB-INF/lib directory of the Activiti Tomcat instance.

5 Change the Activiti engine configuration in webapps/activiti-explorer/WEB-INF/applicationContext.xml with the `RulesDeployer` enabled, like you saw in section 12.3.1. This means adding the following property configuration to the `processEngineConfiguration` bean:

```
<property name="customPostDeployers">
  <list>
    <bean class="org.activiti.engine.impl.rules.RulesDeployer" />
  </list>
</property>
```

6 Start the Activiti Tomcat instance. Run the `ant tomcat.start` command.

7 Go to http://localhost:8080/activiti-explorer and deploy the BAR file from the dist/deploy directory to the Activiti Engine.

8 Go ahead and start a new process instance from the Activiti Explorer and validate that the business rules are executed as expected.

You've seen how rules can be written in a .drl file and how they can be deployed on Activiti Engine. The way you've implemented the rules in this section is fine when you're still in development. You'll gain real advantage with business rules when you can put the business in the driver's seat and allow them to change the business rules in production in real time. We'll see an example of that in the next section!

12.4 Creating a web-based rule editor

In the previous chapter, you implemented a couple of rules, but how can you make them rapidly changeable, without too much hassle? You want to be able to change the content of a rule so you can directly influence the behavior of your business processes.

In this section, we'll introduce a small application that enables you to edit the rules deployed on the Activiti Engine from a web application and directly deploy the changed rules without the need to redeploy the process. No hassle at all!

12.4.1 Introducing flexibility with a custom rule authoring application

In this book's source code, you can find a small Vaadin web application in the book-rules-app project that you can run on a Jetty web container with Maven. Vaadin is a web framework with a server-driven programming model that enables you to create fancy web applications with Java code. To get started with Vaadin, you can download the *Book of Vaadin* at http://vaadin.com/book.

The idea of the book-rules-app web application is to have a view on the deployed Drools rule files and have a way to open them in the web application, edit the rules, and deploy the edited rules right away. This way, no coding in an IDE is necessary, and rules can be directly viewed and deployed to speed up the process of change.

> **NOTE** We won't be discussing the details of the web application here, because it uses the Activiti API you've been using throughout this chapter. But, to get more details of the structure, you can browse the source code of the web application.

You can start the application from the command line with Maven using the `mvn clean install jetty:run` command. Maven will start compiling the code, package the WAR file, start a Jetty server instance, and deploy the WAR file to it.

To learn what's going on in the Vaadin application, the *Book of Vaadin* is a great start, but what's interesting to know now is that Vaadin applications have a base class that extends from the Vaadin `Application` class. That class is declared in the web.xml file and forms the starting point of a Vaadin application; from there, the user interface starts to build up.

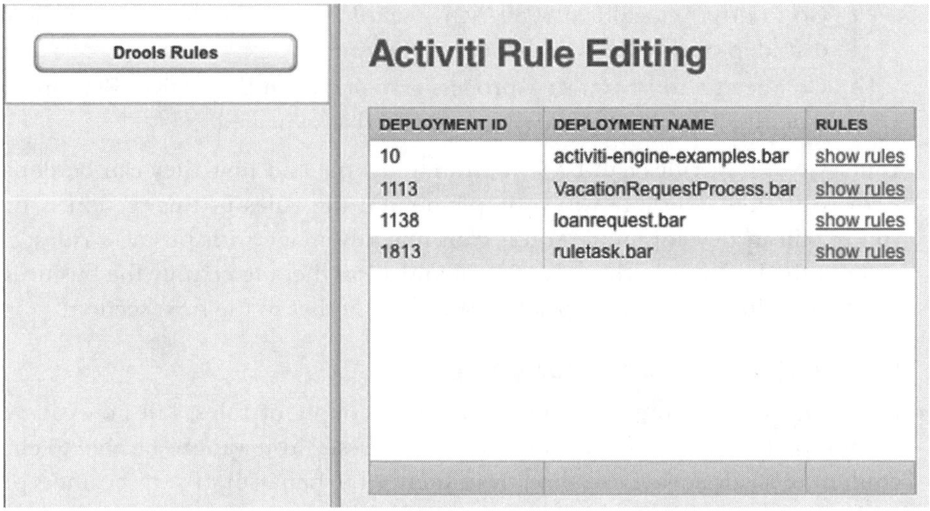

Figure 12.8   Showing Activiti deployments in the Activiti rule editing panel with the help of Vaadin

The `book-rules-app` rules editor application uses the Activiti REST application to deploy updated rules. Therefore, before you can use the `book-rules-app` application, you must execute the steps at the end of section 12.3 again, but this time for the `activiti-rest` application. This ensures the Drools and loan request JARs are deployed to the Activiti REST application and that you can deploy rules in that application. When the Activiti Tomcat instance is started again, you can start the rules web application and go to the http://localhost:8081/book-rules-app URL. Click Drools Rules and you'll see a new panel on the right side of the screen. In the panel, a table is populated with the installed BAR files on the Activiti instance running on Tomcat. In this case, we're interested in the installed loan request process example from the previous section. Take a look at figure 12.8 to see where we are.

You can click the "show rules" links in the table. It looks for .drl files in the installed archives and will either display a message saying that there are no rules installed or display a second table containing the names of the Drools rule files.

Clicking the Show Rules link for the ruletask.bar file, and you'll find yourself looking at the screen in figure 12.9.

In the text field below Edit DRL in figure 12.9, you can directly edit the rule. You can, for example, change the `CreditCheckRule` by making it harder for applicants to get a loan by stating that the applicant's income should be higher than three times the requested amount. After you're done, you can click Deploy Edited Rule and the edited rule will be deployed to the Activiti Engine!

Notice that this results in a new deployment showing in the list of deployments in figure 12.9. You can sort this list by clicking on the column headers: Deployment ID or Deployment Name. You can check that the modified rule is effective immediately by running another instance of the loan request process.

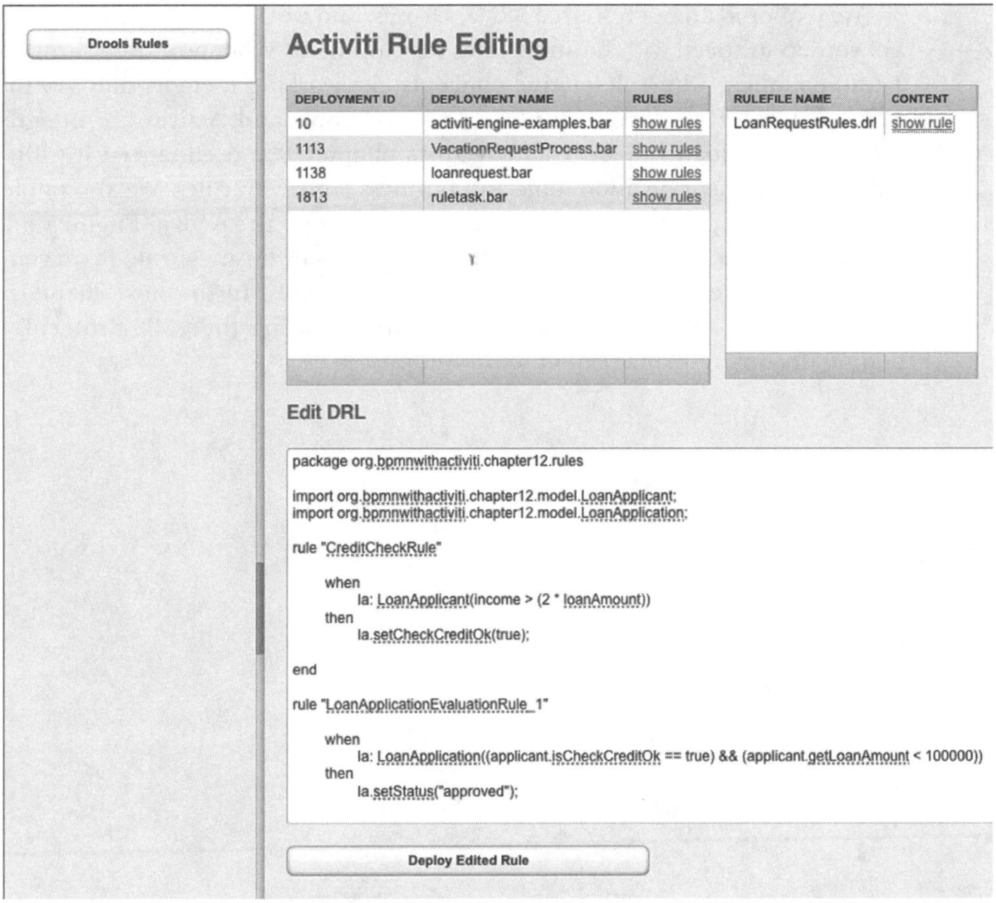

Figure 12.9 Web-based rule authoring and direct deployment of the edited rules on Activiti Engine

Using a simple application like this simplifies the process of changing the business rules quite a bit. Activiti and Drools integrate nicely together to achieve this flexibility with only a few lines of code.

This concludes our journey into the business rule world. There are many more things that could be covered in the vast field of business rule management, but I'm sure that, after this chapter, you're ready to explore that field on your own!

12.5 Summary

In this chapter, you got a thorough introduction to business rule management. We took a look at what relationship between business rule management and business process management, and examined in more detail what kinds of rules you can encounter in business processes. You should now have a good feel for how business rules can make your processes more flexible and dynamic.

We explored an open source BRMS, Drools, and worked through some examples to get you up to speed with business rules development. When working with Drools, you became familiar with rule engine concepts like working memory and saw the execution of rules in practice. You also saw how Drools and Activiti are integrated. We picked up the loan request example from chapter 5 and enhanced it with business rules to implement decision logic and business logic with rules. We also implemented a simple web application to change deployed rules on the Activiti Engine on the fly.

Having done all this, you now know the basics of business rule management and how to implement rule logic with Activiti and Drools. In the next chapter, we'll be looking at how to integrate Activiti with Alfresco using the CMIS protocol. We'll be adding document management to Activiti processes.

Document management using Alfresco

In chapter 1, we talked about the history of the Activiti project and its relation to Alfresco. Alfresco offers a document, web content, and record management solution. Alfresco provides an open source version called Alfresco Community, which we'll be using in this chapter, and a version with enterprise-level support called Alfresco Enterprise. Activiti is used as a workflow engine to provide review and approval processes for items in the Alfresco repository, including documents.

Document management is a natural fit with BPM and BPMN 2.0 processes because a lot of processes create documents or at least access documents in workflow tasks to provide context. A good example is an order process that results in creating an order document and sharing it with the client who placed the order. In an order process, we want to create a document based on process variables like a list of products with amounts and prices. We also want to store this document for future reference in a document management system like Alfresco, so that it can be found easily.

In this chapter, we'll look at how Activiti is used in the open source Alfresco Community product. We'll create new ad hoc and review and approval processes and look at how these processes are implemented with BPMN 2.0 and Activiti.

Then, we'll discuss how you can communicate with a document management product like Alfresco Community using the Content Management Interoperability Services (CMIS) open standard. We'll use the open source Apache Chemistry project, which implements the CMIS standard, to communicate with Alfresco Community in order to retrieve the folder content and store a PDF document.

In the last section, we'll combine what we've seen about how we can communicate with Alfresco using CMIS with running processes in the Activiti Engine. We'll implement a process that accesses an Excel sheet in the Alfresco repository and creates a PDF document that the process will automatically archive in a specific folder in Alfresco. In addition, we'll make sure that we can access the Excel sheet and the PDF document in the Activiti Explorer.

To get an overview of Alfresco document management and how the Activiti Engine is integrated, we'll start with an introduction to Alfresco.

13.1 Introducing Alfresco Community

Alfresco provides an open source product that offers a lot of functionality, including document, web content, and record management. With millions of downloads, Alfresco is used in a lot of enterprises. To accommodate enterprise use, Alfresco provides an Alfresco Enterprise version of the open source Alfresco Community product, which offers more administration tools, a wide range of supported databases, detailed documentation, and 24/7 support.

But in this chapter, we'll be using the Alfresco Community version, because it includes all the document management capabilities we need for this chapter, including CMIS support. We'll start with installing and starting Alfresco Community before looking into the Activiti integration.

13.1.1 Installing Alfresco Community

Alfresco Community can be installed using an easy installer wizard that you can download from www.alfresco.org. The examples in this chapter use Alfresco Community 4.0.a (the latest version available at the time of writing), but go ahead and download the latest available 4.0.x version. Then, start the wizard and choose the advanced installation type so that you can change the port settings of the built-in Tomcat server.

In the next wizard screen, you can select the components you want to install. Figure 13.1 shows the wizard for a Mac OS X system; the Java option is grayed out in this screenshot because it was already installed on the system. If you install Alfresco and have Java 7 installed, it's advisable to keep the Java option selected.

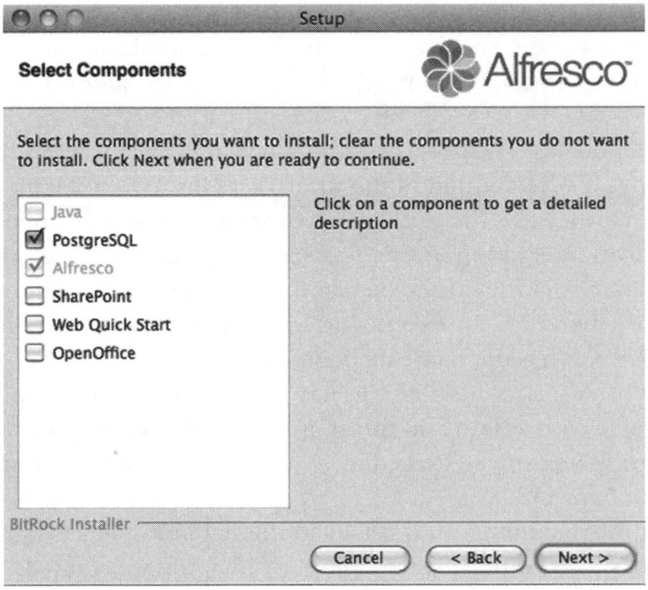

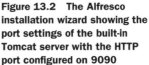

Figure 13.1 The Alfresco installation wizard on Mac OS X showing the installable components

You only need to select the PostgreSQL option so that a ready-to-use database with Alfresco schema is installed. If you don't have OpenOffice installed, you can also select that component in the wizard, so that you can use the document preview functionality available in Alfresco.

In the next screen, you can leave the default database port as is. Then, you need to configure the Tomcat settings of the Alfresco server. To prevent these ports from conflicting with the Activiti Tomcat server, change them as shown in figure 13.2.

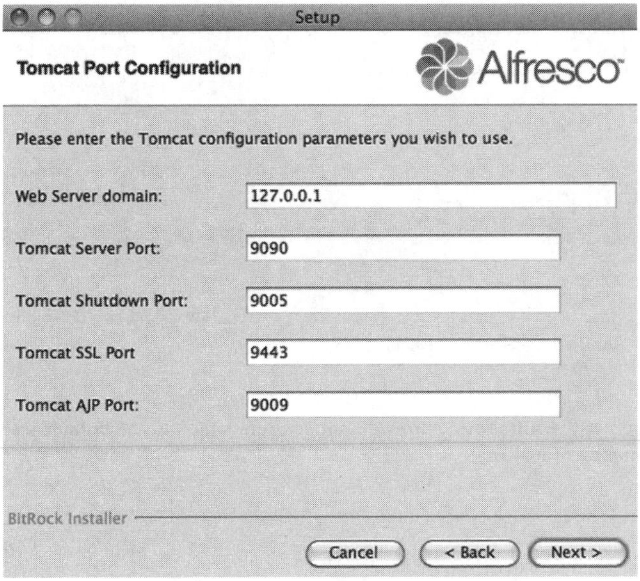

Figure 13.2 The Alfresco installation wizard showing the port settings of the built-in Tomcat server with the HTTP port configured on 9090

For the rest of the wizard screens, except for the last one, you can accept the default settings. In the last wizard screen, you have to configure an administrator password. This password is important because you'll need it in the examples later on; it's a good idea to write it down.

When you've finished the last wizard screen, the Alfresco installation will start with the configuration settings you've defined in the wizard screens. When the installation is complete, enable the check box to start the Alfresco server because you need it running to explore the Activiti integration in the next section. If you want to stop or start the Alfresco PostgreSQL or Tomcat server, you can find a simple management tool in the installation directory. Look for an executable with a name something like manager-osname. On Mac OS X it has the name manager-osx.

To test whether the Alfresco installation has succeeded, go to http://localhost:9090/share and log in with admin and the administrator password you've chosen in the installation wizard. When you're logged in, you should see a web page similar to the screenshot shown in figure 13.3.

When you log in for the first time, you'll get an additional welcome dashlet or portlet that can help you get started with Alfresco. In figure 13.3, this welcome dashlet has already been removed from the dashboard page.

Let's explore some of the functionality provided by Alfresco Share with a focus on its Activiti integration.

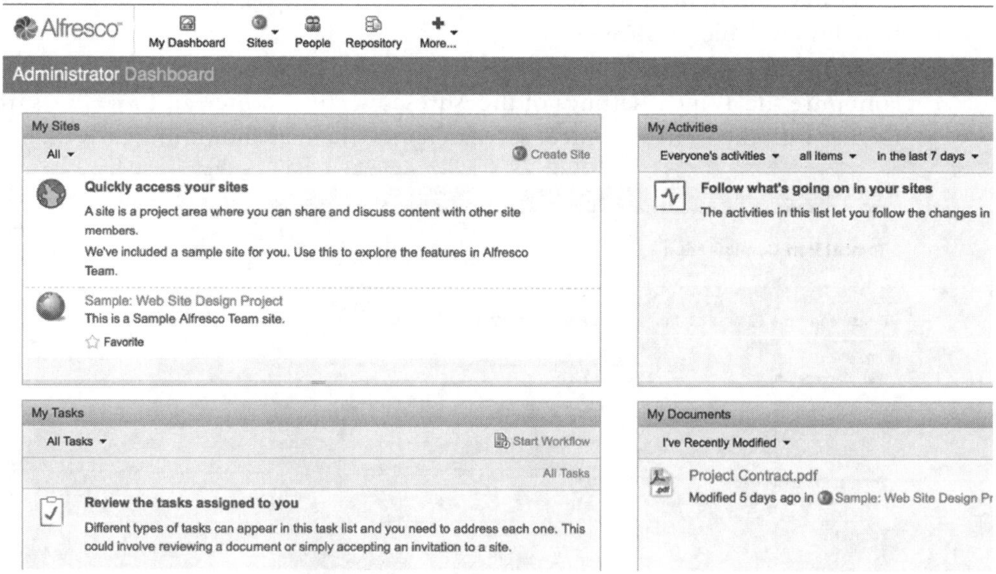

Figure 13.3   The landing page of the Alfresco Share web application, which is the default web application to access the Alfresco repository

13.1.2 *Introducing Activiti integration in Alfresco*

A document management and record management system like Alfresco needs a workflow component to deal with the review and approval processes, but also for simpler ad hoc tasks.

Imagine that you want a document you've written to be reviewed by a group of colleagues. You'd like a document management system to support this need by creating review tasks in Alfresco for your colleagues with pointers to the document. When each of your colleagues has reviewed the document, you'd like the review feedback to be reported back to you. That's exactly the functionality that Activiti provides within Alfresco.

On the dashboard page of Alfresco Share, you can see a dashlet named My Tasks. This dashlet contains the tasks that are assigned to you, and it retrieves these tasks from the Activiti Engine. In the My Tasks dashlet, you can start a new workflow process immediately, but you can also start a process from a document in the My Documents dashlet.

Let's start a process from the Project Contract.pdf document that you can see in the My Documents dashlet. Click on the document, and the Alfresco Share application will show the document detail page (see figure 13.4), including a document viewer, a set of document actions, and document properties.

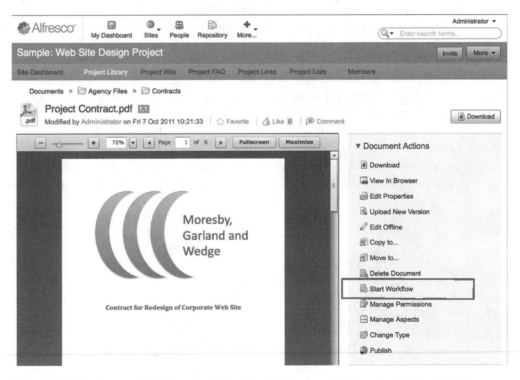

Figure 13.4 The document details page in the Alfresco Share application, showing the Project Contract.pdf document that's available as demo document

Start Workflow

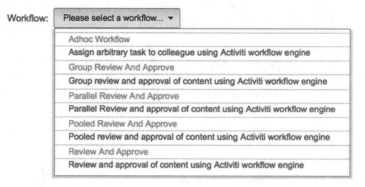

Figure 13.5   **The workflow wizard where you can select the workflow process you want to work with, such as Review and Approve (a specific document)**

In the document details screen, you can scroll through the full document using a PDF reader. But, for now, we're interested in the workflow capabilities as shown in figure 13.4. When you click on the Start Workflow action, you can choose the workflow process you want to start (see figure 13.5).

The five workflow processes shown in figure 13.5 are available by default in Alfresco. You can change these process definitions or create new ones from scratch, just like you're used to with Activiti. These five default processes can also be found in the Activiti Designer in the New Diagram wizard. Figure 13.6 shows the Group Review and Approve process created in the Activiti Designer based on the default template.

As you can see, the Group Review and Approve process consists of standard BPMN 2.0 constructs, like a start event, a user task, and an exclusive gateway. But there's some important additional logic implemented in the process definition. In the next listing, a part of the Group Review and Approve process definition is shown.

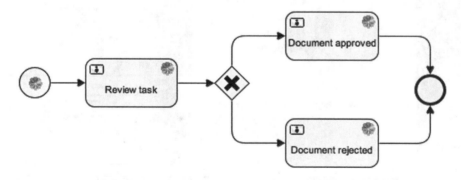

Figure 13.6   **The Group Review and Approve process in the Activiti Designer**

Listing 13.1 Part of the Alfresco Group Review and Approve process definition

```
<startEvent id="start" name="Start"
    activiti:formKey="wf:submitGroupReviewTask" />
<userTask id="reviewTask" name="Review Task"
    activiti:assignee="${reviewAssignee}"
    activiti:formKey="wf:activitiReviewTask">
  <extensionElements>
    <activiti:taskListener event="create"
        class="org.alfresco.repo.workflow.activiti.tasklistener.
            ➥ ScriptTaskListener">
      <activiti:field name="script">
        <activiti:string>
          if (typeof bpm_workflowDueDate != 'undefined')
            task.setVariableLocal('bpm_dueDate',
              bpm_workflowDueDate);
          if (typeof bpm_workflowPriority != 'undefined')
            task.priority = bpm_workflowPriority;
        </activiti:string>
      </activiti:field>
    </activiti:taskListener>
    <activiti:taskListener event="complete"
        class="org.alfresco.repo.workflow.activiti.tasklistener.
            ➥ ScriptTaskListener">
      <activiti:field name="script">
        <activiti:string>
          if(task.getVariableLocal('wf_reviewOutcome')
              == 'Approve') {

            var newApprovedCount = wf_approveCount + 1;
            var newApprovedPercentage =
              (newApprovedCount / wf_reviewerCount)
                * 100;
            execution.setVariable('wf_approveCount',
              newApprovedCount);
            execution.setVariable('wf_actualPercent',
              newApprovedPercentage);
          }
        </activiti:string>
      </activiti:field>
    </activiti:taskListener>
  </extensionElements>
  <multiInstanceLoopCharacteristics isSequential="false">
    <loopDataInputRef>wf_groupMembers</loopDataInputRef>
    <inputDataItem name="reviewAssignee" />
    <completionCondition>
      ${wf_actualPercent &gt;= wf_requiredApprovePercent}
    </completionCondition>
  </multiInstanceLoopCharacteristics>
</userTask>
```

① **Defines Alfresco start form**

② **Uses Alfresco review task form**

③ **Implements task listener with a script**

④ **Calculates approved percentage**

⑤ **Completes review if condition is true**

The Alfresco process definitions use the form key to render a specific task form implemented in the Alfresco server. In this process definition, the start event ① and the first user task ② contain such form key definitions. Besides using the out-of-the-box form definitions, you can also develop your own task form in Alfresco. You can read more about that in the Alfresco documentation at http://docs.alfresco.com.

The task forms produce process variables like you're used to when using Activiti standalone. In the first task listener ❸, the process variables `bpm_workflowDueDate` and `bpm_workflowPriority` are used to set the due date and priority task properties. This is done in a script that's executed by the `ScriptTaskListener` class implemented in Alfresco.

The Review user task is a multi-instance activity, so multiple review tasks are created based on the input provided by the start event form. When a review task is completed, a second script task listener is executed, and the number of approvers and the percentage of approvers ❹ is calculated. In the multi-instance completion condition ❺, the percentage is compared to the required approvers percentage provided in the start event form.

Now let's go back to the Start Workflow wizard in the Alfresco Share web application (from figure 13.4) and start the Group Review and Approve process. Figure 13.7 shows the start form corresponding to the start event form key definition of listing 13.1.

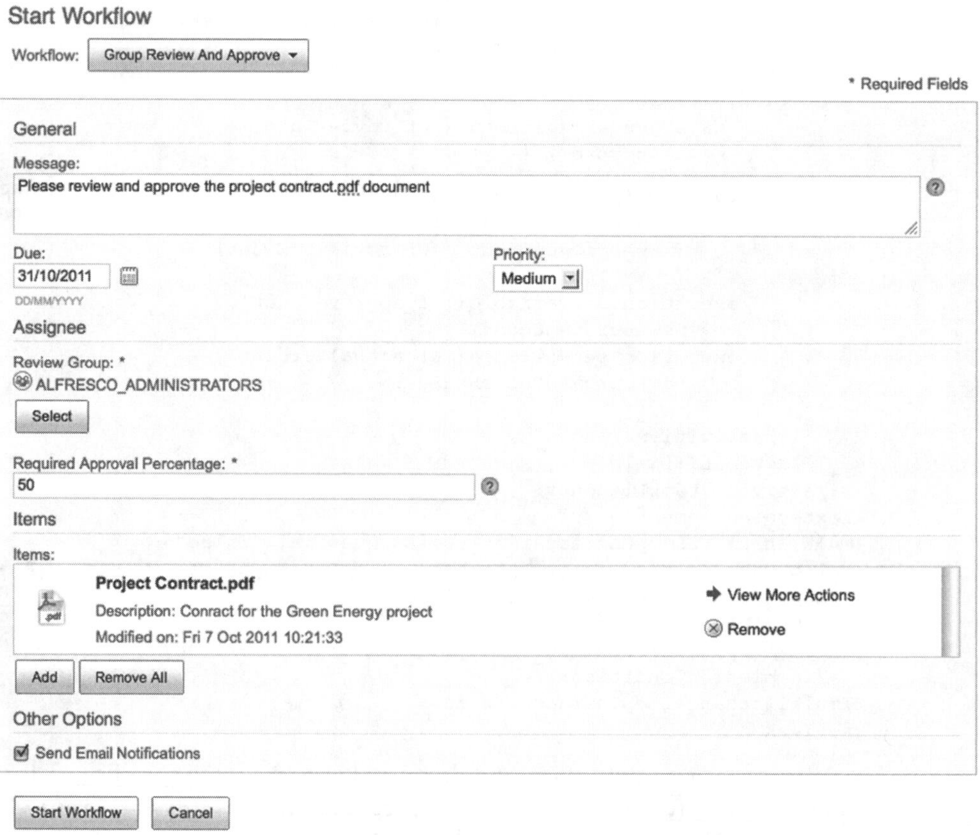

Figure 13.7   The start form of the Group Review and Approve process

You need to select a review group that corresponds to the group of people you want to review the document. Figure 13.7 shows the administrators group selected, but that's just for demo purposes because it only consists of the administrator user you used to log in. You can fill in a required percentage of approvers to complete the multi-instance "Review user" task that you saw in listing 13.1. You can also see the Project Contract.pdf document from which you started the workflow process. When you click the Start Workflow button shown in figure 13.7, the Activiti Engine kicks off the process definition to create a new process instance.

Because you're logged in as the administrator user, a new task appears in the My Tasks dashlet on the dashboard page. When you click this task, a new user task form is shown (see figure 13.8) corresponding to the form key definition of the Review user task of listing 13.1.

In the task form, some details about the user task are shown, including the priority and the due date. In addition, you can look at the contents of the PDF document by clicking on it. With the Approve and Reject buttons you can choose to approve or reject the PDF document. If you reject it, you'll see a new task in the My Tasks dashlet named The Document Was Reviewed and Rejected. When you click on that task, another task form page is shown that provides details about the review process, such as the number of reviewers and the percentage of approvers (0 in this case).

You now know the basics about how Activiti is integrated and used within Alfresco. It's possible to develop your own user task forms and process definitions, but that's

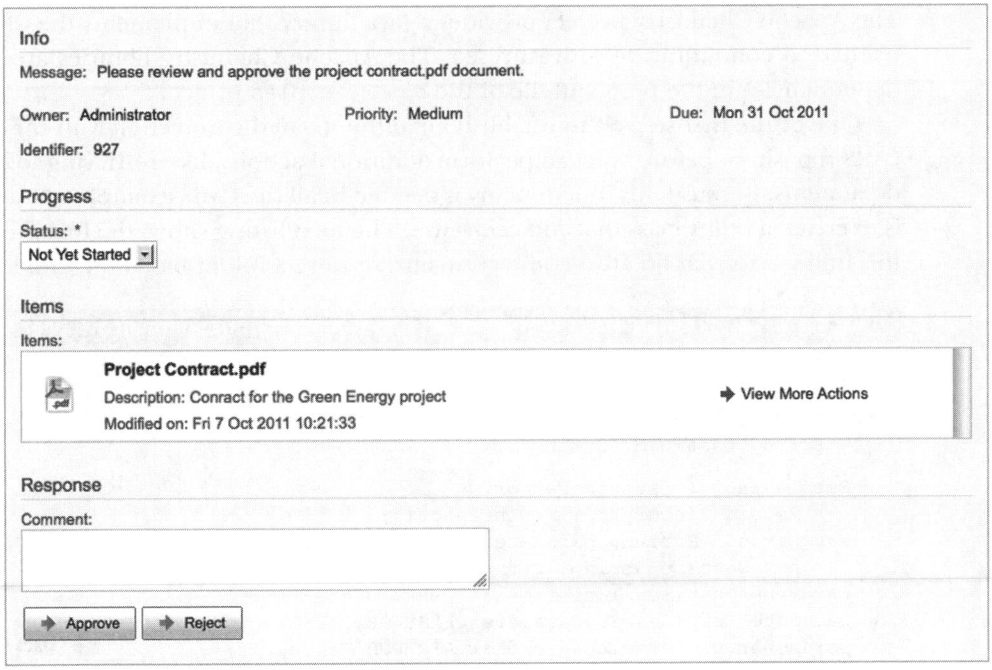

Info

Message: Please review and approve the project contract.pdf document.

Owner: Administrator   Priority: Medium   Due: Mon 31 Oct 2011

Identifier: 927

Progress

Status: *

Not Yet Started ▾

Items

Items:

📄 **Project Contract.pdf**
Description: Conract for the Green Energy project   ➜ View More Actions
Modified on: Fri 7 Oct 2011 10:21:33

Response

Comment:

[   ]

➜ Approve   ➜ Reject

Figure 13.8 The multi-instance "Review user" task form

beyond the scope of this book. The Alfresco documentation website (http://docs.alfresco.com) provides a lot more detail about this.

Using Activiti inside Alfresco is nice, but we'd also like to store and retrieve documents from Alfresco when we're executing a process instance with Activiti. In the next section, we'll discuss the CMIS standard and how to use it to communicate with the Alfresco repository.

13.2 *Using CMIS to store and retrieve documents*

Content Management Interoperability Services (CMIS) is an open standard maintained by OASIS with the goal of standardizing an API to communicate with a content management system like Alfresco or SharePoint. There are two benefits associated with this.

The first benefit is that you can access content management applications via an API from another application to retrieve and store content. A content management application can then be a central hub for content in an organization.

A second benefit is that the API you use to implement the communication logic isn't proprietary for that one content management application; it's an open standard that can be used to communicate with a number of content management applications.

In this section, I'll show you how to use CMIS to retrieve information from Alfresco and how to store a new document version. We'll use the Apache Chemistry framework for the client CMIS implementation.

13.2.1 *Retrieving folder content from Alfresco using CMIS*

The Apache Chemistry project provides a Java library that implements the CMIS logic needed to communicate with Alfresco. The Apache Chemistry libraries are listed as dependencies in the pom.xml file of the bpmn-examples project.

One of the first steps is to establish an authenticated connection with the Alfresco CMIS repository before you can perform additional actions, like retrieving folders and documents. Because this functionality is needed in all the CMIS examples, best practice is to create a utility class that you can reuse. The next listing shows the first methods of this utility class that create a connection and retrieve a folder based on a folder name.

> **Listing 13.2   A utility class that uses Apache Chemistry to communicate over CMIS**

```
public class CmisUtil {

  public static Session createCmisSession(String user,
      String password, String url) {

    SessionFactory sessionFactory =
        SessionFactoryImpl.newInstance();
    Map<String, String> parameter =
        new HashMap<String, String>();
    parameter.put(SessionParameter.USER, user);
    parameter.put(SessionParameter.PASSWORD, password);
    parameter.put(SessionParameter.ATOMPUB_URL, url);
    parameter.put(SessionParameter.BINDING_TYPE,
        BindingType.ATOMPUB.value());
```

1 Uses AtomPub, no web service binding

```
    Repository repository = sessionFactory
        .getRepositories(parameter).get(0);
    return repository.createSession();
}
public static Folder getFolder(
    Session session, String folderName) {

    ObjectType type = session.getTypeDefinition(
        "cmis:folder");
    PropertyDefinition<?> objectIdPropDef = type
        .getPropertyDefinitions()
        .get(PropertyIds.OBJECT_ID);
    String objectIdQueryName =
        objectIdPropDef.getQueryName();

    ItemIterable<QueryResult> results =
        session.query(
            "SELECT * FROM cmis:folder WHERE cmis:name='" +
                folderName + "'", false);
    for (QueryResult qResult : results) {
        String objectId = qResult
            .getPropertyValueByQueryName(objectIdQueryName);
        return (Folder) session.getObject(
            session.createObjectId(objectId));
    }
    return null;
  }
}
```

2 Creates session to Alfresco repository

3 Looks for folders

4 Seeks unique object IDs

5 Gets folder object

In the first method, a CMIS session is created, which is an authenticated connection to the Alfresco repository. Once you have a CMIS session, you can perform actions like creating a document or querying the repository like you do in the second method. The AtomPub binding type is used to communicate with the Alfresco repository **1**. CMIS and Apache Chemistry also support a web service binding type.

With a user ID that's allowed to access Alfresco, you can get a list of Alfresco repositories. By default, you only get one repository here, so you can get the first repository and create a CMIS session **2**. This CMIS session is needed to communicate with the Alfresco repository and retrieve folder and document information from it.

The second method shows how you can perform a query against the Alfresco repository using a CMIS session. In this method, you want to retrieve a folder object based on a folder name, so you can set the query type definition to cmis:folder **3**. Because you want to retrieve the full folder object, the query result type is set to object identifier (OBJECT_ID) **4**. This object identifier is then used to retrieve the full folder object via the CMIS session **5**.

Now let's test both methods with a simple unit test. First, in the Alfresco repository, you have to set up a folder that you can use in your unit test. Follow these steps:

1 Create a new site named Activiti. In the Alfresco Share web application, click Sites > Create Site in the top menu bar. Then, fill in the name Activiti and leave the other fields as is. Then click OK to create the site.

  2   Create a folder named `myExpenses`. In the newly created site, click the Document Library link and choose Create a New Folder. Fill in the name field with `myExpenses` and click Save. The `myExpenses` folder is created.

  3   Open the `myExpenses` folder and upload a document from your hard drive. Confirm that the document is uploaded to the `myExpenses` folder.

Now you can implement a simple unit test to validate the CMIS session and folder query functionality shown in listing 13.2. The next listing shows a test method that retrieves the `myExpenses` folder from the Alfresco repository and then downloads the uploaded document from the folder to a local directory.

Listing 13.3   Unit test to retrieve a folder and document from the Alfresco repository

```
public class CmisTest {

  private static final String ALFRESCO_CMIS_URL =
      "http://localhost:9090/alfresco/service/cmis";

  @Test
  public void retrieveFolder() throws Exception {
    Session session = CmisUtil.createCmisSession(
        "admin", "secret", ALFRESCO_CMIS_URL);
    Folder folder = CmisUtil.getFolder(
        session, "myExpenses");
    assertNotNull(folder);
    assertEquals(1, folder.getChildren()
        .getTotalNumItems());
    CmisObject cmisObject = folder.getChildren()
        .iterator().next();
    assertTrue(cmisObject instanceof Document);
    Document document = (Document) cmisObject;
    System.out.println("document name " +
        document.getName());
    System.out.println("document type " +
        document.getType().getDisplayName());
    System.out.println("created by " +
        document.getCreatedBy());
    System.out.println("created date " +
        document.getCreationDate().getTime());
    FileOutputStream output = new FileOutputStream(
        document.getName());
    InputStream repoDocument = document
        .getContentStream().getStream();
    byte[] buffer = new byte[1024];
    while(repoDocument.read(buffer) != -1) {
      output.write(buffer);
    }
    output.close();
    repoDocument.close();
  }
}
```

① The Alfresco CMIS server URI

② Logs in to Alfresco repository

③ Gets myExpenses folder

④ Gets document in myExpenses folder

⑤ Gets document content

To communicate with the CMIS server in the Alfresco repository, you need to define the URI at `/alfresco/service/cmis` **①**. Then you can log in to the Alfresco CMIS repository using the admin user and the password you configured in the Alfresco Community installation wizard (I used `secret` in this listing) ❷.

Once you're logged in to the CMIS repository, you can query the repository for the `myExpenses` folder ❸. You've uploaded one document to the folder, so you'll expect only one document in the child list of the `folder` object ❹. Then you print some information about the document to the console, such as the document name and the create date.

At the end of the unit test method, the contents of the document are downloaded using the `getContentStream` method on the document object ❺. The document is downloaded to the root directory of the `bpmn-examples` project and can be opened when you run this unit test.

Try running the unit test to make sure you can retrieve the uploaded document as expected.

The CMIS API offers a wide range of functionality that goes far beyond querying capabilities. Next, we'll take a look at a more complex capability to upload a new document version to the Alfresco repository.

13.2.2 *Storing a new document version*

Versioning is an important feature of a document management system like Alfresco, and it can allow you to perform complex operations with CMIS.

For an important document there can be a lot of different versions. After each round of review, the document is revised based on the reviewer's comments, and a new document version is created. For auditing and traceability purposes, it's nice to have the latest and the previous version available to see exactly what has changed. There are also cases where version 1.0 is the latest public version and version 1.2 is being worked on by a group of people. A document management system should provide support to make these two versions available to the right people.

You can upload a new version of a document via the Alfresco Share web application and then find out if there are multiple versions available of that document available, and which is the latest version. But you can also do this via a number of CMIS operations. In the next listing, a unit test is shown with the CMIS operations to upload a new version of a document.

Listing 13.4 Unit test with CMIS operations to upload a new document version

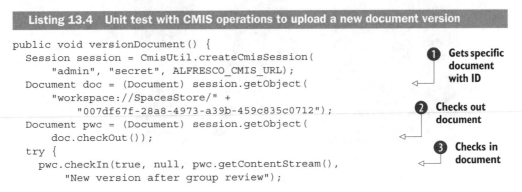

```
public void versionDocument() {
    Session session = CmisUtil.createCmisSession(
        "admin", "secret", ALFRESCO_CMIS_URL);
    Document doc = (Document) session.getObject(
        "workspace://SpacesStore/" +
            "007df67f-28a8-4973-a39b-459c835c0712");
    Document pwc = (Document) session.getObject(
        doc.checkOut());
    try {
        pwc.checkIn(true, null, pwc.getContentStream(),
            "New version after group review");
```

❶ Gets specific document with ID

❷ Checks out document

❸ Checks in document

```
  } catch (Exception e) {
    e.printStackTrace();
    System.out.println("checkin failed, cancel checkout");
    pwc.cancelCheckOut();
  }
System.out.println("Document version history");
List<Document> versions = doc.getAllVersions();
for (Document version : versions) {
  System.out.println("\tname: " + version.getName());
  System.out.println("\tversion label: " +
      version.getVersionLabel());
  System.out.println("\tlast modified by: " +
      version.getLastModifiedBy());
  System.out.println("\tlatest version: " +
      version.isLatestVersion());
  System.out.println("\tcheckin comment: " +
      version.getCheckinComment() + "\n");
  }
}
```

4 Gets all document versions

This unit test method is part of the same `CmisTest` class as the one shown in listing 13.3. When you've created a session to the Alfresco repository, you can retrieve a specific document directly using a unique identifier **1**. The unique identifier shown here is the identifier of the document uploaded in the previous section.

You can find the unique identifier for a document in the Alfresco Share application as shown in figure 13.9.

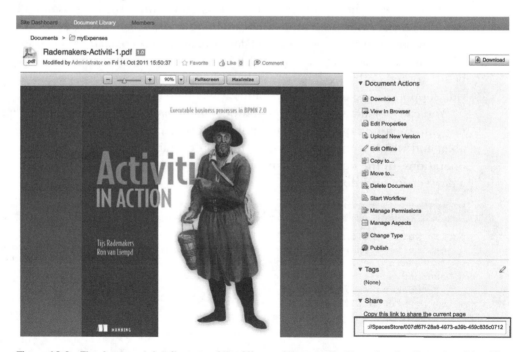

Figure 13.9   The document details page of the Alfresco Share application, showing the unique identifier of the document (in the rectangle at the bottom right of the figure)

The unique identifier can be found on the document details page in the Share section, as shown in figure 13.9. You can also find the unique identifier at the end of the URL shown in your web browser. An alternative way of getting a document using CMIS is to use a query like you did in listing 13.3.

When you've found the document, you can perform a check out operation ❷, which will lock the document so it can't be edited by someone else. In this example, you perform the check-in operation ❸ immediately after the check out, but, when there's more time between these operations, the Alfresco Share application will show a locked message (see figure 13.10).

When the check-in operation is executed, a new version of the document is created in the Alfresco repository. In this unit test, you upload the exact same document as the previous version, but you could alternatively upload another document. You can also provide a check-in message; in listing 13.4, it's "New version after group review".

In the last part of the unit test, you print information about all the versions of the document to the console ❹. This shows that you can access each version of the document individually and even download them. When you execute the unit test a couple of times, you can see that the same number of new document versions is created. In the document details of the Alfresco Share application, you can also see the version history, as shown in figure 13.11.

In the screenshot shown in figure 13.11, three document versions are created. In the unit test in listing 13.4, you created major versions of the document. But you can also create minor versions, like version 2.1 or 3.2, by setting the first input parameter of the checkIn method invocation to false.

Now that you're familiar with the document management features of Alfresco and have experimented with the CMIS standard, it's time to look at integrating documents in a BPMN 2.0 process flow using the Activiti Engine and Explorer.

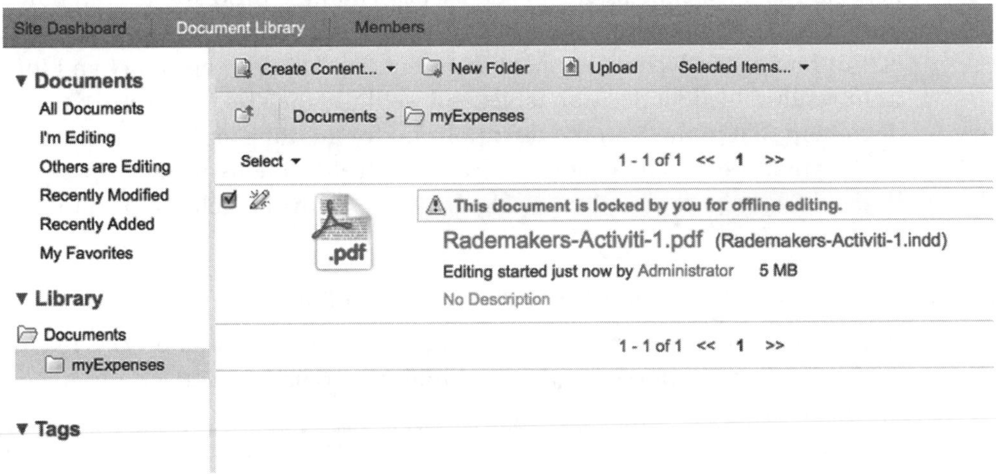

Figure 13.10   The Alfresco Share application showing a locked message when you perform a check-out CMIS operation on the document

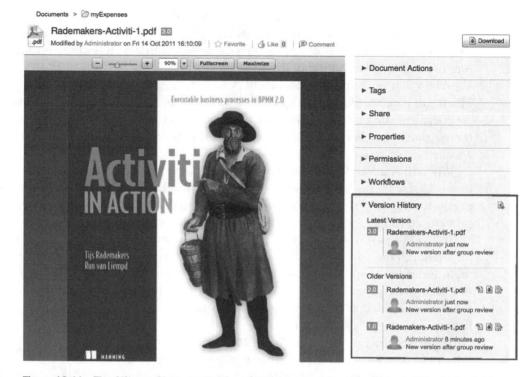

Figure 13.11   The Alfresco Share application with the document version history at the lower right

13.3   *Adding documents to a BPMN 2.0 process definition*

A lot of business processes deal with documents for a lot of different reasons, including auditing and traceability, informing customers, and formal communication with business partners. It can be useful for service tasks in these processes to communicate with a document management system like Alfresco. Later on in this section, we'll use Apache POI to retrieve an Excel document stored in the Alfresco repository and look up the right result value in a decision table, and we'll use the iText framework to store a PDF document sent to the loan request applicant for auditing and traceability purposes.

But first, we'll look at how you can attach documents to user tasks and process instances so you can easily view them in the Activiti Explorer or another process application.

13.3.1   *Working with task and process instance attachments*

When you want to implement a document review and approval process like the one in section 13.1, it's important that you can also automatically attach the to-be-reviewed document to the reviewers' user tasks.

The Activiti task service interface provides service methods to upload attachments and to couple them to user tasks or process instances. Let's implement a unit test that uses the task service interface to upload a PDF document and attach it to a user task.

Listing 13.5 Adding attachments to a user task with the task service interface

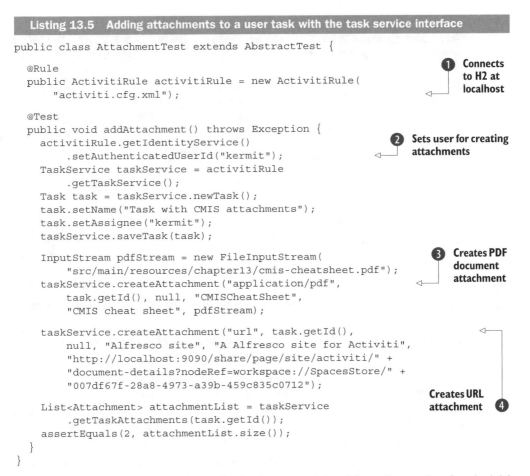

```
public class AttachmentTest extends AbstractTest {

    @Rule
    public ActivitiRule activitiRule = new ActivitiRule(
        "activiti.cfg.xml");

    @Test
    public void addAttachment() throws Exception {
        activitiRule.getIdentityService()
            .setAuthenticatedUserId("kermit");
        TaskService taskService = activitiRule
            .getTaskService();
        Task task = taskService.newTask();
        task.setName("Task with CMIS attachments");
        task.setAssignee("kermit");
        taskService.saveTask(task);

        InputStream pdfStream = new FileInputStream(
            "src/main/resources/chapter13/cmis-cheatsheet.pdf");
        taskService.createAttachment("application/pdf",
            task.getId(), null, "CMISCheatSheet",
            "CMIS cheat sheet", pdfStream);

        taskService.createAttachment("url", task.getId(),
            null, "Alfresco site", "A Alfresco site for Activiti",
            "http://localhost:9090/share/page/site/activiti/" +
            "document-details?nodeRef=workspace://SpacesStore/" +
            "007df67f-28a8-4973-a39b-459c835c0712");

        List<Attachment> attachmentList = taskService
            .getTaskAttachments(task.getId());
        assertEquals(2, attachmentList.size());
    }
}
```

① Connects to H2 at localhost

② Sets user for creating attachments

③ Creates PDF document attachment

④ Creates URL attachment

Because you want to view the task that's created in this unit test in the Activiti Explorer, the unit test uses the activiti.cfg.xml configuration, which points to the H2 database running at localhost **①** (not the in-memory H2 database). You set the authenticated user **②** because an authenticated user is needed to invoke the create-Attachment methods to show the name of the attachment uploader in the event stream (see the right column in figure 13.12).

Then you create a task and assign it to Kermit. With the task identifier, you can invoke the createAttachment method on the task service interface to upload a PDF document **③** to the Activiti Engine database and add it as related content to the newly created task. You also create another attachment that points to a URL **④**. In this example, you point it to the uploaded document created in section 13.2.

When you run this unit test, a task is created in the Activiti Engine database with two attachments. You can view this task in Kermit's inbox in the Activiti Explorer, as shown in figure 13.12.

In the Activiti Explorer, you can see that two related content items are shown in the task details page. When you click on the CMISCheatSheet PDF document, you can

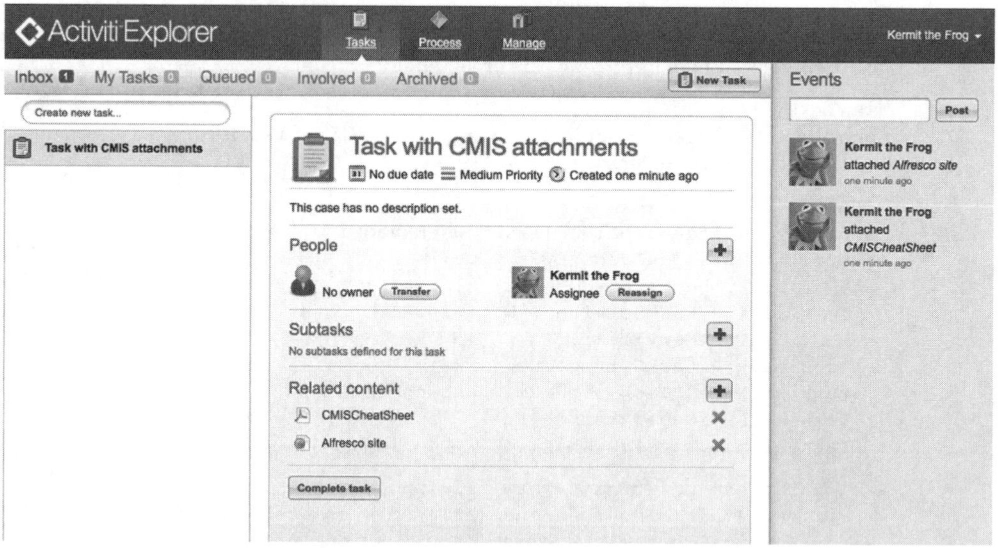

Figure 13.12   The Activiti Explorer showing the newly created task with two attachments

download and view it directly. In addition, you can click the Alfresco site link to point your web browser to the uploaded document in Alfresco Share.

There are also two events added in the event stream on the right side of the task page shown in figure 13.12. This is why you needed to set the authenticated user in listing 13.5—the event needs a valid user identifier to render the user picture. If you hadn't set the authenticated user, an exception would've been thrown in the Activiti Explorer and the task detail page wouldn't have been shown.

Now let's go ahead and use what you've learned in previous sections. In the next section, you'll implement a process definition that uses CMIS to communicate with the Alfresco Community repository, and you'll add an attachment to the process instance that can be viewed in the Activiti Explorer.

13.3.2   *Implementing a document-aware process definition*

A typical business process in a financial organization involves retrieving, creating, or storing a document. In this section, we'll use the same loan request example we used in previous chapters, but here we'll add logic to retrieve and store Excel and PDF documents.

Figure 13.13 presents an overview of the process definition and the interaction with the Alfresco repository. The loan request process definition hasn't changed much on a BPMN level. The main difference is that, in the last service task, you create a PDF document that can be sent as a letter to the customer to provide information about the outcome of the loan request approval process. Under the hood, though, there are quite a lot of changes.

In the previous chapter, you implemented the credit check task with a business rule task and a Drools rule file. In this chapter, you'll replace this with a service task

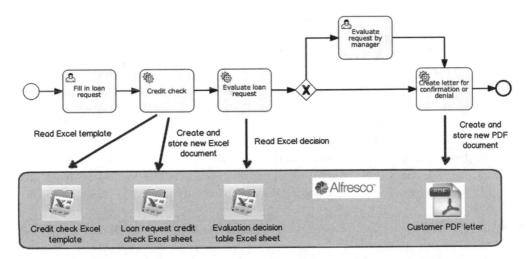

Figure 13.13 An overview of the loan request process definition we'll be implementing in this section. It shows the interaction with the Alfresco repository to retrieve and store Excel and PDF documents.

that will retrieve an Excel document from the Alfresco repository; the Excel document contains formulas used in the credit check. In addition, a new Excel sheet that contains the loan request details and the outcome of the credit check for that specific loan request is created.

In the second service task, you'll also retrieve an Excel document, but this time it contains a decision table. The "Evaluate loan request" service task will read the decision table and determine the right evaluation value based on the values found. Based on the evaluation value, the "Evaluate request by manager" user task will either be executed or not.

Let's start with implementing the "Credit check" service task that reads an Excel template and then, based on this template, stores a new Excel document containing the loan request details. But, before we do that, let's take a look at the Excel template you'll be using (see figure 13.14).

	A	B	C
1	Customer name		
2	Email address		
3			
4	Income	Loan amount	Loan amount * 2
5	0	0	0
6			
7	Credit check	=A5 > C5	
8			

Figure 13.14 The Credit Check Excel template showing the simple formula for the credit check calculation

The Credit Check Excel template shown in figure 13.14 is simple. In cell C5, the value of the loan amount entered in B5 is doubled. Then, in the credit check formula in cell B7, a check is implemented to see if the income is higher than double the loan amount. The great thing about using Excel templates and a document repository like Alfresco for this kind of logic is that business users can create the formulas themselves without the need for coding. Note that there is a tradeoff when the Excel sheets become large and complex.

In the "Credit check" service task implementation, you'll retrieve the Excel sheet from the Alfresco repository and read it using the Apache POI library, a well-known Apache framework to read and write Microsoft Office documents from Java. In listing 13.6, the service task implementation of `CreditCheckCMISTask` is shown.

Listing 13.6   Credit check service task implementation using CMIS and POI

```java
public class CreditCheckCMISTask implements JavaDelegate {
  private static final String EXCEL_MIMETYPE =
    "application/vnd.openxmlformats-" +
      "officedocument.spreadsheetml.sheet";

  @Override
  public void execute(DelegateExecution execution)
      throws Exception {

    LoanApplication loanApplication = (LoanApplication)
        execution.getVariable("loanApplication");
    POICMISHelper helper = new POICMISHelper();
    helper.openWorkbook("workspace://SpacesStore/" +
      "a5715b04-7422-4e8c-bb8f-def83031103a");

    helper.setCellValue(loanApplication
        .getApplicant().getName(), 0, 1, true);
    helper.setCellValue(loanApplication
        .getApplicant().getEmailAddress(), 1, 1, true);
    helper.setCellValue(loanApplication
        .getApplicant().getIncome(), 4, 0, false);
    helper.setCellValue(loanApplication
        .getApplicant().getLoanAmount(), 4, 1, false);

    helper.evaluateFormulaCell(4, 2);
    helper.evaluateFormulaCell(6, 1);
    loanApplication.getApplicant().setCheckCreditOk(
      helper.getBooleanCellValue(6, 1));

    helper.recalculateSheetAfterOpening();


    Document document = helper.saveWorkbookToFolder(
        loanApplication.getApplicant().getName(),
          ".xls", EXCEL_MIMETYPE);

    helper.attachDocumentToProcess(
        execution.getProcessInstanceId(), document, "xls",
          "Credit check sheet for " +
              loanApplication.getApplicant().getName());
```

1. Gets credit check Excel template

2. Sets loan application name

3. Sets loan amount value

4. Executes Excel formula

5. Recalculates formula fields when opening

6. Attaches Excel sheet to process context

```
    execution.setVariable("loanApplication",
        loanApplication);
    execution.setVariable("documentFolderId",
        helper.documentFolder.getId());
  }
}
```

The service task contains quite a bit of logic, but the core CMIS and POI logic is implemented in the POICMISHelper class that you can find in the bpmn-examples project of the book's source code. This class has a variable (ALFRESCO_ADMIN_PASSWORD) that holds the password of the Alfresco admin user. You should change this password to the password you specified while installing Alfresco.

The first step in the service task retrieves the Excel template shown in figure 13.14 from the Alfresco repository using the unique identifier ❶. To be able to retrieve the Excel template from the Alfresco repository, you first have to upload it to the Activiti site you created in section 13.2. Create a folder named loanapplication and upload the creditcheck.xlsx file from the src/main/resources/chapter13/cmis directory (see the bpmn-examples project of the book's source code) to that folder. Then, retrieve the object identifier for that object by looking at the document details page or its URI. Finally, replace the object identifier mentioned in CreditCheckCMISTask with the object identifier of the uploaded document in your Alfresco environment.

When you retrieve the credit check Excel template from the Alfresco repository, it's parsed by the Apache POI framework in the POICMISHelper class. You can now set values like the loan applicant name ❷ and the loan amount ❸ by referencing a cell in the template with a row and column number. For the loan applicant name, you have to create the cell first because the template doesn't yet contain a value. To do this, you set the last parameter of the setCellValue method to true. For the loan amount, you don't have to create the cell; you can just set the value because there's already a value of 0 in the template. In addition to setting values, you can also execute a formula in the Excel sheet ❹ and get the result value afterwards.

At this point, you have used the credit check logic in the Excel template to get a value of true or false for the credit check attribute in the loan application process variable. To make sure the formula cells in the Excel sheet contain the right values, you tell the Excel sheet to recalculate all formula cells when the sheet is reopened ❺.

In the last steps of the service task, the Excel document with the loan request information filled in is stored in the Alfresco repository in a subfolder of the loanapplication folder with the subfolder name that's equal to the value of the name of the loan applicant. Then the new document is coupled to the process instance as a new attachment ❻. You also set the subfolder with the applicant name as a process variable because you need it in the last service task where you'll create the PDF letter.

The credit check service task definition in the loanrequest.cmis.bpmn20.xml process definition, which you can find in the src/main/resources/chapter13/cmis folder of the bpmn-examples project, contains the class attribute configuration pointing to the CreditCheckCMISTask, as you'd expect. But there's also an asynchronous attribute, shown in the following code snippet:

```
<serviceTask id="checkCredit"
    activiti:async="true"
    activiti:class="org.bpmnwithactiviti.chapter13.process.task.
        ⮑ CreditCheckCMISTask" />
```

By adding the asynchronous attribute, you make sure that the user doesn't have to wait for the whole process instance to finish after completing the first user task. Starting from the credit check service task, the process instance is executed asynchronously, so the user can go on with their work. In this example, the asynchronous execution fits perfectly because the communication with the Alfresco repository, the Excel reading and writing, and the PDF document generation all take some time to complete.

Now that you've got the first service task communicating with the Alfresco repository and reading and writing an Excel document, you can go on with a similar second service task. The loan request evaluation service task differs a bit because it only reads an Excel document containing a decision table. The service task looks up the evaluation outcome in the decision table (see figure 13.15) and adds this value to the loan application process variable.

◇	A	B	C
1	Credit check	Loan amount	Status
2	TRUE	< 10000	approved
3	TRUE	>= 10000	needs manager approval
4	FALSE	N/A	denied
5			

Figure 13.15   The Excel decision table you'll use in the loan request evaluation service task

The decision table contains the credit check and loan amount columns for the `if` conditions and the status column for the evaluation result. Let's look at the implementation of the `EvaluationCMISTask` using this decision table. Note that it's a long listing due to the logic needed to process the decision table.

Listing 13.7   Implementing a service task using an Excel-based decision table

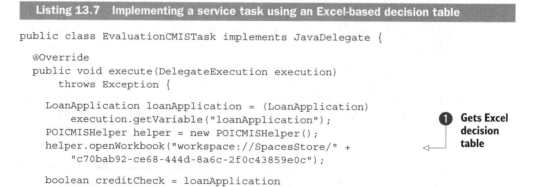

```
public class EvaluationCMISTask implements JavaDelegate {

  @Override
  public void execute(DelegateExecution execution)
      throws Exception {

    LoanApplication loanApplication = (LoanApplication)
        execution.getVariable("loanApplication");
    POICMISHelper helper = new POICMISHelper();
    helper.openWorkbook("workspace://SpacesStore/" +
        "c70bab92-ce68-444d-8a6c-2f0c43859e0c");

    boolean creditCheck = loanApplication
```

① Gets Excel decision table

```
        .getApplicant().isCheckCreditOk();
long loanAmount = loanApplication
        .getApplicant().getLoanAmount();
boolean foundMatch = false;
boolean reachedEndOfRules = false;
int rowCounter = 1;
while(foundMatch == false && reachedEndOfRules == false) {
  Cell cell = helper.getCell(rowCounter, 0);
  if(cell == null) {
    reachedEndOfRules = true;
  } else if(creditCheck == helper.getBooleanCellValue(
        rowCounter, 0)) {

    String loanAmountRule = helper.getStringCellValue(
        rowCounter, 1);
    if("N/A".equalsIgnoreCase(loanAmountRule)) {
      foundMatch = true;
    } else {
      int spaceIndex = loanAmountRule.indexOf(" ");
      String loanAmountRuleCompare =
          loanAmountRule.substring(0, spaceIndex);
      String loanAmountRuleValue = loanAmountRule
          .substring(spaceIndex + 1,
              loanAmountRule.length());
      if("<".equals(loanAmountRuleCompare)) {
        if(loanAmount < Long.valueOf(
            loanAmountRuleValue)) {
          foundMatch = true;
        }
      } else if("<=".equals(loanAmountRuleCompare)) {
        if(loanAmount <= Long.valueOf(
            loanAmountRuleValue)) {
          foundMatch = true;
        }
      } else if("=".equals(loanAmountRuleCompare)) {
        if(loanAmount == Long.valueOf(
            loanAmountRuleValue).longValue()) {
          foundMatch = true;
        }
      } else if(">".equals(loanAmountRuleCompare)) {
        if(loanAmount > Long.valueOf(
            loanAmountRuleValue)) {
          foundMatch = true;
        }
      } else if(">=".equals(loanAmountRuleCompare)) {
        if(loanAmount > Long.valueOf(
            loanAmountRuleValue)) {
          foundMatch = true;
        }
      }
    }
  }
  if(foundMatch == false) {
    rowCounter++;
```

② Starts at decision table first row

③ Gets rule value

④ Gets rule comparator

⑤ Gets rule number value

⑥ Compares loan amount to rule value

```
      }
    }
    if(foundMatch == false) {
      throw new ActivitiException(
          "No match found in decision table");
    }
    loanApplication.setStatus(                          ❼ Gets status
        helper.getStringCellValue(rowCounter, 2));         value
    execution.setVariable("loanApplication",
        loanApplication);
  }
}
```

Note that you start with retrieving the Excel decision table document ❶ using the unique document identifier. As in the previous service task, you have to replace the document identifier with the value of your local Alfresco repository after uploading the evaluation.xlsx Excel sheet, which can be found in the src/main/resources/chapter13/cmis directory.

To process the decision table, you loop through the contents starting with row 1 ❷, which corresponds to row 2 in the Excel sheet shown in figure 13.15 (remember that Java often starts with 0 instead of 1). You then check if the Excel credit check Boolean value is equal to the process variable value. If it is, you retrieve the loan amount condition from the Excel sheet ❸.

When the value is "N/A", you've found your match in the decision table. For the other cases, you implement logic to validate the comparator ❹ and the loan amount value ❺ used in the condition. For example, when the comparator is >, you check whether the loan amount value in the process variable is larger than the one defined in the condition ❻. As you can see, the service task contains this kind of conditional logic for the common comparators.

If a match is found in the decision table, the `while` loop is ended and the value in the status column is retrieved on the same row number as the match ❼. With the loan request evaluation status found, you can update the loan application process variable.

In the exclusive gateway that's connected to the "Evaluate loan request" service task (you can look back at figure 13.13 for the process definition), the status value is used to determine which sequence flow should be followed. When there's a need for manager approval, a new user task is created. In the other cases, the PDF letter service task is executed. In this service task, you'll generate a PDF document using the process variables to inform the customer about the loan request outcome. An example of this PDF document is shown in figure 13.16.

To implement the logic needed to generate the PDF document, the iText framework (www.itextpdf.com) is used. The iText libraries are listed as Maven dependencies in the pom.xml file of the `bpmn-examples` project, available in the book's source code.

Loan Sharks
4543 1st Street
Bay City, 38989

E-mail: info@loansharks.com

Dear Mr/Mrs Rademakers,

After analysis regarding your loan request we are happy to inform you that your loan request for $1000 is approved. Enclosed, you'll find all the details regarding the next steps in the process of your loan request.

With regards,

John Shark
Manager Loan Sharks

Figure 13.16 A sample PDF letter generated by the last service task of the loan request process definition. Process variables are used to fill in the values in the PDF document.

In the following code snippet, a part of the service task implementation is included. You can find the full source code in the bpmn-examples project:

```java
public class PDFLetterTask implements JavaDelegate {
  public void execute(DelegateExecution execution) throws Exception {
    LoanApplication loanApplication = (LoanApplication)
        execution.getVariable("loanApplication");
    com.itextpdf.text.Document pdf = new com.itextpdf.text.Document();
    pdf.add(new Paragraph("Dear Mr/Mrs " +
        loanApplication.getApplicant().getName() + ","));
    pdf.add(new Paragraph(" "));

    if("approved".equalsIgnoreCase(loanApplication.getStatus()) ||
        "approved by manager".equalsIgnoreCase(
            loanApplication.getStatus())) {
      pdf.add(new Paragraph("After analysis regarding your loan request" +
          " we are happy to inform you that your loan request for $" +
          loanApplication.getApplicant().getLoanAmount() +
          " is approved. Enclosed, you'll find all the details regarding" +
          " the next steps in the process of your loan request."));
    } else {
      pdf.add(new Paragraph("After analysis regarding your loan request" +
          " we regret to inform you that your loan request for $" +
```

```
                    loanApplication.getApplicant().getLoanAmount() + " is denied."));
        }
      }
    }
}
```

The `PDFLetterTask` service task contains more code than is shown here (to include the header and the shark image), but this code snippet shows how you can use iText to create a new PDF document without a lot of boilerplate code. To personalize the letter, you make use of the process variables to fill in the customer name and the loan request evaluation outcome. At the end of the service task implementation, the newly created PDF document is uploaded to the same folder in the Alfresco repository where you store the credit check Excel document:

```
POICMISHelper helper = new POICMISHelper();
helper.createCmisSession();
helper.saveDocumentToFolder(outputStream,
    (String) execution.getVariable("documentFolderId"),
    loanApplication.getApplicant().getName(), ".pdf", "application/pdf");
```

The `POICMISHelper` is used to create a new CMIS session, and the PDF document is uploaded to the folder corresponding to the `documentFolderId` process variable.

It's good to take some time to read through the full process definition implementation at this point, starting with the loanrequest.cmis.bpmn20.xml file in the src/main/resources/chapter13/cmis folder. In the next section, we'll deploy the solution to the Activiti Explorer and start a couple of process instances.

13.3.3 *Deploying and testing the document-aware process definition*

To test the loan request process definition with the Activiti Explorer, you must deploy the solution to that web application first. Because you're using external libraries like Apache POI and iText, you have to copy additional JAR files to the WEB-INF/lib directory of the Activiti Explorer web application.

Execute the following steps to get the process definition deployed:

1 Execute the build.xml Ant build file in the src/main/resources/chapter13/cmis directory by running its default target, `create.cmis`.

2 In the dist/enginelibs subdirectory, the cmis.jar file is created in step 1 containing the service task and listener classes. In addition, the libraries needed for Apache POI and iText are copied there (also by the Ant script of step 1). Copy all of these JAR files to the WEB-INF/lib directory of the Activiti Explorer web application in Tomcat.

3 If the Activiti Tomcat server is still running, stop it by executing the command `tomcat.stop` in the setup directory of your Activiti installation. Then, start it up again by running the `tomcat.start` command from that same setup directory.

4 Open the Activiti Explorer in a web browser and log in with Kermit.

5 In the dist/deploy subdirectory, a cmis.bar file containing the BPMN 2.0 XML process definition is generated. In the deployments tab, upload this BAR file to the Activiti Explorer.

After executing these steps, you're good to go and can start a new process instance. Fill in the required fields of the user task form using an income value of 50,000 and a loan amount value of 20,000. This should lead to creating a new user task with management as the candidate group.

At this point, the credit check and loan request evaluation service tasks are executed, and the credit check Excel document should be attached to the process instance. Figure 13.17 shows a screenshot of the claimed manager approval user task that contains the credit check Excel document as related content. You can open the Excel document by clicking on it to see if the right values are filled in.

Now approve the request and complete the user task. When you do, the PDF letter will be generated and stored in the Alfresco repository.

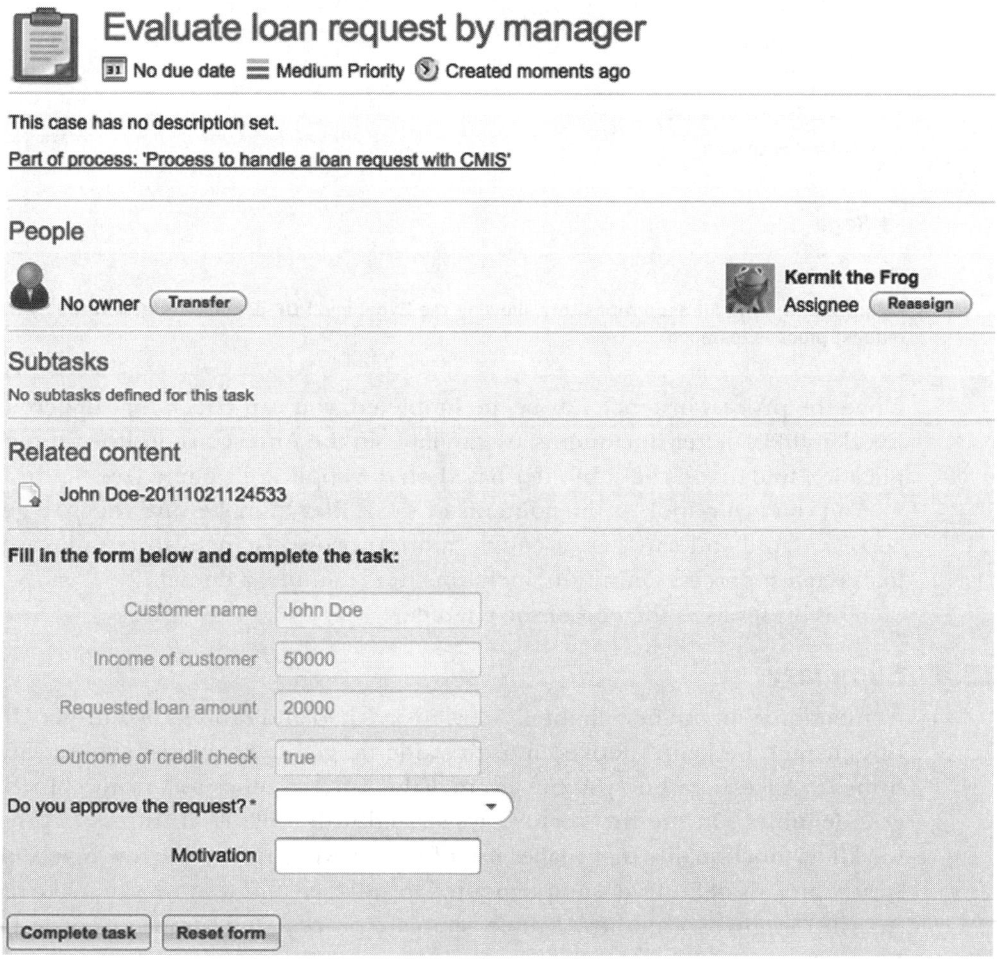

Evaluate loan request by manager

`31` No due date ≡ Medium Priority ⟩ Created moments ago

This case has no description set.

Part of process: 'Process to handle a loan request with CMIS'

People

No owner (Transfer)

Kermit the Frog
Assignee (Reassign)

Subtasks

No subtasks defined for this task

Related content

John Doe-20111021124533

Fill in the form below and complete the task:

Customer name	John Doe
Income of customer	50000
Requested loan amount	20000
Outcome of credit check	true
Do you approve the request? *	▼
Motivation	

(Complete task) (Reset form)

Figure 13.17   The Activiti Explorer showing the claimed manager approval user task with the credit check Excel document as related content

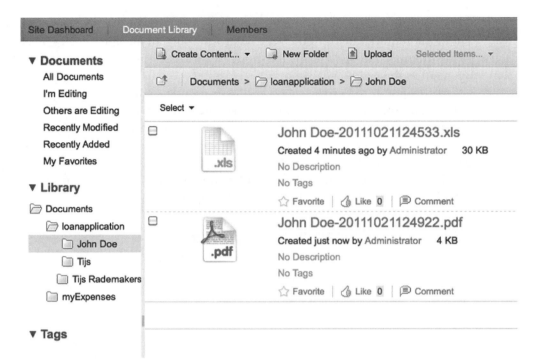

Figure 13.18   The Alfresco repository showing the Excel and PDF documents generated by the loan request process instance

Once the process instance has been completed, you can check that the credit check Excel and PDF letter documents are available in the Alfresco repository in the loanapplication folder and the subfolder based on the applicant's name (see figure 13.18).

You can again look at the contents of these files to make sure they are generated correctly. And you can start a couple more process instances to test all cases of the loan request process definition, including, for example, a denial.

This brings us to the end of the chapter.

13.4   *Summary*

As mentioned in the first chapter, Activiti is created and funded by Alfresco. But, until this chapter, we hadn't looked into the wide range of capabilities the Activiti Engine brings to Alfresco or how you can leverage the Alfresco repository from a BPMN 2.0 process definition. In the first section, we started with looking at Alfresco's process and workflow functionality that makes use of the Activiti Engine. We saw how a BPMN 2.0 review process definition is implemented in Alfresco and that we can make use of the Activiti Designer to modify Alfresco template process definitions or create new ones from scratch.

Then, we looked into the details of the CMIS standard and its implementation in the Apache Chemistry framework. The CMIS specification was defined to standardize the interfaces and data formats amongst different vendor implementations of content and document management systems like Alfresco. Alfresco is one of the supporters of this standard, maintained by OASIS, so we can use CMIS to communicate with the Alfresco repository to retrieve document contents, store new document versions, and so on.

In the last section, you implemented a process definition making heavy use of documents and the Alfresco repository. You saw how to utilize Excel documents and their powerful formulas to implement conditional logic. The logic implemented with Drools in the previous chapter can easily be implemented using Excel formulas. In addition, you saw that a framework like iText can be used to generate a PDF document with a few lines of code.

In the next chapter, we'll take a look at how you can leverage the Activiti Engine to create real-time dashboards. We'll be using the Esper framework to handle business events created by Activiti process instances and using Vaadin to create graphical dashboards.

14

Business monitoring and Activiti

This chapter covers

- Business activity monitoring (BAM)
- Introducing complex event processing (CEP)
- Open source CEP with Esper
- Monitoring Activiti processes with Esper
- Implementing a Vaadin BAM dashboard application

When many different business processes are running in an organization, it's difficult to get a good sense of the status of all of these processes. You can imagine that decision-making becomes a whole lot easier when there's a dashboard that can give you real-time insight into all of these running processes: What is currently being ordered? Are stock levels dropping? To provide this real-time information about what's happening in an organization, business monitoring or business activity monitoring (BAM) comes to the rescue. This chapter will cover what business monitoring is and show how you can extend Activiti to implement it.

We'll start off by explaining what business monitoring is and we'll introduce a number of monitoring concepts that will be used throughout the rest of the chapter. We'll take a good look at what complex event processing (CEP) is because this technique is often used while implementing business monitoring.

After you've seen how business monitoring works, we'll take Esper, an open source CEP engine, for a spin. When we're fully up to speed with Esper, we'll integrate the Esper engine with Activiti in section 14.3. Finally, in section 14.4, we'll introduce a Vaadin application that visualizes the state of the loan request process instances to give you an idea of the real-time business monitoring capabilities of Esper and Activiti.

We have quite a bit of ground to cover, but we'll take it one step at a time!

14.1 Monitoring business processes

This first section will provide you with an introduction to business monitoring. We'll take a look at what business monitoring is and discuss the differences between it and business intelligence. To conclude the section, we'll introduce complex event processing. This technique is often used in business monitoring environments and plays an important role in the code examples of this chapter.

14.1.1 Introducing business activity monitoring (BAM)

Business monitoring, or business activity monitoring (BAM), is all about knowing what's going on in an organization at any given moment in time. Knowing what goes on in real time can help managers quickly identify problem areas and risks, guide businesses to make better decisions, and lets companies adapt faster to external changes.

An example of the practical use of business activity monitoring is the monitoring of credit card transactions to prevent possible fraud. If large cash withdrawals are suddenly charged on a credit card, business activity monitoring can help in signaling this situation and, possibly, even alert a bank security officer to call the cardholder to verify that the monitored transactions were intended.

Business activity monitoring is also often used in spotting trends or forecasting events. An increase in a department's workload can quickly be detected using business monitoring, alerting management to add extra employees to handle peaks.

A work field that's closely related to BAM is business intelligence (BI). The main difference is that BAM is about real-time monitoring, and BI is about analyzing historic data (see the sidebar). We're only focusing on BAM in this chapter, but the Activiti database can also be used for BI analysis.

> **BAM versus BI**
>
> Business activity monitoring (BAM) is often used in the same context as business intelligence (BI). Although both have the shared goal of providing a business with vital information concerning the business state, there are differences between the two.

(continued)

The biggest difference concerns the kind of data used to provide the business with its information. In BAM, monitoring takes place on live events; it's real time. In the remainder of this chapter, we'll be monitoring *running* business processes, focusing on BAM.

BI, on the other hand, is a discipline that focuses mainly on *historic data* to perform its analyses. Information is gathered from different systems and stored in data warehouses, where it can be analyzed and processed to produce reports and possibly forecasts. In the context of Activiti, the source of BI data analysis would be the history tables in the Activiti database.

Although BI and BAM serve similar goals of improving businesses in the future, BI focuses mainly on the past to achieve those goals, whereas BAM focuses on the present.

Monitoring itself is nothing new. For example, your thermostat, which shows the current temperature and which is ready to alert the heater when temperature drops below a predefined value, performs simple at-home monitoring. Business activity monitoring is no different from these examples.

A business monitoring solution uses a common pattern to deal with business events, and this pattern consists of three main components, as shown in figure 14.1.

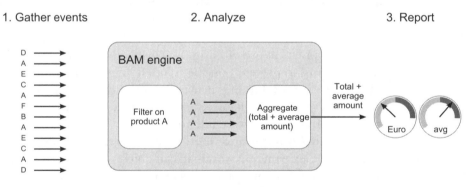

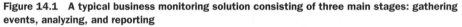

Figure 14.1   A typical business monitoring solution consisting of three main stages: gathering events, analyzing, and reporting

These are the three main steps when implementing a BAM solution:

1 *Gather events*—This involves inputting data by receiving events from as many sources as needed. Events are typically sent from other applications and contain short messages of information, such as, "customer A bought 10 items of product B for $300."

2 *Analyze the gathered data*—An example of analysis in this step is filtering. When a certain product has recently been heavily advertised, a company might be

interested in how many people are in the process of buying it; filtering takes place on the shopping baskets to retrieve only the information that's needed for a specific measurement.

3 *Report the results of the analysis*—After the information has been analyzed, the results need to be communicated. Dashboards, like the one illustrated in figure 14.1, can help to quickly display trends and spot exceptional situations. This step also covers the signaling function we talked about in the thermostat example a couple of paragraphs back. When values reach certain limits, actions can be taken, such as sending an email.

NOTE The signaling function in the reporting step can also trigger the start of a new business process execution. For example, when stock values drop below a certain level, a new order process can be started to get the stock level back to normal. This is a typical example that shows how business monitoring can fulfill a thermostat-like function and help to regulate the business.

To conclude this introduction to BAM, we need to take a look at an important concept in the business monitoring world: the key performance indicator (KPI). Before you start monitoring, you need to know why you want to monitor something. After the business has defined the goals it wants to reach, measurement is needed to check if the business is on track to reach the goals or not. KPIs are defined to enable that measurement; they form the building blocks of the dashboards you need to monitor.

A KPI is a value, usually numeric, that represents performance. Suppose the business defined a goal of doubling the number of visitors to the company's web shop. The visitor count metric would be the KPI that would indicate whether the goal has been reached. As another example, suppose the goal was to reduce employee turnover in a company. To measure whether the goal has been reached, one of the KPIs could be the total number of employees that terminated their jobs or were fired divided by the number of employees at the beginning of the year. In the loan request example further in this chapter, you'll see some KPIs and get a good grasp of what kind of stuff you can show and how.

Now that you know what BAM is, let's discuss the technique of complex event processing and look at how it can be used to implement a BAM solution.

14.1.2 *Introducing complex event processing (CEP)*

Before we can dive into code examples with the Esper open source CEP engine in the next section, you need to know a little bit more about complex event processing (CEP) in general and why it's of importance in BAM.

What is CEP? Let's look at an example and consider the following three events coming from the same event source:

- Church bells ring.
- A man wearing a tuxedo appears, with a woman in a white gown at his side.
- Rice flies through the air.

From these basic events, an event processing system may infer a complex event; in this case, a wedding. CEP is the technology that performs filtering, correlation, aggregation, and computing on volumes of real-time event data. It does all this to take subsequent action, mostly by creating new events and passing those on to listeners.

A CEP engine looks like an inverted database. Where you first store data in a database and then start querying, a CEP system lets you define the queries first and then starts running data through those queries. Take a look at figure 14.2 to get a better idea.

In figure 14.2, you see a stream of different event types entering the CEP engine. The engine performs different types of operations on the events, like filtering the events worth watching, aggregating similar events, and joining different types of events together. While these operations are performed on the events, a pattern matching mechanism runs on the results to search for combinations of data the engine needs to put out. Finally, the output is sent to possible listeners to act upon.

The events that enter the CEP engine are processed immediately, so there's no database underneath this mechanism. What does exist, though, is the concept of *windows*. In figure 14.2, the timeline suggests there's some sort of *life* of the event in the engine during which processing takes place.

Let's return to the wedding example. If you hear bells ringing one day, see a guy in a tuxedo with a woman in a white gown the next day, and some other time rice is thrown on the ground, there could be three weddings going on or none. The window during which these events are analyzed is set to a certain period of time in order to deduce that a wedding must be going on. We'll talk more about windows in the next section.

Now that you have some background information on both BAM and CEP, it's time to move on to what we like most: coding!

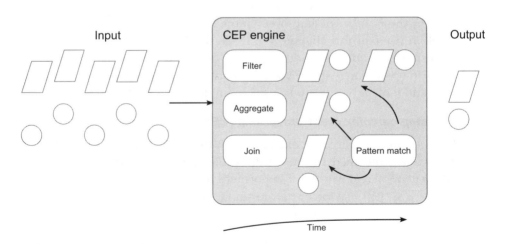

Figure 14.2 Basic overview of a CEP engine in action

14.2 *Meeting the Esper framework*

We'll start with a Hello World Esper example to get you up and running. In the remainder of this section, we'll take events from the loan request process and start working our way into more advanced Esper examples. Those examples will be used again in section 14.3 when we integrate Esper and Activiti.

14.2.1 *Kick-starting Esper*

The Esper project was started some six years ago with the goal of creating a lightweight and easy-to-integrate open source Java CEP engine, and it's available under the LGPL license. Esper provides an Event Processing Language (EPL) that looks a lot like SQL.

Let's start with a Hello World Esper example.

Listing 14.1   Hello World with Esper

```
public class HelloWorldEsperTest {

  public class HelloWorldEvent {                                    ← Defines
    private String value;                                          ❶ event class

    public HelloWorldEvent(String value){
      this.value = value;
    }

    public String getValue(){
      return value;
    }
  }

  @Test
  public void helloEsper() {
    Configuration configuration = new Configuration();
    configuration.addEventType(HelloWorldEvent.class);             ❷ Creates
    EPServiceProvider epService =                                     Esper engine
        EPServiceProviderManager                                     instance
            .getDefaultProvider(configuration);               ←

    EPStatement epStatement = epService.getEPAdministrator()       ❸ Creates
        .createEPL("select value as eventValue" +                    basic EPL
            " from HelloWorldEvent");                                 statement

    epStatement.addListener(new UpdateListener(){           ←
      public void update(EventBean[] newEvents,
          EventBean[] oldEvents){                                    Adds
        Assert.assertEquals("Hello!",                                event
            (String) newEvents[0].get("eventValue"));           ❹ listener
      }
    });

    HelloWorldEvent helloworld =
        new HelloWorldEvent("Hello!");                             ❺ Sends
    epService.getEPRuntime().sendEvent(helloworld);         ←        event
  }
}
```

Events can be map based, represented with XML, or, as you can see in this example, represented by a Java POJO class like the `HelloWorldEvent` class ❶. You configure the Esper CEP engine to handle the event class `HelloWorldEvent` and then obtain an engine instance ❷.

The next line of code defines an EPL query and registers it to be executed continuously when new events arrive in the Esper engine ❸. This simple query doesn't perform any filtering; it returns every `HelloWorldEvent` it comes across.

Then, a listener is created and attached to the EPL statement ❹. Listeners are invoked by the Esper engine when the EPL query returns new values. An Esper listener implements the `UpdateListener` interface and acts upon `EventBean` instances.

Finally, a `HelloWorldEvent` instance is instantiated and sent to the Esper engine ❺ to run the test in the listener.

EPL, the event processing language

EPL follows an SQL-like syntax. It has `SELECT`, `FROM`, `WHERE`, `GROUP BY`, `HAVING`, and `ORDER BY` clauses, just like SQL.

The `SELECT` clause in an EPL query specifies the event or the event properties to retrieve. The `FROM` clause refers to the event type, and `WHERE`, just like in SQL, specifies filter conditions in the statement. For example, the following statement returns the loan amount for a `LoanRequestEvent` that Kermit has applied for:

```
SELECT loanAmount AS amount FROM LoanRequestEvent WHERE name="Kermit"
```

Besides filtering using the `WHERE` clause, EPL supports the concept of windows. With this concept, you're looking at a stream of events. We'll look at examples of this later in the chapter, but let's take a quick peek now. Suppose you're looking for `LoanRequestEvent`s that were sent in the last 30 seconds. The EPL would look like this:

```
SELECT * FROM LoanRequestEvent.win:time(30 seconds)
```

EPL supports some standard functions as well, such as `sum`:

```
SELECT sum(loanAmount)
FROM LoanRequestEvent.win:time(30 seconds)
```

With the `sum` function, the sum of all loan requests over the last 30 seconds is returned. Other functions calculate, for example, the median or average of a stream.

The last feature, which we'll cover in more depth later on, is the joining of different event types:

```
SELECT * FROM LoanRequestEvent.win:time(30 seconds) as lr,
OrderEvent.win:time(30 seconds) as oe WHERE lr.Id = oe.Id
```

Two different event types occurring in a window of 30 seconds are joined by their IDs here. We'll come back to examples of these more advanced uses of EPL later in the chapter.

You'll see that the EPL syntax is straightforward to read, so I won't provide a very detailed explanation of the grammar and keywords of the language. If you want to know more, check out the Esper documentation; EPL is well covered in there.

From now on, we'll start diving deeper. We'll create some more interesting events, perform many of the Esper operations on them, and explore some serious business monitoring possibilities.

14.2.2 *Introducing event windows*

In the introduction to CEP (section 14.1.2), we briefly touched on the subject of event windows. Most of the time when you're monitoring applications or processes, you won't be interested in single events because they don't often mean much by themselves.

Take, for example, the fraud detection problem. When somebody tries to log in and uses a wrong username/password combination, this doesn't mean a lot by itself. In fact, it's something that happens to most of us. It starts to be different, though, when dozens or even thousands of login attempts fail from one certain location within a couple of minutes. That series of events is interesting!

In Esper, event windows define how many events the CEP engine is going to "remember" when performing its pattern matching. There are two different types of windows:

- *Length windows*—A length window instructs the CEP engine to keep the last N events. When the length window is full and a new event arrives, the oldest events are pushed out of the window.
- *Time windows*—A time window instructs the CEP engine to keep events for the specified amount of time. If the age of an event exceeds the time interval, it's pushed out of the window.

Both types of event windows work basically the same way. To show how Esper deals with event windows, we'll first try out an example with the length window.

LENGTH EVENT WINDOWS

Before we start coding, take a look at figure 14.3 to see how the length event window mechanism handles events.

On the left side, events start entering the engine one by one. The length window in the engine is set to 3, as you can see in the middle of the figure. When the fourth event enters the window, event 1 is pushed out.

The UpdateListener is the interface you saw in the Hello World example. It gets notified when events enter the CEP engine. Its only method has the following signature:

```
public void update(EventBean[] newEvents, EventBean[] oldEvents);
```

On the right side of figure 14.3, you can see when and with which values the listener is called. After the first event is moved out of the window, it will be available in the oldEvents array when the update method is called.

Let's put the length event window to work; it's time to pick up our loan request business process again! Business has been going pretty well since Loan Sharks made the move to BPM. They now get so many loan requests that sometimes the company is in danger of running out of money to lend. One simple metric that would help the employees figure out how much money they need to have available is the total amount lent.

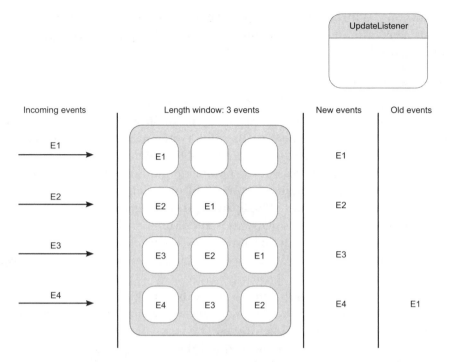

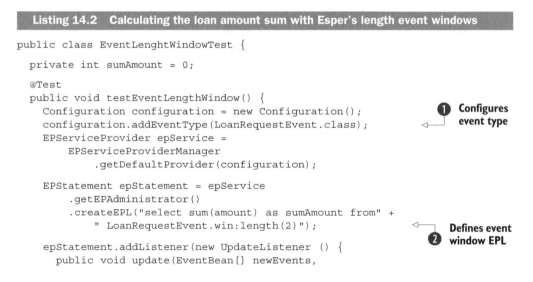

Figure 14.3   An Esper length event window with a defined length of three events

Obviously, the total amount lent since the company was founded isn't very informative. Management needs to be able to act upon situations that are happening right now, so, in calculating the total amount lent, we're only interested in the last loan requests that have been made. To keep this code easy to read, we'll only focus on the last two loan requests, which means a length window of two events.

Listing 14.2   Calculating the loan amount sum with Esper's length event windows

```
public class EventLenghtWindowTest {

  private int sumAmount = 0;

  @Test
  public void testEventLengthWindow() {
    Configuration configuration = new Configuration();       ❶ Configures
    configuration.addEventType(LoanRequestEvent.class);         event type
    EPServiceProvider epService =
        EPServiceProviderManager
          .getDefaultProvider(configuration);

    EPStatement epStatement = epService
      .getEPAdministrator()
      .createEPL("select sum(amount) as sumAmount from" +
        " LoanRequestEvent.win:length(2)");                   ❷ Defines event
                                                                 window EPL
    epStatement.addListener(new UpdateListener () {
      public void update(EventBean[] newEvents,
```

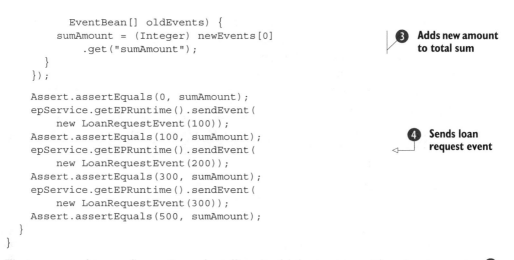

```
            EventBean[] oldEvents) {
         sumAmount = (Integer) newEvents[0]
             .get("sumAmount");
      }
   });

   Assert.assertEquals(0, sumAmount);
   epService.getEPRuntime().sendEvent(
       new LoanRequestEvent(100));
   Assert.assertEquals(100, sumAmount);
   epService.getEPRuntime().sendEvent(
       new LoanRequestEvent(200));
   Assert.assertEquals(300, sumAmount);
   epService.getEPRuntime().sendEvent(
       new LoanRequestEvent(300));
   Assert.assertEquals(500, sumAmount);
  }
}
```

❸ Adds new amount to total sum

❹ Sends loan request event

First, you need to configure Esper by telling it which event type it's going to receive ❶. In this case, the LoanRequestEvent class is a simple POJO with just one attribute named amount of type int. Then you define the EPL statement where you set a length window of 2, meaning that you're only going to be interested in the last two events that arrive in the Esper engine ❷. The sum of the amounts of the last two events is calculated in the update method of the UpdateListener instance ❸. To see if all works well, you kick in a few loan request events ❹ and test the sum amounts.

TIME EVENT WINDOWS

Often, it's not enough to know what happened with a specific number of events; you also want to know what happened in a certain period of time. To support this kind of functionality, Esper introduced the concept of time windows, which we'll use in the next example.

Take a look at the following code snippet. It shows a newly defined LoanRequest-ProcessedEvent:

```
public class LoanRequestProcessedEvent {

  private final String processInstanceId;
  private final long processedTime;
  private final int requestedAmount;
  private final boolean requestApproved;

  public LoanRequestProcessedEvent(String processInstanceId, long
      processedTime, int requestedAmount, boolean requestApproved) {
    this.processInstanceId = processInstanceId;
    this.processedTime = processedTime;
    this.requestedAmount = requestedAmount;
    this.requestApproved = requestApproved;
  }
  ...
}
```

This LoanRequestProcessedEvent has four attributes, which will be populated when the event is instantiated via the constructor. It contains values for a process instance

ID, a requested loan amount, a `boolean` indicating whether the loan request has been approved or not, and a `processedTime` field. The value of this field is of type `long` and defines the time (the well-known number of milliseconds since the Unix epoch) in which the loan request is processed.

The next listing shows the first part of the test class, including the setup method that's called before the test is run, to configure Esper.

Listing 14.3 Configuring Esper before testing the time window example

```java
public class TimeWindowTest {

  private EPRuntime epRuntime;
  private EPAdministrator epAdmin;

  @Before
  public void startEsper() {
    Configuration configuration = new Configuration();
    configuration.addEventTypeAutoName
      ("org.bpmnwithactiviti.chapter14.bam.event");
    EPServiceProvider epService =
        EPServiceProviderManager.getDefaultProvider(
            configuration);
    epRuntime = epService.getEPRuntime();
    epAdmin = epService.getEPAdministrator();
  }
  ...
}
```

1 Configures event types for Esper to handle

You can see in the `TimeWindowTest` class that you can easily configure Esper to handle multiple events by stating the name of the package in which the events are defined **1**.

Now let's get the test case implemented and up and running. You'll filter out loan requests that haven't been approved and validate the events in Esper's time window.

Listing 14.4 Testing Esper time windows while firing `LoanRequestEvents`

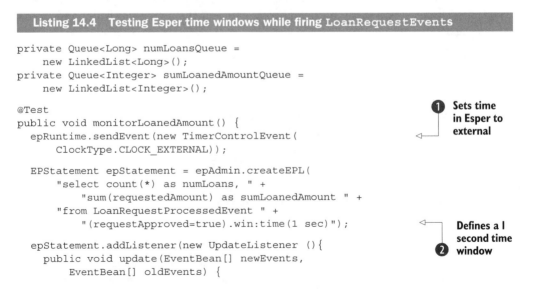

```java
private Queue<Long> numLoansQueue =
    new LinkedList<Long>();
private Queue<Integer> sumLoanedAmountQueue =
    new LinkedList<Integer>();

@Test
public void monitorLoanedAmount() {
  epRuntime.sendEvent(new TimerControlEvent(
      ClockType.CLOCK_EXTERNAL));

  EPStatement epStatement = epAdmin.createEPL(
      "select count(*) as numLoans, " +
          "sum(requestedAmount) as sumLoanedAmount " +
      "from LoanRequestProcessedEvent " +
          "(requestApproved=true).win:time(1 sec)");

  epStatement.addListener(new UpdateListener (){
    public void update(EventBean[] newEvents,
        EventBean[] oldEvents) {
```

1 Sets time in Esper to external

2 Defines a 1 second time window

```
            Assert.assertEquals(1, newEvents.length);
            Assert.assertNull(oldEvents);
            Long numLoans = (Long) newEvents[0].get("numLoans");
            Integer sumLoanedAmount = (Integer)
              newEvents[0].get("sumLoanedAmount");
            numLoansQueue.add(numLoans);
            sumLoanedAmountQueue.add(sumLoanedAmount);
        }
    });

    sendLoanRequestProcessedEvent(1000, "1", true, 100);
    assertMonitoredLoans(1L, 100);
    sendLoanRequestProcessedEvent(1300, "2", true, 200);
    assertMonitoredLoans(2L, 300);
    sendLoanRequestProcessedEvent(1600, "3", false, 1000);
    assertMonitoredLoans(null, null);
    sendLoanRequestProcessedEvent(1900, "4", true, 300);
    assertMonitoredLoans(3L, 600);
    sendLoanRequestProcessedEvent(2200, "5", true, 400);
    assertMonitoredLoans(2L, 500);
    assertMonitoredLoans(3L, 900);
    sendLoanRequestProcessedEvent(2400, "6", false, 900);
    assertMonitoredLoans(2L, 700);
    assertMonitoredLoans(null, null);

    epStatement.destroy();
}
```

❸ Sends loan's quantity variable to queue

❹ Expects no new number on the queue

❺ Fires update after 2 seconds

To test the time window of 1 second, you need to be able to time travel in the Esper engine. The easiest way to do this in Esper is to send a CurrentTimeEvent to the Esper engine, which sets the time. But before you can send a CurrentTimeEvent you need to tell Esper that the time will be externally managed by sending a TimerControlEvent ❶.

To set the time window to 1 second, you implement an EPL statement ❷. In the EPL statement, you select the number of loan request events and the total loan amount of the available events in the window. As you can see, you also apply a filter. The (requestApproved=true) part of the EPL ensures that you'll only handle approved loan requests.

The UpdateListener will be invoked when a new event arrives in the Esper engine, as you saw in listing 14.2. When you use a time window, the UpdateListener will also be invoked after a cycle in the time window has passed. In the unit test, you can see this when a new event is sent to the Esper engine after 2,200 milliseconds. After 2,000 milliseconds, a cycle of the time window has passed and the UpdateListener is invoked ❺. Then, you can expect two messages on the queue: the time cycle message and the new event message. To be able to test this properly, you use a Queue implementation ❸.

To fill the Esper engine with loan request events, you start firing a couple of events and test the results. If the loan request isn't approved, you have no new message on the queue ❹ because the EPL statement ignores those types of events.

Let's take a closer look at the firing of the events:

```
private void sendLoanRequestProcessedEvent(long time,
    String processInstanceId, boolean requestApproved, int loanedAmount) {

  sendEvent(time, new LoanRequestProcessedEvent(processInstanceId,
      time, requestApproved, loanedAmount));
}
private void sendEvent(long time, Object event) {
  epRuntime.sendEvent(new CurrentTimeEvent(time));
  epRuntime.sendEvent(event);
}
```

Before a loan request event is sent to the Esper engine, you need to test the time window of 1 second. You use the Esper `CurrentTimeEvent` class to inform Esper about the current time to use in the engine.

Now that you've implemented the CEP logic, you need a few lines of code to validate the number of loan requests and the total value of loan amounts:

```
private void assertMonitoredLoans(Long numLoans,
    Integer sumLoanedAmount) {
  Assert.assertEquals(numLoans, numLoansQueue.poll());
  Assert.assertEquals(sumLoanedAmount, sumLoanedAmountQueue.poll());
}
```

As previously mentioned, you use a `Queue` to test the `UpdateListener` events. This makes it possible to test multiple events fired by the Esper engine in the right order when a new loan request event is sent.

Because this unit test covers quite a bit of logic, it's good to look at figure 14.4, which provides a graphical overview of the Esper execution in the unit test.

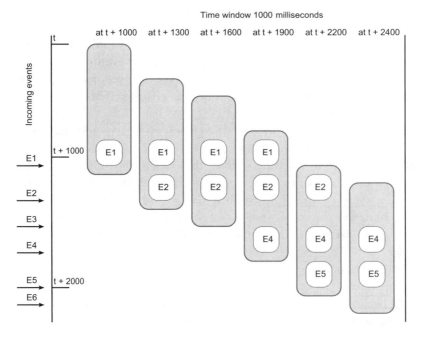

Figure 14.4   An overview of the state of the Esper 1 second time event window used in the unit test. Events 3 and 6 are ignored because these loan requests were not approved.

Here's what happens in figure 14.4:

- *At time t*—Nothing has happened and the window is empty.
- *At time t + 1000 milliseconds*—Event 1 arrives and enters the time window. The engine reports the event to the `UpdateListener`.
- *At time t + 1,300 milliseconds*—Event 2 arrives and enters the time window. The engine reports the event again to the `UpdateListener`, and now two events reside in the window.
- *At time t + 1,600 milliseconds*—Event 3 arrives. It's filtered out and doesn't enter the time window because the loan request isn't approved. The `UpdateListener` isn't invoked.
- *At time t + 1,900 milliseconds*—Event 4 arrives. The engine reports the event to the `UpdateListener`, and now three events reside in the window.
- *At time t + 2200 milliseconds*—Event 5 arrives. The engine reports two events to the `UpdateListener`, because event 1 is first pushed out of the time window and then event 5 is added. There are still three events residing in the window.
- *At time t + 2,400 milliseconds*—Event 6 arrives. Because the request isn't approved, it will not enter the window. But the engine isn't done; it pushes event 2 out of the window because it has now been in longer than a second. Two events remain in the window when the test is finished.

In this example, we used a very short time window to make it easy to understand the concept. But you can imagine that using a longer time window can be useful for BAM, perhaps showing the amount of products sold in the last 24 hours.

You now have a good understanding of the basic use of Esper so let's move on to a more advanced example, where we combine multiple events.

JOINING DIFFERENT EVENT TYPES

We've seen the Esper window concept in action in the last two sections. Now we'll take a look at another powerful concept that will help you monitor important business process information: the joining of different event types. In the earlier wedding example, to infer a complex event, you need to be able to handle different types of simple events and join them into one complex event: the wedding.

Later in the chapter, we'll monitor information related to process duration with Activiti. For now, though, let's focus on two KPIs. We'll look at the average process duration and the maximum process duration. Again, we aren't interested in these metrics from the beginning of time; we'll focus instead on specific intervals. In order to retrieve this kind of information, you need to be informed when a process starts and when a process instance is finished. These are two different event types, and the Esper engine will have to provide a signal when the start and end events for a specific process instance come in.

You need to define a join and a pattern construct in the EPL to handle this. Take a look at the next EPL statement, which shows how to calculate the average process duration:

```
select avg(endEvent.processedTime - beginEvent.receiveTime)
   as avgProcessDuration
from pattern [every beginEvent=LoanRequestReceivedEvent ->
   endEvent=LoanRequestProcessedEvent
       (processInstanceId=beginEvent.processInstanceId)]
```

This advanced EPL statement is selecting the average process duration. To get the process duration of a specific instance, the Esper engine takes the processedTime value, which is an attribute of the LoanRequestProcessedEvent, and subtracts the receiveTime, an attribute of the LoanRequestReceivedEvent. It correlates receive and processed events using a so-called pattern. The EPL statement correlates two event types when the processInstanceId attributes of both events are equal.

Check out the next listing to see how you can use the joining of different event types to get valuable information out of Esper. The test method is implemented in the same TimeWindowTest unit test class as the example in listing 14.4.

> **Listing 14.5 Joining different event types and correlating with an Esper pattern**

```
private Queue<Double> avgProcessDurationQueue =
   new LinkedList<Double>();
private Queue<Long> maxProcessDurationQueue =
   new LinkedList<Long>();

@Test
public void monitorProcessDuration() {
  epRuntime.sendEvent(new TimerControlEvent(
     ClockType.CLOCK_EXTERNAL));

  EPStatement epStatement = epAdmin.createEPL(            ❶ Selects
     new StringBuffer()                                      average
     .append("select avg(endEvent.processedTime - ")        process
     .append("beginEvent.receiveTime) as avgProcessDuration, ")  duration
     .append("max(endEvent.processedTime - ")
     .append("beginEvent.receiveTime) as maxProcessDuration ")
     .append("from pattern [")
     .append("every beginEvent = LoanRequestReceivedEvent ")
     .append("-> endEvent = LoanRequestProcessedEvent(")
     .append("processInstanceId=beginEvent.processInstanceId)")
     .append("].win:time(5 sec)").toString()); #1

  epStatement.addListener (new UpdateListener () {
    public void update(EventBean[] newEvents,
        EventBean[] oldEvents) {
                                                           ❷ Gets new
      Double avgProcessDuration = (Double)                   average
         newEvents[0].get("avgProcessDuration");             duration
      Long maxProcessDuration = (Long)
         newEvents[0].get("maxProcessDuration");
      avgProcessDurationQueue.add(avgProcessDuration);
      maxProcessDurationQueue.add(maxProcessDuration);
    }
  });
                                                   ❸ Sends
  sendLoanRequestReceivedEvent(0, "1", 100);         LoanRequestReceivedEvent
  assertMonitoredProcessDuration(null, null);
```

```
sendLoanRequestReceivedEvent(300, "2", 200);
assertMonitoredProcessDuration(null, null);

sendLoanRequestProcessedEvent(400, "2", true, 200);          ◁─┐  Send
assertMonitoredProcessDuration(100.0, 100L);                   │  LoanRequest-
                                                             ④  ProcessedEvent
sendLoanRequestProcessedEvent(600, "1", true, 100);
assertMonitoredProcessDuration(350.0, 600L);

sendLoanRequestReceivedEvent(1100, "3", 300);
assertMonitoredProcessDuration(null, null);

sendLoanRequestProcessedEvent(1600, "3", true, 300);
assertMonitoredProcessDuration(400.0, 600L);

epStatement.destroy();
}
```

In the test method, you define an EPL statement with the average and maximum process durations within a five second time window ❶. When the Esper engine invokes the UpdateListener, the new average and maximum duration variables are added to a Queue ❷.

In each event, you send the time, process instance ID, and requested loan amount values to the Esper engine; see, for example, the first LoanRequestReceivedEvent ❸. After you send a couple of process start events, you start sending a couple of process end events like those shown with the sendLoanRequestProcessedEvent method ❹. When this first end event is sent for process instance ID 2, this event is correlated with the process start event for the same process instance ID. The expected process duration can now be calculated as 400 − 300 = 100 milliseconds.

This concludes our introduction to Esper. It's time to see what we can do when we combine the power of Esper and Activiti. Time to do some business activity monitoring!

14.3 Monitoring Activiti processes with Esper

In this section, we'll use all your new knowledge of Esper and start monitoring the loan request process on Activiti. First, we'll discuss the position of the CEP engine in relation to Activiti, and then we'll work out an integrated example to run the two side by side in a test environment.

14.3.1 Integrating Activiti and Esper

Take a look at figure 14.5 to see how we'll combine Activiti and Esper to get monitoring information from the processes running on Activiti.

In section 6.4, we covered the Activiti execution listeners. You learned that they can be configured on the process itself, on activities, and on transitions. As you can see in figure 14.5, you can use the execution listeners to create and throw events to the Esper engine. The execution listeners have access to the process variables, and they can create Esper events filled with these process variables and send those events to Esper. This basic setup will be enhanced in section 14.4, where you'll use a Vaadin dashboard to display what's going on in the processes.

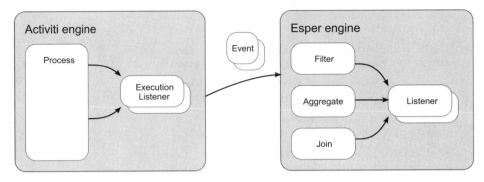

Figure 14.5   Activiti Engine using process execution listeners to feed Esper events

But, first, let's look into the basics of integrating Activiti and Esper in a unit test environment. In such an environment, we can keep the setup of the Activiti and Esper integration simple so we can focus on the implementation logic needed to combine Activiti listeners with Esper events.

14.3.2 *Testing the Activiti and Esper setup*

To run Activiti with Esper in a test environment, you need to follow a few steps. Let's walk briefly through them:

1 Define a BPMN process including execution listeners.
2 Implement the execution listeners to make them send events to Esper.
3 Set up Esper in a unit test, including the creation of the EPL statement.
4 Run the test.

The following code displays a simple business process with one user task and a simple form:

```
<definitions>
  <process id="loanrequest_withespertest">
    <extensionElements>
      <activiti:executionListener
        class="org.bpmnwithactiviti.
            ➥ chapter14.test.ProcessStartExecutionListener"
        event="start" />
      <activiti:executionListener
        class="org.bpmnwithactiviti.
            ➥ chapter14.test.ProcessEndExecutionListener"
        event="end" />
    </extensionElements>
    <startEvent id="theStart" />
    <sequenceFlow sourceRef="theStart" targetRef="evaluateLoanRequest" />
    <userTask id="evaluateLoanRequest" name="Evaluate loan request"
      activiti:assignee="fozzie" />
    <sequenceFlow sourceRef="evaluateLoanRequest" targetRef="theEnd" />
    <endEvent id="theEnd" />
  </process>
</definitions>
```

You can see that this process definition defines two execution listeners. The first will be called when the process is started, and the other when the process finishes. Listing 14.6 shows the code of one of the execution listeners. The other one is included in the source code accompanying the book.

Listing 14.6 Using a process start execution listener to send an event to Esper

```
public class ProcessStartExecutionListener
    implements ExecutionListener {

  public void notify(DelegateExecution execution)
      throws Exception {
    LoanRequestReceivedEvent event =
        new LoanRequestReceivedEvent(
            execution.getId(), new Date().getTime(),
            (Integer) execution.getVariable("loanAmount"));
    EPServiceProviderManager.getDefaultProvider()
        .getEPRuntime()
        .getEventSender("LoanRequestReceivedEvent")          ❷ Sends event
        .sendEvent(event);                                     to Esper
  }
}
```

First, a `LoanRequestReceivedEvent` is created and filled with the process instance ID, current time in milliseconds, and `loanAmount` process variable. The time attribute will be used in Esper to calculate the process duration. When the event is created, it's sent to the Esper engine ❶. This way of sending events to Esper will work fine in a unit test environment because Activiti and Esper are running in the same JVM. In section 14.4, we'll go a bit further and look at how to invoke Esper when it isn't running in the same JVM as Activiti.

There are still two things left to do to run the example. The first is to implement a unit test to run the Activiti and Esper setup. The Esper engine will be started before you deploy the process definition and start a new process instance, as shown in the following code snippet:

```
public class LoanRequestProcessWithEsperTest extends AbstractTest {

  @Rule
  public ActivitiRule activitiRule = new ActivitiRule(
      "activiti.cfg-mem-fullhistory.xml");

  private EPAdministrator epAdmin;

  @Before
  public void startEsper() {
    Configuration configuration = new Configuration();
    configuration.addEventTypeAutoName(
        "org.bpmnwithactiviti.chapter14.bam.event");
    EPServiceProvider epService = EPServiceProviderManager
        .getDefaultProvider(configuration);
    epAdmin = epService.getEPAdministrator();
    epAdmin.createEPL(new StringBuffer()
      .append("select avg(endEvent.processedTime ")
```

```
        .append("- beginEvent.receiveTime)")
        .append(" as avgProcessDuration, from pattern [")
        .append("every beginEvent = LoanRequestReceivedEvent ->")
        .append("endEvent = LoanRequestProcessedEvent")
        .append("(processInstanceId = beginEvent.processInstanceId)]")
        .append(".win:length(20)");
        .toString(), "processDuration");
  }
}
```

The EPL statement is named `ProcessDuration`. With that name, the statement can be accessed later in the test itself when you want to attach the Esper listener to it.

In listing 14.7, the average process duration is validated by comparing start and end times of the process.

Listing 14.7   Testing Activiti Esper integration using process execution listeners

```
private Double avgProcessDuration = null;

@Test
@Deployment(resources={"chapter14/
    ➥ loanrequest_withespertest.bpmn20.xml"})
public void testEsperActivitiSetup() {
  RuntimeService runtimeService =
      activitiRule.getRuntimeService();
  TaskService taskService =
      activitiRule.getTaskService();

  EPStatement epStatement = epAdmin.getStatement(          ❶ Retrieves EPL
      "processDuration");                                     statement
  epStatement.addListener(new UpdateListener () {
    public void update(EventBean[] newEvents,
        EventBean[] oldEvents) {
      avgProcessDuration = (Double)
          newEvents[0].get("avgProcessDuration");
    }
  });

  Map<String, Object> processVariables =
      new HashMap<String, Object>();
  processVariables.put("loanAmount", 10);                  ❷ Starts
  runtimeService.startProcessInstanceByKey(                   process
      "loanrequest_withespertest", processVariables);

  Thread.sleep(1000);

  processVariables = new HashMap<String, Object>();
  processVariables.put("requestApproved", true);           ❸ Finishes
  taskService.complete(taskService.createTaskQuery()          process
      .singleResult().getId(), processVariables);

  assertTrue(avgProcessDuration >= 1000);                  ◁ Validates
                                                              that variable
  processVariables = new HashMap<String, Object>();        ❹ is set
  processVariables.put("loanAmount", 20);
  runtimeService.startProcessInstanceByKey(
      "loanrequest_withespertest", processVariables);

  Thread.sleep(2000);
```

```
    processVariables = new HashMap<String, Object>();
    processVariables.put("requestApproved", true);
    taskService.complete(taskService.createTaskQuery()
        .singleResult().getId(), processVariables);

    assertTrue(avgProcessDuration >= 1500);
}
```

After the process deployment is configured and the necessary services are acquired, you need to add an Esper update listener to the `processDuration` EPL statement **❶** created in the `startEsper` method (see the previous code snippet). Then, you're ready to start your process with the loan amount as the initial process variable **❷**.

Note that, when you start a new process instance, the Activiti Engine invokes the process execution start listener. By completing the user task and approving the loan request, you implicitly finish the process **❸**, and the Activiti Engine will invoke the process execution end listener. Then, you can validate whether the Esper `UpdateListener` has set the `avgProcessDuration` variable **❹**. Because you included a `sleep` in the test execution, the average process duration should be at least 1 second (or 1,000 milliseconds).

Now that you've seen how to send events to Esper from the Activiti Engine, it's time to go one step further; let's implement a monitoring dashboard.

14.4 Monitoring Activiti with a Vaadin dashboard

In this section, we'll use all the material covered so far to build a complete business monitor dashboard application. First, we'll see what the application will look like and talk about the steps needed to build it. Then, we'll look at the process implementation and see how the Esper events are generated. Finally, we'll develop the dashboard web application using Esper and Vaadin.

14.4.1 An Activiti BAM architecture

In the example in the previous section, Activiti and Esper were both running in a single JVM and everything was coordinated from within a unit test. This doesn't represent a production-like situation.

Check out figure 14.6 to get an idea about the setup of Esper and Activiti we're going to use.

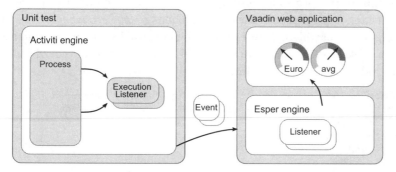

Figure 14.6   Setup of Activiti and a Vaadin-Esper BAM application running in a separate JVM

The idea is to start process instances on the Activiti Engine from within a unit test. The process definition contains the declaration of process execution listeners that will be informed by the Activiti Engine when process events occur. The listeners will then connect with a Jetty server that manages a Vaadin web application and a REST service. One by one, the events will be delivered to a REST service implemented by the dashboard web application, which will then deliver the events to the Esper engine. Esper is also running within the dashboard web application.

After the Esper engine is done filtering, aggregating, and joining events, it will push updates to the Vaadin user interface. That user interface contains some gauges and a table displaying the business monitoring information from the Activiti process.

We'll put this all together in the remainder of this section. It will involve three steps:

1　We'll take a look at the event producer side, the Activiti Engine. We'll discuss the process, the listeners, and how the connection with the REST service is established.

2　We'll move on to the receiving end. We'll look at the REST service itself, followed by the Esper code, and we'll talk a bit about the Vaadin application.

3　We'll start the Jetty server, cover the unit test that starts off process instances, and run it.

To keep the listings interesting, only new pieces of logic are listed. The complete application can be found in the book's source code.

14.4.2 *Producing REST events with Activiti*

To communicate events with the Esper engine, you need to perform two steps:

1　Define the BPMN 2.0 XML, including the process execution listener declarations for the events you're interested in.

2　Implement the listeners to create the Esper events and connect with the REST service.

To keep things focused on the BAM functionality, we'll use the same loan request process definition we used in the previous section. The implementation of the listener is different, though. In the previous section, we could directly communicate with Esper and send the `LoanRequestReceivedEvent` and `LoanRequestProcessedEvent` straight to the Esper engine. This will work differently now, because Esper runs behind the REST service. Take a look at the implementation of the `ProcessStartExecutionListener` that can be found in the package ending with `chapter14.listener`:

```
public void notify(DelegateExecution execution) throws Exception {
  LoanRequestReceivedEvent event = new LoanRequestReceivedEvent(
      execution.getId(), new Date().getTime(),
        (Integer) execution.getVariable("loanAmount"));
  EventSender.send(event);
}
```

When the notify method is called upon by Activiti Engine, the LoanRequestReceived event is created as before, using the execution to obtain the process variables. It now uses the EventSender class to send the event to Esper. Here's how this is implemented.

Listing 14.8 Sending Esper events to a REST service

```
public class EventSender {
  private static String HOST =                                    ❶ Defines REST
      "http://localhost:8081/book-bam-app/events/";                   API location
  public static void send(Object event) {
    HttpURLConnection connection = null;
    try {                                                          ❷ Finds right
      URL url = new URL(HOST +                                        REST service
          event.getClass().getSimpleName());                         for the event
      connection = (HttpURLConnection) url.openConnection();
      connection.setRequestMethod("POST");
      connection.setDoOutput(true);
      connection.setAllowUserInteraction(false);
      connection.setRequestProperty(
          "Content-type", "application/xml; charset=UTF-8");
      OutputStream out = connection.getOutputStream();           ❸ Sends event by
      JAXBContext.newInstance(event.getClass())                     transforming it
          .createMarshaller().marshal(event, out);                  into XML
      out.close();
    } catch (Exception e) {
      log.warn("Event could not be send to BAM application", e);
    } finally {
      if (connection != null) {
       connection.disconnect();
      }
    }
  }
}
```

In the Vaadin web application, which we'll discuss in section 14.4.3 (implemented in the book-bam-app project), you run a Jetty server locally on port 8081 and the REST resource resides at the declared URL ❶. The REST service handles post requests that are named after the event type ❷. Finally, the event is converted to XML and sent to the service ❸.

Events can't be converted to XML messages automatically. You first need to add the necessary JAXB annotations as shown in the following code snippet:

```
@XmlRootElement(name = "loanRequestReceivedEvent")
@XmlAccessorType(XmlAccessType.FIELD)
public class LoanRequestReceivedEvent {

  @XmlElement
  private final String processInstanceId;
  @XmlElement
  private final long receiveTime;
  @XmlElement
  private final int requestedAmount;
  ...
}
```

The `LoanRequestReceivedEvent` will be converted to an XML message with the root tag `loanRequestReceivedEvent`. All three attributes will be converted to XML child elements of this root tag.

Now you can send events to a REST service, so let's see how you can implement this REST service and connect it to an Esper engine.

14.4.3 *Setting up the Vaadin application with the Esper REST service*

Setting up the REST service is a little more work. Let's break it down into a few steps as we did before:

1 Configure the web application to run Esper and the REST provider.
2 Implement the REST resource to handle the different event types and forward them to the Esper engine.
3 Build the Vaadin monitor application containing the Esper update listeners that will update the BAM dashboard.

When the REST service running in the web application (see the `book-bam-app` project in the book's source code) starts receiving events, the Esper engine needs to be up and running. To start the Esper engine, we'll configure and build a `ServletContext-Listener`. It's declared in the web.xml like this:

```
<listener>
  <listener-class>
    org.bpmnwithactiviti.chapter14.bam.EsperStatementsCreator
  </listener-class>
</listener>
```

The `EsperStatementsCreator` class will be called by the web container when the application is started, and it is responsible for configuring the EPL statements you want to use in the example. The class also contains the EPL statement definitions. The following code shows the most important parts of the `EsperStatementsCreator` implementation:

```
public class EsperStatementsCreator implements ServletContextListener {
  ...
  public void contextInitialized(ServletContextEvent context) {
    Configuration configuration = new Configuration();
    configuration.addEventTypeAutoName(
        "org.bpmnwithactiviti.chapter14.bam.event");
    EPServiceProvider epService = EPServiceProviderManager
      .getDefaultProvider(configuration);
    epAdmin = epService.getEPAdministrator();

    epAdmin.createEPL(new StringBuffer()
        .append("select avg(requestedAmount) as avgRequestedAmount, ")
        .append("max(requestedAmount) as maxRequestedAmount, ")
        .append("sum(requestedAmount) as sumRequestedAmount ")
        .append("from LoanRequestReceivedEvent.win:length(10)")
        .toString(), REQUESTED_AMOUNT_STATEMENT_NAME);
    ...
  }
}
```

When the application is started, the contextInitialized method will be invoked on the EsperStatementsCreator. Then Esper is configured and started and the EPL statements are defined.

Because we're using the Apache CXF framework to implement the REST service, you also need to define a CXF REST servlet in the web.xml (see the next code snippet). Note that the EventResource class that's mentioned here will be implemented in listing 14.9:

```xml
<servlet>
  <servlet-name>CXFJAX-RSServlet</servlet-name>
  <servlet-class>org.apache.cxf.jaxrs.servlet.
     ➥ CXFNonSpringJaxrsServlet</servlet-class>
  <init-param>
    <param-name>jaxrs.serviceClasses</param-name>
    <param-value>org.bpmnwithactiviti.EventResource</param-value>
  </init-param>
</servlet>
```

The responsibility of the EventResource class is to receive the REST service calls from the Activiti process execution listeners and send them through to the Esper engine. You can see that class in the following listing.

Listing 14.9 Definition of the REST resource that handles the Esper events

```java
@Path("/events")                                          ◁─┐  Defines
@Consumes("application/xml")                               ❶  resource's URL
public class EventResource {

  @POST
  @Path("LoanRequestReceivedEvent")                       ◁─┐  Handles
  public Response postEvent(LoanRequestReceivedEvent event) {  ❷  POST
    try {                                                          request
      EPServiceProviderManager.getDefaultProvider()
          .getEPRuntime()
          .getEventSender("LoanRequestReceivedEvent")
          .sendEvent(event);                               ◁─┐  Forwards
      return Response.status(Status.OK).build();           ❸  event to Esper
    } catch (RuntimeException e) {
      throw new WebApplicationException(e);
    }
  }

  @POST
  @Path("LoanRequestProcessedEvent")
  public Response postEvent(LoanRequestProcessedEvent event) {
    ...
  }
}
```

The URI path for invoking this REST service is defined by the @Path annotation ❶. You saw this URI path used in listing 14.8, where the EventSender class invokes this REST service.

Then, the `LoanRequestReceivedEvent` `POST` method is defined with an additional URI path for this specific type of event ❷. In the `postEvent` method, you forward the event to the Esper engine ❸.

We saw in the `EventSender` implementation in listing 14.8 that the class name was used to call the right service. The `EventResource` can handle `LoanRequest-ProcessedEvent` types as well.

In the final step, you need to implement the Vaadin application logic to visualize the Esper events. We won't dive deep into the Vaadin application because it's a bit out of scope, and also not important for the business monitoring functionality itself. But, to give you an idea of the Vaadin logic, here's a small snippet from the Vaadin `BAMApplication` class:

```
...
requestedAmountListener = new UpdateListener() {
  public void update(EventBean[] newEvents, EventBean[] oldEvents) {
    Double  avgRequestedAmount = (Double)
        newEvents[0].get("avgRequestedAmount");
    Integer maxRequestedAmount =
        (Integer)newEvents[0].get("maxRequestedAmount");
    Integer sumRequestedAmount =
        (Integer)newEvents[0].get("sumRequestedAmount");

avgRequestedAmountLabel.setValue(avgRequestedAmount);
    maxRequestedAmountLabel.setValue(maxRequestedAmount);
    sumRequestedAmountLabel.setValue(sumRequestedAmount);
  }
};
...
```

Every time the `UpdateListener` is invoked, the event will be processed, leading to updates on the Vaadin labels on the dashboard. Other listener logic updates the Vaadin gauges as well. As you can see, the great thing about Vaadin is that you can directly change the values of labels and gauges using only a few lines of Java code.

Time to check out the dashboard now and start some processes!

14.4.4 *Monitoring Activiti processes with a Vaadin dashboard*

In this last subsection, we'll kick things off with the Vaadin BAM web application and use a unit test to simulate a couple of Activiti processes, so that you have some action going on in your business monitor application.

The Vaadin BAM dashboard is implemented in the `book-bam-app` project. You can run the internal Jetty server with the dashboard application by issuing the `mvn clean install jetty:run` Maven command. After you see the Jetty started message, you can open the application at http://localhost:8081/book-bam-app/ui. You'll see a few gauges that aren't moving yet and an empty table ready to list different kinds of loan request process information. Because there are no processes running, there's nothing more to see yet.

Now, to get a couple of processes up and running, let's walk through the unit test in the following listing, which you can find in the `bpmn-examples` project.

Listing 14.10 Starting multiple loan requests to provide input to the monitoring dashboard

```
public class LoanRequestProcessWithBAMTest extends AbstractTest {

  @Rule
  public ActivitiRule activitiRule = new ActivitiRule(
      "activiti.cfg-mem-fullhistory.xml");

  private RuntimeService runtimeService;
  private TaskService taskService;
  private Random random;

  @Test
  @Deployment(resources={"chapter14/loanrequest_withbam.bpmn20.xml"})
  public void testBAM() throws InterruptedException {
    runtimeService = activitiRule.getRuntimeService();
    taskService = activitiRule.getTaskService();
    random = new Random();
    for (int i = 0; i < 20; i++) {
      startRandomLoanRequestProcess("Person "
          + Integer.toString(i));
    }
  }

  private void startRandomLoanRequestProcess(String name)
      throws InterruptedException {
    Map<String, Object> processVariables =
        new HashMap<String, Object>();
    processVariables.put("name", name);
    processVariables.put("income", 1000);
    processVariables.put("loanAmount", random.nextInt(100));
    runtimeService.startProcessInstanceByKey(
        "loanrequest_withbam", processVariables);

    Thread.sleep(500 + random.nextInt(1000));
    processVariables = new HashMap<String, Object>();
    processVariables.put("requestApproved", true);
    taskService.complete(taskService.createTaskQuery()
        .singleResult().getId(), processVariables);
  }
}
```

❶ Starts processes with random amount

❷ Waits a little time

❸ Completes task and process

After you have the `TaskService` and `RuntimeService` available, you start process instances with a random loan amount ❶. You then simulate the time it takes to complete the user task with a `Thread.sleep` call ❷ and then complete the loan request process instance ❸.

You're all set to monitor these processes now, so start the unit test and watch the Vaadin BAM dashboard in action. If all goes well, you'll see something that looks like figure 14.7.

With this small application, we conclude our business-monitoring trip with Esper and Activiti. You can play around a bit with the test to kick off more processes or wait longer to complete the tasks. Check out the Esper statements in the Vaadin application as well; tweaking them is a bit more tricky, but Esper is well documented and worth checking out!

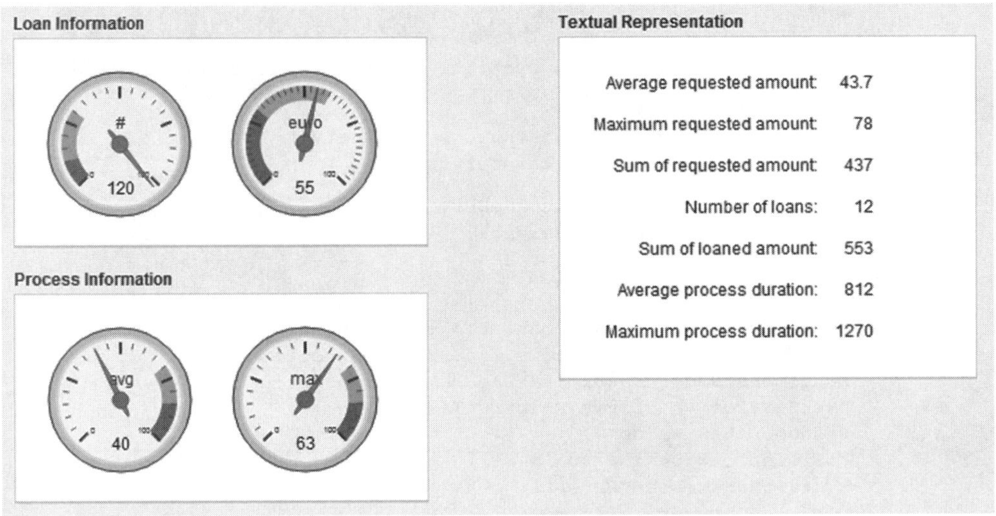

Loan Information

Textual Representation

Average requested amount:	43.7
Maximum requested amount:	78
Sum of requested amount:	437
Number of loans:	12
Sum of loaned amount:	553
Average process duration:	812
Maximum process duration:	1270

Process Information

Figure 14.7   Gauges and a table showing Activiti business activity monitoring in action

14.5   *Summary*

In this chapter, we covered a lot of new material. First, we took a look at what business monitoring is. We saw that CEP can help you analyze large volumes of data, and we checked out the open source CEP engine implementation called Esper.

We worked out some examples with Esper, starting with simple stuff but moving on to some more advanced processes, including length and time windows and the joining of different event types. Integrating your newly acquired Esper knowledge with Activiti was then rather easy.

Finally, we saw the power of business monitoring in action with a simple but quite powerful Vaadin application. By running Activiti processes in a unit test, we used the process execution listeners to shoot process events via a REST service to Esper. Then, with some Vaadin user interface components, we used the Esper listeners to update the UI and saw how all this stuff comes together.

In the next chapter, we'll take a step back from implementing business processes and look in more detail at how to manage the Activiti environment.

Part 4

Managing
BPMN 2.0 processes

In this last, brief part, we step back from developing new process definitions and focus on the remaining components that are important to understand when you want to run the Activiti Engine in a production environment. In chapter 15, we'll talk about the Activiti database model in order to understand the foundation of the Activiti Engine. We'll also discuss process versioning and the asynchronous functionality provided by the job executor. Finally, we'll explore how to extend the Activiti Explorer with additional management functionality.

Managing
the Activiti Engine

This chapter covers

- Understanding the Activiti database model and its scripts
- Versioning process definitions
- Executing asynchronous jobs with the job executor
- Enhancing the Activiti Explorer with additional administration functionality

We've been developing process solutions with the Activiti Engine and additional frameworks like Drools, Esper, and Alfresco, and you've familiarized yourself with the Activiti API and what's happening under the hood. We're almost ready to take our process solutions to production, but we haven't touched on managing the Activiti Engine in a production environment, which is vital to using Activiti within an organization. In this final chapter, we'll look at several topics that are required knowledge when you're working toward a production stage. In this chapter, we'll take the final steps to making you an Activiti expert.

The Activiti framework relies heavily on the database for persisting the process state, the deployment artifacts, and the process history. Therefore, you need to understand the underlying database model and the database scripts provided with the Activiti framework to be able to manage an Activiti Engine environment. We'll also be looking at how to create an Activiti database from scratch and how to upgrade the database when a new version of Activiti that contains database changes is released.

We'll also be looking at two maintenance tasks, the first of which is process versioning. When you use the Activiti Engine, there will come a time when you'll want to deploy a new version of an already existing process definition. We'll look at best practices for dealing with process versioning. The second maintenance task is the job infrastructure. For asynchronous behavior, like timer events and async continuations, the job executor is used by the Activiti Engine to process these jobs. We'll look at how the job executor works and how it can be used when you want to add more servers with the Activiti Engine running on them.

In the last section, we'll implement an administration enhancement to the Activiti Explorer. We'll add functionality to get an overview of all running and completed process instances, including full details. In addition, we'll implement views on the process engine configuration like the database and history configuration.

But let's start with the foundation of the Activiti Engine: the database.

15.1   *Working with the Activiti database*

The Activiti Engine relies heavily on the underlying database to manage running process instances, deployed process definitions, and the job scheduler, among other things. When you're not using another transaction manager, the Activiti Engine also uses the database for transaction management, committing or rolling back transactions of BPMN 2.0 elements that are executed after each other. Therefore, in order to manage the Activiti Engine in a production environment, it's important to understand the database model that's used to store running process instances and user tasks.

In this section, we'll start by looking at the database model. Then we'll discuss how a database administrator can create an Activiti database. Finally, we'll talk about ways to upgrade the Activiti database when a new Activiti version that contains database updates is released.

15.1.1   *Understanding the Activiti runtime execution database model*

The Activiti database can be roughly divided into three separate models:

- Tables that are used for the deployment artifacts and the runtime execution of process instances and user tasks.
- Tables that are used for history purposes, meaning completed process instances and user tasks.
- User and group management tables used for the built-in user and group repository.

In this section, we'll take a look at the first model, which is the runtime execution and deployment data model.

A RUNTIME EXECUTION AND DEPLOYMENT MODEL OVERVIEW

We'll start off by looking at the tables that are used to store deployment information and the data needed for the runtime execution of the process instances. Figure 15.1 shows the tables with their columns, primary keys, and relationships.

As you can see in figure 15.1, the database model of the runtime execution and deployment tables is quite big. Furthermore, in tables like ACT_RU_EXECUTION and ACT_RU_TASK, a lot of additional structure is implemented. In the next sections, we'll therefore walk through the database model with the vacation request example process that's installed with the Activiti Explorer.

TAKING A DETAILED LOOK AT THE DEPLOYMENT TABLES

To start off, imagine that you deploy a new BAR file or BPMN 2.0 XML file to the Activiti Engine. Then, the deployed artifacts are inserted into the ACT_RE_DEPLOYMENT and ACT_GE_BYTEARRAY tables. Out of the box, the Activiti Engine already contains

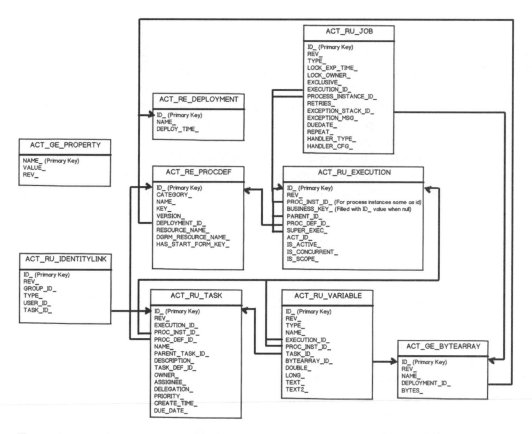

Figure 15.1 Database model of the runtime execution and deployment tables used by the Activiti Engine

the deployment of examples, including the vacation request process definition. The ACT_RE_DEPLOYMENT table contains the following entries:

```
ID_            10
NAME_          activiti-engine-examples.bar
DEPLOY_TIME    2011-10-27 20:18:34.212
```

Only the name column is the same on every environment. It contains the name of the deployment file if no other name has been specified during deployment. As you can see, this table contains almost no information.

The ACT_GE_BYTEARRAY table contains the deployment artifacts:

```
ID_            11
REV_           1
NAME_          org/activiti/examples/taskforms/VacationRequest.bpmn20.xml
DEPLOYMENT_ID_ 10
BYTES_         Byte array

ID_            12
REV_           1
NAME_          org/activiti/examples/taskforms/VacationRequest.png
DEPLOYMENT_ID_ 10
BYTES_         Byte array
```

Here, the deployment artifacts of one of the example processes are shown. The first entry contains the vacation request BPMN 2.0 XML file, with the artifact stored as a byte array in the BYTES_ column. The second artifact contains the picture of the vacation request process definition in the same manner. If the vacation request had contained more deployment artifacts, like a DRL file for the rules definition, they would've been stored here as well.

Another table that contains rows when the Activiti Engine stores a deployment artifact is the ACT_RE_PROCDEF table. The Activiti Engine parses the BPMN 2.0 XML file and stores information about this process definition in the ACT_RE_PROCDEF table:

```
ID_                  vacationrequest:1:21
CATEGORY_            http://activiti.org/bpmn20
NAME_                Vacation request
KEY_                 vacationRequest
VERSION_             1
DEPLOYMENT_ID_       10
RESOURCE_NAME_  org/activiti/examples/taskforms/VacationRequest.bpmn20.xml
DGRM_RESOURCE_NAME_  org/activiti/examples/taskforms/VacationRequest.png
HAS_START_FORM_KEY_  false
```

The ID_ column corresponds to the process identifier of the process definition. The KEY_ column holds the value for the business key of the process definition. Next to these unique process identifiers, the process definition table contains the name of the process, a reference to the deployment artifact, and references to the BPMN 2.0 XML file and to a picture of the process definition, if present.

This is all the information the Activiti Engine stores about a deployment and a process definition. The parsed activities of a process definition aren't stored in the database but are held in memory inside the Activiti Engine, so when a new process instance is started, all the activities of the corresponding process definition are available.

Let's move on to the tables that are used to hold information about a running process instance.

TAKING A DETAILED LOOK AT THE PROCESS EXECUTION TABLES

First, there's the ACT_RU_EXECUTION table, which contains information about the process instance itself. Let's look at the contents of the ACT_RU_EXECUTION table after you have started a new instance of the vacation request process definition:

```
ID_              717
REV_             1
PROC_INST_ID_    717
BUSINESS_KEY_
PARENT_ID_
PROC_DEF_ID_     vacationRequest:1:21
SUPER_EXEC_
ACT_ID_          handleRequest
IS_ACTIVE_       true
IS_CONCURRENT_   false
IS_SCOPE_        true
```

The execution table contains information about the process instance and process definition identifiers. It also holds the state of the process instance with the current activity identifier in the ACT_ID_ column. When a process definition doesn't contain asynchronous continuations, the process instance executes all automatic activities in the same transaction without storing its state to the database. Only when the Activiti Engine encounters a wait state like a user task or a receive task will the process instance state be persisted to the ACT_RU_EXECUTION table. In this vacation request example, the current activity is the Handle Request user task.

When a process instance contains concurrent flow logic like a parallel gateway or an inclusive gateway, there will be more than one entry in the execution table for the same process instance. For example, with the multitasking process example implemented in chapter 6, the ACT_RU_EXECUTION table contains four rows of the multitasking process instance when a new one is started (see figure 15.2).

The first entry shown in figure 15.2 is the parallel gateway fork, which corresponds to the first parallel gateway of the process definition. This entry will be persisted in the table until a joining parallel gateway is executed. The second entry contains the backlog email user task of the first outgoing path of the parallel gateway. The third entry contains the execution of the job that's attached to the intermediate timer event. The fourth entry contains the intermediate timer event that's being executed in the second outgoing path of the parallel gateway. When the job is executed after 30 seconds, the execution table will only contain three entries, with the timer and job executions having been deleted and a new entry added for the "Do work" user task.

Also, in the case of subprocesses, the execution table will contain more than one entry: one for the main process execution and one for the subprocess execution.

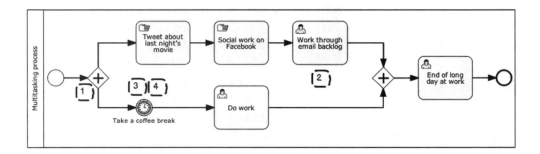

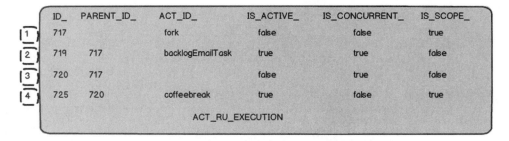

Figure 15.2   Recap of the parallel gateway example from chapter 6, with the database rows that are created in the ACT_RU_EXECUTION table when a new process instance is started

The execution table is the most complex table in the Activiti Engine database model. It can contain a lot of hierarchical relationships concerning parallel execution or subprocesses. In the chapter 6 example, it contains four rows, but, for the vacation request example we used earlier, it only contains one entry or row, so let's stick with that example and not make it overly complex.

TAKING A DETAILED LOOK AT THE USER TASK TABLES

In the execution table of the vacation request process instance, you saw that the current activity identifier was the "Handle request" user task. The details about this user task are stored in the ACT_RU_TASK table:

```
ID_              726
REV_             1
EXECUTION_ID_    717
PROC_INST_ID_    717
PROC_DEF_ID_     vacationRequest:1:21
NAME_            Handle vacation request
PARENT_TASK_ID_
DESCRIPTION_
  kermit would like to take 10 day(s) of vacation (Motivation: Holiday).
TASK_DEF_KEY_    handleRequest
OWNER_
ASSIGNEE_
DELEGATION_
PRIORITY_        50
CREATE_TIME_     2011-10-27 20:56:18.332
DUE_DATE_
```

The task table contains two references to the execution table.

- A reference (PROC_INST_ID) to the process instance for which the user task was created
- A reference (EXECUTION_ID_) to the activity execution corresponding to the user task

For a simple process like the vacation request example, these references point to the same row in the execution table. But when there is a concurrent execution, like there was for the multitasking process definition in chapter 6, these values can be different.

A lot of the columns in the task table hold information details about the user task, like the name, the priority, and the creation time. The task table also contains the owner, assignee, and delegation values for the task assignment state. The task table further contains a parent task identifier column for defining a task hierarchy. When you create a subtask, the corresponding row in the task table points to the parent task.

As you can see, the task table doesn't contain the candidate user or group definition. This information is stored in the ACT_RU_IDENTITYLINK table. For the "Handle vacation request" user task, this table holds the following information:

```
ID_          727
REV_         1
GROUP_ID_    management
TYPE_        candidate
USER_ID_
TASK_ID_     726
```

This user task is available to be claimed by a person of the management group. If you claim the user task with the Kermit user, the assignee column in the task table will be filled.

Now let's look at how process variables are stored in the Activiti database.

INTRODUCING THE VARIABLE TABLE

Another important table for the runtime execution of process instances is the ACT_RU_VARIABLE table. This table contains all of the process variables related to a specific execution. For simple processes, this means that the variable table contains the process variables related to a specific process instance. But, when a process definition contains embedded subprocesses, the variable table will contain process variables for the main process as well as for the embedded process execution.

Let's look at an example row of the variable table for the motivation process variable of the vacation request process:

```
ID_            724
REV_           1
TYPE_          string
NAME_          motivation
EXECUTION_ID_  717
PROC_INST_ID_  717
TASK_ID_
BYTEARRAY_ID_
```

```
DOUBLE_
LONG_
TEXT_            Holiday
TEXT2_
```

A variable can be coupled to a process instance (PROC_INST_ID_) or a user task (TASK_ID_). In this example, the variable is coupled to the vacation request process instance. When the variable contains a complex object like a Java bean, the value is stored as a byte array. The byte array itself is stored in the ACT_GE_BYTEARRAY table, which we've discussed already.

STORING ASYNCHRONOUS JOBS IN ACTIVITI

When a process instance contains asynchronous behavior like a timer event or an async continuation, a job is created in the ACT_RU_JOB table. The job executor will process the jobs in this table when it's activated in the process configuration.

The multitasking example in chapter 6 contains an intermediate timer event in the second flow of the parallel gateway. When the intermediate timer event is processed, the following job entry is created in the job table:

```
ID_                     762
REV_                    1
TYPE_                   timer
LOCK_EXP_TIME_
LOCK_OWNER_
EXCLUSIVE_              false
EXECUTION_ID_           761
PROCESS_INSTANCE_ID_    754
RETRIES_                3
EXCEPTION_STACK_ID_
EXCEPTION_MSG
DUEDATE_                2011-10-27 23:31:33.453
REPEAT_
HANDLER_TYPE_           timer-intermediate-transition
HANDLER_CFG_            coffeebreak
```

The job scheduler we'll be discussing in section 15.3 reads the entries in the job table and tries to execute them. The references to the corresponding process execution (EXECUTION_ID_) and process instance (PROCESS_INSTANCE_ID_) is available, and a job handler type is defined so the scheduler knows which command class should process the job. When the job is completed without errors, the job is deleted from the job table. Otherwise, an exception message is stored and the job is retried three times by default.

STORING HISTORY LEVEL AND ENGINE VERSION INFORMATION

There's one table remaining from figure 15.1, and that's the ACT_GE_PROPERTY table. This table contains property values needed by the Activiti Engine. By default, the history level and the Activiti Engine version can be found here:

```
NAME_   historyLevel
VALUE_  2
REV_    1
```

```
NAME_    schema.version
VALUE_   5.9
REV_     1
```

The value in the history level corresponds to one of the four possible history configuration levels you can find in the `ProcessEngineConfigurationImpl` class of Activiti. The default value is audit, which corresponds to the value of 2:

```
public static final int HISTORYLEVEL_NONE = 0;
public static final int HISTORYLEVEL_ACTIVITY = 1;
public static final int HISTORYLEVEL_AUDIT = 2;
public static final int HISTORYLEVEL_FULL = 3;
```

As you know, you can also configure a history level in the process engine configuration in an activiti.cfg.xml file or in another Spring configuration file. When you set the `databaseSchemaUpdate` property to `false` in the Activiti Engine configuration, the history value configuration should be the same as the history configuration level in the database; otherwise, an error is thrown when the Activiti Engine is initialized. This means that, if you set the `databaseSchemaUpdate` property to `false`, you must change the history value in two places: the database and the Activiti Engine configuration file.

> **WARNING** The history level stored in the ACT_GE_PROPERTY database table should be the same as the history level in your Activiti Engine configuration. If they aren't the same and the `databaseSchemaUpdate` property is set to `false`, an error is thrown when the Activiti Engine is started. When you want to change the default history level from audit to another level, you should change the value in the database and the configuration file. When you change the database history level value, it's important that no process instances are running.

Let's move on to the history tables, where you can find process instance and user task information even after the process instance has ended or the user task is completed. Note that the amount of information stored depends on the history configuration level.

15.1.2 Understanding the Activiti history database model

The database model of the history tables is a lot smaller and easier to understand than the deployment and runtime execution database model. The history tables can be used for reporting and managing information related to all process instances and user tasks that are running or have been completed.

You can choose to store data in the history tables only for a specific lifetime and delete all rows that are older than a specific time period; for example, older than six months. The tables don't have foreign key references, which makes this easy.

Take a look at the database model overview in figure 15.3.

You've already seen the runtime execution database model, so most of the history database tables should almost speak for themselves. When a process instance like the vacation request example is started, the ACT_HI_PROCINST and ACT_HI_ACTINST

ACT_HI_PROCINST
ID_ (Primary Key)
PROC_INST_ID_ (For process instances same as id)
BUSINESS_KEY_
PARENT_ID_
PROC_DEF_ID_
START_TIME_
END_TIME_
DURATION_
START_USER_ID_
START_ACT_ID_
END_ACT_ID_
SUPER_PROCESS_INSTANCE_ID_

ACT_HI_TASKINST
ID_ (Primary Key)
PROC_DEF_ID_
TASK_DEF_KEY_
PROC_INST_ID_
EXECUTION_ID_
NAME_
PARENT_TASK_ID_
DESCRIPTION_
OWNER_
ASSIGNEE_
START_TIME_
END_TIME_
DURATION_
DELETE_REASON_
PRIORITY_
DUEDATE_

ACT_HI_ACTINST
ID_ (Primary Key)
PROC_DEF_ID_
PROC_INST_ID_
EXECUTION_ID_
ACT_ID_
ACT_NAME_
ACT_TYPE_
OWNER_
ASSIGNEE_
START_TIME_
END_TIME_
DURATION_

ACT_HI_DETAIL
ID_ (Primary Key)
REV_
TYPE_
NAME_
EXECUTION_ID_
PROC_INST_ID_
TASK_ID_
ACT_INST_ID_
VAR_TYPE_
TIME_
BYTEARRAY_ID_
DOUBLE_
LONG_
TEXT_
TEXT2_

ACT_HI_ATTACHMENT
ID_ (Primary Key)
REV_
USER_ID_
NAME_
DESCRIPTION_
TYPE_
TASK_ID_
PROC_INST_ID_
URL_
CONTENT_ID_

Figure 15.3 The database model of the history tables used by the Activiti Engine

tables are filled (at the same time that the process instance is stored in the ACT_RU_EXECUTION table). The history tables aren't only filled when a process instance is completed but also when the process instance state is stored in the runtime execution tables.

For a process instance, a number of interesting metrics are stored in the ACT_HI_PROCINST table, including the start and end times and the duration. These values can be used for reporting purposes, for example, to calculate the minimum, maximum, and average duration times of a specific process definition. The ACT_HI_TASKINST table holds similar information about a user task. For every user task that's started or completed in the Activiti Engine, you can find an entry in this table with information like the assignee, the duration, and the due date.

The ACT_HI_ACTINST table contains information about every activity that's being executed as part of a process instance. This table contains quite detailed information about the start time, end time, and duration of every activity executed by the Activiti Engine.

When you set the history level to audit or full, a lot more detailed information is stored in the ACT_HI_DETAIL table. For the audit level, all form property values submitted via the FormService interface are stored in this table. And, for the full history level, all the process variables, including the updates, are stored in this table. Remember that you can retrieve these values using the `HistoryService createHistoricDetailQuery`.

The last table, ACT_HI_ATTACHMENT, isn't really related to the other tables. It contains the process instance or user task attachments discussed in chapter 13. You can add attachments to a process instance and a user task using the `TaskService createAttachment` method, and then these attachments will be stored in the ACT_HI_ATTACHMENT table.

As you can see, we don't need to spend a lot of time explaining the history tables. In section 15.4, we'll use the history tables for the management dashboard to show all process instances that are being executed or are already completed.

Now that you understand the database model, let's discuss the best practices for creating the Activiti database that contains the tables of the database model.

15.1.3 *Creating the Activiti database*

In this book's examples, we took the availability of an Activiti Engine database containing the tables described in the previous section for granted. You used an in-memory H2 database for the unit test examples and the default H2 database for the examples where you made use of the Activiti Explorer. Under the hood, the in-memory database is created every time you start a unit test using the in-memory database configuration.

This is great when you're developing process solutions, but, when you have to set up a test or production environment, a DBA will not allow you to run a Java program to create a new database. Therefore, you need another solution for these kinds of environments. First, you have to get a hold of the database scripts that create tables for your specific database type. When you open the Activiti Engine JAR file, activiti-engine-<version>.jar, you can find the SQL scripts in the `org.activiti.db.create` package (figure 15.4).

You can look at the contents of the JAR file by opening it in a ZIP application or by opening the referenced

Figure 15.4 The database scripts in the Activiti Engine JAR in Eclipse

libraries in Eclipse, as shown in figure 15.4. For every supported database, you can find the `create` scripts. When you want to run the Activiti Engine on a MySQL database, the engine, history, and identity scripts are needed by default. If you won't be using the user and group management tables because you're using an LDAP repository, for example, you can even skip the identity script. The cycle script is legacy and isn't needed anymore. This script will probably be removed in future versions of the Activiti Engine.

When you unzip the appropriate create scripts from the Activiti Engine JAR file, it's time to hand them over to the DBA. By default, the engine database script already contains the primary key, foreign key, and index definitions. But, the index definitions can certainly be improved based on your specific query needs. The following indexes are created by default:

```
create index ACT_IDX_EXEC_BUSKEY on ACT_RU_EXECUTION(BUSINESS_KEY_);
create index ACT_IDX_TASK_CREATE on ACT_RU_TASK(CREATE_TIME_);
create index ACT_IDX_IDENT_LNK_USER on ACT_RU_IDENTITYLINK(USER_ID_);
create index ACT_IDX_IDENT_LNK_GROUP on ACT_RU_IDENTITYLINK(GROUP_ID_);
create unique index ACT_UNIQ_RU_BUS_KEY on ACT_RU_EXECUTION
    (PROC_DEF_ID_, BUSINESS_KEY_) where BUSINESS_KEY_ is not null;
```

If you want to do a lot of querying based on process variable names, it would be good to add an index to the ACT_RU_VARIABLE table. But, with the engine, history, and optional identity database scripts available, your DBA will know how to create a new database for your test or production environment.

Now, let's see what you need to do when you want to upgrade the Activiti database to a new version.

15.1.4   *Upgrading the Activiti database*

In the past, there have been database changes with almost every release of the Activiti framework, but, since version 5.7, the database model may be considered stable. Nevertheless, a new version of the Activiti framework may require database changes. You don't want to clean your database out and start all over again with the new database scripts. Fortunately, the `org.activiti.db.upgrade` package in the Activiti Engine JAR contains the database scripts necessary to upgrade your database (see figure 15.5).

The upgrade scripts are categorized by database type and version upgrade. As you can see in figure 15.5,

```
▼ 🗄 activiti-engine-5.8.jar - M2_REPO/org/activiti/activit
  ▶ 🗄 org.activiti.db.create
  ▶ 🗄 org.activiti.db.drop
  ▶ 🗄 org.activiti.db.mapping
  ▶ 🗄 org.activiti.db.mapping.entity
  ▼ 🗄 org.activiti.db.upgrade
        activiti.db2.upgradestep.53.to.54.engine.sql
        activiti.db2.upgradestep.53.to.54.history.sql
        activiti.db2.upgradestep.53.to.54.identity.sql
        activiti.db2.upgradestep.54.to.55.engine.sql
        activiti.db2.upgradestep.54.to.55.history.sql
        activiti.db2.upgradestep.56.to.57.history.sql
        activiti.h2.upgradestep.50.to.51.engine.sql
        activiti.h2.upgradestep.50.to.51.history.sql
        activiti.h2.upgradestep.52.to.53.history.sql
        activiti.h2.upgradestep.53.to.54.engine.sql
        activiti.h2.upgradestep.53.to.54.history.sql
        activiti.h2.upgradestep.53.to.54.identity.sql
        activiti.h2.upgradestep.54.to.55.engine.sql
        activiti.h2.upgradestep.54.to.55.history.sql
        activiti.h2.upgradestep.56.to.57.history.sql
```

Figure 15.5   Some of the upgrade scripts available in the Activiti Engine JAR

the last database update was from version 5.6 to 5.7 and only contained the following update:

```
alter table ACT_HI_PROCINST
add SUPER_PROCESS_INSTANCE_ID_ varchar(64);
```

This example is for the H2 database, and all it did was add a new column to the ACT_HI_PROCINST table.

When you want to upgrade to a new version of Activiti that contains database upgrades, look in the `org.activiti.db.upgrade` package of the Activiti Engine JAR. Then, take some time to see the database changes and whether you can expect problems with your running process instances. Always make a database backup before you execute the upgrade script and make sure that there are no running process instances.

Also, be aware that if you want to execute the upgrade database scripts manually, you have to configure the Activiti Engine not to update automatically. Otherwise, when you start the Activiti Engine with the JARs of a new version, the Activiti database will automatically be upgraded at startup. Here's the relevant process engine configuration setting:

```
<property name="databaseSchemaUpdate" value="true" />
```

By default, the `databaseSchemaUpdate` property is set to `false`, but you can override this as shown in the preceding code snippet.

To summarize the upgrade process, you can consider an upgrade of the Activiti database model to be much like the upgrade of any other application database model. You have to be careful and make backups, but it's certainly not rocket science.

By now, you've read through a lot of information regarding the Activiti database. Knowing the internal details of the Activiti framework should help when you're developing process solutions. In addition, it's always nice to be able to look up values in the database when you're testing and debugging. In the next section, we'll be talking about process versioning, which is also supported by the Activiti database model. You can look back at figure 15.1 to see that the process definition table contains a version (`VERSION_`) column, which represents the process definition version.

But, there are more challenges to cover before we can fully discuss process versioning. When you're running a process solution in production, it's important to understand what to do when you want to change the existing process solution and deploy a new version. In the next section, we'll discuss a number of best practices for dealing with process versioning.

15.2 *Dealing with process versioning*

Process versioning is an important topic in the rapidly changing environments of most organizations these days. New products have to be delivered to the market today, not tomorrow. And, the ever-increasing importance of the internet requires organizations to provide real-time information to customers about the status of their orders and keep a real-time inventory of products. All of these requirements lead to changes in business processes, so process definitions are mostly dynamic and changing instead of being static artifacts with only one version.

When the first version of a process definition is deployed to the Activiti Engine, the business needs may have already changed and the process definition may need to be adapted. A typical process definition makes use of services for the execution of business logic, so a change in the business logic might not lead to changes in the process definition itself. But, when you're working with process definitions on the Activiti Engine for a longer period of time, there will come a time when you need to deploy a new version of an existing process definition. What then?

Well, the versioning model of the Activiti Engine is quite simple. When a new version of a process definition is deployed, all newly started process instances will run against this new process definition, and all process instances that are already running will keep running against the older process definition version.

That's the default behavior, but the Activiti Engine is also capable of starting new process instances with older process definition versions. In the `RuntimeService` API, there's a method named `startProcessInstanceById` that requires a specific process definition identifier as an input parameter. You can call this method with the process definition identifier of an older process definition to start a new process instance with that specific version.

The versioning of process definitions, therefore, is relatively simple. It gets a lot harder with the Java service task and listener classes that are used in the process definition. When you use a Tomcat server with the Activiti Engine running embedded in a web application like the Activiti Explorer, there can only be one version of a specific Java class on the class path (see figure 15.6).

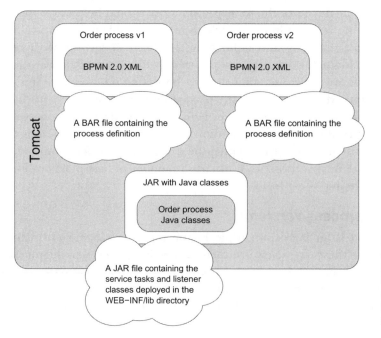

Figure 15.6   Two versions of the order process are deployed on a Tomcat server but there's only one version of the JAR file containing the Java classes of the order process .

In the order process example in figure 15.6, two versions of the process definition have been deployed. But, there can be only one version of a specific Java class on the classpath of the web application. This means that, when you change the implementation of a service task class and deploy a new version of the order process definition to the Tomcat server with a JAR containing the service task classes, this change will have a direct impact on any running process instances of the previous version of the order process definition.

If you want to prevent these issues, a good solution could be to change the class names or, better, the package names of the service task classes you want to update. This overcomes potential issues for the already-running process instances but it also introduces a new challenge for the version management of your process solutions. If you have a lot of process definitions that are changing, it can become a nightmare to keep track of all these different versions of service task classes and listeners. But, for a more static environment, changing the class names can be valid approach.

A more elegant solution is to use more flexible classloading environments like OSGi or JBoss with camunda fox, which we discussed in chapter 9. With camunda fox, for example, you can deploy new versions of a process definition in a single deployment archive, including the service task and listener classes (see figure 15.7).

When you have two versions of the order process running on camunda fox as shown in figure 15.7, the process instances running version 1 of the order process definition use a different classpath than the process instances running version 2. The JBoss server and JEE provide the functionality to run applications with different classpaths on one instance. You can use the same class name for a service task in both process archives, but each process definition will make use of their self-contained version of that Java class.

As you can see, process versioning is quite easy using the Activiti Engine. You have to be aware of its versioning capabilities and limitations, but, with the environment offered by camunda fox, there are no real barriers. Still, you have to keep in mind that the already-running process instances will keep running against the existing version of the process definition.

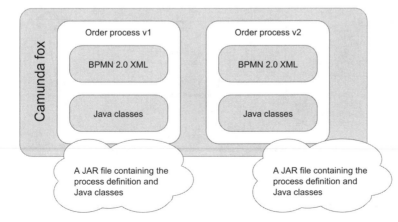

Figure 15.7 Overview of the process definition versioning solution provided by camunda fox. You can deploy two versions of a process definition, including its Java classes, in a single archive.

With that process versioning knowledge in your pocket, it's time to take a look at another important component of the Activiti Engine: the job executor. In a production environment, it's important to understand the functionality of the job executor and know how to deal with failed jobs.

15.3   *Understanding the job executor*

We've used the job executor in a number of process examples in the previous chapters. The job executor is used by the Activiti Engine to execute the asynchronous logic that's mainly needed for the timer and async continuation support.

In chapter 4, you were introduced to the default synchronous behavior of the process execution inside the Activiti Engine. You saw that, by default, the activities of a process instance are executed in a single transaction and Java thread. Only when the Activiti Engine encounters wait states like a user task or a receive task will the current transaction be committed to the Activiti Engine database and the Java thread be ended.

For process definitions consisting of only service tasks, the whole process instance is executed in a single transaction and Java thread. A Java class invoking the `start-ProcessInstanceByKey` method of the `RuntimeService` for this process definition won't get a response until the process instance is ended. In these kinds of process definitions, there's no need for asynchronous behavior, so the job executor isn't used.

But, when you add an `async` attribute with a value of `true` to a service task, you definitely do need asynchronous behavior. Figure 15.8 shows the flow of execution of a process definition with three service tasks, where one has been configured as asynchronous.

When a Java class starts a new process instance for the process definition as shown in figure 15.8, the Activiti Engine will execute the first service task and, then, the process state will be persisted to the Activiti database. When the process state is persisted, the Java class that started the process instance will receive a response containing the process instance object. But, the Activiti Engine has also created a new job in the job table discussed in section 15.1. And, this table is the starting point for the job executor.

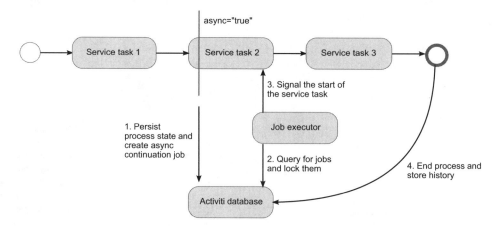

Figure 15.8   Overview of the workings of the job executor for async continuations

The `org.activiti.engine.impl.jobexecutor.JobExecutor` class starts a thread when the Activiti Engine is initialized to search for open jobs. By default, a maximum of three jobs per search are retrieved from the jobs table, and the jobs are locked before this job executor executes them. Locking jobs is important for environments where multiple Activiti Engines are running on the same database, as we'll discuss in a bit. When the job executor locks the jobs successfully, the jobs are executed individually in a thread pool.

For the async continuation example in figure 15.8, the running process instance is signaled, and service task 2 is executed, including the remaining synchronous activities. In this example, the whole process instance is completed, and eventually the Activiti database is updated and the history information is persisted.

It's important to be aware of possible exceptions thrown when the job executor executes the jobs. When you only use synchronous activities like Java service tasks, the Java class starting the process instance will receive exceptions thrown while executing the process logic. But, when the job executor encounters an exception, the Java class that started the process instance won't receive any feedback. The job scheduler will write the exception and its message to the job table in the Activiti database and will retry the job three times by default. After each retry, the job executor will wait for ten seconds by default, but you can change these parameters in the job executor configuration as shown in chapter 8. Therefore, in a production environment, it's important to keep an eye on the job table.

For timers like the timer start event or the intermediate timer event, the Activiti Engine also uses the job infrastructure and the job executor. This is done in a similar manner as described in figure 15.8 for the async continuations. When the Activiti Engine encounters a timer, the process state is persisted in the Activiti database and a new timer job is created in the job table. Because timers can have a complex timer configuration, the job executor contains intelligence to deal with reoccurring timers as well as timers that should be executed at a specific time.

When you're using the job executor with only one instance of the Activiti Engine, the previous information covers Activiti's asynchronous capability. But, in a lot of production environments, there will be more than one Activiti Engine running. This is needed for fail-over purposes but also for horizontal scaling of the environment when you're executing lots of process instances. In these cases, you'll have more than one job executor running on the Activiti database, and there can be potential conflicts with job executors retrieving and executing the same jobs. Figure 15.9 shows the locking implementation that the job executor uses to prevent these kinds of conflicts.

To be sure that only one job executor executes a job, the Activiti engine relies on the underlying database. When there are two job executors querying for open jobs on an Activiti database, the first job executor that's able to lock a job will execute it. When the job executor retrieves a job, it will try to lock that row by setting a lock owner value. The first job executor will be able to do this successfully, but the second job executor that tries to lock the same job will receive a locking exception; only the first job executor will execute the job.

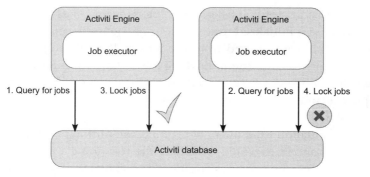

Figure 15.9 An overview of the environment where multiple Activiti Engines and job executors are running on one Activiti database

NOTE When a job executor receives a locking exception from the database, it will also log this exception, with a level of severe. This may be misleading because, in essence, there's no real error that you should worry about. In future versions of Activiti (at the time of writing, the latest version is 5.9) this may be solved by decreasing the logging level.

The job executor is an important component in the Activiti Engine because it provides an implementation for asynchronous capabilities like timer events and async continuations. It's no problem to run multiple job executors in one Activiti environment because there's built-in locking of jobs.

The Activiti Explorer provides a good interface for the current jobs in the Manage section available in the top level menu. This is a handy means to look for possible issues with failing jobs. In the next section, we'll build on the Activiti Explorer's management functionality and extend it with a functionality to be used by an administrator who needs the view of a running Activiti Engine.

15.4 *Building an administrator dashboard*

In order for administrators to maintain the Activiti Engine environment, you need an administration tool that doesn't require deep Activiti knowledge. The Activiti Explorer already provides a number of administration capabilities out of the box, providing deployment features, views on database tables, and lists of waiting jobs. But, this might not be enough to get a good grip on the Activiti environment if we don't dive into the XML configuration.

For example, the database configuration details are only available in the Activiti process engine configuration file. It's also not possible to get an overview of all running and completed process instances with just the Activiti Explorer. You can get a view of the running process instances that are started by the logged-in user, but this isn't usable for an administrator.

In this section, you'll see that it's not hard to enhance the Activiti Explorer and add missing capabilities to it.

The first step in enhancing the Activiti Explorer is to check out the source code from the Activiti SVN repository. This has already been done for you in the `book-manager` project in the book's source code.

Next, it's good to have some knowledge about the Vaadin framework (www.vaadin.com) and the internal workings of the Activiti Explorer. Vaadin is one of the most popular web frameworks today, and you can find a lot of information online, starting with the very good (and free) Vaadin book available on the Vaadin website.

To learn more about the Activiti Explorer architecture, a good way to start is to look at one of the management page implementations like the `UserPage` class that you'll find in the `org.activiti.explorer.ui.management.identity` package of the Activiti Explorer source code or the `book-manager` project. Let's take a look at the administration page you'll be adding to the Manage section of the Activiti Explorer (see figure 15.10).

As you can see in figure 15.10, you'll be adding a new administration menu item to the Manage section of the Activiti Explorer, and you'll offer a number of maintenance capabilities in that menu. First, you'll provide detailed overviews of all running and completed instances. You'll group these instances by process definition so you can also get a nice overview of the number of instances running for a specific process definition. In addition, you'll display information about the database and the history settings of the running Activiti Engine.

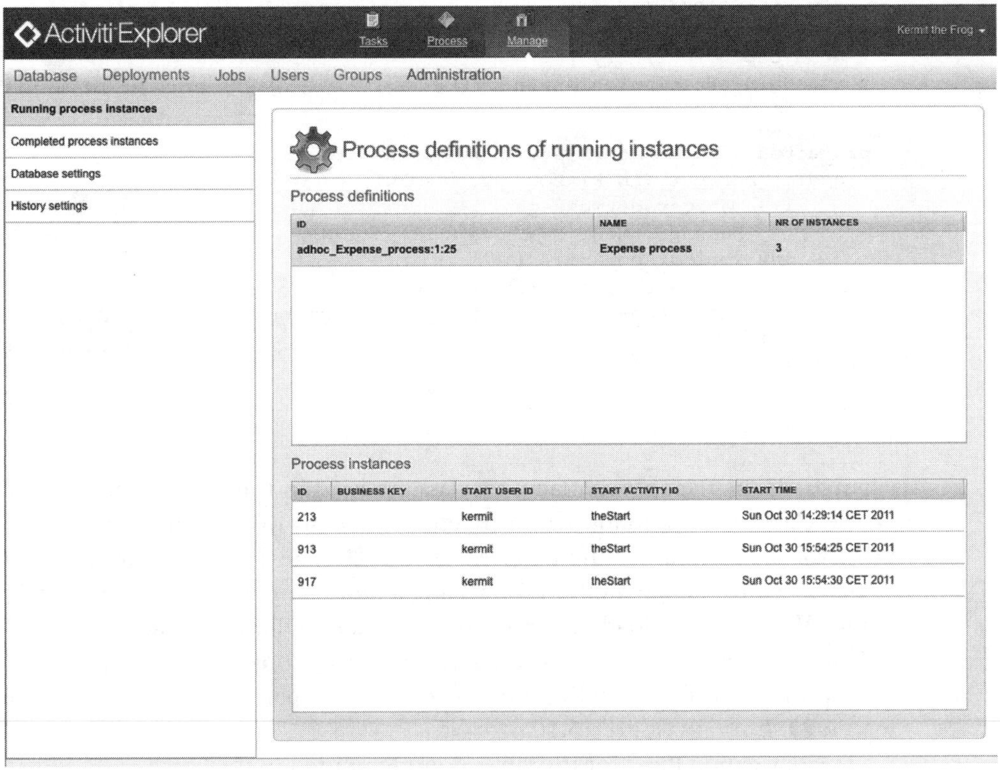

Figure 15.10   The additional administration panel that you'll be adding to the Activiti Explorer

Let's start at the beginning and add a new menu item to the Manage section. You can do this by making some changes to the ManagementMenuBar class in the book-manager project.

> **Listing 15.1   Changes to the ManagementMenuBar class for the new menu item**

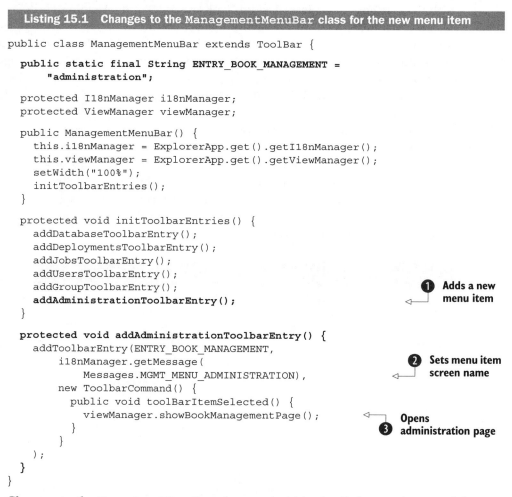

```
public class ManagementMenuBar extends ToolBar {

  public static final String ENTRY_BOOK_MANAGEMENT =
      "administration";

  protected I18nManager i18nManager;
  protected ViewManager viewManager;

  public ManagementMenuBar() {
    this.i18nManager = ExplorerApp.get().getI18nManager();
    this.viewManager = ExplorerApp.get().getViewManager();
    setWidth("100%");
    initToolbarEntries();
  }

  protected void initToolbarEntries() {
    addDatabaseToolbarEntry();
    addDeploymentsToolbarEntry();
    addJobsToolbarEntry();
    addUsersToolbarEntry();
    addGroupToolbarEntry();
    addAdministrationToolbarEntry();                      ❶ Adds a new
  }                                                          menu item

  protected void addAdministrationToolbarEntry() {
    addToolbarEntry(ENTRY_BOOK_MANAGEMENT,
        i18nManager.getMessage(                           ❷ Sets menu item
            Messages.MGMT_MENU_ADMINISTRATION),              screen name
        new ToolbarCommand() {
          public void toolBarItemSelected() {
            viewManager.showBookManagementPage();         ❸ Opens
          }                                                  administration page
        }
    );
  }
}
```

Changes to the ManagementMenuBar class are bold in the listing, and parts of the rest of the class implementation have been omitted so we can focus on these changes. First, you need to add a new toolbar entry ❶. The ToolBar provides an addToolbarEntry convenience method for adding a new menu item. You can provide a screen name ❷, which is loaded from the internationalization files in the src/main/resources folder of the book-manager project (look, for example, at the messages.properties file). Finally, you can define the page class for the administration screen ❸ shown in figure 15.10.

The navigation logic for the views is implemented in the DefaultViewManager class on which you invoke the showBookManagementPage (via its interface ViewManager). In the DefaultViewManager class, you need to add the following method:

```
public void showBookManagementPage() {
  switchView(new BookManagementPage(),
      ViewManager.MAIN_NAVIGATION_MANAGE,
          ManagementMenuBar.ENTRY_BOOK_MANAGEMENT);
}
```

That's all the plumbing code you need to define a new menu item in the Manage section.

We can now start with the implementation of the BookManagementPage, which defines the navigation menu on the left side (see figure 15.10), where you can choose the administration functionality you want to see. To understand a bit better how the navigation logic is implemented, the main part of the createList method is shown in the next listing.

Listing 15.2 Implementation of the administration menu navigation logic

```
managementTable.addContainerProperty(                          Adds one column
    "name", String.class, null);                           ❶ property
managementTable.setColumnHeaderMode(
    Table.COLUMN_HEADER_MODE_HIDDEN);

managementTable.addItem(new String[] {
    "Running process instances"}, 0);
managementTable.addItem(new String[] {                         Adds menu
    "Completed process instances"}, 1);                    ❷ item
managementTable.addItem(new String[] {
    "Database settings"}, 2);
managementTable.addItem(new String[] {
    "History settings"}, 3);

managementTable.addListener(                                    Defines menu
    new Property.ValueChangeListener() {                   ❸ click listener
  private static final long serialVersionUID = 1L;
  public void valueChange(ValueChangeEvent event) {
    Item item = managementTable.getItem(
        event.getProperty().getValue());

    if(item != null) {
      if("0".equals(event.getProperty()
          .getValue().toString())) {
        setDetailComponent(new RunningInstancesPanel());
      } else if("1".equals(event.getProperty()
          .getValue().toString())) {
        setDetailComponent(new CompletedInstancesPanel());     Sets right
      } else if("2".equals(event.getProperty()             ❹ detail panel
          .getValue().toString())) {
        setDetailComponent(new DatabaseSettingsPanel());
      } else if("3".equals(event.getProperty()
          .getValue().toString())) {
        setDetailComponent(new HistorySettingsPanel());
      }
    } else {
      // Nothing is selected
      setDetailComponent(null);
    }
  }
});
```

⚙ Process definitions of completed instances

Process definitions

ID	NAME	NR OF INSTANCES
loanrequestWithRules:1:123	Process to handle a loan request	1
adhoc_Expense_process:1:25	Expense process	2

Process instances

ID	BUSINESS KEY	START USER ID	START ACTIVITY ID	START TIME	END TIME	DURATION
921	kermit	theStart	Sun Oct 30 15:54:33 CET 2011	Sun Oct 30 15:55:02 CET 2011	29578
1013	kermit	theStart	Sun Oct 30 16:37:43 CET 2011	Sun Oct 30 16:38:03 CET 2011	19572

Figure 15.11 First part of the completed process instances screen, showing the process instances grouped by process definition

The left-side menu you want to add to the administration page contains only the name of the maintenance functionality, so you only need one row in the menu table ❶. You then add all the administration links to the menu list, including the completed process instances ❷. To be able to respond to a menu item selection, you add a listener to the menu table ❸. In the listener implementation, you can validate which item has been selected and open the right detail panel ❹. As you can see, this is quite easy to implement in the Activiti Explorer, and that's because of its convenience classes, which provide ready-to-use building blocks.

The implementation of the four detail panels contains quite a lot of Vaadin-specific code, but it's very readable; you can relate it directly to the screens. Let's have a quick look at the complete process instances overview. Because the screen is large, we'll split it up, starting with the process definition and corresponding process instances in figure 15.11.

In the first table of the completed process instances detail panel, the process definitions corresponding to the completed process instances found in the Activiti Engine are shown. The table also shows the number of process instances that have been completed for a specific process definition. When you click a process definition, the corresponding process instances are shown in the second table.

The following code snippet, which is part of the `CompletedInstancesPage` class, uses the `HistoryService` and `RepositoryService` to retrieve the process definition and instance information:

```
historyService.createHistoricProcessInstanceQuery().finished().list();
completedDefinitions = new HashMap<String, ManagementProcessDefinition>();
for (HistoricProcessInstance instance : instanceList) {
```

```
String processDefinitionId = instance.getProcessDefinitionId();
ManagementProcessDefinition managementDefinition = null;
if(completedDefinitions.containsKey(processDefinitionId)) {
  managementDefinition = completedDefinitions.get(processDefinitionId);

} else {
  ProcessDefinition definition = repositoryService
      .createProcessDefinitionQuery()
      .processDefinitionId(processDefinitionId)
      .singleResult();
  managementDefinition = new ManagementProcessDefinition();
  managementDefinition.processDefinition = definition;
  managementDefinition.runningInstances =
      new ArrayList<HistoricProcessInstance>();
  completedDefinitions.put(definition.getId(), managementDefinition);
}
  managementDefinition.runningInstances.add(instance);
}
```

For every completed process instance found in the Activiti database, the corresponding process definition is matched. Then, a map of process definitions with the corresponding completed process instances is constructed.

When you click a process instance in the second table, most of the details about that instance are retrieved and displayed on the screen, as shown in figure 15.12.

In the second part of the completed process instances screen, you retrieve the image of the process definition from the Activiti database and get all of the completed

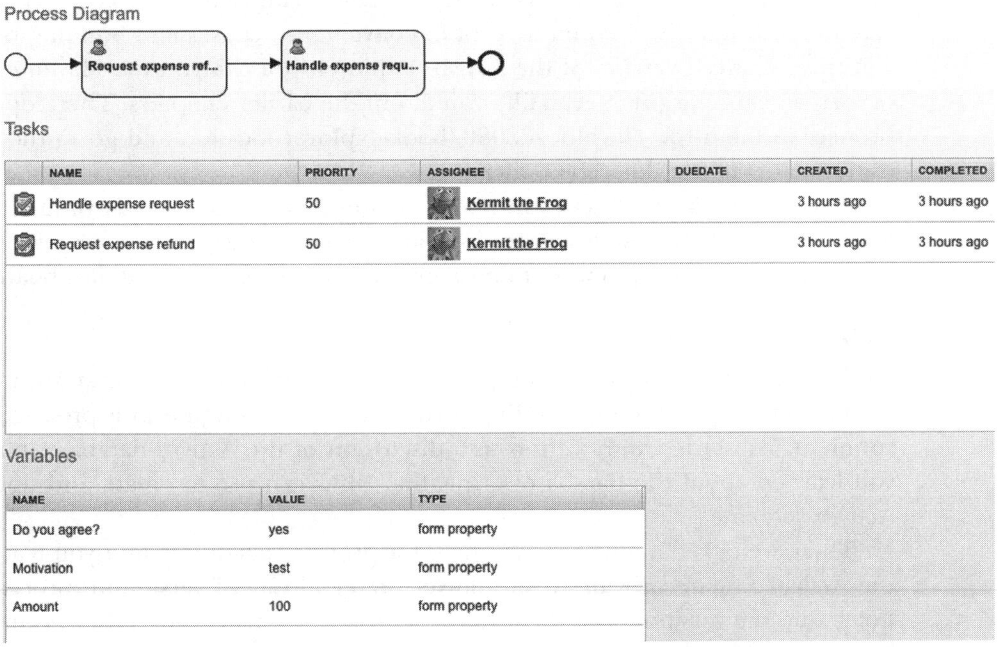

Figure 15.12 Second part of the completed process instances screen, showing the graphical diagram, the completed user tasks, and the form properties, along with other variables

user tasks and variable information, again using the history service. Note that, by default, the Activiti Explorer and the Activiti database are configured with a history level of audit. This means that no process variable updates are logged in the history tables but only the form properties of the user task forms (like the variables shown in figure 15.12).

If you want to change the history level of the Activiti database and the Activiti Explorer, there are two ways of configuring it. First, when the database schema update value is set to `true` in the process engine configuration, like this,

```
<property name="databaseSchemaUpdate" value="true" />
```

you only have to make changes to the history level configuration for the process engine. You can do this by changing the value in the applicationContext.xml file in the src/main/webapp/WEB-INF directory:

```
<property name="history" value="full" />
```

But, when the database schema update value is `false`, you have to make changes in two places. First, you have to change the `historyLevel` property in the Activiti database table ACT_GE_PROPERTY. You can do this by using a SQL GUI client like the open source SQuirrel SQL tool (www.squirrelsql.org). Just change the value of 2 to 3, which corresponds to the highest history level of full. Then, you also have to configure the same value in the applicationContext.xml file.

The `book-manager` project shows that it's not hard to make changes to the Activiti Explorer and add some additional functionality. The Activiti Explorer is built with reusability in mind and contains a lot of convenience classes and building blocks. To run the enhanced version of the Activiti Explorer, you can run the Maven command `mvn clean package jetty:run` like you did in the earlier chapters. Then, open a web browser to the http://localhost:8080/book-explorer location and go to the administration panel to test the web application.

This wraps up our discussion about creating an administration dashboard. One last recommendation: take a closer look at the source code of the `book-manager` project. It's a good start if you want to implement your own customized dashboard.

15.5 Summary

In this chapter, we looked at the parts of the Activiti framework that are important for maintaining and administrating a running Activiti Engine in a production environment. We started with a thorough discussion of the Activiti database model, and you learned about the database scripts that DBAs can use to create and upgrade an Activiti database.

Then, we talked about best practices for process versioning, and you learned that the Activiti Engine provides a simple yet powerful way of versioning process definitions. But, the versioning of the Java classes used by a process definition is more challenging. With some best practices and the optional use of more flexible classloading environments, like camunda fox, these challenges aren't hard to solve.

We also looked at the Activiti implementation of asynchronous behavior with the job executor. The job executor queries the Activiti database for open jobs in a separate ongoing thread and executes these jobs when they become available. The job executor implementation is developed with clustering and horizontal scaling in mind and uses a locking mechanism to make sure a job is executed only once.

Finally, we looked at ways to enhance the Activiti Explorer with additional administration capabilities. We built nice overview screens that display all running and completed process instances with their full details, like attached user tasks and process variables. With some knowledge of Vaadin, you can build great extensions in the Activiti Explorer yourself using the built-in building blocks and rich convenience classes.

This brings us to the end of this book. We've explored the full range of possibilities that the Activiti framework offers. We didn't only focus on the Activiti framework itself; we also explored ways of integrating with other frameworks like Alfresco, Esper, Drools, Mule, and Camel. This book provides a rich set of source code examples for you to use in your own projects.

I hope this book provides you with a good foundation for some great process solutions. I'm always interested to hear about your endeavors. The Activiti forum and the Manning book forum are good places to get in touch!

appendix A
Working with the source code

The source code accompanying this book is an important asset for getting up to speed with Activiti. You can either download the source code package from the Manning book website (www.manning.com/rademakers2) or you can check out the latest source code from the Google SVN repository (http://code.google.com/p/activitiinaction). Note that the Google SVN repository will be more up to date, and will be revised for new versions of the Activiti framework.

In this appendix, I'll provide an overview of the different projects that you'll find in this book's source code. We'll also take a closer look at the bpmn-examples project, which contains most of the code examples.

A.1   Overview of the source code projects

Because the source code contains a lot of different projects, it's good to get an overview of which project relates to which chapter in the book. In table A.1, you'll find all of the projects, with short descriptions and the respective chapters.

Table A.1   Overview of the projects that you can find in the book's source code

Project	Chapter	Short description
book-bam-app	14	The Vaadin web application that implements a BAM dashboard
book-camel	11	The Camel examples that are described in chapter 11
book-cdi-app	9	A web application that uses JSF 2.0 and CDI to implement a custom process and task application
book-explorer-form	10	A customized version of the Activiti Explorer that implements an additional form field type for a text area
book-jee6	9	An example of a JEE6 process and EJB application that can be deployed on a camunda fox server

Table A.1 Overview of the projects that you can find in the book's source code *(continued)*

Project	Chapter	Short description
book-manager	15	A customized version of the Activiti Explorer that implements an additional administration page in the Manage section
book-mule	11	The Mule examples described in chapter 11
book-osgi-app	9	A number of OSGI bundle subprojects that can be deployed on Apache Karaf to implement an OSGi-based process solution
book-rest-app	8	A customized version of the Activiti REST web application that implements an additional REST service
book-rules-app	12	A web application that provides functionality to manage rules deployed on the Activiti Engine
book-sales-app	7 and 11	A web application that implements web services used in the error handling examples of chapter 7 and the web service task example of chapter 11
bpmn-examples	Most of the chapters	Contains most of the code examples of the book (there's more about this project in the next section)

As you can see in table A.1, most of the source code examples can be found in the bpmn-examples project. In later chapters, the examples are implemented in separate projects because they result in different deployment artifacts, like a web application or OSGi bundles. We'll look in more detail at using the bpmn-examples project in the next section.

A.2   *Using the bpmn-examples project*

All the source code projects have Maven pom.xml files to resolve the dependencies and, when mentioned in the example implementation, descriptions to build the deployment artifacts. If you're not familiar with Maven, you can learn about it in a five-minute tutorial on the Maven website (http://maven.apache.org).

Although you can use the example projects in every code editor, the preferred way is to use Eclipse. That's because you'll also use the Activiti Designer Eclipse plugin now and then in this book. Note that, to get the projects installed with the right dependencies in Eclipse, you need to generate the classpath and project files. There are two main ways to do this.

The first and fully supported method is to use the command line to run mvn eclipse:eclipse in every root folder of the different source code projects. If you haven't already imported the projects via the Eclipse Subversion plugin, you can import the projects you want in Eclipse, and the dependencies will point to your Maven repository. To get the bpmn-examples project in Eclipse, you'll have to run mvn eclipse:eclipse (make sure you have installed Maven—the latest available version of 2.x or 3.x—and made the Maven bin directory available on the command line). Then you can import the project in Eclipse via the menu: File > Import > Existing Projects into Workspace.

You can alternatively use the Eclipse Maven plugin, which may not be installed by default but can easily be downloaded via the Eclipse Marketplace (Maven Integration for Eclipse). Following this path, you first have to import the source projects from the source code distribution or check out the sources from the Google Subversion repository. When the source code projects are imported, you can define them as Maven projects by right-clicking on a project and choosing Configure > Convert to Maven Project. When the project is configured as a Maven project, you can right-click on the project and choose Maven > Update Project Configuration, and the dependencies and source folders will be set up for you. For some projects, like the book-bam-app, the Maven Eclipse plugin doesn't recognize the plugin lifecycle. Solutions for this error are described on the Maven Eclipse plugin wiki page (http://wiki.eclipse.org/ M2E_plugin_execution_not_covered). But the easiest way to deal with this is to use the quick fix suggested by Eclipse.

The bpmn-examples project contains a Maven project structure with the unit tests in the src/test/java folder and the implementation classes in the src/main/java folder. As you may have noticed already while working with the examples in the book, I've used a lot of unit tests to easily start up the examples and test them. In the package names of the bpmn-examples project, you can find the chapter where the example is described. For example, the RuntimeServiceTest from chapter 4 has a package of org.bpmnwithactiviti.*chapter4*.api in the src/test/java folder.

For other examples, I've used Activiti Explorer to test the process definition. Because you need to create a BAR and often also a number of JAR files, I've developed Ant build scripts. One of the Ant build scripts is used for the loan request example described in chapter 5. In the src/main/resources/chapter5 folder, you can find an Ant build.xml script, which will generate a BAR file containing the loan request BPMN 2.0 XML file and a JAR file that contains the Java classes used in the loan request process definition. The BAR and JAR files are generated in a new dist directory that's created in the directory that contains the Ant build script.

If you run into issues using the source code, I'm happy to help you solve them. Just post a message on the Manning book forum or create an issue in the Google code repository. I hope you enjoy working with the examples!

appendix B
BPMN 2.0 supported elements in Activiti

As described in chapter 2, the full BPMN 2.0 specification consists of a large range of elements. Activiti provides support for the common BPMN 2.0 elements, so it's important to know which BPMN 2.0 elements are supported and which Activiti extensions are implemented for these elements. The Activiti user guide already provides a good overview of the supported elements, but this appendix is available offline and provides a slightly different angle on the BPMN 2.0 elements, focusing on the usage options.

The BPMN 2.0 elements can be categorized in some basic groups:

- Start and end events
- Tasks
- Other activities
- Intermediate events
- Sequence flows
- Gateways
- Boundary events

In the following subsections, the supported BPMN 2.0 elements are discussed in these element groupings.

B.1 Start and end events

The following start and end events will be described in this section:

- None start event
- Timer start event
- None end event
- Error end event

B.1.1 None start event

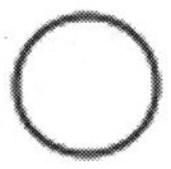

The none start event is the simplest start event element that can be started using the Activiti API, such as with the startProcess-InstanceByKey method of the RuntimeService interface. The graphical representation is shown in figure B.1.

Figure B.1 None start event

The XML representation of the none start event is

```
<startEvent id="startEvent" name="Start event" />
```

The attributes shown in table B.1 can be configured on a none start event.

Table B.1 Attributes of a none start event

Attribute name	Short description	Example
activiti:formKey	The Activiti form key extension attribute can be used to add an external form definition to a start event.	`<startEvent id="startEvent" formKey="test.form" />`
activiti:initiator	An initiator is an Activiti extension attribute to create a process variable that will hold the name of the initiator user—the user who started the process instance.	`<startEvent id="startEvent" initiator="initiator" />`

You can also define form properties on a start event. This is described in the User task description later on.

B.1.2 Timer start event

The timer start event can be used to start a new process instance at a specific time interval or at a specific date. It can be used to start more than one process instance after every time interval, or it can be used to start a process instance only once at a specific date and time. The graphical representation is shown in figure B.2.

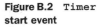

Figure B.2 Timer start event

The XML representation of the timer start event is

```
<startEvent id="timerStartEvent" name="Timer start event">
  <timerEventDefinition>
    <timeCycle>R10/2012-12-12T00:00/PT24H</timeCycle>
  </timerEventDefinition>
</startEvent>
```

This XML configuration example shows the use of a time cycle defined with a recurring time duration according to ISO 8601. It says that a new process instance will be started 10 times, starting at 2012-12-12 midnight with a time interval of 24 hours. Table B.2 shows the different timer event definitions that can be used for a timer start event.

Table B.2   Timer event definition elements for a timer start event

Element name	Short description	Example

timeDate	A specific date and time when a new process instance should be started. You can use static ISO 8601 time definitions with an ISO 8601 string.	`<timeDate>`
		`  ${startTime}`
		`</timeDate>`

timeDuration	A timer interval for which the Activiti Engine waits to start a new process instance. You can use static ISO 8601 duration definitions with an ISO 8601 string.	`<timeDuration>`
		`  PT5M`
		`<timeDuration/>`

timeCycle	A time cycle that's used to start a specific number of process instances after every time interval. You can use static ISO 8601 cycle definitions with an ISO 8601 string.	`<timeCycle>`
		`  R20/2012-01-`
		`01T00:00:00/PT1M`
		`</timeCycle>`

B.1.3   *None end event*

The none end event is the simplest end event element. When a none end event is reached, the process instance will be completed. The graphical representation is shown in figure B.3.

The XML representation of the none end event is

Figure B.3   None end event

```
<endEvent id="endEvent" name="End event" />
```

There are no additional attributes or elements that can be defined on a none end event.

B.1.4   *Error end event*

The error end event can be used to end a process instance by throwing an error. This can be useful in combination with an error boundary event. An error boundary event can be configured on a call activity or an embedded subprocess to catch a potential error and handle it in a different flow. The graphical representation of the error end event is shown in figure B.4.

Figure B.4   Error end event

The XML representation of the error end event is

```
<endEvent id="errorEndEvent" name="Error end event">
  <errorEventDefinition errorRef="anError" />
</endEvent>
```

This XML configuration example shows the use of an error event definition that throws an error with the name anError. You can choose to let the error reference attribute point to an error definition or, if none is specified, to let it use the actual error name.

An error definition looks like the following code snippet:

```
<error id="anErrorId" errorCode="aNewErrorCode" />
<endEvent id="errorEndEvent">
  <errorEventDefinition errorRef="anErrorId" />
</endEvent>
```

Table B.3 shows the error reference attribute with a short description and example.

Table B.3   Error event definition attribute for an `error` end event

Attribute name	Short description	Example
errorRef	An error code pointing to an error definition element or a textual error indicator that can be directly used as the error code that's thrown.	`<errorEventDefinition errorRef="notFound" />`

B.2   Sequence flows

The following sequence flows will be described in this section:

- Sequence flow
- Conditional sequence flow

B.2.1   Sequence flow

A sequence flow is used to define the process flow. The standard sequence flow does nothing more than connect two elements, a source and a target element. The graphical representation of a sequence flow is shown in figure B.5.

Figure B.5   Sequence flow

The XML representation of the sequence flow is

```
<sequenceFlow id="flow" sourceRef="startEvent" targetRef="userTask" />
```

In addition, you can also configure an Activiti-specific extension for a sequence flow, named an *execution listener*. This execution listener class is executed when the sequence flow is executed (see table B.4 for a short description and an example).

Table B.4   Extension elements definition of a sequence flow

Element name	Short description	Example

activiti: executionListener	An execution listener defined on a sequence flow will be executed when the sequence flow is taken by the Activiti Engine. The configuration is very similar to a Java service task, so you can use a class or a delegateExpression attribute. In addition, you can use field extensions when using the class attribute.	`<sequenceFlow`
		`   id="flow"`
		`   sourceRef="startEvent"`
		`   targetRef="userTask">`
		`<extensionElements>`
		`<activiti:executionListener`
		`class="com.TestListener"/>`
		`</extensionElements>`
		`</sequenceFlow>`

B.2.2   Conditional sequence flow

A conditional sequence flow is like a standard sequence flow, but it has a conditional expression attached to it. Only when the conditional expression validates to true will

the Activiti Engine execute the sequence flow path. Usually the conditional sequence flow is used together with an
exclusive or inclusive gateway but it's not limited to that.
The graphical representation is shown in figure B.6.

**Figure B.6   Conditional
sequence flow**

The XML representation of the conditional sequence flow is

```
<sequenceFlow id="invalidOrderFlow"
    sourceRef="startEvent"
    targetRef="userTask">
  <conditionExpression xsi:type="tFormalExpression">
    <![CDATA[${orderValid == false}]]>
  </conditionExpression>
</sequenceFlow>
```

A condition expression typically consists of a combination of process variables with
conditional operators. In addition, you can also configure an execution listener as
shown in the description of the standard sequence flow.

B.3   *Tasks*

The following sequence flows will be described in this section:

- Business rule task
- Email task
- Manual Task
- Receive task
- User task
- Camel task
- Java service task
- Mule task
- Script task
- Web service task

B.3.1   *Generic task configuration*

Some process functionality is supported for every task type when using the Activiti
Engine. In this first subsection, we'll look at these generic task configuration items
before we dive into the details of the different task types.

ASYNCHRONOUS CONTINUATIONS

The first generic configuration item is the asynchronous continuation support. You
can define the `async` attribute for every task type as follows:

```
<serviceTask id="serviceTask" class="com.TestTask" async="true" />
```

When a task is defined to be executed asynchronously, the Activiti Engine will store
the process state and create a job when the task is encountered. The job executor, as
described in chapter 15, will execute the job and, therefore, the task instance.

EXECUTION LISTENERS

Another generic task configuration item is the execution listener. The execution listener configuration has already been shown in the standard sequence flow description. For task types, you can define a start or end event to instruct the Activiti Engine
to execute the execution listener when the task is started or ended.

The following code example shows a start event execution listener implemented
with a Java class:

```
<serviceTask id="task" activiti:class="org.bpmnwithactiviti.TestTask">
  <extensionElements>
    <activiti:executionListener
        class="org.bpmnwithactiviti.TestListener"
        event="start"/>
  </extensionElements>
</serviceTask>
```

You can also define execution listeners using an expression or a delegate expression configuration instead of a class. The following short code snippet shows an execution listener with an expression and an end event definition:

```
<activiti:executionListener
    expression="${testListener.processEvent(execution.eventName)}"
    event="end"/>
```

This example will invoke the processEvent method on the object that's registered in the Activiti context with the name testListener (for example, a Spring bean or a process variable). For an execution listener with a class definition, you can also use field extensions like those we'll see with a Java service task (see B.3.5).

MULTI-INSTANCE

By default, every activity (every task, call activity, and embedded subprocess) is executed only once when the process token reaches the activity. But, sometimes, you'll want to execute an activity multiple times.

In chapter 10, we described a use case of the multi-instance construct with the user task. When you want to let a group of colleagues review a specific document, you need to create a user task for every member of the group. That's exactly the functionality that a multi-instance construct can provide for a process definition. You can configure every activity (every task, call activity, and embedded subprocess) to be a multi-instance construct.

In the following example, a user task is configured to be multi-instance:

```
<userTask id="userTask" activiti:assignee="${assignee}">
  <multiInstanceLoopCharacteristics isSequential="false">
    <loopDataInputRef>userList</loopDataInputRef>
    <inputDataItem name="assignee" />
  </multiInstanceLoopCharacteristics>
</userTask>
```

In this example, you create a user task for every item in the userList collection, which refers to a process variable. Every item in the collection is set as a local process variable assignee for every user task. Then you can use this assignee local variable as the assignee of the user task.

This example also defines the multi-instance user task to be non-sequential (with the isSequential attribute). This means that all user tasks are created in parallel—all at once. When the isSequential attribute is set to true, the next user task is created after the previous user task is completed.

Another way to get a collection that represents the number of multi-instance items is shown in the next code snippet:

```
<userTask id="userTask" activiti:assignee="${assignee}">
  <multiInstanceLoopCharacteristics isSequential="false"
      activiti:collection="${identityBean.resolveAssignees()}"
      activiti:elementVariable="assignee" />
</serviceTask>
```

In this example, the multi-instance items are retrieved via an expression that points to the `resolveAssignees` method of the `identityBean`, which is registered within the Activiti context as a Spring bean.

It's also possible to define a different completion condition. By default, all instances should be completed before the process execution will continue, but you can also define a formula so that only 75 percent of the instances need to be completed before the process execution continues:

```
<userTask id="userTask" activiti:assignee="${assignee}">
  <multiInstanceLoopCharacteristics isSequential="false"
      activiti:collection="userList"
      activiti:elementVariable="assignee">
    <completionCondition>
      ${nrOfCompletedInstances/nrOfInstances >= 0.75 }
    </completionCondition>
  </multiInstanceLoopCharacteristics>
</serviceTask>
```

You can also keep the multi-instance configuration far simpler. When, for example, you want to execute a service task three times, you can do it like this:

```
<serviceTask id="serviceTask" activiti:class="org.ServiceTask">
  <multiInstanceLoopCharacteristics isSequential="true">
    <loopCardinality>3</loopCardinality>
  </multiInstanceLoopCharacteristics>
</serviceTask>
```

You can also use expressions in the `loopCardinality` definition to define a more complex loop instruction.

B.3.2   *Business rule task*

A business rule task can be used to execute business rules with the values of process variables as input. Activiti uses the Drools framework to execute business rules that are deployed with a .drl file together with the process definition. The graphical representation is shown in figure B.7.

Figure B.7   Business rule task

The XML representation of the business rule task is

```
<businessRuleTask id="ruleTask" name="Rule task"
    activiti:ruleVariablesInput="${ruleInputVariable}"
    activiti:resultVariable="ruleOutputVariable"
/>
```

In this example, all rules that are deployed together with the process definition will be executed. The value of the `ruleInputVariable` process variable will be placed on the

Drools rules context and can therefore be used in the rule execution. When the Drools rule execution results in return values, these will be placed in the `ruleOutput-Variable` process variable. This process variable is always a collection of objects that contains all the Drools output variables.

The attributes shown in table B.5 can be configured on a business rule task.

Table B.5   Attributes of the business rule task

Attribute name	Short description	Example
`activiti:ruleVariablesInput`	The Activiti Engine passes these input variables on to the Drools rule context. You can provide more than one variable, using a comma as the separator.	```<businessRuleTask id="ruleTask" activiti: ➥ ruleVariablesInput= ➥ "${var1}, ${var2}" />```
`activiti:resultVariable`	All output variables of the Drools context will be placed in a collection object with the process variable name defined by this attribute.	```<businessRuleTask id="ruleTask" activiti:resultVariable= ➥ "resultVar" />```
`activiti:rules`	When you don't want to execute all rules that are deployed, you can use the `rules` attribute to define the rules you want to execute or exclude (when the exclude attribute is set to `true`).	```<businessRuleTask id="ruleTask" activiti:rules= ➥ "ruleA, ruleB" />```
`activiti:exclude`	The exclude attribute can be used in combination with the `rules` attribute to exclude certain rules. By default, exclude is `false`.	```<businessRuleTask id="ruleTask" activiti:exclude="true" activiti:rules="ruleA" />```

B.3.3   Camel task

The Camel task isn't part of the BPMN 2.0 specification because it implements the Activiti Camel integration. You can invoke a Camel route from a process definition by defining a service task with a delegate expression pointing to the Camel context. The graphical representation, therefore, is a service task, as shown in figure B.8.

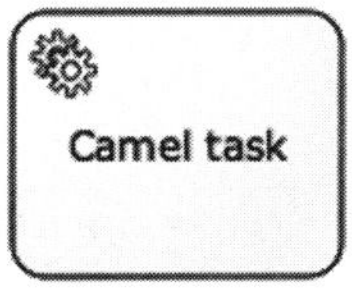

Figure B.8   Camel task

The XML representation of the Camel task is

```
<serviceTask id="camelTask" delegateExpression="${camel}" />
```

Chapter 11 discusses how the delegate expression is coupled to the Camel context via the `CamelBehaviour` class provided by the Activiti Camel module.

B.3.4   *Email task*

An email task can be used to send an email based on the process variables available in the process instance. This task isn't part of the BPMN 2.0 specification but is implemented as a service task with an Activiti-specific type definition. The graphical representation shown in figure B.9, therefore, is the same as for a service task.

Figure B.9   Email task

The XML representation of an email task is

```
<serviceTask id="emailTask" name="Email task" activiti:type="mail">
  <extensionElements>
    <activiti:field name="from"
        stringValue="info@bpmnwithactiviti.org" />
    <activiti:field name="to"
        expression="${recipientVariable}" />
    <activiti:field name="subject"
        expression="Your order request ${orderId} has been received" />
    <activiti:field name="text"
        expression="Thanks for the order" />
  </extensionElements>
</serviceTask>
```

The email task contains all the element definitions that you expect when sending an email, so you can define the `from` and `to` recipients, a `subject`, and an email body. You can use static text values, but also expressions like those shown in the `to` and `subject` field definitions. All the supported field names are shown in table B.6.

Table B.6   Field names for the email task

Field name	Short description	Example

To	The to recipients (comma separated)	`<activiti:field`
		`    name="to"`
		`    expression="${to}"`
		`/>`

From	The from recipient	`<activiti:field`
		`    name="from"`
		`    expression="${from}"`
		`/>`

Subject	The subject of the email	`<activiti:field`
		`    name="subject"`
		`    expression="${subject}"`
		`/>`

Cc	The cc recipients (comma separated)	`<activiti:field`
		`    name="cc"`
		`    expression="${cc1}, ${cc2}"`
		`/>`

Table B.6 Field names for the email task *(continued)*

Field name	Short description	Example

Bcc	The bcc recipients (comma separated)	```xml
		<activiti:field
		    name="bcc"
		    expression="${bcc}"
		/>
		``

Charset	The charset for the email	```xml
		<activiti:field
		    name="charset"
		    expression="${charset}"
		/>
		``

Text	The mail body defined with a simple string	```xml
		<activiti:field
		    name="text"
		    expression="${email}"
		/>
		``

html	The mail body defined with a HTML string	```xml
		<activiti:field
		    name="html">
		    <activiti:expression>
		        <![CDATA[
		        <html>
		            <body>
		                Hello ${male ? 'Mr.' : 'Mrs.'}
		                ${recipientName},
		
		            </body>
		        </html>
		        ]]>
		    </activiti:expression>
		</activiti:field>
		``

B.3.5 *Java service task*

The Java service task isn't a standard BPMN 2.0 element because it's focused on supporting custom Java logic, which isn't defined in the BPMN 2.0 specification. The BPMN 2.0 element used for the definition of a Java service task is the service task element (see figure B.10).

Figure B.10 Java service task

The XML representation of the Java service task is

```xml
<serviceTask id="serviceTask" name="Service task"
    activiti:class="org.bpmnwithactiviti.ServiceDelegate" />
```

This is a simple example of a Java service task that points to a Java class, which implements a `JavaDelegate` or `ActivityBehavior` interface. You can configure a number of attributes in the service task element, and you can add field extensions when using a Java service task class configuration.

The attributes shown in table B.7 can be configured on a Java service task.

Table B.7   Attributes of the Java service task

Attribute name	Short description	Example

`activiti:class`	The logic of the service task class is implemented in a Java class that implements the `Java-Delegate` or `Activit-Behavior` interface.	`<serviceTask`
		`  id="serviceTask"`
		`  activiti:class=`
		`    ➥ "org.ServiceDelegate"`
		`/>`

`activiti:`
`expression`
	The expression points to a UEL method or attribute value. You can, for example, point to a Spring bean and invoke a specific method. You can also pass process variables and the execution instance as input parameters for the method invocation.	`<serviceTask`
		`  id="serviceTask"`
		`  activiti:expression=`
		`    ➥ "#{orderBean.order()"`
		`/>`

`activiti:`
`delegateExpression`
	A delegate expression provides a flexible way to invoke a `JavaDelegate` or `ActivityBehavior` class with an expression pointing to the Activiti registry like a Spring bean.	`<serviceTask`
		`  id="serviceTask"`
		`activiti:delegateExpression=`
		`    ➥ "#{delegateBean}"`
		`/>`

`activiti:`
`resultVariable`
	The result variable attribute defines the process variable name for the result value of the class or the expression invocation.	`<serviceTask`
		`  id="serviceTask"`
		`  activiti:class=`
		`    ➥ "org.ServiceDelegate"`
		`  activiti:resultVariable=`
		`    ➥ "result"`
		`/>`

For Java service task elements with a class attribute, you can specify field extensions to inject static values or process variables in the Java class. Here's an example of a field expression:

```
<serviceTask id="serviceTask" activiti:class="org.ServiceDelegate">
  <extensionElements>
    <activiti:field name="introText"
      expression="Hello ${gender == 'male' ? 'Mr.' : 'Mrs.'} ${name}" />
  </extensionElements>
</serviceTask>
```

It's also possible to use static string values by using the `stringValue` attribute instead of the `expression` attribute.

B.3.6   *Manual task*

The manual task is the simplest task type available in BPMN 2.0. The Activiti Engine will just process the task as an empty node and proceed to the next sequence flow. The graphical representation is shown in figure B.11.

Figure B.11   Manual task

The XML representation of the manual task is

```
<manualTask id="manualTask" name="Manual task" />
```

B.3.7 Mule task

The Mule task isn't a standard BPMN 2.0 element because it implements the Activiti Mule integration. While the Camel task uses a service task type, the Mule task is implemented as a send task (see figure B.12).

The XML representation of the Mule task is

Figure B.12 Mule task

```
<sendTask id="muleTask" activiti:type="mule">
  <extensionElements>
    <activiti:field name="endpointUrl">
      <activiti:string>vm://in</activiti:string>
    </activiti:field>
    <activiti:field name="language">
      <activiti:string>juel</activiti:string>
    </activiti:field>
    <activiti:field name="payloadExpression">
      <activiti:expression>${payload}</activiti:expression>
    </activiti:field>
    <activiti:field name="resultVariable">
      <activiti:string>resultVar</activiti:string>
    </activiti:field>
  </extensionElements>
</sendTask>
```

This example uses an embedded Mule instance because you're sending a message to the VM queue in the same Java virtual machine as the Activiti instance. You can also use JMS or another remote protocol and invoke a Mule instance that runs standalone.

The `language` field defines the language used to evaluate the payload expression, which is usually JUEL. Then you can define the payload with an expression and send a process variable to a Mule instance. You can also define a process variable name to specify where you want to store the return message.

These are all the supported fields for the Mule task.

B.3.8 Receive task

The `receive` task is actually a Java receive task, as it can only be signaled via the Activiti API. The process instance will wait until the signal method is invoked. The graphical representation is shown in figure B.13.

The XML representation of the receive task is

```
<receiveTask id="receiveTask" name="Receive task" />
```

Figure B.13 Receive task

With the `RuntimeService` signal method, you can trigger the process instance to go to the next element in the process definition.

B.3.9 *Script task*

The script task is a handy BPMN 2.0 element that implements a short piece of logic without your needing to write Java. Common scripting languages that can be used are Groovy and JavaScript, but you can use any JSR-223 compliant scripting language as long as the scripting engine is available on the classpath. The graphical representation is shown in figure B.14.

Figure B.14   Script task

The XML representation of the script task is

```
<scriptTask id="scriptTask" scriptFormat="groovy">
  <script>
    def name = "Activiti"
    execution.setVariable("name", name);
  </script>
</scriptTask>
```

This example defines a script task with the Groovy language. A local variable name is created in the script, and its value is set as a new process variable. The Activiti Engine injects the execution variable, so you can use the execution instance in the script logic.

Table B.8 shows the attributes of the script task that you can use.

Table B.8   Attributes of the script task

Attribute name	Short description	Example
scriptFormat	The scripting language that's used to implement the script logic. Languages that are available in Activiti by default are JavaScript, Groovy, and JUEL, but you can use any JSR-223 compatible script engine as long as it's available on the classpath.	`<scriptTask id="scriptTask" scriptFormat="juel" />`
activiti: resultVariable	The process variable name to set the result value of the script logic.	`<scriptTask id="scriptTask" scriptFormat="juel" activiti:resultVariable=` ➥ `"result" />`

B.3.10 *User task*

The user task is a standard BPMN 2.0 element that can be used to implement workflow logic in a process definition. You can set several configuration items on a user task, such as the due date, the priority, and the assignee. The graphical representation of a user task is shown in figure B.15.

The XML representation of the user task is

Figure B.15   User task

```
<userTask id="userTask" activiti:assignee="kermit"
    activiti:dueDate="${deadline}" />
```

This user task will be assigned to Kermit with a due date that's equal to the `deadline` process variable.

The user or group assignment is an important part of a user task configuration. You can use the BPMN 2.0 standard elements or use the Activiti shorthand extensions. Both definitions will result in the same behavior. Let's walk through the different methods of configuration, starting with assigning one user:

```
<userTask id="userTask">
  <humanPerformer>
    <resourceAssignmentExpression>
      <formalExpression>kermit</formalExpression>
    </resourceAssignmentExpression>
  </humanPerformer>
</userTask>
```

The Activiti shorthand equivalent is the following user task definition:

```
<userTask id="userTask" activiti:assignee="kermit" />
```

To define a candidate user or group, you can use the following standard BPMN 2.0 configuration:

```
<userTask id="userTask">
  <potentialOwner>
    <resourceAssignmentExpression>
      <formalExpression>
        user(fozzie), group(sales), management
      </formalExpression>
    </resourceAssignmentExpression>
  </potentialOwner>
</userTask>
```

As you can see, you actually define a potential owner of a user task. You can combine user and group definitions, as shown in the example, or use only one type of candidate definition. When you don't define the type user or group, like was done with management in the previous example, the default type is group. The shorthand definition of this example is

```
<userTask id="userTask"
    activiti:candidateUsers="kermit"
    activiti:candidateGroups="sales, management" />
```

In addition to the assignment of a user task, you can also use the attributes described in table B.9.

Table B.9   Attributes of the user task

Attribute name	Short description	Example

`activiti:dueDate`	Defines the due date of the user task	`<userTask`
		`  id="userTask"`
		`  activiti:dueDate="${deadline}"`
		`/>`

Table B.9   Attributes of the user task *(continued)*

Attribute name	Short description	Example

`activiti:priority`	Defines the priority of the user task	`<userTask`
		`  id="userTask"`
		`  activiti:priority=`
		`      ➡ "${priority}"`
		`/>`

On a user task, you can also define a special type of listener, named the *task listener*. You can use `assignment`, `create`, and `complete` events. In the following example, you define a task listener with the `complete` event:

```
<userTask id="userTask">
  <extensionElements>
    <activiti:taskListener
        class="org.bpmnwithactiviti.TestTaskListener"
        event="complete" />
  </extensionElements>
</userTask>
```

You can use the same method of configuration for a task listener as for an execution listener. You can use an `expression` and a `delegateExpression`, and you can define field extensions when you use the `class` attribute.

B.3.11 *Web service task*

The web service task is a standard BPMN 2.0 element that can be used to invoke an external web service. As you'll see, the web service task configuration contains quite a lot of XML elements. As an alternative, you can use a Java service task to invoke a web or REST service. The graphical representation of a web service task is shown in figure B.16.

Figure B.16   Web service task

The XML representation of the web service task is

```
<serviceTask id="webServiceTask" implementation="##WebService"
    operationRef="tns:hello">
  <ioSpecification>
    <dataInput itemSubjectRef="tns:findCustomerAddressRequestItem"
        id="dataInput" />
    <dataOutput itemSubjectRef="tns:findCustomerAddressResponseItem"
        id="dataOutput" />
    <inputSet>
      <dataInputRefs>dataInput</dataInputRefs>
    </inputSet>
    <outputSet>
      <dataOutputRefs>dataOutput</dataOutputRefs>
    </outputSet>
  </ioSpecification>
  <dataInputAssociation>
    <sourceRef>name</sourceRef>
```

```
      <targetRef>customerName</targetRef>
    </dataInputAssociation>
    <dataOutputAssociation>
      <sourceRef>address</sourceRef>
      <targetRef>webserviceResponse</targetRef>
    </dataOutputAssociation>
</serviceTask>
```

This web service task XML example comes from chapter 11, and only the service task definition is included here. For the full example, including the WSDL import and the item definition, see chapter 11, listings 11.1 and 11.2.

In the XML configuration, you can see that you have to define the input and output definitions. You correlate the WSDL input and output message to process variables. In this example, the process variable name is mapped to the WSDL input message part customerName, and the WSDL output message part address is mapped to a process variable webserviceResponse.

B.4   Gateways

The following gateways will be described in this section:

- Exclusive gateway
- Inclusive gateway
- Parallel gateway

B.4.1   Exclusive gateway

An exclusive gateway offers conditional logic to be used in a process definition. Only one of the outgoing sequence flows connected to an exclusive gateway will be executed. The first sequence flow whose condition equals true will be taken, and the rest of the sequence flows will be ignored. If no outgoing sequence flow can be taken, an exception will be thrown. To prevent this, you can set a default flow that will be executed when no condition is met. The graphical representation of an exclusive gateway is shown in figure B.17.

Figure B.17   Exclusive gateway

The XML representation of the exclusive gateway is

```
<exclusiveGateway id="exclusiveGateway"/>
```

The conditional logic is implemented in the sequence flows connected as outgoing flows to the exclusive gateway.

For more information about conditional sequence flows, you can look in the sequence flow section of this appendix. You can specify a default sequence flow like the one shown in the following example:

```
<exclusiveGateway id="exclusiveGateway" default="defaultFlow" />
```

B.4.2   Inclusive gateway

An inclusive gateway is like a parallel gateway but with conditional logic on the sequence flows. Every outgoing sequence flow connected to an inclusive gateway will be taken when the condition equals true. This is the main difference with the exclusive gateway, where only one sequence flow will be taken. When multiple incoming sequence flows are connected to an inclusive gateway, the gateway will wait until all sequence flows with a process token are completed, so an inclusive gateway has fork behavior with multiple outgoing sequence flows and join behavior with multiple incoming sequence flows. The graphical representation of an inclusive gateway is shown in figure B.18.

Figure B.18   Inclusive gateway

The XML representation of the inclusive gateway is

```
<inclusiveGateway id="inclusiveGateway" />
```

Like the exclusive gateway, you can also define a default flow in case no condition is met for an outgoing sequence flow.

B.4.3   *Parallel gateway*

A parallel gateway can be used to run multiple sequence flows. Every outgoing sequence flow connected to a parallel gateway will be executed; a defined condition will be ignored. You can also use a parallel gateway to join multiple incoming sequence flows. The graphical representation of a parallel gateway is shown in figure B.19.

Figure B.19   Parallel gateway

The XML representation of the parallel gateway is

```
<parallelGateway id="parallelGateway" />
```

B.5   *Other activities*

Besides the tasks already discussed, there are some other BPMN activities that are supported by the Activiti Engine. The following two activities will be described in this section:

- Call activity
- Embedded subprocess

B.5.1   *Call activity*

A call activity can be used to invoke another process definition as a subprocess. This is primarily interesting for reusability purposes. A process definition can be reused as a subprocess by multiple other process definitions. Every process definition can be used as a subprocess invoked by a call activity. The graphical representation of the call activity is shown in figure B.20.

Call activity

Figure B.20   Call activity

The XML representation of the call activity is

```
<callActivity id="callActivity" name="Call activity"
    calledElement="subProcess" />
```

In this example, the called element will result in the invocation of another process definition with an `id` attribute that's equal to `subProcess`.

The process variables of the parent process instance aren't shared with the subprocess instance by default. When you want to pass variables to and from the subprocess, you can use the following Activiti extensions:

```
<callActivity id="callActivity" name="Call activity"
    calledElement="subProcess">
  <extensionElements>
    <activiti:in source="parentProcessVar" target="subProcessVar" />
    <activiti:in sourceExpression="${order.hasForeignAddress}"
        target="anotherSubProcessVar" />
    <activiti:out source="resultSubProcessVar"
        target="anotherParentProcessVar" />
  </extensionElements>
</callActivity>
```

As you can see, you can pass along process variables from the main process to the subprocess using the `in` element. With the `source` attribute, you can specify the process variable name of the parent process instance. The `target` attribute contains the process variable name that will be set in the subprocess instance. With the `sourceExpression` attribute, you can specify a more complex expression to get a value from the parent process instance context.

The `out` element can be used to specify the variable values that will be passed back from the subprocess instance to the parent process instance. Once you've done that, the `source` attribute refers to the subprocess variable and the `target` attribute is used for the name of the process variable that will be set in the parent process. You can also use a `sourceExpression` here.

B.5.2 Embedded subprocess

An embedded subprocess can be used as a child scope in a process definition. This is most useful when you want to set a boundary error or timer event on a group of task elements. The process instance context, including the process variables, is shared between the parent process and the embedded subprocess. Embedded subprocesses can't be reused across multiple process definitions. The graphical representation of an embedded subprocess is shown in figure B.21.

The XML representation of an embedded subprocess without any tasks is

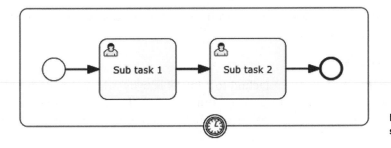

Figure B.21 Embedded subprocess

```
<subProcess id="subProcess">
  <startEvent id="startEvent" />
  <sequenceFlow id="flow" sourceRef="startEvent" targetRef="endEvent" />
  <endEvent id="endEvent" />
</subProcess>
```

An embedded subprocess must have a none start event and at least one end event. This can be an error end event or a none end event. The sequence flows inside the embedded subprocess can't cross the boundaries of the embedded subprocess itself, so you can only connect outgoing sequence flows to the embedded subprocess or to a boundary event that's attached to the embedded subprocess.

B.6 Boundary events

The following boundary events will be described in this section:

- Error boundary event
- Timer boundary event

B.6.1 Error boundary event

An error boundary event can be attached to a BPMN activity, which means every task, a call activity, or an embedded subprocess. But it only makes sense on a call activity or an embedded subprocess in Activiti. That's because a subprocess can define an error end event, which can be caught by this error boundary event. The graphical representation of an error boundary event is shown in figure B.22.

Figure B.22 Error boundary event

The XML representation of the error boundary event is

```
<boundaryEvent id="boundaryEvent" attachedToRef="subProcess">
  <errorEventDefinition errorRef="logicalError" />
</boundaryEvent>
```

A boundary event is always attached to a specific activity, and often this is a call activity or an embedded subprocess. This is configured using the attachedToRef attribute. The logical error code that's caught with this boundary event is defined with the errorRef attribute. The value of this attribute can be used directly as the error code definition, but you can also make a reference to an error definition like this:

```
<error id="myError" errorCode="logicalError" />
```

If you want to catch every logical error with the error boundary event, you can even omit the errorRef attribute.

B.6.2 Timer boundary event

A timer boundary event can be attached to a BPMN activity, which means every task, a call activity, or an embedded subprocess. But it makes the most sense on non-automated tasks, like a user task or a grouping of BPMN elements when using a call activity

or an embedded subprocess. The graphical representation of a
timer boundary event is shown in figure B.23.

The XML representation of the timer boundary event is

**Figure B.23   Timer
boundary event**

```
<boundaryEvent id="boundaryEvent"
    cancelActivity="false"
    attachedToRef="userTask">
  <timerEventDefinition>
    <timeDuration>PT2H</timeDuration>
  </timerEventDefinition>
</boundaryEvent>
```

A boundary event is always attached to a specific activity, like the user task activity in
this example. This is configured using the `attachedToRef` attribute. You can also specify whether the activity to which you attach the boundary event should be cancelled
when the timer is due. In this example, the user task will not be cancelled.

With the timer event definition, you can define the time configuration for the
timer boundary event. In table B.2 with the `timer` start event, you already saw the possible timer configurations. The difference with the `timer` start event is that you can
also use process variables to define the timer.

B.7   Intermediate events

The following intermediate event will be described in this section:

- Timer intermediate catching event

B.7.1   Timer intermediate catching event

The timer intermediate catching event is very similar to the timer
boundary event. The only difference is that the timer intermediate catching event is used in the process flow itself and isn't
attached to another activity. This means you can define an incoming sequence flow to a timer intermediate catching event, and this
will trigger a timer to be executed. The process execution will
continue when the timer is due. The graphical representation is
shown in figure B.24.

**Figure B.24   Timer
intermediate
catching event**

The XML representation of the timer intermediate catching event is

```
<intermediateCatchEvent id="timerCatchEvent">
  <timerEventDefinition>
    <timeDuration>PT2H</timeDuration>
  </timerEventDefinition>
</intermediateCatchEvent>
```

The timer event definition has already been described in table B.2 with the `timer` start
event. The difference between these two events is that with the `timer` start event, you
can also use process variables to define the timer.

index